AF597847

Rhythmic Cycles and Structures in the Art Music of the Middle East

ISTANBULER TEXTE UND STUDIEN

HERAUSGEGEBEN VOM
ORIENT-INSTITUT ISTANBUL

BAND 36

Rhythmic Cycles and Structures in the Art Music of the Middle East

Edited by
Zeynep Helvacı
Jacob Olley
Ralf Martin Jäger

WÜRZBURG 2017

ERGON VERLAG WÜRZBURG
IN KOMMISSION

Umschlaggestaltung: Taline Yozgatian

Umschlagabbildung: Cantemir, Dimitri [Kantemiroğlu], Kitâb-ı ʿİlmü'l-Mûsıkî ʿalâ Vechi'l-Hurûfât, [manuscript copy] İstanbul Üniversitesi Kütüphanesi Nadir Eserler Koleksiyonu T.Y. 1856, fol. 13b-14a.

Bibliografische Information der Deutschen Nationalbibliothek
Die Deutsche Nationalbibliothek verzeichnet diese Publikation in der Deutschen Nationalbibliografie; detaillierte bibliografische Daten sind im Internet über http://dnb.d-nb.de abrufbar.

Bibliographic information published by the Deutsche Nationalbibliothek
The Deutsche Nationalbibliothek lists this publication in the Deutsche Nationalbibliografie; detailed bibliographic data are available in the Internet at http://dnb.d-nb.de.

ISBN 978-3-95650-172-2
ISSN 1863-9461

 Gedruckt mit Unterstützung des Orient-Instituts Istanbul, gegründet von der Deutschen Morgenländischen Gesellschaft, aus Mitteln des Bundesministeriums für Bildung und Forschung.

Ergon-Verlag GmbH
Keesburgstr. 11, D-97074 Würzburg

Gedruckt auf alterungsbeständigem Papier

Contents

Preface and Dedication

This volume presents the proceedings of the international congress "Rhythmic Cycles and Structures in the Art Music of the Middle East" that took place at Westfälische Wilhelms-Universität, Münster, on 27–28 February 2014. The congress was organized by the Ethnomusicology and European Music History Section of the Department for Musicology and Music Education in cooperation with Orient-Institut Istanbul (part of the Max Weber Foundation). The present volume follows on thematically from the book *Writing the History of "Ottoman Music"*[1], which discusses the foundations and current problems of research on music and music history in the Ottoman context, thereby contributing to the development of new perspectives and methods.

The authors and editors dedicate this volume, with much respect and gratitude, to our esteemed teacher, honored colleague and dear friend Eckhard Neubauer, an international pioneer and originator of innovative methodological approaches to research on the historical contexts, interconnections and details of Middle Eastern music cultures, who reached his 75th birthday on 13 January, 2015. The idea of publishing this volume as a *Festschrift* for the esteemed scholar's jubilee was discussed during the initial preparations for the congress. However, two strong arguments dissuaded the editors: In the first place, Eckhard Neubauer by no means presents all the characteristics usually associated with *Festschrift* dedicatees, especially that of having more or less finished his or her life's work. On the contrary, at an age when many have long since retired intellectually, he displays an awe-inspiring scholarly energy, finally finding the time to realize long-cherished research and publication plans, to participate more in scholarly discourse with inspiring ideas and, furthermore, to support a new generation of young scholars with advice and assistance. The second argument against a *Festschrift* in fact results from the first, since a dedicatee is celebrated in this type of publication but does not personally contribute to it. In the case of the present volume on "Rhythmic Cycles and Structures in the Art Music of the Middle East", this would have meant excluding one of the most renowned scholars in the field. Readers will notice what a substantial gap the absence of Eckhard Neubauer's contribution would have caused. So, Dr. Neubauer, please consider this volume as an individually tailored *Festschrift*, which, the authors and editors are convinced, suits you much better – because it places you there, amongst a circle of international colleagues, where you will hopefully be fruitfully active for a long time to come. In this, we wish you all the best.

---

1 Greve, Martin (Ed.) 2015, *Writing the History of "Ottoman Music"*, Istanbuler Texte und Studien: 33, Würzburg: Ergon.

In conclusion, I would like to thank those people without whose help this volume could not have been completed. I thank the authors for their helpful communication and for their support in the process of revising the submitted manuscripts. I cordially thank Martin Greve for much good advice, for encouraging words at the right moments and for accepting the volume as part of the publication series of Orient-Institut Istanbul. Jacob Olley (Münster) undertook the revision of the manuscripts diligently, with great finesse and firm commitment; he not only improved the linguistic standards of the papers but also provided helpful scholarly and editorial suggestions.

Special thanks are due to Zeynep Helvacı, who was involved in developing the content of the congress, together with Salah Eddin Maraqa (Würzburg), whom I also sincerely thank. She carried the main burden of the publication of this volume, self-effacingly, but at the same time with outstanding expertise and with (mostly) affectionate labor. She undertook the correspondence with authors for the most part, substantially edited individual contributions, standardized the formatting, partially undertook the music-setting, and with laborious attention to detail even completed missing footnotes. The whole volume is marked with traces of her labor, without which it could not have been finished.

For the funding of the congress "Rhythmic Cycles and Structures in the Art Music of the Middle East", which helped to open a new research field in the musicological branch of Middle Eastern Studies, and whose fruits resulted in the present volume, I cordially thank Westfälische Wilhelms-Universität, Münster.

Münster, November 2015

Ralf Martin Jäger

Introduction

Ralf Martin Jäger

Along with *makams*, which provide the complex guidelines for melodic structures in Middle Eastern art musics, rhythmic cycles (*usûl* or *iqāʿ*) are of fundamental significance for the complete conception of a musical work. While the *makam* system has been documented and researched in a broad range of scholarly studies, the issue of *usûl* has been the subject of only a limited number of publications until now, which, moreover, cover little more than selected aspects of this multifaceted phenomenon.

Among fundamental studies to date are Heinz Peter Seidel's "Studien zum Usûl Devri kebir in den Peşrev der Mevlevi"[1], published in 1973, as well as Owen Wright's 1988 article "Aspects of historical change in the Turkish classical repertoire"[2], Walter Feldman's article "Melodic progression, rhythm and compositional form in the Ottoman peşrev: 1500-1850"[3] from 1992 and Yalçın Tura's thoughts on "Darb-ı Fetih Usûlü ve Bu Usûlle Yapılmış Peşrevler"[4] ("*Usûl Darb-ı Fetih* and *Peşrevs* Composed With This *Usûl*"), published in 1988. Certain writings of Eckhard Neubauer are also of central importance for the subject, among them his two publications on the theory of *īqāʿ*[5], as well as his thoughts on the early history of Arabic theories of pitch and musical metre[6].

There are a number of publications dealing with the question of transmission history, theory and notation[7], while Rûhî Ayangil has worked on *usûl*-related prob-

1 Seidel, Heinz-Peter 1972/3, "Studien zum Usul 'Devri kebîr' in den Peşrev der Mevlevi", *Mitteilungen der deutschen Gesellschaft für Musik des Orients* 11, 7-69.

2 Wright, Owen 1988, "Aspects of historical change in the Turkish classical repertoire", in: *Musica Asiatica 5*, Richard Widdess (Ed.), Cambridge: Cambridge University Press, 1-107.

3 Feldman, Walter 1992, "Melodic progression, rhythm and compositional form in the Ottoman peşrev: 1500-1850", in: *Regionale maqām-Traditionen in Geschichte und Gegenwart: Materialien der 2. Arbeitstagung der Study Group 'Maqām' des International Council for Traditional Music vom 23. bis 28. März in Gosen bei Berlin*, Jürgen Elsner and Gisa Jähnichen (Ed.), Berlin, 191-251.

4 Tura, Yalçın 1988b, "Darb-ı Fetih Usûlü ve Bu Usûlle Yapılmış Peşrevler", in: *Türk Mûsıkîsinin Mes'eleleri*, Yalçın Tura (Ed.), Istanbul, 87-103.

5 Neubauer, Eckhard 1968/1969, "Die Theorie vom īqāʿ. I: Übersetzung des Kitāb al-Īqāʿāt von Abū Nasr al-Fārābī", *Oriens 21/22*, 196-232, and 1994, "Die Theorie vom īqāʿ: II. Übersetzung des "Kitāb Iḥṣāʾ al-īqāʿāt von Abū Naṣr al-Fārābī", *Oriens 34*, 103-173.

6 Neubauer, Eckhard 1995, "Al-Ḫalīl ibn Aḥmad und die Frühgeschichte der arabischen Lehre von den 'Tönen' und den musikalischen Metren, mit einer Übersetzung des Kitāb an-naġam von Yaḥyā ibn 'alī al-Munaǧǧim", *Zeitschrift für Geschichte der arabisch-islamischen Wissenschaften 10*, 255-323.

7 Jäger, Ralf Martin 1996, *Türkische Kunstmusik und ihre handschriftlichen Quellen aus dem 19. Jahrhundert* (=*Schriften zur Musikwissenschaft aus Münster* 7, ed. Klaus Hortschansky), Eisenach; 1998, "Die Metamorphosen des Irak Elçi Peşrevi", in: *Berichte aus dem ICTM-*

lems in performance practice since the 1980s. The first recording of the *ilâhî* "*Uyan Ey Gözlerim*" (as documented by Ali Ufukî (1610–1675) in his *Mecmuâ-ı sâz ü söz*[8]) by the Ayangil Turkish Music Orchestra and Chorus in 1988 is regarded as a milestone in the historical performance practice of Ottoman art music.

The function of the *usûl* is of complex structural relevance and goes well beyond accompanying a melodic line with a more or less defined sequence of beats. It is a substantial parameter for every metricized melodic structure and shapes the form of both vocal and instrumental compositions. *Usûl* is not only a subject of music theoretical and music aesthetical discourses, but is also a field of research for (historical) performance practice. It represents a musical concept whose central importance was already visible in the time of the Arab music theoretician Xalīl ibn Aḥmad (d. *ca.* 170/786), who differentiated between "musical disciplines of 'pitches' (*naġam*), 'rhythmical time measurement' (*īqāʿ*) and 'composition' (*taʾlīf*)".[9]

Almost a millennium later, the polymath, theoretician and composer of Ottoman art music Dimitrie Cantemir (Tr. Kantemiroğlu, 1673–1723) highlighted the importance of this concept in his still much acclaimed *Book of the Science of Music* (*Kitâb-ı ʿilmü'l Mûsikî*), writing that a sequence of notes "is not a musical melody" without *usûl*, which is the "balance and measure of music".[10] To this day, the realisation of the *usûl* is essentially equivalent to *makam*-based melodic construction, with which it interacts in various ways, and is a core element in the organisation of musical time and formal structure in the composition of Middle Eastern art music, indispensable both formally and aesthetically. In vocal compositions, its relation to poetic metre additionally plays an important role.

Rhythmic cycles, just like the *makam* system and canon of musical forms, went through the process of musical transformation that, beginning in the seventeenth century, is increasingly documented in theoretical writings and (hitherto hardly studied) sources of musical performance, and which still continues. As well as political, social and religious phenomena, commercial and technological factors have been of growing significance in this process since the last decades of the nineteenth century.

A fundamental change in Ottoman cultural life was brought about especially by Sultan Mahmud II's (1785–1839) reforms of the state apparatus, beginning

---

Nationalkomitee, Band VI/VII, Marianne Bröcker (Ed.), Bamberg, 31-57; 2004 "The Aesthetic of Time in Traditional Ottoman Art Music", in: *Proceedings of the 1st International Conference of the Cyprus Musicological Society*, Panikos Giorgoudes (Ed.), Nikosia, 75-96. On the visualisation of *usûls* cf. also Klebe, Dorit 2006, "Visualization-Forms of the Ottoman-Turkish Rhythmic Mode Usûl from the 17th Century on: Discussed in the Context of the Emic/Etic Concept", in: *Shared Musics and Minority Identities*, Naila Ceribašić and Erica Haskell (Ed.), Zagreb, 141-155.

8 British Museum, Sloane 3114.

9 Neubauer 1968/69, p. 196.

10 Dimitrie Cantemir,1 *Kitâb-ı ʿilmü'l Mûsikî ʿalâ vechi'l hurûfât*, İstanbul Üniversitesi Türkiyat Araştırmaları Enstitüsü Kütüphanesi, Arel Collection, Nr. 100, p. 78.

with the destruction of the Janissaries in 1826. The elite culture of Ottoman art music was gradually replaced by Western music from around 1835, and it lost considerable prestige. During the nineteenth century, many important Ottoman musicians received training in both traditional and Western music through the *Mızıka-ı Hümâyûn*, or the "Imperial Orchestra", which included learning European musical notation. In the same period, new coffee houses, casinos and night clubs were established in the Beyoğlu district of Istanbul, distinguished by its "European" character, where an urban, intellectual-educated entertainment music was cultivated by the newly emerging middle classes.

Furthermore, the musical forms of traditional art music changed profoundly due to the changing conditions of musical life. Traditional vocal forms such as the *kâr, beste, ağır semâi, nakış semâî* and *yürük semâi*, typical of the *fasıl* performance cycle, were gradually replaced by the *şarkı*, a form central to the music culture of the middle classes. Almost no composer born after 1870 based his works on these older musical forms.

From the 1840s, together with older musical forms, numerous *usûl*s began to disappear from contemporary performance practice, and even more so from compositional practice. Whereas earlier composers had grappled intellectually with larger rhythmic cycles such as *hâvî* (64 beats), *darb-ı fetih* (88 beats) or *zencîr* (120 beats), shorter and rhythmically more concise structures such as *düyek* and *katakofti* (both 8 beats), *aksak* (9 beats) or *curcuna* (10 beats) now dominated. Thanks to the availability of printed music from the late nineteenth century onwards and of sound recordings from the beginning of the twentieth century[11], *şarkı* culture gained extraordinary popularity in the urban centres of the eastern Mediterranean region. In Turkey, it prevails even today.

* * *

The fact that such a central aspect of this region's art music has until now been studied only rudimentarily by international scholars in the twentieth and twenty-first centuries might partly reflect the perspective of the young field of musicology, which, from the late nineteenth century, tended also to be Western-oriented in Turkey and the Arabic-speaking lands. But the cultural politics of the nation-states that emerged in the territory of the former Ottoman Empire after 1918 also played their part in the gradual eclipse of the structural and performance-related functions of rhythmic cycles. This process is particularly apparent in Turkey. Mustafa Kemal Atatürk, against the background of the resolute Turkicization of numerous cultural arenas by the nation-state, gave a programmatic speech in which he postulated that contemporary traditional art music was "all in all not especially valuable", and that folk music was better suited to "skilfully and sensi-

11 On the cultural history of sound recordings in Turkey see Ünlü, Cemal 2004, *Git Zaman Gel Zaman. Fonograf – Gramofon – Taş Plak*, Istanbul.

tively express the ideas of our people".[12] Consequently, traditional art music was supressed by the cultural policies of the state. In this critical situation, Mes'ud Cemil (1902–1963) thus began to consciously alter not the music itself, but the performance practice of classical Ottoman music. In this he was able to draw upon the previous efforts of Münir Nurettin Selçuk (*ca.* 1900-1981). The establishment of the first distinguished classical choir in 1937 was his most influential step: A performance practice that, due to tradition and certain musical–aesthetic concepts, was primarily soloistic became a choral performance practice. Simultaneously, the figure of the musical director appears for the first time in the history of Ottoman–Turkish music.[13] The internationalization that Atatürk desired was achieved by the Europeanization of performance practice. This concept was refined by Nevzad Atlığ (b. 1925), successor to Mes'ud Cemil and the founder of *Cumhurbaşkanlığı Klasik Türk Müziği Korosu* (Presidential Classical Turkish Music Choir). Not only did Atlığ replace a heterophonic performance style with a strictly homophonic one, he also abandoned rhythmic instruments completely. *Usûls* no longer play a central role in performance practice, at least not in that of the State Choir of Classical Turkish Music. Yet the rhythmic cycle never completely disappeared from sophisticated urban entertainment music, and the historical performance practice that began in 1980s was aware of its importance.

* * *

The nature of the *usûl* phenomenon is supra-national, supra-ethnic and supra-regional. Despite all the differences in detail, it fundamentally shapes musical works from Turkey as well as the Arabic-speaking lands and functions as a shared concept as far as Central Asia. More or less thorough explanations of rhythmic models are found in Ottoman song anthologies from the late nineteenth century as well as in secular Greek music prints or instructions in Greek Orthodox liturgical chants[14], in Armenian music manuscripts from the late nineteenth century[15] as well as in Arabic writings on music theory, explicitly those after 1500[16].

---

12 Akdemir, Kemal Hayrettin 1990, *Die neue türkische Musik: Dargestellt an Volksliedbearbeitungen für mehrstimmigen Chor*, Berlin, pp. 28-29.

13 Cf. Aksoy, Bülent, 2008, *Geçmişin Musikî Mirasına Bakışlar*, Istanbul, pp. 194-198. Mes'ud Cemîl was able here to build upon the experiment in the choral performance of traditional art music that Ali Rifat Çağatay had already attempted in Kadıköy in 1920 (p. 196).

14 As seen in Keltzanides, Chatzi Panagiotes 1881, *Μεθοδικη διδασκαλια θεωρητικη τε και πρακτικη προς εκμαθησιν και διαδοσιν του γνησιου εξωτερικου μελους*, Konstantinopel.

15 For instance using two different musical notations as in the manuscript Y.209/7 from the collection of İstanbul Üniversitesi Devlet Konservatuvarı, today in İstanbul Üniversitesi Nadir Eserler Kütüphanesi.

16 An excellent overview is given by Salah Eddin Maraqa (2015, *Die traditionelle Kunstmusik in Syrien und Ägypten von 1500 bis 1800. Eine Untersuchung der musiktheoretischen und historisch-biographischen Quellen* (=*Würzburger Beiträge zur Musikforschung* 4, ed. Ulrich Konrad), Tutzing. The index of "Musikalisch- und prosodisch-metrische[n] Begriffe[n]" (Musical and Prosodical-Metrical Terms) provides a useful compilation of the terminology used in Arabic-speaking lands, pp. 386-389.

Alongside diachronic developments are synchronic processes, which are marked by regional peculiarities on the one hand, but also by a supra-regional understanding based on a more or less common pool of *usûls*. The current situation of international research on the *usûl* phenomenon in music cultures of the eastern Mediterranean region is marked by this historical and regional disparity; a systematic approach is lacking.

The aim of the present volume is to bring together, deepen and, by posing new questions, further develop these somewhat piecemeal studies. A systematic scientific approach to the central parameter "*usûl*" in all its complex multidimensionality in past and present, which remains an urgent desideratum for research, is here the subject of a discourse between leading international experts and already prominent young scholars. The contributions should at the same time provide directions for future research in terms of both content and methodology.

Due to the historical interconnectedness of the region, contributions focus firstly on the art music cultures of the Ottoman Empire, then on neighbouring cultures and finally on the contemporary Republic of Turkey.

Owen Wright (London), Eckhard Neubauer (Frankfurt), Yalçın Tura (Istanbul) and Judith Haug (Münster) take up a range of topics concerning *usûl* in historical context from different perspectives. While Wright[17] and Haug present overviews of early history and a specific historical repertoire, Neubauer and Tura focus in their contributions on historical changes of specific *usûls* in all their fascinating complexity. These texts complement each other and provide a basis for the understanding of rhythmic cycles in their historical context.

Walter Feldman (New York), Jacob Olley (Münster) and Ralf Martin Jäger (Münster) investigate specific topics based on this foundation. The aim of each of these studies is to musically and contextually analyse the relationship between *usûl* and musical structure in one or more art music works, based on emic transcriptions handed down from the seventeenth to the nineteenth century. The *peşrev* form is the main focus of these chapters. Unlike the *sâz semâî*, the *peşrev* is not necessarily associated with a certain group of *usûls*, nor is it bound by the prosodic rules that must be considered in vocal music; it therefore presents an especially interesting and fruitful research field.

Nilgün Doğrusöz-Dişiaçık (Istanbul) and Şehvar Beşiroğlu (Istanbul) analyse in their contributions central themes of music theoretical discourse on the issue of *usûls* in different eras. While Doğrusöz-Dişiaçık explores concepts of rhythmic cycles in the fifteenth century based on the *edvâr* of Yusuf Kırşehrî, written in Persian in 1411 and translated into Ottoman in 1469 by one Hariri bin Muhammed, which is among the most important sources of its type, Beşiroğlu deals

17 During the preparation of this volume, Wright extended his analysis of Amir Ḫān Gurji's (1697) treatise significantly; it is presented separately from the chapter based on his conference presentation in order to provide a more balanced treatment of topics.

with the still fertile question of *usûl* and relative time structure in Cantemir's *Kitâb-ı ʿilmü'l Mûsikî*. Ruhi Ayangil (Istanbul) brings music theoretical discourse together with questions of historical performance practice and shows, based on the example of *usûl havî*, the significance of specific intra-cyclic periodic structures for the understanding of larger *usûl*s in theoretical, but also especially practical performance contexts.

The contributions of Angelika Jung (Weimar) and Salah Eddin Maraqa (Würzburg) provide an overview of the regional traditions of neighbouring cultures from Central Asia and the Arabic-speaking countries. In her investigation of the rhythmic cycles of the *shashmaqam* in Bukhara (Uzbekistan), Angelika Jung focuses on mythical and speculative connotations whose importance, alongside primarily musical parameters, should not be underestimated for the contextual understanding of the latter. Based on the Arabic manuscript of Kubaisî (1686), a compilation of song texts, Salah Eddin Maraqa poses a question fundamental to our understanding of locality and supra-regionality in Ottoman music culture, namely: How Turkish *are* the so-called "*al-uṣulāt at-turkīya*"?

Finally, John Morgan O'Connell (Cardiff), Martin Stokes (London) and Songül Karahasanoğlu (Istanbul) examine the changing meanings of *usûl*s in the music of the modern Turkish Republic. The contribution of John Morgan O'Connell deals with the interesting phenomenon of the "*usûl*-lessness" of rhythmic structures in Münir Nurettin Selçuk's concerts between 1923 and 1938. At the centre of Martin Stokes' study is the meaning of rhythmic concepts in the urban entertainment music form *fantezi*, which dates back to the 1980s and is still popular among younger generations. Finally, Songül Karahasanoğlu makes a substantial contribution to the topic through an analysis of the impact of Republican cultural politics on Turkish folk music, which assumed an identity-defining function from the 1930s onwards.

* * *

The authors and editors equally are aware that, more often than not, this volume presents questions rather than gives answers. Each individual contribution marks a specific research area that requires systematic scholarly study in the future. Central questions concerning the change and continuity of rhythmic cycles in diachronic and synchronic dimensions, phenomena related to rhythmic, metric and formal structures in their entire complexity, or to related transcultural processes, are still mostly unanswered. We still know very little about music theoretical discourses, the musical realisation of rhythmic cycles, the extent to which they can be reconstructed from the available practical music sources of the seventeenth to twentieth centuries, or the transmission of *usûl*s in different traditions and regions.

All of the contributors therefore hope that future research on the music cultures of the Middle East will give greater attention to the essential and multidimensional parameter of rhythmic structure in all its complexity.

1.
Usûl in Historical Context

A Historical Sketch of the Musical Metre Called *Ramal*

Eckhard Neubauer

This is a short survey of the musical metre *ramal* from its first appearance at the end of the 7th century in Arabia to its latest period in the contemporary Middle East. Together with the metres called *thaqīl* ("heavy"), *khafīf* ("light") and *hazaj*, it was one of the four metres of the early urban art music performed in Medina, Mecca and Damascus and later in Baghdad. *Ramal* as well as *hazaj* were dance metres comparable to their distant western relatives *zarabanda*, *folia* and *menuet*, and to the Caucasian and Mediterranean 6/8-dances such as *lezginka*, *tarantella* and *siciliana*.

Ramal was favoured by the effeminate so-called *mukhannath* singers in Mecca, who dressed like women, sang with head voice (in falsetto), and did not play the lute but instead marked the metre with a stick (*qaḍīb*). Another group devoted to *ramal* were the players of the long-necked lute *ṭunbūr*, also known for their preference for "light" music. When the four earlier metres were split into a "heavy" and a "light" form each in the middle of the 2nd/8th century, *ramal* was divided accordingly into *al-ramal al-thaqīl* ("heavy" *ramal* of 3/2) and *khafīf al-ramal* ("light" *ramal* of 3/4). In the local theory of music the basic beats or time units of the metres were first represented by mnemonic syllables and later by numbers.

I have combined here the basic patterns of *ramal* as listed by Isḥāq al-Mawṣilī (d. 235/850) in Baghdad with the mnemonic syllables *ta*, *tan* and *tanna* (or *tannan*) later used by Abū Naṣr al-Fārābī (d. 339/950). Al-Fārābī was the first to define unambiguously three fundamental values of duration in the relation of 1 : 2 : 4:

4th/10th century (al-Fārābī)

1 = syllable *ta*	= time unit of *hazaj*	=	♪
2 = syllable *tan*	= time unit of the "light" *ramal*	=	♩
4 = syllable *tanna* or *tannan*	= time unit of the"heavy" *ramal*	=	𝅗𝅥

Accordingly, the two versions of *ramal* can be represented as follows:
khafīf al-ramal ("light" *ramal*):

1st period (*dawr*):				2nd period (*dawr*):			
tan +	*tan* +	| rest (*fāṣila*)	|	*tan* +	*tan* +	| rest (*fāṣila*)	||
2 +	2 +	| 2 +	|	2 +	2 +	| 2 +	||
♩	♩	| 𝄽	|	♩	♩	| 𝄽	||

al-ramal al-thaqīl ("heavy" *ramal*):

1st period *(dawr)*:						2nd period (*dawr*):					
tanna(n) +	*tan* +	*tan* +	| rest	|		*tanna(n)* +	*tan* +	*tan* +	| rest	||
4	+ 2	+ 2	+ | 4	|		4	+ 2	+ 2	+ | 4	||
𝅗𝅥	♩	♩	| 𝄼	|		𝅗𝅥	♩	♩	| 𝄼	||

The construct of one "metre" (Arabic *īqāʿ*) as a sequence of two "periods" (*dawr*, pl. *adwār*) was conceived after the model of the two-part structure of the verses in *qaṣīda* and *ghazal* poetry, and was applied to all the musical metres. Consequently, two "periods" of *ramal* were regarded as one metrical unit.[1] The "rest" between the periods was called "separation" (*fāṣila*). It was understood as analogous to the pause between hemistichs and verses of poetry in recitation.

Because of the fundamental formal dependence of *īqāʿ* on the elements of prosody (*ʿarūḍ*), I am inclined to speak of "metres" instead of "rhythmic cycles" or the like. According to the theorists the main function of *īqāʿ* was to measure musical passages or periods, to give them a metrical skeleton. The aspect of rhythm *per se* was of secondary importance.

It seems, however, that it was not only the analogy to the two-part verse that led to the concept of the two-part *īqāʿ* but also an intrinsic musical element. The binary structure of melodies is a frequent phenomenon in folk songs, dance tunes, religious hymns and in the art music of the Middle East. Thus, we can suppose that the early definition of *īqāʿ* as being a unit of two "periods" was not only an imitation of prosody but also represented a widespread musical reality.

Furthermore, a poem written in the prosodic metre *ramal* was usually not composed in the musical metre *ramal*. Attention was given, however, to the fact that the metrical scansion of the verse (*tajziʾa*) should tally with the metrical structure of the melody (*qisma*).[2] In general, the text of a song consisted of only two to four verses while the melody of a single verse could encompass more than 50 "periods".[3] In these songs all kinds of metrical modifications could occur, such as *rubato*, *accelerando*, the combination of different metres in one melody or

---

1 This can explain the fact that the name of the prosodic metre *rajaz* was not given to a musical metre. *Rajaz*, a metre used in didactic *urjūza* poems, was evidently "musical" as these poems were cantillated. It lacked, however, the necessary formal preconditions, for *rajaz* verses were not composed of rhyming distichs but of rhyming monostichs, and thus were not considered proper "poetry" (*shiʿr*).

2 For both terms see Sawa, George Dimitri 2015, *An Arabic Musical and Socio-Cultural Glossary of* Kitāb al-Aghānī, Leiden: Brill.

3 See al-Iṣfahānī, Abū l-Faraj 1936, *Kitāb al-Aghānī al-kabīr*, vol. 9, Cairo: Dār al-Kutub al-Miṣriyya, pp. 60-61.

the inclusion of extra measures. These modifications were described by al-Fārābī.[4]

The duration of the notes was written down by the theorists in different ways. Here we see three different approaches to defining one period of the "heavy" *ramal* by prosodic means:

"heavy" *ramal*:	4 +		2 +	2
1. al-Mawṣilī + al-Fārābī:	*tanna(n)*		*tan*	*tan*
2. Ibn al-Sīd, ca. 1100:	*lā-*	*tu*	*maf-*	*'ū*
3. al-Urmawī et al.:	*fā-*	*'i-*	*lā-*	*tun*
	–	∪	–	–
	♩.	♪	♩	♩
or:	𝅗𝅥 (3)	♩ (3)	♩	♩

Isḥāq al-Mawṣilī (d. 235/850) and Abū Naṣr al-Fārābī (d. 339/950) in the East, Ibn al-Sīd al-Baṭalyawsī in Muslim Spain (ca. 500/1100), and Ṣafī al-Dīn al-Urmawī in Baghdad (d. 693/1294) all agree that a note of four time units has the same duration as the sequence of a long and a short syllable.[5] The two syllables long *fā-* and short *-ʿi* are not considered mathematically as a sequence of long and short with a ratio of 2:1. Rather, *fāʿi* is seen as an entity having the same duration as the two long syllables *lā-* and *-tun* together. This seems to have been the reason why the musical *ramal* was named after its prosodic counterpart: *fāʿilātun* is the standard metrical pattern of the prosodic *ramal.* The metric- or music-related meaning of the word *ramal*, by the way, is a "trotting pace, between a walk and a run".[6]

---

4 See Sawa, George Dimitri 2009, *Rhythmic Theories and Practices in Arabic Writings to 339 AH / 950 CE.* (= Musicological Studies, vol. XCIII), Ottawa: The Institute of Mediaeval Music. For the relationship between music and verse in early Arabic songs, see Wright, Owen 1983, "Music and verse", in: *Arabic Literature to the End of the Umayyad Period*, A.F.L. Beeston et al. (Ed.), Cambridge etc.: Cambridge University Press, 433-459.

5 To the best of my knowledge, it was ʿAbd al-Ḥamīd Ḥamām who first pointed to this important clue for better understanding both the prosodic system of al-Khalīl ibn Aḥmad (d. ca. 175/791) and the theory and practice of *īqāʿ*, see his studies 1409/1989, "Awzān al-ʿarab al-shiʿriyya", in: *Majallat al-Majmaʿ al-lugha al-ʿarabiyya al-urdunnī* , no. 36, ʿAmmān, 233-275; 1989, "al-Ahammiyya al-mūsīqiyya li-l-ishbāʿ wa-l-taḥrīk fī l-shiʿr al-ʿarabī", in: *Abḥāth al-Yarmūk (Jāmiʿat al-Yarmūk)*, vol. 5, 287-302; 1991, *Muʿāraḍat al-ʿarūḍ*, ʿAmmān, and review by Sawa, George D. 1995, "*Muʿaradat al-ʿArud*, by ʿAbd al-Hamid Hamam",*The World of Music*, vol. 37(2), 106-108.

6 See Lane, Edward William 1968 [1867], *Madd al-Qāmūs. An Arabic-English Lexicon ...*, Book I, part 3, Beirut: Librairie du Liban, p. 1159.

Now, the basic patterns of the slow and the fast *ramal*, first recorded in the 2nd/8th century, continued to be transmitted in the same way up to the middle of the 5th/11th century. Our last witness is Ibn Zayla (d. 440/1048), the pupil of Ibn Sīnā (d. 428/1037), in Iran.[7]

The 6th/12th century is, generally speaking, a "dark" period due to a manifest lack of source material. But when we proceed to the 7th/13th century we discover that *ramal* continued to be described, in the books on music theory, essentially in the same way as before. Its patterns were described by Ṣafi al-Dīn al-Urmawī, Quṭb al-Dīn (al-) Shīrāzī (d. 710/1311), ʿAbd al-Qādir (al-) Marāghī (d. 838/1435) and others. Their terminology includes the following four time values:

letter *alif* (= 1)	= syllable *ta*	= called *sarīʿ* = time unit of *hazaj*	=	♪
letter *bāʾ* (= 2)	= syllable *tan*	= called *sabab* or *khafīf*	=	♩
letter *jīm* (= 3)	= syllables *tanan*	= called *watid* or *khafīf al-thaqīl*	=	♩.
letter *dāl* (= 4)	= syllables *tananan*	= called *fāṣila* or *thaqīl*	=	𝅗𝅥

Compared with al-Fārābī's three values the dotted crotchet is new. The most striking novelty, though, is seen in the last line by "letter *dāl*". The 4-time-unit note is represented here by the syllables *tananan* instead of the earlier *tanna* or *tannan* known from al-Fārābī. This means that *tananan* does not represent a series of two short notes and one long note, but simply one long note of four time units. Accordingly, *tanan* is a note of three time units, not a short note followed by a long one. These mnemonics, together with numbers representing the duration of notes and letters indicating their pitch, were a perfect means of memorizing and writing down melodies such as those recorded by al-Urmawī and his successors at the end of their books on music theory.

The new patterns of the metre *ramal* are represented here together with their precursor in al-Mawṣilī and al-Fārābī:

khafīf al-ramal ("light" *ramal*, 2nd/8th-4th/10th cent.):

	1st period:			2nd period:			
al-Mawṣilī + al-Fārābī:	*tan* +	*tan* +	rest	*tan* +	*tan* +	rest	‖
	(2 +	2 +	2)	(2 +	2 +	2)	=12
	(2 +	4)		(2 +	4)		=12

7 See Ibn Zayla, *al-Kāfī fī l-mūsīqī*, Zakariyyā Yūsuf (Ed.) 1964, Cairo: Dār al-Qalam, pp. 55-59.

ramal (7th/13th – 9th/15th cent.):

1. *ramal* (*Adwār*; Marāghi)[8]:	(2 +	2 +	2)		(2 +	2 +	2)	=12
2. *khafīf al-ramal* (*Sharafiyya*):	(2 +	1+ 1+	2)	+	(2 +	1+1+	2)	=12
3. *ramal* (var. *Adwār*; Jāmi; var. Lādhiqī, *Zayn*):	(2 +	2 +	2)	+	(2 +	4)		=12
4. *ramal* (Quṭb al-Dīn):	**(2 +**	**4)**		+	**(2 +**	**4)**		=12
5. *ramal* (var. Quṭb al-Dīn):	(4 +		2)	+	(4 +		2)	=12
6. *ramal* (var. Quṭb al-Dīn; Marāghī):	2 +	2 +	4	+		4		=12
7. *ramal qaṣīr* (Lādhiqī):	2 +	6 +				4		=12

The new patterns show one essential change. What previously was thought of as two "periods" plus one "rest" is now a single basic form called *aṣl* (hence the plural *uṣūl* that is still used as a generic term in addition to the plural forms *īqāʿāt* and *awzān*): the complete *khafīf al-ramal* of old has become one period of the new standard *ramal* (no. 1). The patterns in bold, the traditional *khafīf al-ramal* (p. 20) and the basic form of the new *ramal* recorded by Quṭb al-Dīn (al-) Shīrāzī (no. 4) are identical.[9] In addition, patterns no. 1-5 have the same inner structure regardless of some differences in detail, and they reveal that the former *fāṣila*s are now completely integrated into the new standard *ramal*. The underlined points of nos. 1 and 3, now called "basic beat" (*ḍarb al-aṣl*), are the first beat of the previous first "period" and the last beat of the former second "period". Examples 6 and 7 represent variants of one period of the former *al-ramal al-thaqīl*.

In addition to the above *ramal* of 12 time units, an enlarged "heavy" or "doubled" form of 24 time units also occurs in the writings of al-Urmawī, (al-) Marāghī and al-Lādhiqī (d. after 890/1485). It is shown below together with its predecessor, the former "heavy" *ramal* of al-Fārābī. Here again, in nos. 1 and 2 the underlined "basic beat" (*ḍarb al-aṣl*) corresponds to two of the previous main points of the metre, whereas no. 3 deviates at the end:

al-ramal al-thaqīl ("heavy" *ramal*):

	1st period:				2nd period:			
al-Fārābī:	*tanna(n)* +	*tanna(n)* +	rest |		*tanna(n)* +	*tanna(n)*+	rest ‖	
	(4 +	4 +	4)		(4 +	4 +	4)	= 24

[8] For the sources mentioned here and later in abbreviated form see the bibliographical survey at the end of the present volume. The works of Arab and Persian authors up to the 15th century were evaluated by Eckhard Neubauer: "Quṭb al-Dīn Shīrāzī (d. 1311) on musical metres (*īqāʿ*)", in: *Zeitschrift für Geschichte der arabisch-islamischen Wissenschaften* (Frankfurt), vol. 18 (2008-9), pp. 357-371.

[9] It was also the pattern of the two *ramal* melodies written down by Ṣafī al-Dīn al-Urmawī at the end of his *Kitab al-Adwār*.

*ramal, thaqīl al-ramal, ramal ṭawīl, muḍā*ᶜ*af al-ramal* (13th-15th cent.):

1. *ramal* (*Adwār* + Marāghī):	(4 + 4 + 4)	+	(4 + 4 + 4)	= 24
2. *ramal* (var. *Adwār*, Lādhiqī: *ramal ṭawīl*):	(4 + 4 + 4)	+	(4 + 8)	= 24
3. *thaqīl al-ramal* (Marāghī; Lādhiqī: *muḍā'af al-ramal*):	(4 + 4 + 2 + 2)	+	(2 + 2 + 2 + 2 + 4)	= 24

Al-Urmawī, (al-) Marāghī and al-Lādhiqī state that the "heavy" or "doubled" *ramal* was the most favoured *īqā*ᶜ among the Persians.[10] Marāghī adds two further augmented patterns, one of 48 time units, and another of 96 time units.

When we consider these extended versions of the early 9th/15th century we understand that multiple amplification was not a special characteristic of the later Ottoman period. Its beginning could even be dated back to the differentiation between "light" and "heavy" metres in the early Islamic period. In the period between al-Urmawī and al-Lādhiqī, augmentation had become one of the main impulses towards the further development of the *uṣūl*. We also learn that a piece of music could begin "before" (*qabl*), "together with" (*ma*ᶜ*a*) or "after" (*ba*ᶜ*d*) the metre.[11] In multipart compositions this could result in an enjambment between two parts of different *uṣūl*s. The study of a song began by beating the metre with the help of fingers, hands and knees. ᶜAbd al-Qādir (al-) Marāghī (d. 1435) describes the practice of beating with both hands and knees four different metres at the same time, including the simple and the "heavy" *ramal*, and he adds that an experienced person should be able to mark with different fingers differing metres simultaneously.[12]

The late 9th/15th and the 10th/16th centuries were a period of far-reaching renewal and change in the music of the eastern Islamic world. This was the result of the emancipation of Ottoman-Turkish music in the West, Persian music under the Safavids in Iran, the Central Asian development under the Shaybanids in Bokhara and the Irano-Mogul musical "marriage" in India. From the 10th/16th century onwards these countries followed individual directions. As a result, musical modes,

---

10 Ṣafī al-Dīn al-Urmawī, *al-Risāla al-Sharafiyya fī l-nisab al-ta'līfiyya*, latest edition by Quraiᶜa [Kriaa], Muḥammad al-Asᶜad 2009, Sīdī Bū Saᶜīd: *Markaz al-Mūsīqā al-ᶜArabiyya wa-l-Mutawassiṭiyya* (= *Iṣdārāt al-Najma al-Zahrā'*), p. 261; ᶜAbd al-Qādir b. Ghaybī al-Marāghī, *Sharḥ-i Adwār*, ed. Bīnesh, Taqī 1370/1991, Tehran: Markaz-e nashr-e dāneshgāhī, p. 262; Muḥammad b. ᶜAbd al-Ḥamīd al-Lādhiqī, *Zayn al-alḥān fī ᶜilm al-ta'līf wa-l-awzān*, Ms. İstanbul, Nuruosmaniye 3655, fol. 84r (p. 166).

11 References occur in Arabic, Persian and Turkish treatises from the 8th/14th to the 10th/16th century (see Popescu-Judetz, E. and E. Neubauer (Ed.) 2004, *Seydī's book on music: A 15th century Turkish discourse*, The Science of Music in Islam, vol. 6, Frankfurt am Main: Institute for the History of Arabic-Islamic Science, pp. 208-209, note 399). They were resumed by ᶜAlī Ufuḳī in the third quarter of the 17th century (see his collection of texts and musical notations, Ms. Paris, Bibl. Nat., turc 292, fol. 51v).

12 See Marāghī, *Sharḥ-i Adwār*, p. 341.

metres and forms changed; local idioms complemented or superseded foreign influences; and traditional instruments like the harp and the lute disappeared to the benefit of members of the family of long-necked lutes. The metre *ramal* was no exception to this trend of change. Its traditional form either disappeared or was renamed.

To demonstrate this development, I will follow a geographical order beginning in Iran and proceeding to Central Asia, then to Syria and Egypt, and finally to Ottoman Turkey.

Iran (10th/16th-11th/17th century):

1. *ramal* (Nasīmī, 16th cent.):	*ta-na*	*ta-na*	*tananan*		
	1+1+	1 +1+	4		= 8
2. *ramal* (Mortażā Shāmlū, ca. 1650):	*tan*	*tan*	*tananan*		
	2 +	2 +	4		= 8
3. *ramal-i ṭawīl* (Nasīmī, 16th cent.):	*tanan*	*tanananan*	*tan tan*	*tan tan*	
	3 +	5 +	2 + 2 +	2 + 2	= 16
4. *ramal* (*Taqsīm al-naghamāt*, 16th cent.):	*tanan*	*tanan*	*tananan*	*tan*	
	3 +	3 +	4 +	2	= 12
5. *ramal-i ṣaghīr* (Amīr Khān, ca. 1700):	*dīk dak dak dak dak dak*			*dīk dak*	
muḍā'af al-ramal (Lādhiqī):	<u>4</u> + 4 + 2 + 2 + 2 + 2 + 2 + <u>2</u>			+ 4	= 24

In Persian writings of the 16th and 17th centuries the name *ramal* is still present, yet the metre has assumed new structures. Completely new patterns of 8 and 16 time values appear in a treatise written in the 16th century by an author named Nasīmī, who probably lived in Gīlān by the Caspian Sea (no. 1). His *ramal* of 8 time units seems to have been a local north-eastern Iranian version. It was later confirmed by Mortażā Qolī Shāmlū from Azerbayjan (no. 2).

The traditional version of 12 time units reappears, though in different forms. The anonymous *Taqsīm al-naghamāt* (no. 4) has a version of its own. Amīr Khān Gorjī, who lived around 1700 in Isfahan, also mentions a "small *ramal*" (*ramal-i ṣaghīr*) of 12 time units but with eight beats (no. 5). His pattern seems to resemble al-Lādhiqī's above-mentioned "doubled" *ramal* (*muḍāʿaf al-ramal*), but we are not able to arrive at a harmonization between Amīr Khān's *dīk* and *dak* and al-Lādhiqī's numerical pattern. While in the traditional method it was the duration or the quantity of the notes that was specified, it is now the quality of "high" and "low" beats on percussion instruments (where Persian *dīk* and *dak* and Turkish *düm* and *tek* can be either long or short). This new and purely pedagogical method used by drum players first appears in Persian and Turkish sources of the 17th century and superseded the older teaching. So any attempt at verifying the *ramal-i ṣaghīr* of Amīr Khān by the help of al-Lādhiqī's *muḍāʿaf al-ramal* remains fruitless. The underlined "basic beat" (*ḍarb al-aṣl*) even contradicts any sense of close resemblance. The two idioms could complement one another; but they can hardly replace or be used to interpret one another. As of the 11th/17th century the *tan-tanan* terminology was totally replaced by the new *düm-tek* terms.

In any case, in Amīr Khān's day, at the end of Safavid rule, the former splendour of courtly and urban music in Iran was vanishing. In the course of the 12th/18th century, the repertoire of traditional Persian metres fell into oblivion. The present-day metrical repertoire in Iran is, apart from some *aksak* and traditional 6/8 metres, reduced to simple 3/4- and 4/4-time. In doing so the Persians have preserved and returned to the early Islamic metres, one of them being a version of the original *ramal.*

Central Asia (Uzbekistan):

1. *ramal* (Kawkabī, 1509):	*tana*	*tananan*		*tana*			
	1+1+	4 +		1+1			= 8
2. *ramal* (Mortażā Shāmlū, ca. 1650):	*tan*	*tan*		*tananan*			
	2 +	2 +		4			= 8
3. *taṣnīf-i dūgāh* (*shashmaqōm*):	*bum*	*bum*	*bak*	*īst*	*bak*	*īst*	
	2 +	2 +	4 +		4		= 12
ramal (var. Quṭb al-Dīn; Marāghī):	2+	2+	4+		4		= 12
jār al-arba'a wa-l-'ishrīn (Shihāb al-Dīn al-'Ajamī):	2+	2+	4+		4		= 12
4. *naqāra* (*shashmaqōm*):	*bum*	*bak*	*ba-ka*	*bum*	*bak*	*īst*	
	2 +	2 +	1 + 1	+ 2	+ 4		= 12
ramal (var. *Adwār*, Jāmī; var. Lādhiqī, *Zayn*):	2 +	2 +	2 +	2	+ 4		= 12

In Central Asia the situation in the 10th/16th century was similar to that in Iran, with the difference that the name *ramal* seems to have disappeared earlier in Bokhara than in Isfahan. First we find a *ramal* of 8 time units described in a Persian text written in Bokhara by Najm al-Dīn Kawkabī (no. 1). This version is comparable to that of Nasīmī from Gīlān (see above) and is also confirmed by Mortażā Shāmlū (no. 2). Thus, we can assume with greater probability that it was a northeastern Iranian variant of *ramal.* Kawkabī, incidentally, made a general distinction between "heavy" (*thaqīl*), "medium" (*awsaṭ* or *nīm thaqīl*) and "light" (*khafīf*) metres.[13] In doing so he resumed al-Fārābī's tripartite scheme and passed it on to following generations and finally to Cantemir (d. 1723), who describes a "stable"

---

13 See his *Risāla-i mūsīqī*, ed. Rajabov, ʿAskarʿalī, 1985, Doshanbe: ʿIrfān, Persian text p. 21.

(*thābit*) relation of 4:2:1 between the "large" metre (*vezn-i kebīr*), the "small" metre (*vezn-i ṣaghīr*) and the "smallest" metre (*vezn-i aṣgharü ṣ- ṣaghīr*) of *uṣūl*.[14]

Later, the name *ramal* is absent from the metrical terminology used in Central Asia, especially in the local *shashmaqōm* of Uzbekistan.[15] Nevertheless, two of the *uṣūls* of the *shashmaqōm* can be regarded as successors to the *ramal* family. The first is called *taṣnīf-i dūgāh* (no. 3). Its pattern was recorded with the name *ramal* in Iran in the 8th/14th and 9th/15th centuries and, with a new Arabic name, in 9th/15th century Syria (both are indented in the above list). Uzbek *bum* corresponds to Persian *dīk* and Turkish *düm*. Uzbek *bak* corresponds to Persian *dak* and Turkish *tek*, and *īst* is a Persian word in Uzbek meaning "rest".

The second of these metres used in the *shashmaqōm* (no. 4) is called *naqāra* ("kettle drum", pronounced *naghora*). The name refers to the practice of the military bands, yet it does not follow the typical equal-measured march rhythm in 4/4 time but has a soft, dance-like 6/4 measure. Its structural affinity with one of the earlier patterns of *ramal*, listed by al-Urmawī, Jāmī and al-Lādhiqī, is obvious. Thus, some variants of the traditional *ramal* seem to have survived incognito in Central Asia.

Syria and Egypt (9th/15th century):

1. Saylakūnī (ca. 1500):					
arba'a wa-'ishrūn [*thaqīl al-ramal*]:	4 + 4 + 2 + 2 + 2 + 2 + 2 + 2 + 4				= 24
thaqīl al-ramal (Marāghī),					
muḍā'af al-ramal (Lādhiqī):	4 + 4 + 2 + 2 + 2 + 2 + 2 + 2 + 4				= 24
2. Saylakūnī (ca. 1500):					
niṣf arba'a wa-'ishrīn = niṣf al-aṣl:	4 +	4 +		4	= 12
al-ramal al-thaqīl (Fārābī):	*tanna(n)* +	*tanna(n)* +		rest	
	4 +	4 +		4	= 12
ramal (var. Quṭb al-Dīn):	4 +	2 +	4 +	2	= 12
3. Shihāb al-Dīn al-'Ajamī (15th cent.):					
jār al-arba'a wa-l-'ishrīn:	*tan*	*tan*	*tananan*	*tananan*	
	2 +	2 +	4 +	4	= 12
ramal (var. Quṭb al-Dīn; Marāghī):	2 +	2 +	4 +	4	= 12

---

[14] See Tura, Yalçın 2001, *Kitābu ʿilmi'l-mūsiḳī ʿalā vechi'l-ḥurūfāt. Mûsikîyi harflerle tesbît ve icrâ ilminin kitabı, I. cilt, Edvâr (tıpkıbasım – çevriyazı – çeviri – notlar)*, İstanbul, pp. 16-21. Certain discrepancies regarding metre and tempo caused by this statement as against indications in the practical part of the Cantemir corpus cannot occupy us here. I refer the reader to the study by Wright, Owen 1988, "Aspects of historical change in the Turkish classical repertoire", in: *Musica Asiatica 5*, Richard Widdess (Ed.), Cambridge: Cambridge University Press, 1-108, esp. p. 13.

[15] I am indepted to Angelika Jung for kindly sharing with me her knowledge of the recent Uzbek metres.

In Syria and Egypt we come across, in the 9th/15th century, the new Arabic name just alluded to in Central Asia. It reads literally as "24" (*arbaʿa wa-ʿishrūn*) and was given to the pattern of the traditional "heavy" or "doubled" *ramal* of 24 time units described by Marāghī and Lādhiqī (no. 1 in the table above).

The diminished version of "24" (nos. 2 and 3) had a basic pattern identical to that of Fārābī's "heavy" *ramal.* It was called "half of 24" (*niṣf arbaʿa wa-ʿishrīn)* or "half of the basic pattern" *(niṣf al-aṣl*), or "neighbour of 24" *(jār al-arbaʿa wa-l-ʿishrīn).*

The new names were used by Shihāb al-Dīn al-ʿAjamī in the second half of the 9th/15th century in Syria (no. 3) and by ʿAlī ibn ʿUbayd Allāh al-Saylakūnī around 1500 in Egypt (nos. 1 and 2).

The correspondence between the Persian patterns (indented in the above list) and the Arab patterns confirms the historical fact that in this period Syria and Egypt cultivated, besides their own tradition, a musical fashion imported from Iran by pupils and followers of ʿAbd al-Qādir (al-) Marāghī.

Syria and Egypt (12th/18th-14/20th century):

Kubaysī (comp. 1785); *Sulāfat al-ḥān* (comp. 1860); Cairo Congress (1932):

arbaʿa wa-ʿishrūn:

dum	*tak*	*dum*	*tak*	*dum*	*dum*	*[dum]*	*tak*	*dum*	*tak*	*tak*	*dum*	*tak*	*tak*	*dum*	*tak*	*tak*	*dum*
1 +	1 +	1 +	1 +	1 +	½ +	½ +	1 +	1 +	1 +	1 +	1 +	1 +	1 +	1 +	1 +	1 +	1 +
tak	*tak*	*tak*	*dum*	*tak*	*tak*												
1 +	1 +	1 +	2 +	1 +	1	= 24											

Kubaysī (comp. 1785); *Sulāfat al-ḥān* (comp. 1860); Cairo Congress (1932):

niṣf arbaʿa wa-ʿishrīn:

dum	*tak*	*dum*	*dum*	*dum*	*tak*	*dum*	*tak*	*tak*	*dum*	*tak*	*tak*	
1 +	1 +	1 +	1 +	1 +	1 +	1 +	1 +	1 +	1 +	1 +	1	= 12

The metre called "24" *(arbaʿa wa-ʿishrūn*) has survived in the Eastern Arab countries until today. It retained its name and the number of 12 or 24 time units in Arabic sources from the 12th/18th century onwards, here represented by al-Kubaysī from Syria and others.

The inner structure of the metre, however, does not bear any resemblance to its former namesake. Here we first meet with the break in tradition between the 9th/15th and the 11th/17th century that in a different form we will also find in Turkey. In Syria and Egypt it coincided with a loss of political sovereignty. Courtly and urban secular art music lost importance in relation to the growing artistic performance of religious *qaṣīda*s and *muwashshaḥāt.*

Irak is a special case. The origin and early development of the present-day *al-maqām al-ʿirāqī* is hidden from us. Neither the name *ramal* nor any of its historical patterns seem to have survived. In the contemporary urban repertoire the number of metres (*awzān*) is reduced to eight with a preference for short patterns such as 2/4, 3/4, 4/4 and 6/4.

North Africa seems to have ignored *ramal* as a musical metre. Instead the name was given to one of the melodic modes. Yet some triple patterns (today written in 6/4, 3/4 or 6/8), such as *basīṭ* in Morocco, *khalāṣī* in Algeria or *mṣaddar* in Tunisia, can be interpreted as modifications of the old Arabic *ramal* of Isḥāq al-Mawṣilī and al-Fārābī.[16]

Ottoman Turkey (1450-1500):

remel-i ṭavīl ("long" *remel*):

1. Seydī:	2 + 2 + 4 + 4 + 2 + 2 + 2 = 18
2. Seydī (var.):	1+1+2 + 4 + 4 + 2 +1+1+ 2 = 18

remel-i ṭavīl :

3. Khıżır b. ʿAbdullāh and Yūsuf b. Niẓāmeddīn:	4 + 3 + 3 + 2 + 2 + 2 + 2 = 18

remel-i ḳaṣīr ("short" *remel*):

4. Seydī:	2 + 2 + 2 + 2 + 4 + 2 = 14
5. Seydī (altern.):	4 + 2 + 2 + 4 + 2 = 14
6. Khıżır b. ʿAbdullāh and Yūsuf b. Niẓāmeddīn:	2 + 2 + 2 + 3 + 3 + 2 = 14
7. *remel-i nıṣfü 'l-aṣıl* (Seydī):	4 + 2 + 4 + 2 = 12
(= *ramal*, var. Quṭb al-Dīn):	4 + 2 + 4 + 2 = 12

In Anatolia in the second half of the 9th/15th century, we find new types of *ramal* in local variants. They are described in the *edvār* books by Khıżır b. ʿAbdullāh, Yūsuf b. Niẓāmeddīn al-Rūmī from Kırşehir, and by a certain Seydī. These metres have 18 or 14 time units (instead of 12 in former times) and no visible relation to any of the earlier or contemporaneous patterns of the *ramal* family.

---

16 See al-Mahdī, Ṣāliḥ 1990, *Īqāʿāt al-mūsīqā al-ʿarabiyya wa-ashkāluhā* (= Wizārat al-Thaqāfa wa-l-Iʿlām, Silsilat maʿārif li-l-jamīʿ: funūn jamīla), Qarṭāj (Carthago): Bayt al-Ḥikma, p. 46, 47, 48.

There is only one exception. It is the "half of the original" (*nişfü 'l-aşıl*) listed by Seydī (no. 7). This metre of 12 time units looks identical to the short *ramal* listed by Quṭb al-Dīn Shīrāzī (above). But whether this variant was still used in Anatolia or was simply a historicizing relic cannot be answered without further evidence.

Ottoman Turkey (11th/17th-14th/20th century):

1. *remel* (Cantemir etc., 17th and 18th cent.):

düm teke düm teke teke düm teke düm ***tek*** *tek düm tek düm düm tek* ***teke teke***

(2)+ (2)+ (2)+ (2)+ (2)+ (2)+ (2)+ (2)+ (2)+ (2)+ (1)+ (1)+ (1)+ (1)+ (2)+ (1) +(1) = 28

2. *ramal* (Aleppo, Cairo Congress):

dum tak tak dum tak tak tak dum tak tak dum dum dum tak tak tak dum tak ...

(2)+ (1)+ (1)+ (2)+ (2)+ (1)+ (1)+ (2)+ (1)+ (1)+ (1)+ (½)+ (½)+ (2)+ (1)+ (1)+ (1)+ (1) ... = 28

3. *remel* (14th/20th cent.):

düm teke düm teke teke düm teke düm ***düm*** *tek düm tek düm düm tek* ***teke***

(2)+ (2)+ (2)+ (2)+ (2)+ (2)+ (2)+ (2)+ (2)+ (2)+ (1)+ (1)+ (1)+ (1)+ (2)+ (2) = 28

In the 11th/17th and 12th/18th centuries the Ottoman-Turkish *remel* was recorded by Dimitrie Cantemir, Kevs̱erī, Khıżır Āghā, ʿAbdülbāḳī Dede and others (no. 1). By this time it had either 14, 28, 56, or 112 time units.[17] The extent of augmentation corresponds to Marāghī's four-fold series of 12, 24, 48 and 96 time units.

At first sight one might expect that the "short" *remel-i ḳaṣīr* of 14 time units described by Seydī and others in the 9th/15th century could have been the ancestor of this "doubled" version of 28 time units, but no structural resemblance can be ascertained. Here we meet with a similar break in tradition between the 9th/15th and the 11th/17th centuries as that observed before in Syria and Egypt. In this case the change in musical taste seems to have been a consequence of the nearly complete resettlement of Constantinople/Istanbul after the Ottoman conquest in 1453.

Likewise similar to Egypt and Syria, this most recent form of *remel* survived nearly unchanged from the 11th/17th to the 14th/20th century (two minimal variants are given in bold in the table above). This stability, however, was accompanied by a decreasing use of this and other long *uṣūl*s. The extensive Cantemir collection of instrumental *peşref*s and *semāʿī*s from the 1690s contains only two exam-

---

17 See the comparative description in Neubauer, Eckhard 1999, *Der Essai sur la musique orientale von Charles Fonton mit Zeichnungen von Adanson*, Frankfurt: Institute for the History of Arabic-Islamic Science, pp. 287-288.

ples in the metre *remel*[18], and ʿAlī Ufuḳī (d. probably 1677) did not record a single piece in this metre.

The obvious predilection for short *uṣūl*s was intensified by western influence and modern popular music and has resulted in a reduction of the long metres to the benefit of 3/4- and 4/4-time. In this respect most of the countries mentioned here share a common recent development. They have either returned to or have retained the short metres of old.

In conclusion, it may be mentioned that the *ramal* from Aleppo in Syria (no. 2 above) was recorded at the Cairo Congress in 1932. Our journey through time has established that this local Syrian variant was more closely related to the Turkish version of the Cantemir corpus (late 11th/17th century) than to the Syrian-Arab version documented by al-Kubaysī (late 12th/18th century) and in subsequent Syrian sources.

To sum up, it can be stated that the metre *ramal* kept its initial pattern nearly unchanged from early Islamic times up to the 7th/13th century and beyond. The only modification consisted in linking together two "periods" of the original metre (6 + 6 time units) to form one new "basic form" of 12 time units with the same name and structure. *Ramal* shared this kind of augmentation with other principal metres, in some cases combined with a change of name. At the same time, the melodic modes grew in number and some of them also received new names.[19]

In Iran and its cultural sphere of influence *ramal* kept its new, enlarged structure and underwent further augmentation (24 to 96 time units) up to the 9th/15th century.

In the eastern Arab countries the enlarged *ramal* of 24 time units was renamed "24" (*arbaʿa wa-ʿishrūn*). This took place in the 9th/15th century or earlier. In the 10th/16th century a fundamental change resulted in a different inner structure of the pattern, recorded in 12th/18th-, 13th/19th- and 14th/20th-century sources.

In Safavid Iran (16th and 17th centuries) at least two versions of *ramal* existed side by side: the traditional pattern and several namesakes with different structures. In the 12th/18th and early 13th/19th centuries the traditional metres disappeared altogether.

Ottoman Turkey kept the name but changed the pattern as early as in the 9th/15th century. After a period of development (and missing sources), *remel* reap-

---

18 Ms. İstanbul, Türkiyat Enstitüsü, T.Y. 2768, pp. 142-143; Wright, Owen 1992b, *Demetrius Cantemir, The collection of notations, Volume 1: Text*, London, nos. 277 and 278 (28/8), and 2000, pp. 498-500; Tura 2001b, *Kitābu ʿilmi'l-mūsīḳī ʿalā vechi'l-ḥurūfāt. Mûsikîyi harflerle tesbît ve icrâ ilminin kitabı, II. cilt, Notalar (tıpkıbasım –çeviri – notlar)*, İstanbul: Yapı Kredi Yayınları, nos. 277 and 278, pp. 510-512, (both *vezn-i kebīr*, 28/4).

19 Cf. Wright, Owen 2004-5, "Die melodischen Modi bei Ibn Sīnā und die Entwicklung der Modalpraxis von Ibn al-Munağğim bis zu Ṣafī al-Dīn al-Urmawī", *Zeitschrift für Geschichte der arabisch-islamischen Wissenschaften* Bd. 16, pp. 224-308.

peared with a new structure in the 11th/17th century and then remained unchanged until the present.

In several countries of the Middle East a decrease in the use of long metres (such as *ramal*) can be observed, which was to the benefit of shorter metres including 5/4 (the old "second heavy"), 6/8 (the old *hazaj*), and the popular 3/4 and 4/4 times. Cantemir could still point in the early eighteenth century to the latter (*semāʿī* and *ṣōfiyān*) as being the only metric representatives of "the Franks and the Russians" in contrast to the colourful variety of the eastern *uṣūl*s.[20]

20 See Tura 2001, p. 12, 13.

The Ottoman *Usul* System and Its Precursors[1]

Owen Wright

One of the more problematic issues in the history of Ottoman music is how to account for the erosion of the sixteenth-century Persianate court-music repertoire of vocal music and its replacement in the seventeenth by an emergent Istanbul-based repertoire; and related to this is the question of the degree to which the musical grammar of the Persianate repertoire, its interlocking systems of modes, rhythmic cycles and forms, was retained, adjusted or transformed in the course of this major shift. While the former question is of some complexity, demanding the sifting of scattered and sometimes elusive historical and social evidence in order to contextualize what musicological materials seem to suggest[2], it might be thought that the latter should be somewhat easier, at least to the extent that it can be largely conducted within a narrower framework, by observing alterations to the patterns of occurrence of technical terms and, above all, by interrogating the definitions of them supplied by the theoretical literature.

It is, however, a literature with frustrating gaps, not least with regard to the repertoires of rhythmic cycles. One may venture the generalization that the evolution of the Ottoman *usul* system is reasonably clear from the time of Cantemir (1674-1732) on[3]: its course can be tracked through theoretical texts as well as through notations, and although additions and losses to the stock occur as well as internal changes in individual cycles, in neither case are they so drastic as to call into question the notion of continuous development within an essentially unitary tradition; and a comparably coherent state of affairs is suggested by the equally precise and largely consistent definitions provided throughout the fif-

1 The present introductory sketch draws heavily upon the work, amongst others, of Mehrdad Fallahzadeh, Walter Feldman, Angelika Jung and Amir Hosein Pourjavady, but most especially upon the scholarship of Eckhard Neubauer, of particular relevance here being his 1999-2000, "Glimpses of Arab music in Ottoman times from Syrian and Egyptian sources", *Zeitschrift für Geschichte der Arabisch-Islamischen Wissenschaften 13*, 317-365.

2 See Feldman, Walter 1996, *Music of the Ottoman court: makam, composition and the early Ottoman instrumental repertoire* (Intercultural Music Studies: 10, ed. Max Peter Baumann), Berlin: VWB, pp. 28-84; and more particularly Feldman, Walter 2015, "The Musical Materials of Ali Ukfi Bey (1610-1675) in the Light of The Musical 'Renaissance' of Late 17th Century Ottoman Turkey, with Some Observations on the 'Maraghi' Repertoire", in: *Writing the History of "Ottoman Music"*, Martin Greve (Ed.), Istanbuler Texte und Studien: 33, Würzburg: Ergon Verlag (I am grateful to Walter Feldman for allowing me to see this prior to publication).

3 Tura, Yalçın (Ed.) 2001, *Kitābu ʿilmi'l-mūsīḳī ʿalā vechi'l-ḥurūfāt. Mûsikîyi harflerle tesbît ve icrâ ilminin kitabı, I. cilt, Edvâr* (*tıpkıbasım – çevriyazı – çeviri – notlar*) and 2001b *Kitābu ʿilmi'l-mūsīḳī* [...], *II. cilt, Notalar* (*tıpkıbasım –çeviri – notlar*), Istanbul: Yapı Kredi Yayınları; facsimile and tr. in Popescu-Judeţ, Eugenia 1973, *Dimitrie Cantemir: cartea ştinţei muzicii*, Bucharest: Editura Musicala; Wright, Owen 2000, *Demetrius Cantemir, The collection of notations, Volume 2: Commentary*. (SOAS Musicology Series), Aldershot: Ashgate, pp. 389-527.

teenth century by Marāġī (d. 1435)[4] and his Timurid successors, most notably Awbahī[5] and Banā'ī[6]. The major question is thus establishing what happened in between, and what continuities and ruptures there might be between the late Timurid state of affairs and that to which Cantemir bears witness at the dawn of the eighteenth century. An initial narrowing of this lengthy period may be achieved by accepting that the great majority of the cycles Cantemir describes, and especially the most commonly used ones, were known in virtually the same form to Ali Ufuki (d. 1677). If we set aside those mentioned in his collections[7] and others indubitably represented among his notations,[8] there are just six further cycles cited by Cantemir, one a later innovation, the other five marginal, while Ali Ufuki for his part refers in just one composition to a cycle unknown to Cantemir. Further, Ali Ufuki's definitions may be identical or nearly identical with those of Cantemir, or clearly related, as with *düyek*[9]:

Ali Ufuki	*düm tek . tek düm düm tek teke*
Cantemir	*düm tek . tek düm . tek .* [10]

Elsewhere there may be slightly different perceptions of internal segmentation[11], but the general picture is nevertheless one of near unanimity. Accordingly, from 1700 we may move back at least to 1650, and quite possibly to 1630, and if Cantemir's account is retained here as the primary term of reference it is only because of its greater scope and precision.

Approaching the now slightly reduced gap from the other side, one may note, first, a line linking Marāġī, through his son and grandson, to the fifteenth-century Ottoman court, and to suppose the naturalization there, or at least acceptance, of Timurid norms. Equally, it is reasonable to suppose the retention or evolution of aspects of Timurid practice during the sixteenth century among later generations of musicians in the wider Persianate sphere, some of whom would come or be brought as captives to the Ottoman court, as also happened later during the reign of Murat IV (1623-40).[12] However partial and fragile, how-

4 ʿAbd al-Qādir al-Marāġī, *jāmiʿ al-alḥān*, ed. Taqī Bīniš 1366/1987, Tehran.

5 ʿAlīšāh b. Būka Awbahī, *muqaddima-yi uṣūl*, İstanbul Üniversitesi Kütüphanesi MS F 1079.

6 ʿAlī b. Muḥammad Miʿmār (mašhūr be-Banā'ī) 1368š/1990, *risāla dar mūsīqī*, facsimile, Tehran: markaz-i našr-i dānišgāhī. The treatise is dated 888/1484.

7 Although not necessarily by him: see Behar, Cem 2008, *Saklı mecmua. Ali Ufkî'nin Bibliothèque Nationale de France'taki [Turc 292] yazması*, Istanbul: Yapı Kredi Yayınları.

8 Also in *mecmûa-i sâz ü söz*, British Library Ms Sloane 3114, facsimile in Elçin, Şükrü 1976, *Ali Ufkî: hayatı, eserleri ve mecmûa-i sâz ü söz*, Istanbul, transcription in Cevher, M. Hakan 1991, *Hâzâ mecmûa-i sâz ü söz*, Izmir. Ali Ufuki frequently omits the name of the cycle, and in some pieces there is more than one possibility.

9 In relation to the Ottoman tradition names are given in Turkish form, but in relation to earlier texts Arabic or Persian forms are preferred. Variants are largely ignored.

10 The differences between these versions are discussed in Behar 2008.

11 For further details see the following chapter.

12 See Feldman 1996, pp. 66-67.

ever ideologically inflected the surviving accounts might be, one could thus still anticipate, on the basis of the kind of indebtedness that they suggest, some degree of continuity between Timurid and Ottoman rhythmic structures, whatever the fate of the Persianate repertoire the former had underpinned. Continuity, though, is a comfortably vague concept: at best it points to the survival of certain cycles, whether intact or exhibiting changes brought about by observable and non-random processes, while accepting at the same time that some will be discarded and others added, a scenario seemingly confirmed, at least at the level of their names, by comparing (in fig. 1) those recognized by Cantemir with those found in the late Timurid treatises of Awbahī and Banāʾī.

Timurid only	common	Ottoman only
čahār żarb	*berefşan*	*devr-i kebir*
dawr-i šāhī	*çenber*	*devr-i revan*
farᶜ	*darb-ı fetih*	*ferᶜ-i muhammes*
ġūriyāna	*düyek*	*frenkçin*
ḫafīf al-ramal	*evfer*	*havi*
ḫafīf al-ṯaqīl	*evsat*	*horezm*
miʾatayn	*fahte*	*nim devir*
rāh-i samāᶜ	*hafif*	*semai*
rāh-i sawārī	*hezec*	*semai-i lenk*
šādiyāna	*muhammes*	*sofyan*
ṯaqīl ṯānī	*nim sakil*	*yek darb*
turkī sarīᶜ	*remel*	
żarb al-qadīm	*sakil*	
	türki darb	

Figure 1

Ignoring two complex entities that combine pre-existing cycles, Cantemir thus cites 25 names of which a little over a half are mentioned by Awbahī and/or Banāʾī, while the remainder are counterbalanced by a similar number that fail to survive until the time of Cantemir. This tabulation is, it must be conceded, imprecise and only indicative, as variant forms defined as *kabīr*, *awsaṭ* or *ṣaġīr* have simply been omitted from the Timurid list, and various alternatives and possible equivalences (e.g. *farᶜ* and *ferᶜ-i muhammes*) have likewise been disregarded.[13] It indicates, nevertheless, that we are faced with corpora of approximately similar size in which the substantial stock of common names points to the survival, if not necessarily in exactly the same form, of at least a half, and given the level of

---

13 For further details see Neubauer 1999-2000.

obsolescence and innovation that might reasonably be expected over a period of over a century this would point to a considerable level of continuity.

However, given that the survival of a name does not guarantee that the cycle itself remained unchanged, account also needs to be taken of the various definitions available. In some cases these appear confirmatory, the trail left by the theoretical literature pointing to structural stability, and as a first example we may assemble (in fig. 2) a chronological spread of definitions of *fāḫitī/fahte*, a cycle of particular interest as one might have thought it potentially unstable, given that it was variable in length.[14] Beginning with the definitions of the shorter form given by the pre-Timurid Systematist theorists al-Urmawī (d. 1294) and Šīrāzī (d. 1311), the survey juxtaposes a segmented time-unit abstraction derived from the precise articulations given by Cantemir, who provides both the contrastive attack qualities and the durations between them, with analogous abstractions derived from the earlier texts which give internal segmentation by using the syllable strings *tan*, *tanan*, *tananan* and so forth. The dates point to the approximate mid point of the period for which the definition may be deemed valid.

1250-	al-Urmawī	20	(4+2+4)+(4+2+4)		
1275			(2+4+4)+(2+4+4)		
1300	Šīrāzī	20	(2+4+4)+(2+4+4)		
1400	Marāġī	20	(4+2+4)+(4+2+4)		
1475	Awbahī	20	2+8 +10	10	2+4+4
	al-Lāḏiqī	20	(2+4+4)+(2+4+4)	10	2+4+4
1650	Ali Ufuki			10	(2+4)+4
1700	Cantemir			10	(2+4)+4

Figure 2

As there would be nothing untoward in recalibrating a cycle that consisted of two seemingly identical halves as two separate cycles, there is, it seems, only the slight vacillation of 2+4+4 versus 4+2+4 to note. It should be added, though, as a salutary reminder of the dangers of extrapolating from inadequate evidence, that on the basis of the disposition of *düm/tek* strokes in Cantemir's definition:

düm . tek . . düm tek . teke teke

one might wish to analyse it, rather, as 2+3+(3+2), but that the melodic morphology of the corpus fails to align itself with this distribution, being more akin to that implied by Ali Ufuki's definition:

düm . tek . . . düm tek teke teke

14 It could be extended from 20 time units to 28 (see Arslan, Fazlı 2007, *Safiyyüddîn-i Urmevî ve şerefiyye risâlesi*, Ankara: Atatürk Kültür Merkezi, pp. 254-256.)

A similarly tenacious example of survival is provided by *warašān/berefşan*:

1250	al-Urmawi[15]	16	3+3+4+2+4
1300	Šīrāzī	16	3+3+4+2+4
1400	Marāġī	16	3+3+4+2+4
1475	Banā'ī/ al-Lāḏiqī	16	3+3+4+2+4
1650	Ali Ufuki	16	3+3+2+4+4
1700	Cantemir	16	3+3+2+4+4

Figure 3

The overall total of time units also remains the same for *hafif*, *sakil*, *çenber* and *muhammas* but, as *muhammas* demonstrates (with Ibn Kurr and Seydi added as witnesses to fourteenth-century Egyptian and fifteenth-century Anatolian perceptions respectively), there may be internal redistribution:

1250	al-Urmawi[16]	16	4+4+4+4		
1300	Šīrāzī			8	2+2+4
1340	Ibn Kurr	16	4+4+4+4		(3+3+2)+(3+3+2)
1400	Marāġī	16			(3+3+2)+(3+3+2)
				8	3+3+2
1475	Banā'ī/al-Lāḏiqī	16			(3+3+2)+(3+3+2)
				8	3+3+2
	Seydī			8	3+3+2
1650	Ali Ufuki	16	4+4+4+4		
1700	Cantemir	16	4+4+4+4		

Figure 4

Thus despite the stability of the time-unit total, *muhammas* presents us with the puzzle of the Timurid (and possibly early Ottoman as well as Mamluk) preference for 3+3+2 being supplanted by what is apparently (but perhaps only apparently) a reversal to the earlier 4+4: if actually a continuation rather than a coincidence, it is an undocumented one.

However, in other cases the surviving definitions are variable, with few or no apparent connections between them. Time unit totals do not remain the same in *düyek*, *hezec* and *remel*, and to take two further examples, *evsat* seems to wander erratically between different totals and internal segmentations:

15 For whom it is an alternative name for *ṯaqīl awwal.*

16 For whom it is an alternative name for *ḫafīf al-ṯaqīl.*

1400	Marāġī	20	(4+2+4)+(4+2+4)
		5	3+2
1475	Banāʾī	24	4+4+2+6+8
	al-Lāḏiqī	24	8 +16
1700	Cantemir	26	(2+3+4+4) + (2+3+4+4)

Figure 5

while *darb-ı fetih* rapidly puts on weight, rising from an original 50 time units[17] to as high as 88[18]. It is also important to note a general typological contrast that is not merely a function of a difference in descriptive approach: whereas Cantemir's definitions are quite specific, Timurid accounts are often more fluid, allowing different internal dispositions and subsuming cycles of different length under the same rubric. The general picture, then, seems to be one in which stability is now confined to a significantly smaller area, indicative of a survival rate markedly lower than that suggested by the nomenclature: among these often complex and lengthy cycles fewer than might be supposed can be identified as surviving largely unscathed from their fifteenth-century Timurid to their seventeenth-century Ottoman manifestations.

Also broadly in alignment with this conclusion is the supplementary evidence of the fifteenth to sixteenth-century song-text collections[19], which contain no definitions but both name cycles and, importantly, give some indication of their relative popularity. The forty-odd names that occur in them include more than twenty that are unknown to Cantemir, several evidently marginal, but some central: indeed, to judge by the most populous collection they include three of most frequently occurring cycles (*se darb*, *ʿamal* and *ṭarab angīz*), ones that also leave no trace in the Timurid literature down to Awbahī. We thus have a situation where a third of the vocal repertoire represented in this collection is in cycles seemingly unknown both to the later Ottoman tradition and to the earlier Timurid mainstream.[20] Several of them are, however, recorded by al-Lāḏiqī, the one late Sys-

17 Or 49. One might be tempted to dismiss this as a slip, but both totals are given by Marāġī, its creator. For details see Neubauer 1999-2000.

18 A total already reached before the end of the fifteenth century: it is recorded by both Awbahī and al-Lāḏiqī.

19 For data see Wright, Owen 1992, *Words without songs: a musicological study of an Ottoman anthology and its precursors* (SOAS Musicology Series, 3), London: School of Oriental and African Studies.

20 Their incidence is *se darb*: 116 occurrences, *ʿamal*: 86 and *ṭarab angīz*: 26, giving 228 out of a total of 691. These results are partially confirmed by a control sample, the first 200 entries in the contents list of another collection (Dāniš Pažūh, Muḥammad Taqī 2535/1976, "*advār-i sulṭānī*", Hunar va-Mardum 173, year 15, 18-25). Here *ṭarab angīz* rather surprisingly fails to appear, but *ʿamal* and *se ḍarb* dominate again, accounting between them for 45% of the total, while the marginality of such cycles as *jarr*, *muḥajjal* and *sarandāz* is demonstrated by the fact that each appears only once.

tematist theorist to contrast with an inherited account of modes and rhythms what had replaced them in contemporary practice, while a few also appear in the Arabic terminology recorded by Šihāb al-Dīn al-ᶜAjamī[21] and one or two in the late sixteenth-century Persian treatise attributed to Mīr Ṣadr al-Dīn Muḥammad Qazvīnī[22]. However, this by no means exhausts the cycle names found in the anthologies, and even if it suggests for several of them reasonably wide currency it would hardly justify continuing to examine in simple diachronic terms levels of continuity that might or might not validate the perception of a Timurid to Ottoman transmission, in part via Persianate intermediaries: attention also needs to be paid to the extent of synchronic differentiation resulting from regional particularism. It is only in this way, for example, that one could account for the marked differences in the time-unit totals noted in relation to *żarb al-fatḥ*, for in the late fifteenth century we find one version with a total of 88 time-units alongside another with 48[23], while in the sixteenth century one Persian text has 58 and another 78. Had these occurred chronologically in ascending order one would assume a gradual and hence comprehensible process of distension, but the textual trace we have suggests, rather, random mutations, each in a different locality, with just one being tenacious enough to survive and be incorporated into the Ottoman canon.

The situation is further complicated by the possibility that different local names were used for the same cycle. Širwānī, for example, states that *hazaj* is called *čanbar* in Azerbaijan (and especially Tabriz)[24], Banāʾī that it is called *čanbar* in Iraq (i.e. the west) and *rah-i samāᶜ* in Khorasan (i.e. the east), while al-Lādiqī, without specifying localities, similarly equates *hazaj ṣağīr* with *čanbar* and, further, *ravān* with *ṭarab angīz* and *ᶜamal* with *turkī ḍarb*.[25] Similarly, towards the end of the sixteenth century Mīr Ṣadr al-Dīn Muḥammad Qazvīnī states that *ramal* is now known as *čanbar* and that *samāᶜī* is known as *dawr-i šāhī* in Khorasan[26]. As a result, distinctions may become blurred (and these are not the only instances of name substitution), while a further and more significant difficulty is created by the fact that beyond language we may have few or no clues to the provenance of an anonymous

21 For which see Neubauer 1999-2000, pp. 346-353. Thus in addition to *se ḍarb*, *ᶜamal* and *muḥajjal*, al-Lādiqī mentions *ḍarb jadīd*, *jarr*, *rikāb*, *sarandāz* and *ṭarab angīz* (further names that will disappear later), while al-ᶜAjamī also mentions *se ḍarb*, *ḍarb jadīd* and the variant *muḥajjar*.

22 Mīr Ṣadr al-Dīn Muḥammad Qazvīnī 2003, *risāla-yi ᶜilm-i mūsīqī*, ed. Rustamī, Āriyū, *faṣlnāma-yi mūsīqī-yi māhūr 18*, pp. 81-96. He mentions *sarandāz*, *ḍarb al-mulūk* and *ᶜamal* (and also two cycles not cited elsewhere, *mujammar* and *pirjāmālī*).

23 Recorded by al-ᶜAjamī (Neubauer 1999-2000).

24 Fatḥ Allāh al-Muʾmin al-Širwānī 1986, *majalla fī al-mūsīqī*, facsimile (of MS Topkapı Ahmet III 3449) in Publications of the Institute for the History of Arabic-Islamic Science, series C, 29, Frankfurt, p. 174.

25 Neubauer 1999-2000.

26 Qazvīnī 2003, pp. 91-92. He also states that *sarandāz* is derived from *farᶜ-i muḫammas* and *żarb al-mulūk* from *faḫita-yi kabır*, and that in both cases they are more or less the same; and that the name *hazaj* is being abandoned in favour of *doyak*.

text, and even when authorship is known the local affiliations of the writer may be unascertainable. With such a key witness as al-Lāḏiqī, for instance, we have, apart from his name, in any case an unreliable indicator, only the dedication of his *kitāb al-fatḥiyya* to an Ottoman sultan as a possible indication of the area to which his terminology relates, but it is in any event one that only overlaps partially with what we find in fifteenth-century Turkish texts from Anatolia. Distinctive of such writers as Kırşehirlī[27] and Seydī[28] is the assignment of the cycles to two groups, one subsumed under *ṯaqīl*, the other *ḫafīf*, the former including the familiar *varašān*, *ravān*, *żarb-i turkī*, *fāḫita*, *hazaj* and *awsaṭ*, but also *samāʿī* and *sarandāz* among the further terms mentioned by al-Lāḏiqī. The latter group similarly includes *čār żarb*, *muḫammas*, *rāh (-i kurd)* and *se żarb*, and presents, again like al-Lāḏiqī (and Marāġī before him) variant forms of *ramal*.[29] However, that still leaves unmentioned a considerable number of names included by al-Lāḏiqī (even if he characterizes some as rare or obsolete) and, as might by now have been predicted, the definitions they provide differ from his, often markedly so. Indeed, evident parity is only present in *ṯaqīl* (24 time units for Seydī, 48 for al-Lāḏiqī) and *ḫafīf* (16 for Seydī, 32 for al-Lāḏiqī), whereas they do not correspond at all for *varašān*, *żarb-i turkī* and *fāḫita* (where we have 12 vs. 16, 10 vs. 14 and 14 vs. 10/20 respectively).

Both corpora differ even more clearly from that (or those) exhibited in Arabic texts. Evidence for a distinct Cairene tradition appears already in the account of early fourteenth-century practice provided by Ibn Kurr[30], which stands at a considerable remove even from the earliest Systematist description, despite this relating to cycles stated by the Baghdad-based al-Urmawī to be characteristic of Arab practice[31]. However, Ibn Kurr's terminology is only faintly echoed by the fifteenth-century Arab theorists al-ʿAjamī and al-Saylakūnī, and despite the fact that we encounter in them a further development of the trend to name cycles according to the number of time units they contain, they only have one such in common with Ibn Kurr, *sittat ʿašar*, and this they define as 3+2+3+3+2+3[32] whereas Ibn Kurr points to 4+4+4+4. The earlier of the two, al-ʿAjamī, has the fuller account, but there is still little overlap with Ibn Kurr: common to them both are only *warašān*, with 14 time units, *ḫusrawānī*, with 18, and *fāḫit(a)*, with 20 in one and 10 in the other–but in all three cases with a somewhat different internal segmentation. For

---

27 See the chapter by Nilgün Doğrusöz-Dişiaçık in the present volume.

28 See Popescu-Judetz, E. and E. Neubauer (Ed.) 2004, *Seydī's book on music: A 15th century Turkish discourse*, The Science of Music in Islam, vol. 6, Frankfurt am Main: Institute for the History of Arabic-Islamic Science.

29 For further details see Neubauer 1999-2000.

30 See Wright, Owen 2014, *Music theory in Mamluk Cairo. The ġāyat al-maṭlūb fī ʿilm al-anġām wa-'l-ḍurūb by Ibn Kurr*, Farnham: Ashgate.

31 Ṣafī al-Dīn al-Urmawī 1980, *kitāb al-adwār*, ed. al-Rajab, Hāšim Muḥammad, Baghdad, p. 143. Of these cycles only *ṯaqīl al-ramal* (p. 149) was common among Persians (who called it *ḍarb al-aṣl*). Just one cycle is included that is stated to be specific to them, *fāḫitī* (p. 153).

32 Neubauer 1999-2000, p. 346.

his part, al-Saylakūnī introduces a further complication by reproducing exactly one of the patterns given by al-Urmawī for the 24 time-unit cycle *ṯaqīl al-ramal*, 4+4+2+2+2+2+2+2+4, calling it *arbaʿa wa-ʿišrūn*, while Ibn Kurr acknowledges neither name, offering instead as a cycle of 24 time units *ḫurāsānī*, with a fundamental 6+6+6+6 structure. We thus have a rather unsettled picture of rhythmic nomenclature and practice(s) in Mamluk territories, but at the same time an indication of a major line of cleavage between the Mamluk and Persianate worlds evident from the fourteenth century, compounded in the fifteenth by further, if less marked, variations between early Ottoman (assuming that al-Lāḏiqī and the song-text collections reflect Ottoman preferences), Anatolian and Timurid practice, the widespread (if incomplete) use of a common terminology masking the frequent and seemingly unpredictable contrasts from area to area between the structures to which a given name was attached.

What we have not yet considered is evidence from the problematic sixteenth century. With the stabilization of Ottoman and Safavid power during this period the geopolitical and hence cultural map changes yet again, but not necessarily towards greater centralization. On the Ottoman side provincial cities retained a degree of vitality, and court patronage in Istanbul was insufficiently enthusiastic to foster a prestigious metropolitan style,[33] while the Safavid picture is more fragmented still: the implacable hostility to music shown by Shah Ṭahmāsb for much of his lengthy reign (1524-76) resulted in the dispersal (when not death) of musicians, with patronage only being sustained outside the court, and especially at the peripheries by distant provincial governors.[34] For both, informative texts are in short supply: on the Ottoman side there is a dearth of theoretical writing, and most of the surviving Persian texts are somewhat unhelpful in that they fail to add definitions to their enumerations, which for the rhythmic cycles centre upon what increasingly appears to be a canonical set of seventeen–even if neither the number nor the names are always the same. A typical example is the early sixteenth-century *risāla al-karāmiyya*[35], where we encounter, first, *żarb al-qadīm*, conceived as a form of proto-rhythm, followed by the primary set of seventeen names that, with occasional minor variations, includes all fourteen in the central column (those common to Timurid and Ottoman texts) in fig. 1. Of the remaining three, *čahār żarb* and *miʾatayn* will not survive to the end of the seventeenth century and may well already have been obsolescent, while *dawr*, relatable to the Ottoman *devr-i kebir*, is a recent addition. This indicates, then, the same high level of reten-

33 There is thus a considerable delay before Istanbul begins to export rhythmic cycles to the Arab provinces (see the chapter by Salah Eddin Maraqa in the present volume). For a survey of this period see Feldman 1996 and 2015.

34 For a general survey see Pourjavady, Amir Hoseyn 2005, "*The musical codex of Amir Khān Gorji (c. 1108-1697)*", PhD dissertation, University of California, Los Angeles.

35 Published in Fallahzadeh, Mehrdad 2009, *Two treatises – two streams: treatises from the post-scholastic era of Persian writings on music theory*, edited, translated into English and annotated by Mehrdad Fallahzade, Bethesda, Maryland: Ibex Publishers.

tion of terminology and, to judge by the presence of much of the same name set in the treatises of Najm al-Dīn Kawkabī and Darvīš ʿAlī,[36] suggests with regard to post-Timurid developments that the Ottoman and Persianate traditions (including both Safavid Persia and Shaybanid Central Asia) may have been proceeding in tandem, with cultural ties and exchanges being relatively unaffected by political antagonism.

The *risāla al-karāmiyya* takes us no further, but there are other Persian texts that do: the mid sixteenth-century treatise by Nasīmī, *nasīm-i ṭarab*[37], and the anonymous *taqsīm al-naġamāt*,[38] probably to be ascribed to the same period. In considering the evidence they provide we may begin with yet another list of cycle names, but one that extends into the period of Ali Ufuki and Cantemir by taking account also of the mid to late seventeenth-century treatise by Āqā Muʾmin, the late seventeenth-century treatise by Amīr Ḫān Gurjī,[39] and the elusive *bahjat al-rūḥ*[40]. Common to all five Persian texts are nine core names that are also mentioned by Cantemir: *awfar*, *do(bar)yak*, *fāḫita*, *ḫafīf*, *muḫammas*, *ṯaqīl*, *turkī żarb*, *barafšān* and *żarb al-fatḥ*; and there are a further seventeen that occur in more than one text, distributed as in fig. 6. As this shows, the two mid sixteenth-century texts thus still record three cycles cited in the early song-text collections that will disappear later (*miʾatayn*, *šāhnāma*, *ḫʷājak*), while absent from them are a number of cycles cited in later texts, whether Safavid or Ottoman (*dawr*, *čanbar*, *farʿ*, *nīm dawr*, *ḥarbī*, *ṣūfiyāna*, *żarb al-mulūk*)[41]. Nevertheless, as in fig. 1, which compares Timurid and Ottoman terminology, the rate of turnover is hardly disquieting, and certainly fails to provide evidence for a period of radical transformation: adding in the common core of nine names we have a grand total of twenty-six, of which only six are not recorded in the Ottoman tradition, while no fewer than fifteen, nearly two thirds of the total, are attested in both early and late texts. There is, then, contrary to the rupture that the song-text collections seem to indicate, nothing to suggest other than a smooth progression, a gradual and wholly predictable process of change continuing until we come to the second half of the seventeenth century. It is, though, not one affecting a more or less closed corpus, for in addition to the cycles listed two of these treatises in-

---

36 See Jung, Angelika 1989, *Quellen der traditionellen Kunstmusik der Usbeken und Tadschiken Mittelasiens*, Beiträge zur Ethnomusikologie 23, Hamburg, pp. 132-134 for further details. The absence from Kawkabī's treatise of the newer names listed by al-Lāḏiqī is interpreted as a sigh of regional differentiation.

37 Pourjavady, Amir Hosein (Ed.) 2007, *Nasīm-i Ṭarab (The Breeze of Euphoria). A Sixteenth-Century Persian Musical Treatise by Nasīmī*, Tehran: Iranian Academy of Arts.

38 The full title is *taqsīm al-naġamāt wa-bayān al-daraj wa-'l-šuʿab wa-'l-maqāmāt*, Österreichische Staatsbibliothek MS Flügel 1516 (Mxt. 674).

39 Both published in Pourjavady 2005.

40 ʿAbd al-Muʾmin b. Ṣafī al-Dīn al-Jurjānī (?) 1346/1968, *bahjat al-rūḥ*, Bodleian MS Ouseley 117, ed. H. L. Rabino de Borgomale, Tehran.

41 Although the emergence of *ḥarbī*, *ṣufiyāna* and *żarb al-mulūk* does not post-date the sixteenth century, as they are mentioned by Qazvīnī (2003).

	taqsīm	*nasīm*	*b. al-rūḥ*	Āqā M.	Gurjī	Cantemir
miʾatayn	*	*	*			
šāhnāma	*		*			
ḫʷājak[42]	*	*				
čahār żarb	*	*	*	*		
żarb al-mulūk			*	*		
ḥarbī			*		*	
dawr			*	*	*	*
ramal	*	*	*		*	*
awsaṭ	*	*	*			*
hazaj	*	*	*			*
nīm ṯaqīl		*	*	*	*	*
ravān		*	*	*	*	*
samāʿī		*	*	*		*
čanbar			*	*	*	*
farʿ[43]			*	*	*	*
nīm dawr				*	*	*
ṣūfiyāna					*	*

Figure 6

clude names that are peculiar to them. How marginal they may have been is unclear, but they certainly suggest an element of regional particularism.[44]

Nevertheless, the crucial question, as before, is whether we can progress beyond drawing cautious inferences from a mere tabulation of names to a more informed comparison of structures. Here we are fortunate in that the *nasīm-i ṭarab* and the *taqsīm al-naġamāt* both give time unit totals and some indication of internal segmentation, information of sufficient specificity to allow us a reliable insight into mid sixteenth-century Safavid norms, and hence to reduce the pre-Ottoman gap to less than a century.

What they emphatically do not do, however, is reinforce the picture sketched above. Contrary to the broad continuity observable at the level of nomenclature the evidence they provide with regard to structure yields a landscape markedly different to the seventeenth-century one, for their time unit totals for the common name stock immediately reveal significant discrepancies:

42 Lacking pointing, the reading is uncertain. Pourjavady (2007) prefers *juvājak* in his edition of the *nasīm-i ṭarab*. Neither form appears in the *luġat-nāma*.

43 In addition to *farʿ*, the *bahjat al-rūḥ* also mentions *farʿ-i muḫammas*.

44 Ignoring *kabīr/ṣaġīr* variants, the *nasīm-i ṭarab* includes *bišārat*, *ḥijāzī*, *sulṭān*, *faraḥ* and *ḫafīf-i ṣarīḥ*, the *bahjat al-rūḥ muqaddam* and *ākil*–to which it adds a number of cycle names having a particular association with the military and ceremonial band (*naqqāra-ḫāna*).

	taqsīm	*nasīm*	Cantemir
awfar	6	6	9
ravān		6/8	14
fāḫita (kabīr)	7	7	
fāḫita (ṣaġīr)		5	10
hazaj	8	10	22
samāʿī		9	6
do(bar)yak	10	8	8
nīm ṯaqīl		10	24
ramal[45]	12	8	28
varafšān	14	14	16
turkī żarb	17	12	18
awsaṭ	18	18	26
muḫammas	20	20	16
ḫafīf	28	24	32
ṯaqīl	44	36	48
żarb al-fatḥ	78	58[46]	88

Figure 7

Extraordinarily, from the sixteenth to the seventeenth century there is, on this evidence, coincidence in only one cycle, *do(bar)yak*, and even here the two earlier treatises fail to agree. In the great majority of cases the number of time units increases in the Ottoman version, but not in a predictable way, and certainly not by doubling, which might suggest a change of analytical method, of appearance rather than substance. Equally surprising, disconcerting even, is that the *taqsīm al-naġamāt* and *nasīm-i ṭarab* themselves agree as to the number of time units in only five of the twelve cycles they have in common, although for these, at least, agreement is confirmed by the fact that the internal segmentation is also the same, or virtually the same, so that if we ignore the distinction between *tan* and *tana* these five cycles may be represented as:

45 Specifically *ramal-i ṣaġīr* in the two Safavid texts.

46 Pourjavady 2007 has the correct figure on p. 35, but on p. 103 and p. xxi has, instead, 18. This results from the omission of part of the description (pp. 102-103), which specifies 9 segments (*faṣl*), 2+2+6+6x(1+1+1+1+4): the last element is counted once instead of six times.

awfar	6	2+4
fāḫita	7	3+2+2
varafšān	14	3+3+4+4
awsaṭ	18	4+4+2+2+4+2
muḫammas	20	5+5+5+5

These are, though, structures having little or nothing in common with other versions, whether earlier or later. The only points of resemblance appear to be with the triple (3+3) + duple arrangement of *varafšān* (fig. 3), and the symmetrical structure of *muḫammas* (fig. 4), where one might be tempted to view the substitution of five for four in each segment as lexically inspired[47]. With regard to the other seven cycles described in both treatises, it might be argued that despite the differences in their time unit totals the internal distribution points to the possibility of connections in three further cases:

	taqsīm al-naġamāt		*nasīm-i ṭarab*	
hazaj	8	2+4+2	10	2+4+4
doyak	10	2+4+4	8	4+4
turkī żarb	17	2+5+4+4+2	12	2+4+4+2

A simple deletion, addition or variation of just one segment would lead from one of each pair to the other, and it could be argued that such processes would not be intrinsically different to those that yielded the variant forms to be found in the earlier Systematist literature. The relationship between the two forms of the remaining cycles is, however, of a different order of complexity:

	taqsīm al-naġamāt		*nasīm-i ṭarab*	
ramal	12	3+3+4+2	8	2+2+4
ḫafīf	28	4+4+5+3+5+3+4	24	4+4+2+4+2+4+4
ṯaqīl	44	11x4	36	4+4+6+6+6+7+3[48]
żarb al-fatḥ	78	4+4+3+3+2+4+2+4+ 2+4+4+3+3+2+2+4+ 2+2+4x(4+2)	58	2+2+6+6x8

47 A seemingly unconvincing notion, but one that can draw support from Ibn Kurr, who derives the name precisely from the segments of five time units that it contains (Wright 2014, p. 46).

48 The definition is incomplete but can be reconstructed, as the total number of time units is not in question. The description (Pourjavady 2007, p. 103) states that there are seven segments (*faṣl*), and of these the first and the last two are defined while the third, fourth and fifth are stated to be the same, so that the whole can be summarized as 4+x+y+y+y+7+3, and since the logic of the description requires that y does not equal 7, the only possible solution is x=4 and y=6. Pourjavady suggests x=3 and y=6, but this yields a total of 35 time units.

Indeed, there would seem to be nothing to justify the arbitrary moves required to transfer from one form of *ramal* to the other, while with *ḫafīf* the removal or addition of a segment of four time units, unexceptional in itself, would still leave two unrelated sequences. With *ṯaqīl* and *żarb al-fatḥ* not only are the variations in time unit totals more marked, but any possible internal similarities are masked by the opacity of presentation in one version or the other, the definition of *ṯaqīl* as eleven repetitions of *tananan*, for example, having an air of simplified abstraction. The question, then, is less how these various manifestations might be related to each other than whether they can be convincingly derived from a common source. Given the earlier observation that the five cycles these two texts have in common are seemingly unrelated to previous versions, this may be thought unlikely, and points of resemblance are indeed few. For *hazaj* al-Lāḏiqī mentions a version with 10 time units, but with a different segmentation to that of the *nasīm-i ṭarab*; corresponding to *turkī żarb* he includes a *turkī ḫafīf* with 12 time units and a 2+2+4+4 segmentation that rotates the 2+4+4+2 of the *nasīm-i ṭarab* (it is, though, a cycle he declares obsolete); for *ramal* there are two earlier versions with 12 time units, but in neither case does the segmentation resemble that of the *taqsīm al-naġamāt*[49]; and for the remaining three, *ḫafīf*, *ṯaqīl* and *żarb al-fatḥ*, there are no matches in the earlier literature for the time unit totals offered here. The possibility may therefore be entertained that contrary to the general stability of the seventeenth-century Ottoman cycles sixteenth-century practice was still partially characterized by an approach to rhythmic structures that can be discerned in Timurid texts, one that allowed a degree of creative latitude in altering an existing cycle without necessarily inventing a new name. An obvious example would be the deletion of a segment in the line of development of *barafšān* represented by the Persian 3+3+4+4, with a related form being recorded by al-ʿAjamī, who gives 4+4+6, which apart from the insignificant recasting of 3+3 as 6 could be construed simply as a reordering of the constituent elements[50]. Elsewhere, however, relationships are less clear: corresponding to the 2+4+4 segmentation of *hazaj* in the *nasīm-i ṭarab* al-Lāḏiqī offers 3+2+3+2, which seems fundamentally distinct, and elsewhere significant and unpredictable differences in time unit totals offer further hurdles: instead of 18 for *awsaṭ* al-ʿAjamī has a mere 8; instead of 7 for *fāḫita* both al-ʿAjamī and al-Lāḏiqī have 10.

The conclusion that they represent divergent traditions may be reasonable, but lacks explanatory power. Thus alongside cases involving only minor, or at least comprehensible, variations, others confront us with disparate structures for which, in the absence of further documentation, we must either assume a capricious reassignment of names or the existence of evolutionary steps that cannot now be traced linking them to a putative common origin. As far as the *taqsīm al-naġamāt*

49 Marāġī's grandson, Maḥmūd b. ʿAbd al-ʿAzīz, has 2+2+4+4, al-Lāḏiqī 2+2+2+2+4.

50 For a later example of this phenomenon see the chapter in the present volume by Salah Eddin Maraqa.

and the *nasīm-i ṭarab* are concerned, if the assumption that they are not very far apart in date is correct, their lack of agreement about several cycles (and the presence in each one of them of cycle names not attested in the other) would need to be explained in terms of regional differences within the Persianate world[51], adding yet further lines of fracture to the map, and by the same logic one might wish to make a simple appeal to geographical distance as a sufficient explanation for the more obvious contrasts that they exhibit with the Ottoman definitions, although as these are only attested the best part of a century later one could equally appeal to innovation as the driving force. Unfortunately, given the absence of sixteenth-century Ottoman witnesses no firm conclusions can be drawn about the extent to which earlier Ottoman practice might have been closer to what is presented in one or other of these Safavid texts, but what speaks in favour of the second explanation having some validity is that when we do encounter contemporary Safavid and Ottoman witnesses, in the second half of the seventeenth century, they suggest not continuing or, indeed, increasing divergence but rather the opposite, the consolidation of a new common set of normative structures.

Crucial to this conclusion are the similarities between the definitions of the Ottoman cycles given by Ali Ufuki and Cantemir and those, however cryptically expressed, contained in the treatise by Gurjī and discussed in greater detail in the following chapter. Of the later Persian sources Āqā Muʾmin unfortunately adds nothing further beyond the names, but for most cycles Gurjī gives a total of *żarb* followed by a description expressed in terms of mnemonic syllables reminiscent of the Ottoman ones. To take the first and shortest cycle, *ṣūfiyāna*, defined as consisting of three *żarb*, by aligning the two sets of mnemonic syllables it can readily be seen that Gurjī's version corresponds precisely to the Ottoman definition:

dik *da ka*

düm . *te ke*[52]

and similar correspondences can be observed in other cycles: at least eleven can be stated with confidence to coincide exactly or very closely with the definitions given by Cantemir[53], while varying degrees of similarity can also be observed elsewhere. In one or two cases it seems likely that the time unit totals were different, but as there are still extensive stretches of syllable mnemonics that match it is clear that we are dealing with related forms. Considering such non-identical

51 Pourjavady (2007) makes a case for associating the *nasīm-i ṭarab* with Gilan. The regional affiliations of the *taqsīm al-naġamāt* are unclear.

52 Each syllable has the duration of one time unit, as does the symbol . (signalling a time unit without an attack). The correspondence is noted in Kurdmāfī, Saʿīd 2013, "Bar rasī-yi barḫī janbahā-yi ʿamalī-yi īqāʿ dar risālāt-i qadīm-i mūsīqī-yi ḥawza-yi islāmī (qurūn-i haftum tā davāzdahum-i hijrī-yi qamarī)", *faṣlnāma-yi mūsīqī-yi māhūr 60*, 167-198.

53 In addition to *ṣūfiyāna*, Kurdmāfī (2013) notes such resemblances for *doharyak*, *awfar*, *muḫammas* and *ṯaqīl*, and these are not the only cases.

pairs in isolation, one might conclude that the Persian versions sometimes represent a slightly earlier stage of development, the Ottoman *turkī żarb*[54], for example, evolving from an earlier form with 14 time units reported by Gurjī, but in the wider context of, say, the evidence for continuity marshalled in fig. 3 for *berefşan* as a cycle of 16 time units, the conclusion has to be that the Ottoman *berefşan* represents the mainstream, while Gurjī's version, if of 14 time units, would be a descendant of the offshoot recorded in the two sixteenth-century Persian texts. Similarly, the Ottoman *darb–ı fetih* cannot be regarded as other than standing in a direct line of descent from one or other of the forms described by Awbahī and al-Lāḏiqī, while Gurjī's version appears to diverge, with a lower total of time units that aligns it rather with the earlier Safavid version with 78 time units recorded in the *taqsīm al-naġamāt*.

Reference is also made in the following chapter to the even more condensed account of the rhythmic cycles in the *bahjat al-rūḥ*, which fails to confirm the general appearance of Ottoman-Safavid cohesiveness derivable from Gurjī, and it is difficult not to reach the facile but eminently sensible conclusion that it represents a distinct local tradition. What is indisputable is that Gurjī's evidence is sufficient to demonstrate a high degree of congruence between the cycle repertoires used at the mid to late seventeenth-century Ottoman court and their equivalents as defined by a Safavid court musician, a common structural underpinning that would have facilitated reception and the transfer of compositions. It is thus not surprising that among those cited by Gurjī are items that also appear in the song-text collection of Hafiz Post[55], and that Ali Ufuki and Cantemir include a number of *peşrev*s to which the label *acemler* is attached. Although the sample is too small for conclusions to be drawn with any confidence, it is at least worth noting that of the fifteen such pieces included by Cantemir the great majority are in cycles where there appears to be a good match, and only one is in a cycle that Gurjī fails to define[56].

We began, then, with evidence suggestive of long-range Timurid to Ottoman connections, only to be faced with the paradox that along with the progressive narrowing of the gap between them the case for a substantial level of continuity dwindled. It was called into question first by the intervening song-text collections, with their array of cycles neither mention, and then by the unrelated definitions offered in sixteenth-century Persian texts that, in addition, frequently fail to agree among themselves. As well as synchronic lines of cleavage separating off Arab and

---

54 Not described by Cantemir, but defined as a cycle of 18 time units by Ali Ufuki (see Behar 2008).

55 Pourjavady 2005, p. 168, Wright 1992, p. 150. In these two collections Pourjavady identifies two items of the 'Marāġī' repertoire with the same title, verse, mode and rhythmic cycle, and another Ottoman song-text collection provides further pieces attributed to Marāġī that are settings of verse included by Gurjī. In at least three cases there are sufficient levels of coincidence in the nonsense-syllable sections to indicate that we are faced with variants of the same composition.

56 For a characterization of early *acemler* pieces see Feldman 1996, pp. 339-345.

Anatolian preferences from Ottoman and Persian ones, we thus appear to have possible internal distinctions within what we are obliged to label, however loosely, as Persian practice. Further, we have significant diachronic differences between the sixteenth- and seventeenth-century Persian texts, while the evidence supplied by Gurjī points, paradoxically, to renewed uniformity, indicating that for the second half of the seventeenth century it would be prudent not to categorize the Ottoman *usul* system as something distinct and *sui generis*, but to speak of a common Otto-man-Safavid core set of rhythmic structures. The degree to which this was also current in Astarkhanid Central Asia cannot unfortunately be determined, although one can at least point to the fact that neither the set of names recorded earlier by Kawkabī nor that given by Darvīš ʿAlī[57] contains anything exceptional that might point to Central Asian particularism, even if a few new names do creep in in the late seventeenth-century *muḥīṭ al-tawārīḫ* by Buḫārī[58]. For the most part, the modern *šašmaqām* cycles differ markedly from their earlier namesakes, but compelling evidence for at least partial congruence at an earlier stage is provided by *sakil* and *muhammes*, in places still akin to the seventeenth-century Safavid-Ottoman cycles, while the drastically reduced fragmentary forms of both found in the Khwarazmian tradition[59] result from radical and unpredictable transformations echoing those that doubtless lay behind some of the more extreme contrasts revealed above, even extending to the complete eclipse of the once dominant *ʿamal* and *se ḍarb*. Within this constant flux it is difficult to determine any pattern from which could be derived a taxonomy of change, but given the variety of factors at work it may be unrealistic to expect there to have been one. Qazvīnī's pithy account contains clear notions of derivation, even if their nature is not explained, but he also claims that certain cycles are virtually identical to others, thus confusing the picture further[60]. One may at least observe that, quite unexpectedly, the cycles most resistant to change are to be found among those with 16 time units and above, their stability contrasting with volatility among the shorter cycles. Yet length is still no guarantee of longevity: *ḍarb al-fatḥ* survives, but *muḥajjal* (56 time units), *čahār ḍarb* (24, 48 or 96) and *miʾatayn* (200) fall by the wayside. For the more tenacious longer cycles one might hypothesize a period of relatively greater popularity resulting in an association with a prestigious corpus of serious songs, while elsewhere fashion could change more readily, with new rhythms being adopted from the domain of folk song and dance. But when we do find evidence for the latter, in the

57 Jung 1989, pp. 132-134.

58 Fallahzadeh 2009, pp. 152-153.

59 Jung 1989, pp. 174-179.

60 For him (2003, p. 91) *čahār żarb* is derived from *muḥammas*, *samāʿī* (known as *dawr-i šāhī* in Khorasan) from *turkī żarb*; but only with *ḥāvī* is the nature of the relationship specified: it results from the omission of six consecutive *żarb* from *żarb al-fatḥ*. Further, *sarandāz* is said not merely to be derived from *farʿ-i muḥammas* but to be virtually identical with it – and Qazvīnī adds the acerbic comment that it would have been better if its inventor, Mullā Šams-i Rūmī, hadn't bothered.

prominence of the folk genres *türkü* and *varsağı* in Ali Ufuki's notations, it is accompanied by effacement of the older complex vocal forms, so that survival of the longer cycles at the Ottoman court appears to be have been guaranteed above all by the instrumental *peşrev* repertoire.[61] Among the shorter cycles one might suspect the persistence of fundamental elements concealed behind a change of name, and posit a link, say, between *sofyan* (2+1+1) and what Banāʾī calls *ḫafīf al-ṯaqīl* (= *muḫammas ṣağīr*)[62]. Documentary support is, however, lacking, and such elementary structures are just as likely to be reinvented: with allowance made for the constant inflation of cycle lengths (or at least the representation thereof) one could even see in *se ḍarb*, defined by al-Lāḏiqī as 4+4+8 or 8+8+16, an avatar of an early Abbasid pair definable as 1+1+2 (*ḫafīf*) and 2+2+4 (*ṯaqīl*). What is surprising among the shorter cycles is not the variety they exhibit (there are, after all, twenty-seven possible combinations of just three segments of 2, 3 and 4 time units), but the deceptive reuse of the same names to designate quite different and seemingly unrelated combinations. The cases of continuity with which we started are thus a minority, and we do not need to go back very far to encounter significant differences in relation to the Ottoman *usul* system: it appears to be a matter not merely of regional variation but of there having been an earlier structural flexibility that could be interpreted as pointing to different attitudes to creative freedom in performance. The stages by which this was replaced by mid seventeenth-century Safavid-Ottoman uniformity remain, however, unclear.

---

61 For further contextualization see Feldman 2015.
62 Banāʾī 1368š/1990, p. 109.

Amīr Ḫān Gurjī and Safavid-Ottoman *Usul* Parallels

Owen Wright

Threaded through the occasional remarks made in the surviving sources about the historical development of Ottoman musical culture are repeated, indeed insistent, indications of indebtedness to the Persianate world. They hark back, first, to the Timurid period, and concern primarily the foundational role of ʿAbd al-Qādir Marāġī (d. 1435), to whom are attributed several compositions recorded in Ottoman song-text anthologies. For Evliya Çelebi (1611-82) imagined performances at the court of Ḥusayn Bāyqarā at Herat were still a yardstick of excellence, and stress continued to be laid upon the influential role played later by musicians who were either themselves Persian or had a Persian cultural formation: by Hasan Can during the sixteenth century, and during the early seventeenth by those captured by Murat IV and brought back to Istanbul.[1]

Beyond their recognition of cultural indebtedness, such references imply a stylistic and structural pedigree, but it is one that the historical record fails to endorse: the message conveyed, for example, by the surviving song-text collections is of discontinuity. The post-Marāġī Persianate art-music repertoire, with its frequently complex vocal compositions, appears to fall into neglect during the course of the sixteenth century, to be largely replaced in the seventeenth, at least at the Istanbul court, by a new locally-produced vocal repertoire incorporating significant popular and folk elements.[2] It cannot therefore be simply assumed that the Ottoman and Safavid traditions, for all that they may be considered joint heirs to late Timurid practice, continued to march in step; but neither does it follow that major structural lines of cleavage were beginning to emerge: Persian texts occasionally refer to regional differences of terminology, but not of substance[3]; Murat's Persian imports evidently performed in an idiom that audiences appreciated; the re-emergence of lengthy vocal forms attested in the Hafiz Post collection implies that knowledge of

1 For an analysis of these accounts see Feldman, Walter 1996, *Music of the Ottoman court: makam, composition and the early Ottoman instrumental repertoire* (Intercultural Music Studies: 10, ed. Max Peter Baumann), Berlin: VWB, pp. 45-54, 64-67.

2 See Wright, Owen 1992, *Words without songs: a musicological study of an Ottoman anthology and its precursors* (SOAS Musicology Series, 3), London: School of Oriental and African Studies, and Feldman, Walter 2015, "The Musical "Renaissance" of Late Seventeenth Century Ottoman Turkey: Reflections on the Musical Materials of Ali Ufki Bey (ca. 1610-1675), Hafiz Post (d. 1694) and the 'Maraghi' Repertoire", in: *Writing the History of "Ottoman Music"*, Martin Greve (Ed.), Istanbuler Texte und Studien: 33, Würzburg: Ergon.

3 For example, Mīr Ṣadr al-Dīn Muḥammad Qazvīnī 2003, *risāla-yi ʿilm-i mūsīqī*, ed. Rustamī, Āriyū, *faṣlnāma-yi mūsīqī-yi māhūr 18*, 81-96, identifies a number of regional variations in nomenclature.

them had not been completely lost[4]; and the court instrumental repertoire, in any case possibly retaining a larger proportion of older pieces, included a number of 'Persian' *peşrevs*. Indeed, that more than mere mutual intelligibility of idiom continued well into the eighteenth century is demonstrated by the career of Arutin, an Istanbul-trained musician who was sent as part of a diplomatic mission to Persia and was integrated into the court ensemble of Nadir Šāh.[5]

The nature and extent of the similarities between Ottoman and Persian practice that may accordingly be presumed to have persisted for some time after the demise of the early Persianate court-music repertoire are, however, difficult to assess. Above all, investigation is hampered by a general lack of Safavid sources with documentation analogous to that provided for the seventeenth century by Ali Ufuki (d. 1677) and Cantemir (1673-1723), who between them provide an extensive body of notations, while the latter adds an informative theoretical work engaging directly with contemporary practice.[6] There are, nevertheless, two Persian treatises from the same period, one by Āqā Mu'min, probably of the mid seventeenth century, the other, completed in 1697, by Amīr Ḫān Gurjī (henceforth Gurjī)[7], from which we may glean comparative data with regard to repertoire and, particularly, its constitutive systems of forms, modes and rhythmic cycles.

For the last, with which the present chapter is concerned, the key text is the treatise by Gurjī. Given that one of the major distinctions between the twentieth-century art-music traditions of Turkey and Iran is the retention in the former of a complex system of rhythmic cycles largely derived from seventeenth-century practice and the absence of any equivalent system in the latter, it is a matter of especial interest to encounter a work that sheds light on the nature of the rhythmic cycles in use in Persia, or at least in Isfahan court circles, towards the end of the seventeenth century. As with earlier Persian texts, both Āqā Mu'min and Gurjī provide lists of cycle names, by themselves of limited usefulness for comparative purposes, but the latter, crucially, adds definitions, and although these would remain opaque if considered in isolation, as they give an idea of the characteristic pattern of contrastive attacks but fail to show how they are spaced

---

4 See Feldman 2015 on the key role played by Osman Efendi in ensuring the survival of these forms outside the court environment.

5 See Popescu-Judetz, Eugenia 2002, *Tanburî Küçük Artin. A musical treatise of the eighteenth century*, Istanbul: Pan Yayıncılık.

6 Ali Ufuki, *[Album de poésies turques […]*, Paris Bibliothèque nationale MS Turc 292; *mecmûa-i sâz ü söz*, British Library MS Sloane 3114, facsimile in Elçin, Şükrü 1976, *Ali Ufkî: hayatı, eserleri ve mecmûa-i sâz ü söz*, Istanbul, transcription in Cevher, M. Hakan 1991, *Hâzâ mecmûa-i sâz ü söz*, Izmir. Cantemir's treatise and notations in Tura, Yalçın (Ed.) 2001, *Kitābu ʿilmi'l-mūsīḳī ʿalā vechi'l-ḥurūfāt. Mûsikîyi harflerle tesbît ve icrâ ilminin kitabı, I. cilt, Edvâr* (*tıpkıbasım – çevriyazı – çeviri – notlar*) and 2001b *Kitābu ʿilmi'l-mūsīḳī* […], *II. cilt, Notalar* (*tıpkıbasım –çeviri – notlar*), Istanbul: Yapı Kredi Yayınları.

7 Both published in Pourjavady, Amir Hoseyn 2005, "*The musical codex of Amir Khān Gorji (c. 1108-1697)*", PhD dissertation, University of California, Los Angeles. The approximate date given for the former is that proposed by Pourjavady.

out within the cycle, juxtaposing them with contemporary Ottoman definitions allows crucial insight into their structure.

Scrutiny of individual cases may usefully be set in the context of an initial comparative survey of cycle names. This takes account in addition of two other Persian texts, the *bahjat al-rūḥ*[8] and an anonymous treatise included in the manuscript containing those by Āqā Muʾmin and Gurjī, both difficult to date with any precision, but probably also to be assigned to the seventeenth century[9]. Here, and likewise below, names that are not specifically Ottoman will normally be cited only in the form given by Gurjī. There are ten that are common to all six sources:

barafšān	*čanbar*	*dobaryak*	*fāḫita*
farʿ[10]	*ḫafīf*	*muḫammas*	*nīm ṯaqīl*
ṯaqīl	*żarb al-fatḥ*		

while a further seven occur in at least one Ottoman and one Safavid source (and normally several more):

awfar	*awsaṭ*	*nīm dawr*	*ramal*
ravānī	*samāʿī*	*ṣūfiyāna*	*turkī żarb*

In addition, the Safavid cycle *dawr* may confidently be related to the Ottoman *devr-i kebir*, and for *havi*, recorded by Cantemir, a reference can be found in a late sixteenth-century Persian treatise,[11] thus yielding a common pool of nineteen names. A further six (*čahār żarb*, *żarb al-mulūk*, *miʾatayn*, *šāhnāma*, *żarb al-qadīm* and *ḥarbī*) appear solely in Safavid texts, but only the first two are mentioned by Āqā Muʾmin and, even more tellingly, only the last one by Gurjī, so that it is possible that by the end of the seventeenth century most had been abandoned, at least by musicians at the Safavid court. On the Ottoman side we encounter an equivalent number of cycles that do not appear in Safavid texts, but it is clear from the corpus of notations that some (*devr-i hindi*, *hezec*, *horezm*, *remel*, *yek darb*) were marginal in the extreme, while the other two (the equally marginal *frenkçin* and the ten time-unit form of *semai*) were in all probability recent Ottoman innovations. The dominant impression is thus of a sizeable core set of shared names, a degree of overlap that points strongly towards the likelihood of Safavid-Ottoman commonalities.

If these can be investigated effectively from only one Safavid source, on the Ottoman side we have two, roughly half a century apart, but the differences between

8 (Attributed to) ʿAbd al-Muʾmin b. Ṣafī al-Dīn al-Jurjānī, *bahjat al-rūḥ*, MS Bodleian Ouseley 117; ed. H. L. Rabino de Borgomale, Tehran, 1346.

9 The dating of the *bahjat al-rūḥ* is that proposed by Rabino de Borgomale. The anonymous treatise is likely to be the earlier of the two, so a late sixteenth-century date is not to be excluded.

10 Variously *farʿ* or *farʿ-i muḫammas*.

11 Qazvīnī 2003.

them, even if interesting, are slight. The fact that in his notations Ali Ufuki frequently omits the cycle name sometimes occasions a degree of uncertainly as to identity, but all but one of the cycles named in his two collections are included among those defined by Cantemir[12], while the ones In Cantemir's catalogue that Ali Ufuki fails to exemplify are principally the marginal cycles cited above, for three of which Cantemir himself records not a single composition. Ali Ufuki's definitions also tend to be congruent with Cantemir's, although there are one or two cases, to be referred to below, where a slightly different internal structure is indicated. Despite these minor variations the general picture is thus one of near identity, pointing to the maintenance of a high degree of stability over more than half a century in the stock of Ottoman cycles. Equally clear is that the overwhelming majority of the compositions notated by Ali Ufuki and Cantemir are in cycles the names of which are also present in Safavid sources. There is just one striking exception, for absent from Gurjī's account is any mention of *semai*, but even here it is possible that the same rhythmic structure occurred under another name.

All this points straightforwardly towards a shared repertoire of rhythmic cycles, yet consideration of their previous history gives pause. Even if comparisons are not always easy to make, given the descriptive methods used, earlier (thirteenth to fifteenth-century) and later (seventeenth-century) definitions that relate to the same cycle name frequently yield quite different results[13], so that in order to advance beyond reasonable assumption to certainty with regard to shared structures further confirmatory evidence is required. Crucial here is the descriptive account provided by Gurjī, for all that it is in varying degrees elliptical and in need of elucidation. He names nineteen cycles and provides definitions for seventeen[14], in each case giving an initial total of *żarb* and then a description expressed in terms of the mnemonic syllables *dīk*, *dak* and *daka*, immediately reminiscent of the Ottoman *düm*, *tek* and *teke*. The first and shortest cycle, for example, *ṣūfiyāna*, is defined as consisting of three *żarb* and *dīk daka*, from which we may conclude that *żarb* gives either the number of time units (in which case either *dīk* = 2 and *daka* = 1 or *dīk* = 1 and *daka* = 2) or the number of attacks, expressed by the syllable-initial consonants, or both. The earlier preference for *naqra* (or *ḥarf*) as the technical term for time unit might point to the latter as the more likely, but it would be unwise to discard *a priori* the possibility of *żarb* = time unit, as this equation would work in certain other cycles if *dīk* (and likewise *dak*) = 1 and *daka* = 2. Thus in *nīm dawr* we would have:

12 For Ali Ufuki see Behar, Cem 2008, *Saklı mecmua. Ali Ufkî'nin Bibliothèque Nationale de France'taki [Turc 292] yazması*, Istanbul: Yapı Kredi Yayınları, pp. 72-132.

13 Further, for an incisive analysis of the functional implications of the diachronic differences in descriptive method see Behar 2008, pp. 99-106.

14 The two for which there is no description are *farʿ* and *nim sakil*. No reason for the omission is given, and as nineteen have been listed it can hardly be in order to arrive at a total often regarded as canonical in other texts: scribal error is the most likely cause.

dīk da ka dīk dak da ka da ka dak

yielding the correct sum of ten *żarb*, while in *čanbar* we would have:

dīk da ka dīk dīk dak dīk dak da ka da ka

yielding the correct sum of twelve *żarb*. But if *daka* is assumed to have two attacks the equation *żarb* = attack works equally well in both cases: in other words, on the basis of this evidence *żarb* could indicate the time unit total and/or the number of attacks. The matter may be resolved, however, by reference to the contemporary Ottoman equivalents, in which the durations associated with the mnemonic syllables confirm that it is in fact only the latter that is intended.

1. ṣūfiyāna

This is already apparent in the case of the first cycle, with its three *żarb* and the mnemonic syllables *dīk daka*. As Gurjī's syllable strings fail to specify the distance between attacks there is no symbol in this form of notation for an unmarked time unit, but we may arrive in this case at a perfect match with the Ottoman version if

1) we include a corresponding unmarked time unit (indicated within Gurjī's syllable string by Ø); and
2) assume that *daka* may have the value of two time units:

dīk Ø da ka
düm . te ke[15]

Given that the three *żarb* of *ṣūfiyāna* are now spaced out over four time units, it follows that here *żarb* = attack, and this conclusion also holds elsewhere.

2. ravānī

This is stated to have five *żarb*, and the syllable string is *dīk daka dīk dak*. The obvious term of comparison here is the Ottoman *devr-i revan*, pointing therefore to a total of either seven time units, which is what Ali Ufki's notation suggests[16], or fourteen, as specified by Cantemir, and in either case we can arrive at a match involving just one discrepancy (marked here, and likewise in similar cases below, in bold), if

[15] The correspondence between *dīk daka* and *düm . te ke* has also been noted in Kurdmāfī, Saʿīd 2013, "Bar rasī-yi barḫī janbahā-yi ʿamali-yi iqāʿ dar risālāt-i qadīm-i mūsiqī-yi ḥawza-yi islāmī (qurūn-i haftum tā davāzdahum-i hijrī-yi qamarī)", *faṣlnāma-yi mūsiqī-yi māhūr 60*, 167-98, with the clear implication, even if not spelled out, that they relate to the same structure. Kurdmāfī goes on to note similar parallels for other cycles, as indicated below.

[16] Reproduced in Behar 2008, p. 92.

3) we allow Gurjī's *dak(a)* to correspond on occasion to an unmarked time unit in the Ottoman version; and likewise
4) allow the Ottoman *tek(e)* to correspond on occasion to a hypothetical unmarked time unit in Gurjī's version:

	dīk	***da***	*ka*	*dīk*	Ø	*dak*	Ø
Ali Ufuki	*düm*	***düm***	*tek*	*düm*	.	*teke*	*teke*

	dīk	Ø	Ø	***da***	Ø	ka	Ø	*dīk*	Ø	Ø	*dak*	Ø	Ø	Ø
Cantemir	*düm*	.	.	***düm***	.	*tek*	.	*düm*	.	.	*tek*	.	*tek*	.

The second version may appear initially unconvincing, especially with regard to the expansion of *daka* to *da Ø ka Ø*, but it needs to be noted that within the Ottoman set of cycles *devr-i revan* forms a pair with *devr-i kebir*: for Cantemir both have fourteen time units, and it is fairly clear from the melodic evidence that *devr-i revan* would have been performed at a rather faster tempo[17], thus accounting for the above-average number of unmarked time units. Within the Safavid set of cycles it is likely that a similar relationship obtained between *ravānī* and *dawr*, again with the former being characterized by a relatively faster performance tempo[18], from which it follows that what appears here as *da Ø ka Ø* would not have differed much from *da ka* in a slower cycle. The ***da/düm*** discrepancy could readily be explained as resulting from a development within the evolution of the Ottoman version, a form of differentiation designed to avoid identity between the two halves subsequent to the addition of an extra attack in the second half, i.e.

**düm*	.	.	*tek*	.	*tek*	.	*düm*	.	.	*tek*	.	.	.	→
**düm*	.	.	*tek*	.	*tek*	.	*düm*	.	.	*tek*	.	*tek*	.	→
düm	.	.	*düm*	.	*tek*	.	*düm*	.	.	*tek*	.	*tek*	.	

However, it should be noted that although such a reconstruction could relate only to the fourteen time-unit cycle described by Cantemir, and not to the seven time-unit cycle proposed by Ali Ufuki, Gurjī's account cannot be taken as evidence in favour of the former version.

3. ḥarbī

The syllable string is the same as that of *ravānī*, as is the number of *żarb*, so that unless the text is at fault *ḥarbī* must either have had a different time-unit total or a different distribution of unmarked time units within the same total. However, there is no reason to suspect error: if anything, the more likely assumption is

---

17 See Wright, Owen 2000, *Demetrius Cantemir, The collection of notations, Volume 2: Commentary*. (SOAS Musicology Series), Aldershot: Ashgate, pp. 459-463 and 519-520.

18 Āqā Mu'min lists both *ravānī* and *dawr*, and notes two performance styles/tempi for the former, lively (*sabuk*) and heavy (*sangīn*) (Pourjavadi 2005, p. 198).

that *ḥarbī* was placed after *ravānī* precisely because the definitions coincide. There is in this case no direct seventeenth-century Ottoman point of reference, in the sense that neither Ali Ufuki nor Cantemir mention a cycle called simply *ḥarbī*: neither was concerned to represent cycles specific to the military and ceremonial Janissary *mehter* band. However, the former entitles one song *semai-i harbi*, while the latter cites a form of *semai* called *semai-i harbi*[19], and one could readily map Gurjī's *ḥarbī* syllable string onto the Ottoman *semai*:

dīk da ka dīk dak ∅
düm tek tek düm tek .

Although this equation must remain conjectural in the absence of direct supporting evidence, it has the attraction of resolving the problem of the otherwise inexplicable absence from the Safavid set of one of the more frequently occurring Ottoman cycles; and one could adduce as further circumstantial evidence the presence in the anonymous Persian text that accompanies the treatises of Āqā Muʾmin and Gurjī of a list of seven cycles known to the military and ceremonial band (*naqqāračiyān*)–one that fails to mention *ḥarbī* but does include *samāʿī*[20].

4. dobaryak

With the next cycle there are no such problems: *dobaryak* corresponds straightforwardly to the Ottoman *düyek*[21]. It has five *żarb*, and the mnemonic syllables match perfectly over the eight time-unit span of the Ottoman structure:

dīk dak ∅ *dak dīk* ∅ *dak* ∅
düm tek . *tek düm* . *tek* .

5. fāḫita

If

5) we assume that *daka*, like the Ottoman *teke*, may also cover one time unit then for *fāḫita* we may again plot a distribution containing a discrepancy in just one time unit, but in this case the Safavid version, which has nine *żarb*,

19 See Cevher 1991, p. 319, Wright 2000, p. 523. However, as a cautionary note it may be observed that in the mid sixteenth century Nasīmī (Pourjavady, Amir Hoseyn [Ed.] 2007, *Nasīm-i Ṭarab (The Breeze of Euphoria). A Sixteenth-Century Persian Musical Treatise by Nasīmī*, Tehran: Iranian Academy of Arts, p. 110) recognized *samāʿī* and *ḥarbī* as separate and apparently unrelated: the former is defined as a cycle of nine time units, the latter one of ten.

20 Pourjvady 2005, p. 185.

21 The correspondence has also been noted in Kurdmāfī 2013 (p. 192).

contains one attack more than the Ottoman one. For this, however, Ali Ufuki and Cantemir give slightly different versions, so that we could have either:

	dīk	***dīk***	*dak*	Ø	Ø	Ø	*dīk*	*dak*	*daka*	*daka*
Ali Ufuki	*düm*	.	*tek*	.	.	.	*düm*	*tek*	*teke*	*teke*

or:

	dīk	***dīk***	*dak*	Ø	Ø	*dīk*	*dak*	Ø	*daka*	*daka*
Cantemir	*düm*	.	*tek*	.	.	*düm*	*tek*	.	*teke*	*teke*[22]

As with *ravānī*, Gurjī's definition contains nothing that would point towards one version rather than the other.

6. dawr

This cycle has thirteen *żarb*, and although there is once more no exact correspondence in Ottoman terminology we may reasonably confront Gurjī's sequence of syllables with those in *devr-i kebir*. They can be arranged to match with just one discrepancy at the same point in each seven time-unit half cycle:

dīk	**Ø**	*daka*	*dīk*	Ø	*dak*	Ø	;	*daka*	**Ø**	*dīk*	*dak*	Ø	*daka*	*daka*
düm	***düm***	*tek*	*düm*	.	*tek*	.	;	*tek*	***düm***	*düm*	*tek*	.	*teke*	*teke*

but whereas in the previous cycles the distribution of Gurjī's mnemonic syllables was generally uncontroversial, in this case we begin to be troubled by interpretative uncertainty: it might be thought, in particular, that the pairing *daka* + *Ø* at the beginning of the second half is less than convincing, and that a more persuasive match would be:

dīk	***da***	*ka*	*dīk*	Ø	*dak*	Ø	;	*da*	***ka***	*dīk*	*dak*	Ø	*daka*	*daka*
düm	***düm***	*tek*	*düm*	.	*tek*	.	;	*tek*	***düm***	*düm*	*tek*	.	*teke*	*teke*

Whichever version is preferred, the *düm düm tek* / *tek düm düm* reversal between the two halves of the Ottoman form has a corresponding reversal in the Safavid one (*dīk Ø daka* / *daka Ø dīk* or *dīk da ka* / *da ka dīk*), and the degree of correspondence overall is sufficiently strong to make it certain that Gurjī's account presents a variant form of essentially the same cycle.

With regard to the correspondence between the fast vs. slow pairings, Safavid *ravānī* vs. *dawr* and Ottoman *devr-i revan* vs. *devr-i kebir*, it may be noted that the syllable string *dīk **da** ka dīk dak* / *düm **düm** tek düm tek* is common to all four cycles: it accounts for a whole cycle of the faster one and the first half cycle of the slower:

22 The correspondence has also been noted in Kurdmāfi 2013 (p. 192). The Ali Ufuki version is not taken into consideration.

dīk Ø Ø ***da*** Ø *ka* Ø *dīk* Ø Ø *dak* Ø Ø Ø /
düm . . ***düm*** . *tek* . *düm* . . *tek* . *tek* . /
dīk ***da*** *ka* *dīk* Ø *dak* Ø ;
düm ***düm*** *tek* *düm* . *tek* . ;

but more interesting than this simple observation is to note the difference in distribution whereby to the initial 1+1+1 of the slower corresponds 3+2+2 in the faster, while corresponding to the following 2+1+1 the faster has again 3+2+2. Thus although the 7 : 14 relationship between them suggests a simple distinction of tempo, the two do not in fact match, for if, for purposes of comparison, we simply double the durations of Ali Ufuki's definition, we arrive at:

Ali Ufuki *düm* . *düm* . *tek* . *düm* . . . *te* *ke* *te* *ke*
Cantemir *düm* . . *düm* . *tek* . *düm* . . *tek* . *tek* .

and rather than draw the simplistic conclusion that one of them is mistaken we may entertain the possibility that we are faced here with different solutions to the problem of expressing in whole integer terms durations that were somewhat variable and thus intermediate. If so, the two forms of representation exhibit a hesitation or cognitive shift in the perception of the duration of the constituent cells, with the definition of the faster version revealing aksak characteristics concealed in the other. An extreme form of variation in practice is noted by Cantemir in relation to *evfer* (see 10. *awfar* below), while perhaps more directly comparable to the case of *ravānī* is that of the cognitive complex signalled by the emergent recognition in the Ottoman tradition of forms of *semai* with eight and ten time units as a distinct entities alongside the six time-unit form *semai*[23].

7. nīm dawr

Although evidently related to *dawr*, *nīm dawr* is not, as the name would appear to suggest, half as long: it has ten *żarb*, difficult to accommodate within the seven time units of half of *dawr*. Here, as elsewhere, *nīm* designates more generally a related but shorter cycle, in this case one that begins with the same mnemonic syllables as *dawr* and then deviates towards the end in a way that mirrors the relationship between the Ottoman *devr-i kebir* and the nine time-unit *nim devir*. Following the versions of *dawr* proposed above we may arrive at an arrangement whereby the two coincide, like their Ottoman counterparts, over the first six time units, so that there is again only the one divergence in this area between the Safavid and Ottoman forms:

23 For the definitions of these various forms see Neubauer, Eckhard 1999, *Der Essai sur la musique orientale von Charles Fonton mit Zeichnungen von Adanson*, Frankfurt am Main: Institute for the History of Arabic-Islamic Science, pp. 273-274.

dīk ***da*** *ka dīk* Ø *dak daka daka dak*
düm ***düm*** *tek düm* . *tek* . *teke teke*[24]

Despite the fact that the correspondences proposed for the last three time units carry rather less conviction there is no case to be made for attempting to improve the fit by emending the final *dak* to *daka*, as this would result in a total of eleven attacks as against the ten specified by the text, still less for omitting the first of the two consecutive *daka*.

8. čanbar

No such discrepancies occur in the next cycle, *čanbar*, where we may readily arrive at a perfect fit:

dīk daka dīk dīk dak Ø Ø *dīk dak* Ø *daka daka*
düm teke düm düm tek . . *düm tek* . *teke teke*

9. barāfšān

They recur, however, in *barāfšān*. Here, exceptionally, Gurjī's text is faulty, for corresponding to the initially mentioned ten *żarb* there are only eight attacks in the syllable string. On the assumption that the missing two are both *dīk* syllables a reasonable degree of congruence could readily be established:

dīk Ø *dak dīk* Ø *dak* [*dīk* Ø *dīk*] *da* ***ka*** *dīk* Ø Ø *dak* Ø
düm . *tek düm* . *tek düm* . *düm tek* ***düm*** *düm tek* . *teke teke*

and given the clear 3 + 3 + 2 structure of the first half of the Ottoman *berefşan* the reconstruction of the beginning appears straightforward, and likewise the position of the first hypothetical *dīk*, but the interpretation of the remainder is less secure, and the ending, especially, is unconvincing, to the extent, indeed, that a more persuasive case could be made that the form to which Gurjī's incomplete account relates consisted not of the same number of time units as its Ottoman counterpart but rather of fourteen, with the stable initial 3 + 3 + 2 being followed by either 2 + 2 + 2 or 3 + 3:

dīk Ø *dak* + *dīk* Ø *dak* + [*dīk* Ø ; + *dīk*] *daka* + *dīk* Ø + *dak* Ø
+ *dīk*] *da ka* + *dīk dak* Ø

Despite observing that definitions in earlier Persian sources often have different time unit totals and hence are not good guides to seventeenth-century norms, in this case it is still tempting to note that fourteen is the number of time units

24 As Kurdmāfī (2013, p. 192) points out, the Ottoman syllable string incidentally matches the Safavid one for *fahte*, *dīk dīk dak dīk dak daka daka*, but such is not to suggest that the two are related.

specified in the sixteenth-century treatise by Nasīmī[25], and confirmed in another Persian treatise probably of the same period, the *taqsīm al-naġamāt*[26]. Both give the syllable string *tanan tanan tananan tananan*, representing a basic 3+3+4+4 framework, which thus accords rather better with the first of the above conjectural reconstructions, and suggests:

3 + 3 + 2 ; + 2 + 2 + 2 → 3 + 3 + 2 ; + 2 + 2 + 4

as a possible line of development leading to the Ottoman form, adding, initially, one further attack, so that, setting aside the stable 3 + 3 + 2 beginning, we have:

[*dik*] *daka* + *dīk* ∅ + *dak* ∅	→ [*dīk*] *daka*	+	*dīk*	∅	+	*dak* ∅	+	*dak* ∅
	düm tek		*düm*	***düm***		*tek* .		*teke teke*

The case for such a scenario is, however, weakened by the existence of a more likely ancestor in the shape of a sixteen time-unit cycle with a basic 3+3+4+2+4 framework recorded by Banā'ī, which suggests that the Safavid and Ottoman lines run in parallel. However, a descendant of the Safavid structure may be identified in the fourteen time-unit *lenk* (or *aksak*) *berefşan* recorded in the eighteenth century on the Ottoman side by Kevseri and Fonton.[27] This partially differs from *berefşan* by replacing the repeated initial *düm . tek* cell with repeated *düm tek* . , which corresponds better to the initial *dakkā dakkā* of the anonymous Safavid version. Accordingly, we might wish to conclude that *lenk berefşan* is a better term of comparison for Gurjī's definition than Cantemir's *berefşan*, and so arrive at versions that also correspond more closely to the sixteenth-century 3+3+4+4 framework:

lenk berefşan	*düm*	*tek*	.	*düm*	*tek*	.	*düm*	*düm*	*tek*	*düm*	*düm*	*tek*	.	*teke*
anonymous	*dak*	*kā*	*Ø*	*dak*	*kā*	*Ø*	*dak*	*kā*	*Ø*	*dak*	*dik*	*daki*	*Ø*	*Ø*
Gurjī	*dik*	*dak*	*Ø*	*dik*	*dak*	*Ø*	*[dik*	*dik]*	*da*	*ka*	*dik*	*dak*	*Ø*	*Ø*

10. awfar

Eight *żarb* are specified, and we can again hypothesize a high level of initial congruence, specifically over the first five of the nine time units of the Ottoman form, but with a less secure correspondence thereafter so that, without involving further discrepancies, one could equally well entertain the possibility of alternative arrangements[28]:

25 Pourjavady 2007, p. 42.
26 *taqsīm al-naġamāt wa-bayān al-daraj wa-'l-šuʿab wa-'l-maqāmāt*, Österreichische Staatsbibliothek MS Flügel 1516 (Mxt. 674), fols. 35v-36r.
27 Neubauer 1999, p. 278. The slight differences between their versions are elided here.
28 The two definitions are juxtaposed in Kurdmāfī 2013 (p. 192), but without indicating how they might be related: the final *dak* of Gurjī's version is simply marked, in relation to Cantemir's, as an extra element.

1) *dīk* Ø *daka* *daka* *dīk* Ø ***dīk*** *dak* Ø
2) *dīk* Ø *daka* *daka* *dīk* ***dīk*** *dak* Ø Ø
düm . *teke* *teke* *düm* . *tek* . .

What makes this lack of a clear match in the latter part of the cycle more readily comprehensible is that it may reflect a considerable degree of variability in performance practice, for Cantemir states specifically that singers (and for him *evfer* was only used in the vocal repertoire) were able to ignore the pulse from the second *düm* on, treating the area as unmetred.[29]

11. ramal-i kabīr

12. ramal-i ṣaġīr

We then have two forms of *ramal*, but to judge by the number of *żarb* the second is not slightly shorter, as with *nīm dawr*, but considerably so, for it has only 12 as against the 28 of *ramal-i kabīr*. Consequently, it is the longer form that appears to offer a potential term of comparison for the 28 time units of Ottoman *remel*. Unfortunately, Gurjī's text is again faulty, giving a total of 26 or 27 attacks, depending on whether the reading *dak* or *daka* is preferred at one point.[30] To supply the missing one or two attacks would hardly be a problem if there were otherwise general congruity between Gurjī's version and the Ottoman form, but the coincidence between the number of attacks in the former and the number of time units in the latter is of no help, and the syllable strings fail to signal a high level of similarity. In particular, Gurjī's sequence *dak* (or *daka*) *daka daka daka daka* has no obvious counterpart in Cantemir's definition, so that while it is possible to map one onto the other with no more than four discrepancies, which within a total span of 28 time units hardly seems excessive, the general impression conveyed by the following tentative version is of a rather artificial and awkward fit:

dīk Ø *da* *k[a]* *dīk* *dak* ***dīk*** *dak* ***dīk*** *daka* *dīk* *dak* *da* *ka*
düm . *te* *ke* *düm* . ***te*** *ke* ***te*** *ke* *düm* . *te* *ke*

da *ka* *da* *ka* *da* *ka* *dīk* *dak* *dīk* *[dīk]* *daka* Ø ***dīk*** *dak*
düm . *tek* . *tek* . *düm* *tek* *düm* *düm* *tek* . ***teke*** *teke*

Considering *ramal-i kabīr* in isolation, one could nevertheless point to a satisfactory degree of correlation over the first six and last eight time units, amounting to half of the total cycle, and venture the hypothesis that for the remainder the reduction in the degree of similarity could result from a process of differentiation designed to introduce variety into two rather repetitive strings, in each case inserting a contrastive central element, marked in bold and underlined:

---

29 Wright 2000, p. 396.

30 The text as presented in Pourjavady 2005, p. 256 combines both possibilities.

dīk dak dīk dak dīk daka dīk dak *da ka da ka da ka da ka*
düm . te ke te ke düm . *te ke* ***düm*** *. tek . tek .*

However, there is also *ramal-i ṣaġīr* to take into account, and the latter part of its syllable string aligns itself with the end of *ramal-i kabīr* in a way that strongly suggests that the missing *dīk* in the latter should be inserted at a different point, either *dīk daka dīk [dīk] dak* or *dīk daka [dīk] dīk dak*, but to do so would further reduce the degree of correlation with Ottoman *remel*. This could be accounted for readily enough by positing a substitution in the Ottoman version of the common concluding formula *düm tek . teke teke* for an earlier ending that still survived in the Safavid form, but overall it must be conceded that the case for a connection between the two versions of this cycle is not wholly convincing.

There is yet another factor to be taken into consideration, for the *ramal* pair also exhibits an interesting type of derivational relationship that proceeds (assuming the *ṣaġīr* form to be the secondary one) not merely by the fairly simple procedure of omitting the first ten time units of the longer form, but also by excising an internal segment (*daka daka + dīk dak*) that mirrors its surrounds, so that we have, corresponding to the remainder of the *ramal-i kabīr* syllable string:

kabīr dīk dak daka daka daka daka dīk dak dīk daka [dīk] dīk dak
ṣaġīr dīk dak daka daka dīk daka dīk dīk dak

and on the basis of the distribution of attacks proposed above the twelve *żarb* of *ramal-i ṣaġīr* would constitute a cycle of twelve time units:

dīk dak da ka da ka dīk daka dīk Ø dīk dak

Although by no means conclusive as evidence of historical continuity, it may be noted that the same time-unit total is given in the *taqsīm al-naġamāt*, and even if no correlation can be established with the internal 3+3 distribution of the first half of the definition given there, *tanan tanan*, a satisfactory fit can at least be found in the second half with the 4+2 indicated by *tananan tan*.

There is, though, no obvious relationship between Gurjī's syllable string for *ramal-i ṣaġīr* and an Ottoman cycle with twelve time units: apart from *çenber* the only other one is the very different *frenkçin*. Yet if we look within longer cycles for resemblances to what might be suggested as a hypothetical counterpart of the above (that is, before the substitution of the concluding formula):

dīk dak da ka ***da*** *ka dīk daka dīk Ø dīk dak*
düm . te ke ***düm*** *. düm teke düm . düm tek*

we may consider possible parallels with both *ferʿ-i muhammes* and *türki zarb*. The former adds two time units to each half of this structure, has a slightly different disposition in the second half, but a perfect fit in the first:

düm . te ke düm . [te .] ; düm tek düm düm tek . [te ke]

The resemblance is sufficiently striking to suggest, indeed, that the arrangement proposed above for the second half of *ramal-i ṣaġīr* might be revised accordingly, yielding *dīk daka dīk dīk dak Ø* , and we may consequently venture the same change in the longer cycle, to arrive finally at:

ramal-i kabīr *dīk Ø da k[a] dīk dak dīk dak dīk daka dīk dak da ka*
düm . te ke düm . ***te*** *ke* ***te*** *ke düm . te ke*

da *ka da ka da ka dīk dak dīk* ***daka dīk [dīk]*** *dak Ø*
düm *. tek . tek . düm tek düm* ***düm tek*** *. teke teke*

However, as within the Ottoman corpus *ferᶜ-i muhammes* relates straightforwardly to the first half of *muhammes* (which is identical in its Safavid manifestation):

muhammes *dīk daka dīk dak dīk dīk dak daka*
düm teke düm tek düm düm tek teke

ferᶜ-i muhammes *düm . te ke düm . tek . düm tek düm düm tek . te ke*

ramal-i ṣaġīr *dīk dak da ka* ***da*** *ka dīk daka dīk dīk dak Ø*

any direct form of derivation connecting *ramal-i ṣaġīr* and *ferᶜ-i muhammes* seems to be excluded: it is rather a case of sequences being shared between cycles. On the Safavid side, even if it is easy to show how *ramal-i ṣaġīr* might have been derived from *ramal-i kabīr*, the relationship between them, one a cycle of 28 time units, the other of 12, is anything but straightforward, and it is not inconceivable that the label *ramal-i ṣaġīr* was a survival from an earlier stage, while the structure and syllable string had evolved by assimilation to coincide with various segments of other cycles, including not only *muḫammas* but also *turkī żarb*.

13. turkī żarb

Indeed, placing *turkī żarb* immediately after *ramal-i ṣaġīr* was surely deliberate, not because it has thirteen *żarb* as against the twelve of *ramal-i ṣaġīr*, but rather because, apart from the initial *dīk* (identifiable as the extra *żarb*), its syllable string is identical. However, for the structure of the cycle we need to look at its Ottoman counterpart, and this time a high degree of correlation can immediately be observed, even if the relationship is oblique in that it appears to involve not only cycles with different time-unit totals but also ones that do not start at the same point. Despite mentioning *turkī żarb*, Cantemir fails to describe it or exemplify it with a notated piece, so that for the Ottoman form we have to turn to Ali Ufuki, who likewise provides no notated examples but does define it as a cycle of eighteen time units:[31]

tek . tek tek düm tek düm . düm . tek . teke teke düm . düm düm

[31] Behar 2008, p. 117.

which at first sight seems quite unrelated to Gurjī's syllable string. However, if this is positioned so as to begin at time unit 7 of the Ottoman form the two can be aligned without any discrepancies:

dīk Ø *dīk* Ø *dak* Ø *daka daka dīk daka dīk dīk dak* Ø
tek . tek tek düm tek düm . düm . tek . teke teke düm . düm düm / tek .

(and the perfect match at the end lends support to the identical reading finally arrived at for the end of the two *ramal* cycles).

Thus even more surely than with *barāfšān*, where the Persian form probably consisted of 14 time units as against the 16 of its Ottoman counterpart, we have here a disparity in length, a Persian cycle of 14 time units with an Ottoman counterpart of 18. It would be reasonable to hypothesize that the difference again resulted from a process of extension rather than contraction, the Ottoman form repeating an internal segment of Gurjī's version with minor variations:

dīk Ø *dīk* Ø *dak* Ø [*daka daka dīk daka*] *dīk dīk dak* Ø[*daka daka dīk daka*]
düm . düm . tek . teke teke düm . düm düm tek . tek tek düm tek

and subsequently shifting the additional segment from the end to the beginning[32], a change for which, however, no obvious explanation suggests itself, especially as it involves abandoning a standard *düm* beginning in favour of the much less common *tek* one and ending equally unexpectedly with *düm düm*, something found in no other cycle. If anything, one might suggest a reaction against what had come to be perceived in the sequence */tek . teke teke / düm . düm düm / tek . tek tek/*, as a rather lame final repetition.

Given the difference in length between the two forms, it is interesting to note a seemingly parallel contrast between the two sixteenth-century Safavid accounts: for Nasīmī *turkī żarb* had twelve time units with a 2 + 4 + 4 + 2 organization (*tan tananan tananan tan*)[33], while in the *taqsīm al-naġamāt* it was defined as consisting of seventeen time units, with an interpolated block of five to give the structure 2 [+ 5] + 4 + 4 + 2[34]. The former could be viewed as a possible forerunner of Gurjī's version, statable as 2 + 4 + 4 + 4 or 4 + 4 + 4 + 2 (although 4 + 4 + 2 + 4 would seem preferable).

14. muḫammas

The relationship between the Persian and Ottoman versions of *muḫammas* is far more straightforward, despite the slight inconsistency in Gurjī's text, which specifies 20 *żarb* whereas the syllable string has 21 attacks. If we read *dak* for the

32 For parallel phenomena see the chapter by Salah Eddin Maraqa in the present volume.
33 Pourjavady 2007, p. 106.
34 Vienna MS Flügel 1516, fols. 34v-35r.

third *daka*[35] we arrive at 20, and we then only need the insertion of one unmarked time unit within the syllable string to arrive at a perfect fit with the 16 time units of Cantemir's definition[36]:

dik daka dik dak dik dik dak daka dik daka daka dik dak ∅ daka daka

düm teke düm tek düm düm tek teke düm tek teke düm tek . teke teke

15. ḫafif

With *ḫafīf*, which for Cantemir is twice the length of *muḫammas*, the fit is not quite perfect, but substantial nonetheless, as Gurjī's syllable string of 25 *żarb* can be accommodated with only three discrepancies over the 32 time-unit span:

dik dak dak ∅ dik dak dak ∅ dik ∅ dak ∅ dik ∅ dak ∅
düm tek tek . düm tek tek . düm . te ke düm tek tek .

dik ∅ dak dak dik ***∅*** *da ka dik* ***dik*** *daka dik daka* ***dik*** *dak ∅*
düm . te ke düm ***düm*** *tek teke düm* ***tek*** *teke düm tek* **.** *teke teke*

The particular arrangement proposed for the end of the cycle is by analogy with *turki żarb* and *ramal*, for both of which *dik daka dik dik dak Ø* has been suggested.

16. ṯaqīl

No such guesswork is need with the even longer *ṯaqīl*, however, for the Ottoman *düm tek . teke teke* final formula also occurs in Gurjī's version, thereby allowing us to arrive at a perfect match for its 36 *żarb* spaced out over the whole 48 time-unit span[37]:

dik ∅ da ka dik ∅ da ka da ka dik ∅ da ka dik ∅ dak ∅ dak ∅
düm . te ke düm . te ke te ke düm . te ke düm . tek . tek .

dik ∅ dik ∅ dak ∅ dik ∅ dak ∅ dak ∅ dik ∅ da ka dik dik
düm . düm . tek . düm . tek . tek . düm . te ke düm düm

da ka dik da ka dik dak ∅ daka daka
tek teke düm tek teke düm tek . teke teke

35 One might even suspect editorial oversight here, although Pourjavady is scrupulous in indicating manuscript variants.

36 The correspondence has also been noted in Kurdmāfi 2013 (p. 193), although the Ottoman source used in this case is Abdülbaki Dede.

37 The correspondence has also been noted in Kurdmāfi 2013 (p. 193), although the Ottoman source used in this case is again Abdülbaki Dede.

17. żarb al-fatḥ

The final cycle in Gurjī's list, *żarb al-fatḥ* is stated to have 59 *żarb*, and the syllable string includes an extra element that is unique to it, *dykk*, which occurs twice. As the rest of the string adds up to 53, *dykk*–presumably to be realized as either *dīkak* or *dīkaka* or even *dīkkak*–accordingly has the value of three *żarb*, but how that might be converted into a time unit value is not clear. In fact, the sprawling length of *żarb al-fatḥ*, which in its Ottoman form has 88 time units, gives sufficient latitude for a variety of possible layouts for Gurjī's syllable string, and as there is no patently correct version much of what is proposed here is decidedly tentative. After the first 28 time units, where a high level of correlation with the Ottoman version may be established, the fit is patchy at best, especially as the distribution of *dykk* is such that there seems to be no obvious corresponding segment in the Ottoman version that would help situate it. However, if we assign to it four time units we may arrive, after an ill-matched stretch of 22 time units, at an area extending from time unit 49 to time unit 78 within which only five discrepancies occur. It may be objected that there would be no apparent difference between *dykk* with the value four and *dīk Ø da ka*, but if it were thought to occupy three time units the resulting match would be inferior, and likewise with two. We thus have in all, tentatively:

dīk Ø da ka dīk Ø da ka da ka dīk Ø da ka dīk Ø dak Ø
düm . tek tek düm . tek tek te ke düm . tek tek düm . tek .

dīk Ø dak Ø dīk Ø daka daka dīk Ø ***dīk*** *Ø dī- k ka-k* ***dīk dīk***
düm . tek . düm . te ke düm . ***tek*** *. düm . te ke* ***te ke***

dī- k ka-k ***dīk*** *Ø dīk Ø da ka* ***da*** *ka dīk daka dīk Ø* ***dīk*** *Ø*
düm . te ke te ke düm . tek . ***düm*** *.* ***düm*** *. düm .* ***te*** *ke*

da ka dīk Ø da ka dīk ***dak dīk*** *Ø dīk dak dīk* ***Ø dīk*** *Ø da ka*
te ke düm . te ke düm ***düm tek*** *. düm tek düm* ***düm tek*** *. te ke*

dīk Ø dak Ø dīk dak
düm tek tek . düm tek tek . düm tek düm düm tek . te ke

For the discrepancies in the central area one could again invoke, as with *ramal-i kabīr*, a process of differentiation, one designed in the present case to break up an uninterrupted stream of *dīk* attacks and provide alternating contrasts (*dīk* ***dīk*** *dīkkak* ***dīk dīk*** *dīkkak* ***dīk*** *dīk*), but it can hardly be said that this provides a wholly adequate explanation for the extent to which the two versions fail to coincide. There is also the question of the considerable difference in the total number of time units, and although such discrepancies have been noted elsewhere it is still of some significance that with the distribution proposed here Gurjī's version consists of 78 time units, the total given in the sixteenth-century *taqsīm al-naġamāt*, even if that version fails to suggest similarities in internal segmentation. It would be necessary to force matters unduly to stretch it to arrive at the Ottoman total of

88, although it would certainly be possible to argue for 80 rather than 78, and adduce in evidence the mid eighteenth-century treatise by Arutin, which lists *darb-ı fetih* with 88 time units, as expected, but then at a later stage appears to include alongside it another version with 80[38], and given that he spent an extended period in Persia and subsequently in the entourage of Nadir Shah it may well be supposed that this second version could be a reflection of Persian practice.

Such differences, not just in length but also in the patterning of the syllable strings, serve as a warning against facile assumptions of equivalence: several of the versions offered above are by no means automatic and hence interpretation-free; and even where the relationship is beyond dispute there are specific areas where alternative correspondences would be possible. In the final section of *ṯaqīl*, for example, in place of:

da ka dīk da ka dīk dak Ø daka daka
tek teke düm tek teke düm tek . teke teke

as suggested above, an equally plausible alternative would be:

Ø daka dīk Ø daka dīk dak Ø daka daka
tek teke düm tek teke düm tek . teke teke

In places, then, the versions that have been proposed here are indicative rather than definitive, their purpose being to demonstrate degrees of relatedness rather than to claim that in the Persian tradition the rhythmic cycles listed by Gurjī were performed with exactly the layout of attacks proposed.

Despite these reservations, the overwhelming impression is one of near identity between the two corpora. Although fewer cycles are described on the Safavid side, the readings proposed suggest a comparable range of length (of 4, 6, 8, 9, 10, 12, 14, 16, 18, 28, 32, 48 and 80 time units), and among them the syllable strings match the Ottoman forms perfectly or almost perfectly in eleven (in order of length *ṣūfiyāna, dobaryak, awfar, nīm dawr, fāḫita, čanbar, ravānī, dawr (= devr-i kebir), muḫammas, ḫafīf* and *ṯaqīl*). In *ramal-i kabīr (=remel)* the match is less good, but not quite to the extent of invalidating the presumed connection between them, while in four of the remaining five (*ramal-i ṣaġīr, barāfšān, turkī żarb* and *żarb al-fatḥ*) we encounter not an absence of similarity but rather more complex relationships involving displacement, differentiation, and extension and consequent variations in time unit totals. That leaves only *ḥarbī,* for which there is at least the possibility of a correspondence–and another perfect one–with the Ottoman *semai.* In five cycles (*čanbar, dawr, muḫammas, ṯaqīl* and one version of *fāḫita*) we encounter, according to the readings proposed, the same final formula (*dīk dak Ø daka daka / düm tek . teke teke*), while in a further two, *ḫafīf* and *ramal-i kabīr*, it occurs in the Ottoman versions while the Safavid ones have *dīk daka dīk*

[38] Popescu-Judetz 2002: the longer version is on p. 62, the shorter, which also has a different stroke pattern, on p. 97. The text, however, may not be reliable, since for both a slow (*ağır*) form with 44 time units is mentioned.

dak Ø. Accordingly, it may well be that in the Ottoman tradition we are confronted here with cases of assimilation, and that an earlier *düm teke düm tek .* ending has been replaced. If so, one might speculate that the contrast in the ending of *ravānī* (Safavid *da ka dīk Ø dak Ø* vs. Ottoman *düm tek düm . teke teke*) might be similarly explained as resulting from a variant of the same process, an earlier final *düm . tek .* being replaced by *düm . teke teke.* Similarly, it would be reasonable to assume that the move in Ottoman *fahte* from the *düm tek teke teke* ending recorded by Ali Ufki to Cantemir's *düm tek . teke teke* constitutes a further case of assimilation.

The eleven matching cycles account for 72% of the instrumental repertoire recorded by Cantemir,[39] and if the equation of *ḥarbī* with *semai* is allowed the figure rises to 82%, while as a negative correlation we find that nearly all the cycles that are under-represented in the repertoires notated by Ali Ufuki and Cantemir (*evsat, frenkçin, havi, hezec, horezm, nim sakil, remel* and *yek darb*) are absent from Gurjī's inventory[40]. There are, though, two cycles, *barāfšān* and *żarb al-fatḥ*, both well represented in the Ottoman repertoire[41], where the evidence points to differences in the time unit totals, and here it appears plausible to interpret Gurjī's version of *barāfšān* as the more conservative, embodying an antecedent stage, and his version of *żarb al-fatḥ* as being likely to represent an independent line of development.

Mention has been made of two further Persian texts containing material analogous to Gurjī's definitions, but both present interpretative difficulties. The information contained in the *bahjat al-rūḥ* is coded in two places and in two ways. In the first we have, as with Gurjī, a total number of *żarb*, followed, however, not by a string of mnemonic syllables but by a division of the total into *bam* and *zīr*. These, we might reasonably suppose, could represent a distinction of timbre, *bam* equating with *dīk* and *düm*, *zīr* with *dak*, *daka*, *tek* and *teke*. Syllable strings, significantly more varied, are given elsewhere, and on the basis of the information coded in both forms we could establish a correspondence between the first cycle mentioned, *fāḫita*, which is described as consisting of seven *żarb*, three *bam* and four *zīr*, and the interpretation of Gurjī's account given above:

bahjat al-rūḥ	*tan*	*tan*	*ta*	*na*	*nah*	*dir*	*tā*	*ta*	*na*	*nah*
	bam	*bam*	*zīr*	*Ø*	*Ø*	*bam*	*zīr*	*Ø*	*zīr*	*zīr*
Gurjī	*dīk*	*dīk*	*dak*	*Ø*	*Ø*	*dīk*	*dak*	*Ø*	*daka*	*daka*
Ottoman	*düm*	.	*tek*	.	.	*düm*	*tek*	.	*teke*	*teke*

But quite apart from the questionable status of the syllable string, which has the air of the beginning of a *tarannum* section from a representative composition, the promise of this first example is short-lived, for the *bahjat al-rūḥ* stubbornly re-

39 Ignoring pieces in two (*darbeyn*) or more (*zencir*) rhythmic cycles.

40 In his initial list he includes *nim sakil*, but fails to provide a definition.

41 They account for almost 13% of Cantemir's notations.

fuses further such tempting alignments. For *doyak*, for example, it specifies nine *żarb*, more than the expected number of time units, and for *ṯaqīl* and *ḫafīf* twelve and eleven respectively, far fewer.

The other source, the anonymous and undated work in the same manuscript as the treatises of Āqā Muʾmin and Gurjī, contains definitions of seven cycles in familiar-looking mnemonic syllables[42], while an earlier chapter cites the number of *żarb* in twenty cycles[43]. Some belong to an earlier period, and for the ones held in common with Gurjī there is not a single instance in which the number coincides. With the mnemonic syllables, on the other hand, there are one or two cases where there is a plausible match to be made with the version proposed for Gurjī's syllable string (G). Thus for *muḫammas* one could suggest:

G *dīk daka dīk dak dīk dīk dak daka dīk daka daka dīk dak* ∅ *daka daka*
dakkā dakkā dīk dakkā dakkā dīk dakkā ∅ *dīk dak dakkā dīk dak dakkā dīk dak*

and for *nīm ṯaqīl*:

G *dīk* ∅ *da ka dīk* ∅ *da ka da ka dīk* ∅ *da ka dīk* ∅ *dak* ∅ *dak* ∅
dīk ∅ *dakkā dīk* ∅ ∅ ∅ *dakkā dīk* ∅ *dakkā dīk* ∅ *dak* ∅ *dak* ∅

while with *ṯaqīl* one could arrive at a partial fit on the assumption that we are dealing with a version with 40 rather than 48 time units:

G *dīk* ∅ *da ka dīk* ∅ *da ka da ka dīk* ∅ *da ka dīk* ∅ *dak* ∅ *dak* ∅
dīk ∅ *dakkā dīk* ∅ *dakkā dakkā dīk dīk dakkā dīk* ∅ ∅ ∅ *dīk* ∅

G *dīk* ∅ *dīk* ∅ *dak* ∅ *dīk* ∅ *dak* ∅ *dak* ∅ *dīk* ∅ *da ka dīk dīk*
dīk ∅ *dīk* ∅ *dakkā dīk* ∅ *dak* ∅ *dak* ∅ ∅ ∅ *dakkā dīk* ∅

G *da ka dīk da ka dīk dak* ∅ *daka daka*
dak dak

With the other cycles correspondences are, though, more difficult to find, so that these two texts stand at some distance from Gurjī, and raise again the question of the extent to which Safavid practice during the seventeenth century, in addition to whatever general diachronic developments there may have been, was marked by regional variation. Despite such complications, there can be no doubt as to the strong similarities that existed between the rhythmic structures used during the mid to late seventeenth-century at the Ottoman and Safavid courts. But even if these *usul* parallels are surely highly significant in themselves, they need to be considered in the context of a fuller comparative survey of Ottoman and Safavid structures during this period, one that will also take account of the domains of mode and form.

---

[42] Pourjavady 2007, p. 188.
[43] Pourjavady 2007, p. 187.

Observations on the Use of the Rhythmic Cycle *Darb-ı Fetih* ("Rhythm of Conquest") in Turkish Vocal Music of the 17th – 19th Centuries

Yalçın Tura

ᶜAbd al Qadir al-Marâgî, speaking of rhythmic cycles of his own invention in the third section of the eleventh chapter of his book *Jami al-alhan* ("Collection of Melodies"), presents a cycle of fifty time units which he calls *darb al-fath*. However, in his other works, i.e. *Sharh-i Advar* ("Commentary on the [*Kitab al-*] *Advar* [of Safi ad-Din al-Urmawi]") and *Maqâsid al-alhân*, he presents a cycle of the same name, composed of forty-nine time units, and tells the history of its composition.

After al-Marâgî, other writers who discuss the invention of the same rhythm assert that it is composed of forty-nine time units. Unfortunately, except for some song lyrics, we do not possess a written musical composition in either form of the above-mentioned cycle.

In the books of Muhammad bin ᶜAbd al-Hamid al-Lâdiqî, written after the conquest of Constantinople by the Ottoman sultan Mehmed II and during the reign of Bâyezîd II, we come across a rhythmic cycle with the same name, but composed of eighty-eight time units.[1]

About two centuries later, Ali Ufkî, in his book *Mecmua-i Sâz u Söz*, gives many examples of *peşrev*s (instrumental preludes) composed in this cycle in various *makam*s. He writes this rhythm as twenty-two groups of four quarter-notes. About fifty years after him, Demetrius Cantemir, using the same name, revealed details of this same cycle composed of eighty-eight time units, and wrote the scores of many *peşrevs* with his own notation system.

In a paper presented in a conference held in Istanbul in 1978 and reprinted in my book *Türk Mûsikîsinin Mes'eleleri* ("Problems of Turkish Music"), I analyzed instrumental preludes composed over a time span of five centuries by Ottoman composers in this cycle of eighty-eight units, and corrected many errors committed in the last century due to the misunderstanding of the real structure of this rhythm by musicians and musicologists of the nineteenth and twentieth centuries.

Now, in this paper, I will try to investigate vocal compositions written in this rhythmic cycle by Ottoman-Turkish composers. I hope that this research will help us understand the peculiarities of this interesting rhythm, and show us the secrets of composing in one of the longest rhythmic cycles in usage in Ottoman-Turkish music.

1 For different versions of *darb al-fath* according to al-Marâgî and al-Lâdiqî, see Fig. 1.

When using particular cycles for a vocal composition, especially a long rhythmic cycle, Ottoman-Turkish composers are accustomed to observing some rules in order to adjust their musical phrases to the connecting points of the rhythm in use. For example, the rhythmic cycle *zencîr* ("chain") is composed of five other rhythms joined together, i.e. *çifte düyek* + *fâhte* + *çenber* + *devr-i kebîr* + *berefşân*, with time units arranged as 8+10+12+14+16=60 or 16+20+24+28+32=120. When using this cycle, a composer will try to finish the melody of the verse exactly at the end of the third rhythmic unit, at the middle of the cycle, beginning the *terennüm* (a sort of vocalized syllable section) at the start of *devr-i kebîr* and finishing it at the end of *berefşân*. Some other rhythms, like *lenk fâhte* or *hâvî*, require similar rules.

We observe a similar concern in the use of *darb-ı fetih*. All the vocal compositions that we possess in that cycle observe the same pattern. All of them are in the same musical form: *terennümlü murabbâ beste* (a composition based on a quatrain in four parts, with vocalized sections).

Terennümlü murabbâ beste is composed on two distiches of a *gazel* (a poetical form with many distiches). The melody of the first verse is composed in the principal *makam*, followed by a long vocalized section, named *terennüm*, using in general meaningless syllables denoting rhythmic percussions, such as *tan, ta nan, ta na nan, lal, lal li la la lal* etc., or sometimes with meaningful words such as *cânım, ömrüm* ("my soul", "my life", "my dear"), and so on. The second verse is an almost exact repetition (sometimes with a slight change at the last measure, in order to proceed easily to the melody of the third verse, which is usually in another *makam* or another register). The *terennüm* of this section may use another musical phrase; but at the end we hear the *ritornello* of the previous verses. After this middle section, called *miyân-hâne,* the fourth verse and its *terennüm* are sung exactly as in the first and second verses.

We may schematize the poetic structure of the text and their rhymes as:

Verse 1: A, rhyme a
Verse 2: B, rhyme a
Verse 3: C, rhyme b
Verse 4: D, rhyme a

The musical structure of a *terennümlü murabbâ beste* is:

Verse 1: Melody A + *Terennüm* melody a
Verse 2: Melody A + *Terennüm* melody a
Verse 3: Melody B + *Terennüm* melody a or b
Verse 4: Melody A + *Terennüm* melody a

A verse plus *terennüm* are labelled "*hâne*" ("house"). In a *murabbâ* composed in *darb-ı fetih*, each *hâne* occupies one complete cycle, so the rhythm is repeated four times.

There are ten *murabbas* composed in the rhythm *darb-ı fetih* that we possess as written musical scores. The oldest of these compositions is a *murabbâ* with *terennüm* composed by Küçük İmam (? -1675) in *makam hicâz* (*zîrgüle*) (Fig. 2) on the following verses[2] of an unknown poet:

Tâ be key sûz-î gamımla derdli sînem dağlayım,
Yâr cânım ya le lel le le lel le lel te re li lel le lel lel lel lel yâr işvebâzım
çâresâzım yâr yâr ah dağlayım

Nice bir sûlar gibi dağlar başında çağlayım
Yâr cânım ya le lel le le lel le lel te re li lel le lel lel lel lel yâr işvebâzım
çâresâzım yâr yâr ah çağlayım

Çünki dökmezsin nem-i eşkin benimçün sevdiğim
Yâr cânım ya le lel le le lel le lel te re li lel le lel lel lel lel yâr işvebâzım
çâresâzım yâr yâr ah sevdiğim

Bâri koyver hâlime kendim be kendim ağlayım
Yâr cânım ya le lel le le lel le lel te re li lel le lel lel lel lel yâr işvebâzım
çâresâzım yâr yâr ah ağlayım

We may schematize the structure of this piece as follows:

A (Verse 1) + a (*terennüm*)
A (Verse 2) + a (*terennüm*)
B (Verse 3, called *miyanhâne*) + b (new *terennüm*)
A (Verse 4) + a (*terennüm*)

The rhythm of the piece is notated as eighty-eight half notes, played very slowly (half note = MM.40) four times, each verse and *terennüm* occupying one cycle. But if we carefully examine the structure of the melodies, we may notice a curious usage of the time units: the melody of each verse occupies exactly thirty-two time units, then the first phrase of the *terennüm* begins, followed by a repetition of the last words of the verse, occupying altogether fourteen units. The *terennüm* continues for twenty-six units, after which comes a new melodic phrase, which occupies sixteen units and closes the first part. The second and fourth verse plus their *terennüms* are constructed on exactly the same scheme. The third verse or *miyanhâne* with its own *terennüm* follows the same scheme; but the last phrase of the *terennüm*, which occupies the last sixteen time units, is repeated exactly in each part.

2 Written in the poetic metre *hezec* (*fâ i lâ tün fâ i lâ tün fâ i lâ tün fâ i lün*).

Structural Analyses of the Murabbâs

1. *Hicâz Murabbâ* by Küçük İmam (? – 1675)[3]

(Time units: 88 half notes)

Music:

Hâne-i evvel (1st Part): 32 (verse 1) + 56 (*terennüm*) = 88 time units (no closing section)
Hâne-i sânî (2nd Part): 32 (verse 2) + 56 (*terennüm*) = 88 time units (no closing section; same music as the first part)
Miyânhâne (3rd Part): 32 (verse 3) + 56 (*terennüm*) = 88 time units (no closing section; different music but last 16 units function as a *ritornello* and are the same as previous parts)
Hâne-i râbî (4th Part): 32 (verse 4) + 56 (*terennüm*) = 88 time units (same music as the first and second parts)

2. *Beste-Nigâr Murabbâ* by Buhûrîzâde Mustafa Itrî (1638? – 1712)[4]

(Time units: 88 half notes)

Song-text:[5]

Gamzen ki ola saki-i çeşm-i siyeh-i mest
Yar cânım, siyeh-i mest
Tir yel le lel le le lel le lel lel li ah te ne li yel lel lel lel lel li ya lel ye lel lel li
yâr hey dost hey siyeh-i mest

Mest etmeğe uşşakı yeter bir nigeh-i mest
Yar cânım, nigeh-i mest
Tir yel le lel le le lel le lel lel li ah te ne li yel lel lel lel lel li ya lel ye lel lel li
yâr hey dost hey siyeh-i mest

Rezmî, hazer et ol saçı leylin nigehinden
Yar cânım, nigeh-i mest
Tir yel le lel le le lel le lel lel li ah te ne li yel lel lel lel lel li ya lel ye lel lel li
yâr hey dost hey siyeh-i mest

Mecnûn eder insânı o çeşm-i siyeh-i mest
Yar cânım, siyeh-i mest
Tir yel le lel le le lel le lel lel li ah te ne li yel lel lel lel lel li ya lel ye lel lel li
yâr hey dost hey siyeh-i mest

---

3 See Fig. 2 for the music and above for the song-text.
4 *Darü'l-elhan Külliyatı, no: 72,* Istanbul.
5 Poetic metre *hazaj* (*mef û lü me fâ î lü me fâ î lü fe û lün*).

Music:

Hâne-i evvel (1st Part): 32 (verse 1) +56 [13.5 (end of the verse/beginning of *terennüm*) + 42,5 (*terennüm*)] = 88 time units

Hâne-i sânî (2nd Part): 32 (verse 2) + 56 [13.5 (end of the verse/beginning of *terennüm*) + 42,5 (*terennüm*)] = 88 time units (same music as the first part.)

Miyânhâne (3rd Part): 32 (verse 3) + 56 [13.5 (end of the verse/beginning of *terennüm*) + 42,5 (*terennüm*)] = 88 time units (different music but the last 16 units function as a *ritornello* and are the same as previous parts.)

Hâne-i râbî (4th Part): 32 (verse 4) + 56 [13.5 (end of the verse/beginning of *terennüm*) + 42,5 (*terennüm*)] = 88 time units (same music as the first and second parts)

3. *Nühüft Murabbâ* by Seyyid Nûh (? – 1714)[6]

(Time units: 88 half notes)

Song-text:[7]

Ta kim hattın ey mâh-ı cebînim yüze çıkdı
Hey cânım, ah, yüze çıkdı
Beli beli beli yel le lel li, cânım ye lel lel lel lel lel li ya la ye le la li
yar dost beli yar-i men

Esrâr-ı dil-i kalb-i hazinim yüze çıkdı
Hey cânım, ah, yüze çıkdı
Beli beli beli yel le lel li, cânım ye lel lel lel lel lel li ya la ye le la li
yar dost beli yar-i men

Ruhsârına hatt geldi deyu ağlamam amma
Hey cânım, ah, yüze çıkdı
Beli beli beli yel le lel li, cânım ye lel lel lel lel lel li ya la ye le la li
yar dost beli şah-i men

Baht-ı siyeh-i serd ü kemînim yüze çıkdı
Hey cânım, ah, yüze çıkdı
Beli beli beli yel le lel li, cânım ye lel lel lel lel lel li ya la ye le la li
yar dost beli yar-i men

A (Verse 1) + a (*terennüm*)
A (Verse 2) + a (*terennüm*)
B (Verse 3, "*miyânhâne*") + a (*terennüm*)
A (Verse 4) + a (*terennüm*)

6 Ezgi, Subhi 1953, *Nazarî ve Amelî Türk Mûsıkîsi*, vol. 5, pp. 497-498.
7 Poetic metre *hazaj* (*mef û lü me fâ î lü me fâ î lü fe û lün*).

Music:

Hâne-i evvel (1st Part): 32 (verse 1) +56 [14 (end of the verse/beginning of *terennüm*) + 42 (*terennüm*)] = 88 time units
Hâne-i sânî (2nd Part): 32 (verse 2) + 56 [14 (end of the verse/beginning of *terennüm*) + 42 (*terennüm*)] = 88 time units (same music as the first part)
Miyânhâne (3rd Part): 32 (verse 3) + 56 [14 (end of the verse/beginning of *terennüm*) + 42 (*terennüm*)] = 88 time units (different music but the last 16 units function as a *ritornello* and are the same as previous parts)
Hâne-i râbî (4th Part): 32 (verse 4) + 56 [14 (end of the verse/beginning of *terennüm*) + 42 (*terennüm*)] = 88 time units (same music as the first and second parts)

4. *Uşşâk Murabbâ* by İsmâîl Dede Efendi (1778 – 1846)
(Time units: 88 half notes; 1 unit = MM. 40)

Song-text:[8]

Dil nâle eder bülbül-i şeydâ revişinde
Yâr cânım ah revişinde
Ye lel le lel le lel le lel lel lel lel li te re lel lel lel lel lel lel li
ya la yel lel lel li
Hey yâr hey dost beli yâr-i men

Gül işvelenir dilber-i rânâ revişinde
Yâr cânım ah revişinde
Ye lel le lel le lel le lel lel lel lel li te re lel lel lel lel lel lel li
ya la yel lel lel li
Hey yâr hey dost beli yâr-i men

Mecnun da ederdi nazarın gayriye mâil
Yâr cânım gayriye mâil
Ye lel le lel le lel le lel lel lel lel li te re lel lel lel lel lel lel li
ya la yel lel lel li
Hey yâr hey dost beli yâr-i men

Bulsaydı eger bir dahi Leylâ revişinde
Yâr cânım ah revişinde
Ye lel le lel le lel le lel lel lel lel li te re lel lel lel lel lel lel li
ya la yel lel lel li
Hey yâr hey dost beli yâr-i men

A (Verse 1) + a (*terennüm*)
A (Verse 2) + a (*terennüm*)
B (Verse 3, "*miyanhâne*") + b (new *terennüm*)
A (Verse 4) + a (*terennüm*)

---

8 Poetic metre *hazaj* (*mef û lü me fâ î lü me fâ î lü fe û lün*).

Music:

Hâne-i evvel (1st Part): 32 (verse 1) +56 [13.5 (end of the verse/beginning of *terennüm*) + 42,5 (*terennüm*)] = 88 time units
Hâne-i sânî (2nd Part): 32 (verse 2) + 56 [13.5 (end of the verse/beginning of *terennüm*) + 42,5 (*terennüm*)] = 88 time units (same music as the first part.)
Miyânhâne (3rd Part): 30 (verse 3) + 58 [15 (end of the verse/beginning of *terennüm*) + 43 (*terennüm*)] = 88 time units (different music but last 12 units -part of the *ritornello*- are the same as previous parts)
Hâne-i râbî (4th Part): 32 (verse 4) + 56 [13.5 (end of the verse/beginning of *terennüm*) + 42,5 (*terennüm*)] = 88 time units (same music as the first and second parts)

5. *Sûz-i Dîl Murabbâ* by Eyyûbî Mehmed Bey (1804 – 1850)
(Time units: 88 half notes; 1 unit = MM.40)

Song-text:[9]

Derdim nice bir sînede pinhan ederim ben
Yâr yâr cânım âh ederim ben
Yel lel le le lel le le lel le le lel lel lel li yâr
Bî menendim dim dîl pesendim
Hey yâr yâr ah Belî yâr-i men

Bir ah ile bu canımı kurban ederim ben
Yâr yâr cânım âh ederim ben
Yel lel le le lel le le lel le le lel lel lel li yâr
Bî menendim dim dîl pesendim
Hey yâr yâr ah Belî yâr-i men

Yâr olmayıcak cevr ü sitemdir bana bâde
Yâr cânım bana bâde
Yel lel le le lel le le lel le le lel lel lel li yâr
Bî menendim dim dîl pesendim
Hey yâr yâr ah Belî yâr-i men

Bilmem nice def-î gam ü hicrân ederim ben
Yâr yâr cânım âh ederim ben
Yel lel le le lel le le lel le le lel lel lel li yâr
Bî menendim dim dîl pesendim
Hey yâr yâr ah Belî yâr-i men

A (Verse 1) + a (*terennüm*)
A (Verse 2) + a (*terennüm*)
B (Verse 3, "*miyanhâne*") + b (new *terennüm*)
A (Verse 4) + a (*terennüm*)

9 Poetic metre *hazaj* (*mef û lü me fâ î lü me fâ î lü fe û lün*).

Music:

Hâne-i evvel (1st Part): 32 (verse 1) +56 [13 (end of the verse/beginning of *terennüm*) + 43 (*terennüm*)] = 88 time units
Hâne-i sânî (2nd Part): 32 (verse 2) + 56 [13 (end of the verse/beginning of *terennüm*) + 43 (*terennüm*)] = 88 time units (same music as the first part, no *ritornello*)
Miyânhâne (3rd Part): 32 (verse 3) + 56 [13 (end of the verse/beginning of *terennüm*) + 43 (*terennüm*)] = 88 time units
Hâne-i râbî (4th Part): 32 (verse 4) + 56 [13 (end of the verse/beginning of *terennüm*) + 43 (*terennüm*)] = 88 time units (same music as the first and second parts)

6. *Hicazkâr Murabbâ* by Zekâî Dede (1825 – 1897)[10, 11]
(Time units: 88 half notes)

Song-text:[12]

Bir kerre iltifâtın ile hurrem olmadık
Yâr cânım yâr olmadık
Dâd ey dâd ey dâd ey dâd ey yâr ey yâr ey yâr ey yâr ey bî karârem
Sabr edemem ah ah dost dost yâr olmadık

Bîgâne denlu sohbetine mahrem olmadık
Yâr cânım yâr olmadık
Dâd ey dâd ey dâd ey dâd ey yâr ey yâr ey yâr ey yâr ey bî karârem
Sabr edemem ah ah dost dost yâr olmadık

Etvârımız müsellem erbâb-ı tâb iken
Yâr cânım yâr olmadık
Dâd ey dâd ey dâd ey dâd ey yâr ey yâr ey yâr ey yâr ey bî karârem
Sabr edemem ah ah dost dost yâr olmadık

Yalnız senin yanında iken âdem olmadık
Yâr cânım yâr olmadık
Dâd ey dâd ey dâd ey dâd ey yâr ey yâr ey yâr ey yâr ey bî karârem
Sabr edemem ah ah dost dost yâr olmadık

A (Verse 1) + a (*terennüm*)
A (Verse 2) + a (*terennüm*)
B (Verse 3, "*miyânhâne*") + a (*terennüm*)
A (Verse 4) + a (*terennüm*)

10 İstanbul Belediye Konservatuvarı 1940, *Türk Mûsikîsi Klâsiklerinden: Hâfız M. Zekâî Dede Efendi Külliyâtı*, vol. 1, p. 23f.

11 Half of the scores of *murabbâs* on *darb-ı fetih* that we possess are Zekâî Dede's compositions.

12 Poetic metre *muzârî* (*mef û lü fâ î lâ tü me fâ î lü fâ i lün*).

Music:

Hâne-i evvel (1st Part): 32 (verse 1) +56 [14 (end of the verse/beginning of *terennüm*) + 42 (*terennüm*)] = 88 time units
Hâne-i sânî (2nd Part): 32 (verse 2) + 56 [14 (end of the verse/beginning of *terennüm*) + 42 (*terennüm*)] = 88 time units (same music as the first part)
Miyânhâne (3rd Part): 32 (verse 3) + 56 [14 (end of the verse/beginning of *terennüm*) + 42 (*terennüm*)] = 88 time units (different music but the last 16 units function as a *ritornello* and are the same as previous parts)
Hâne-i râbî (4th Part): 32 (verse 4) + 56 [14 (end of the verse/beginning of *terennüm*) + 42 (*terennüm*)][13] = 88 time units (same music as the first and second parts)

7. *Sabâ Murabbâ* by Zekâî Dede (1825 – 1897)[14]

(Time units: 88 half notes)

Song-text:[15]

Bir lahza nihân olsa o mehrû nazarımdan
Yâr cânım ah nazarımdan
Yel le lel le lel le le lel lel li yen tir ye lel lel lel lel lel li mîrim ye le lâ lî
Hey yâr hey dost belî yâr-î men

Bîzâr olurum hâsılı nûr-î basarımdan
Yâr cânım ah nazarımdan
Yel le lel le lel le le lel lel li yen tir ye lel lel lel lel lel li mîrim ye le lâ lî
Hey yâr hey dost belî yâr-î men

Ben tâir-i evc-î harem-î sûz-i güdâzım
Yâr cânım ah nazarımdan
Yel le lel le lel le le lel lel li yen tir ye lel lel lel lel lel li mîrim ye le lâ lî
Hey yâr hey dost belî yâr-î men

Âteş saçılırsâ ne aceb bâl ü perimden
Yâr cânım ah nazarımdan
Yel le lel le lel le le lel lel li yen tir ye lel lel lel lel lel li mîrim ye le lâ lî
Hey yâr hey dost belî yâr-î men

A (Verse 1) + a (*terennüm*)
A (Verse 2) + a (*terennüm*)
B (Verse 3, "*miyânhâne*") + a (*terennüm*)
A (Verse 4) + a (*terennüm*)

---

13 The vocalised sections may also be considered as 13 + 43 = 56 units.
14 İstanbul Belediye Konservatuvarı 1940, *Türk Mûsikîsi Klâsiklerinden: Hâfiz M. Zekâî Dede Efendi Külliyâtı*, vol. 1, p. 39f.
15 Poetic metre *hazaj* (*mef û lü me fâ î lü me fâ î lü fe û lün*).

Music:

Hâne-i evvel (1st Part): 32 (verse 1) +56 [14 (end of the verse/beginning of *terennüm*) + 42 (*terennüm*)] = 88 time units
Hâne-i sânî (2nd Part): 32 (verse 2) + 56 [14 (end of the verse/beginning of *terennüm*) + 42 (*terennüm*)] = 88 time units (same music as the first part)
Miyânhâne (3rd Part): 32 (verse 3) + 56 [14 (end of the verse/beginning of *terennüm*) + 42 (*terennüm*)] = 88 time units (different music but the last 16 units function as a *ritornello* and are the same as previous parts)
Hâne-i râbî (4th Part): 32 (verse 4) + 56 [14 (end of the verse beginning of *terennüm*) + 42 (*terennüm*)] = 88 time units (same music as the first and second parts)

8. *Muhayyer Murabbâ* by Zekâî Dede (1825 – 1897)[16]

(Time units: 88 half notes)

Song-text:[17]

Hengâm-ı safâdır yine nûş-i mey eyle
(Dem be dem eyle)
Yâr cânım dem be dem eyle
Cânım cânım cânım Ten ne nen ni ten nen ne nenn en nenn en ni tâ nâ dir nâ

til lil len nâ
Yâr dost belî yâr-i men

Zevk et bu gece defter-i âlâmı tay eyle
(Gel kerem eyle)
Yâr cânım dem be dem eyle
Cânım cânım cânım Ten ne nen ni ten nen ne nenn en nenn en ni tâ nâ dir nâ

til lil len nâ
Yâr dost belî yâr-i men

Mutrîb ederek perde muhayyerle ser-âğâz
(Sâz ile hem-âvâz)
Yâr cânım dem be dem eyle
Cânım cânım cânım Ten ne nen ni ten nen ne nenn en nenn en ni tâ nâ dir nâ

til lil len nâ
Yâr dost belî yâr-i men

Bû Zarb-ı Fetîh Besteyi dem-sâz-ı ney eyle
Def-i gam eyle
Yâr cânım dem be dem eyle
Cânım cânım cânım Ten ne nen ni ten nen ne nenn en nenn en ni tâ nâ dir nâ

til lil len nâ
Yâr dost belî yâr-i men

---

16 İstanbul Belediye Konservatuvarı 1940, *Türk Mûsikîsi Klâsiklerinden: Hâfız M. Zekâî Dede Efendi Külliyâtı*, vol. 1, pp. 75-77.

17 Poetic form *müstezâd*, metre *hazaj* (*mef û lü me fâ î lü me fâ î lü fe û lün*).

Music:

Hâne-i evvel (1st Part): 32 (verse 1) +56 [16 (end of the verse/beginning of *terennüm*) + 40 (*terennüm*)] = 88 time units
Hâne-i sânî (2nd Part): 32 (verse 2) + 56 [16 (end of the verse/beginning of *terennüm*) + 40 (*terennüm*)] = 88 time units (same music as the first part)
Miyânhâne (3rd Part): 32 (verse 3) + 56 [16 (end of the verse/beginning of *terennüm*) + 40 (*terennüm*)] = 88 time units (different music but the last 16 units function as a *ritornello* and are the same as previous parts)
Hâne-i râbî (4th Part): 32 (verse 4) + 56 [16 (end of the verse/beginning of *terennüm*) + 40 (*terennüm*)] = 88 time units (same music as the first and second parts; last 16 units function as a *ritornello* and are the same in all parts)

9. *Hisâr-Bûselik Murabbâ* by Zekâî Dede (1825 – 1897)[18]

(Time units: 88 half notes)

Song-text:[19]

Yâr olmayıcak câm-ı safâyı çekemez dîl
Yâr cânım âh çekemez dîl
Yel lel lele lel lel lel lele lel lel lel li yel le lel lel lel lel lel lel li yâ lâ yel lel li
Yâr yâr dost belî yâr-i men

Her ne ise çeker böyle cefâyı çekemez dîl
Yâr cânım âh çekemez dîl
Yel lel lele lel lel lel lele lel lel lel li yel le lel lel lel lel lel lel li yâ lâ yel lel li
Yâr yâr dost belî yâr-i men

Hûn-î dîlî bir zevk ile nûş etmede Gammî
Yâr cânım âh çekemez dîl
Yel lel lele lel lel lel lele lel lel lel li yel le lel lel lel lel lel lel li yâ lâ yel lel li
Yâr yâr dost belî yâr-i men

Ol lezzet ile zehr-i safâyı çekemez dîl
Yâr cânım âh çekemez dîl
Yel lel lele lel lel lel lele lel lel lel li yel le lel lel lel lel lel lel li yâ lâ yel lel li
Yâr yâr dost belî yâr-i men

Music:

Hâne-i evvel (1st Part): 32 (verse 1) +56 [13 (end of the verse/beginning of *terennüm*) + 43 (*terennüm*)] = 88 time units
Hâne-i sânî (2nd Part): 32 (verse 2) + 56 [13 (end of the verse/beginning of *terennüm*) + 43 (*terennüm*)] = 88 time units (same music as the first part)

---

18 İstanbul Belediye Konservatuvarı 1940, *Türk Mûsikîsi Klâsiklerinden: Hâfız M. Zekâî Dede Efendi Külliyâtı*, vol. 1, p. 92f.
19 Poetic metre *hazaj* (*mef û lü me fâ î lü me fâ î lü fe û lün*).

Miyânhâne (3rd Part): 32 (verse 3) + 56 [13 (end of the verse/beginning of *terennüm*) + 43 (*terennüm*)] = 88 time units (different music but the last 16 units function as a *ritornello* and are the same as previous parts)
Hâne-i râbî (4th Part): 32 (verse 4) + 56 [13 (end of the verse/beginning of *terennüm*) + 43 (*terennüm*)] = 88 time units (same music as the first and second parts; last 16 units function as a *ritornello* and are the same in all parts)

10. *Muhayyer-Kürdî Murabbâ* by Zekâî Dede (1825 – 1897)[20]

(Time units: 88 half notes)

Song-text:[21]

Arz-ı niyâzımız sana gerçi cemîledir
Yâr cânım âh cemîledir
Ye le lel li ye le lel le le lel li te re lel lel lel lel li yâ lâ lel lel li
Ah işvebâzım çâre-sâzım belî yâr-i men

Maksûdumuz heman hâk-î-pâye vesîledir
Yâr cânım âh cemîledir
Ye le lel li ye le lel le le lel li te re lel lel lel lel li yâ lâ lel lel li
Ah işvebâzım çâre-sâzım belî yâr-i men

Sâz-âşinâ-yı bezm-i tarabdır hünerverî
Yâr cânım âh cemîledir
Ye le lel li ye le lel le le lel li te re lel lel lel lel li yâ lâ lel lel li
Ah işvebâzım çâre-sâzım belî yâr-i men

Bu mûsikî terâne-künân bir kabîledir
Yâr cânım âh cemîledir
Ye le lel li ye le lel le le lel li te re lel lel lel lel li yâ lâ lel lel li
Ah işvebâzım çâre-sâzım belî yâr-i men

Music:

Hâne-i evvel (1st Part): 32 (verse 1) +56 [14 (end of the verse/beginning of *terennüm*) + 42 (*terennüm*)] = 88 time units
Hâne-i sânî (2nd Part): 32 (verse 2) + 56 [14 (end of the verse/beginning of *terennüm*) + 42 (*terennüm*)] = 88 time units (same music as the first part)
Miyânhâne (3rd Part): 32 (verse 3) + 56 [14 (end of the verse/beginning of *terennüm*) + 42 (*terennüm*)] = 88 time units (different music but the last 16 units function as a *ritornello* and are the same as previous parts)
Hâne-i râbî (4th Part): 32 (verse 4) + 56 [14 (end of the verse/beginning of *terennüm*) + 42 (*terennüm*)] = 88 time units (same music as the first and second parts; last 16 units as a *ritornello* are the same in all parts)

---

20 İstanbul Belediye Konservatuvarı 1941, *Türk Mûsikîsi Klâsiklerinden: Hâfız M. Zekâî Dede Efendi Külliyâtı*, vol. 2, pp. 169-171.
21 Poetic metre *muzârî* (*mef û lü fâ î lâ tü me fâ î lü fâ i lün*).

Concluding Remarks

In nine of the ten compositions, verses have fourteen syllables. Only the first composition has verses of fifteen syllables. The number of syllables in the *terennüms* varies between thirty-five and forty-six.

We encounter three different poetic metres in the poems utilized in these compositions:

1. *Fâ i lâ tün fâ i lâ tün fâ i lâ tün fâ i lün* (*hazaj*)
Tan ta nan tan tan ta nan tan tan ta nan tan tan ta nan
o . o . . o . o . o . . o . o . o . . o . o . o . .
8 *sabab-i hafîfe*, 4 *watad* (only in the first piece)

2. *Mef û lü me fâ î lü me fâ î lü fe û lün* (*hazaj*)
Tan tan ta na nan tan ta na nan tan ta na nan tan
o . o . o . . . o . o . . . o . o . . . o .
5 *sabab-i hafîfe*, 3 *fâsıla-i sugrâ* (in pieces 2, 3, 4, 5, 7, 8 and 9)

3. *Mef û lü fâ i lâ tü me fâ î lü fâ i lün* (*muzârî*)
Tan tan ta nan ta nan ta na nan tan ta nan ta nan
o . o . o . . o . . o . o . o . o . . o . .
3 *sabab-i hafîfe*, 4 *watad*, 1 *fâsıla* (in pieces 6 and 10)

An interesting characteristic of these pieces is the repetition of certain syllables, especially in the beginning of the verses, in order to adapt them to a long melodic line. This process is also used in many other compositions, especially in long and slow-paced cycles.

In all ten pieces the time units attributed to verses are the same: 32 (except in the *miyanhâne* of *Uşşâk Murabbâ* by İsmâîl Dede Efendi, where it is 30 units).

Similarly, in all ten pieces the time units attributed to the *terennüms* are the same: 56. Only the length of the introduction to the *terennüm* and the *terennüm* itself present slight changes, as in 13+43, 13.5+42.5 or 14+42 units, while the total length of the *terennüm* is still 56 units. The sole exception may be observed in the *miyânhâne* of İsmâîl Dede Efendi's *Uşşâk Murabbâ*. However, in other parts of this composition the *terennüms* still occupy 56 units.

All have a repeated melodic phrase, which functions as a *ritornello* at the last sixteen time units. This peculiarity is also found in the *peşrevs* composed in *darb-ı fetih*.

This distribution shows clearly the connecting points of the rhythmic cycle that a composer must observe when using *darb-ı fetih* for a vocal composition, and may lead us to consider this cycle as a chain of smaller cycles assembled together. We already know that the last 16 units look like a well-known rhythm (i.e. *nîm hafîf*), and the preceding 16 units in Rauf Yekta's form resemble another well known rhythm: *muhammes*. The first 24 units of the *terennüms* look exactly like first 24 units of *muhajjal*. However, recognizing the rhythms of other sections is a difficult task and leads us to remember the composition of the original form of the cycle.

We may assert that the version of *darb-ı fetih* with eighty-eight time units was invented towards the end of the fifteenth century by an Ottoman-Turkish composer, probably in honour of the conquest of Constantinople by Mehmed II, or of the conquest of the Crimea by Bâyezîd II. It has no relation with ʿAbd al-Qâdir's invention (except the name) or with the victory of Sultan Giyath ad-Dîn Şayh ʿAli.

We do not know the reason for the choice of eighty-eight time units. It may be to commemorate the year of the composition: 880/1475 or 888/1483.

We may find the oldest form of *darb-ı fetih*, in *Zayn al-Alhan* and in *Risala al-Fathiyya* by Muhammad bin ʿAbd al-Hamid al-Lâdiqî, as mentioned above, and in *Mukaddimat al-Usûl* of Ali Şah bin Büke. According to these writers, it is composed of seventeen *fâsıla-i sugra* (ta na nan) and ten *sabab-i hafife* (tan).

Only the scheme found in the above-mentioned books of al-Lâdiqî is appropriate for this kind of division encountered in the vocal compositions that we have studied.

But neither the division of this cycle shown by Demetrius Cantemir and by all the writers who followed him nor the vocal compositions that we have examined fit the original form of the cycle shown in the books cited above. It is only in Ungay's book[22] that we may find an example (as the first form of *darb-ı fetih*) which corresponds to the original form.

If we carefully examine the original cycle and its later forms we may understand the reason for this discrepancy (Fig. 3).

The original form of this cycle presented in *Zayn al-Alhan* and in *Risâla al-Fathiyya* is used by Ottoman composers in *peşrev*s and in *murabba*s almost unchanged until the end of seventeenth century. Changes we may point out include the use of words like '*düm, tek, teke*', denoting percussions, instead of '*tan, ta nan, ta na nan*', and the division of some long time units into smaller ones, in order to obtain a more varied rhythmic flow. The division of the last thirty-two units into two halves, beating the first half as *muhammes* (in Rauf Yekta's version) and the second half as *nîm hafîf*, contribute to the easy memorization of the connecting points of this long and slow rhythm.

Percussion players, generally, in order to give a more varied form to the rhythm in use, and also to observe and memorize some cue points of the rhythm, have the habit of dividing longer time units into smaller ones. They call this process *velvele* ("noise, trouble, clamour"), and they have special *velvele* patterns for almost all rhythmic cycles (in particular, some patterns are like the

[22] Ungay, M. Hurşit 1981, *Türk Mûsıkîsinde Usûller ve Kudüm*, pp. 227-229.

'break' of jazz drummers at the end of phrases of eight measures). I would suggest that the variations observed in later forms of *darb-ı fetih* are due to this habit.

I argue that, near the beginning of eighteenth century, Demetrius Cantemir, who learned this rhythm from his teachers in Constantinople, made an error when transcribing it into his notebook. He omitted one time unit after the twenty-second unit and in order to complete the cycle he added the forgotten unit after the fifty-fourth unit. After Cantemir, theoreticians who copied his book continued to transmit the scheme of the cycle without correcting this error.

This error did not disturb composers of instrumental music when they composed their *peşrevs*. In general, they did not mind trying to fit their melodies exactly into eighty-eight time units, with the connecting points of the cycle, except the last measures, although in the works of many of them we may find strict observance of the rules. But, from the middle of seventeenth until the beginning of the twentieth centuries, the original form, with its connecting points and learned from masters following the tradition, was keenly observed by composers who used this cycle in their vocal compositions.

Figures

Fig. 1

Al-Marâgî's *darb al-feth* with 50 time units in Jami' al-Alhan

Ta nan ta nan ta na nan ta na nan ta nan ta nan ta na nan ta nan ta nan ta na nan ta na nan ta na nan ta na nan ta na nan
o . . o . . o . . . o . . . o . . o . . o . . . o . . o . . o . . . o . . . o . . . o . . . o . . .

Al-Marâgî's *darb al-feth* with 49 time units in Sherh-i Advar[1]

Ta nan ta nan ta na nan ta na nan ta nan ta nan ta na nan ta nan tan[2] ta na nan ta na nan ta na nan ta na nan ta na nan
o . . o . . o . . . o . . . o . . o . . o . . . o . . o . o . . . o . . . o . . . o . . . o . . .

al-Ladikî's *darb al-feth* with 88 time units in Zayn al-Alhan and in al-Fathiyya

Ta na nan ta na nan tan tan tan ta na nan tan ta na nan ta na nan ta na nan tan ta na nan tan ta na nan ta na nan
o . . . o . . . o. o. o . o . . . o. o . . . o . . . o . . . o . o . . . o . o . . . o . . .

ta na nan ta na nan ta na nan ta na nan ta na nan ta na nan tan tan tan tan ta na nan ta na nan
o . . . . o . . . . o . . . . o . o . o . . . o . . . .

[1] Also reproduced in al-Shirwanî's Majalla.
[2] Reduced unit

Fig. 2

Darb-ı Fetih Usûlünde
Hicâz Murabba'
Küçük İmam
(? -1675)
Verse A B D
Tâ be key sû - zi ga - mım la de derd li sî
Ni ce bir su lar gi bi dağ - lar lar ba sın - - - - -
Bâ - ri koy ver hâ li me ken dim be ken
Te ne nen te ne nen ten ten ten te ne
nem dağ dağ dağ - la - yım,
da çağ çağ çağ la yım.
dim ağ ağ ağ - la - yım
nen ten te ne nen te ne nen te ne nen
Terennüm
Yâr câ nım ya le lel le le lel lel le lel
ten te ne nen ten te ne nen te ne nen

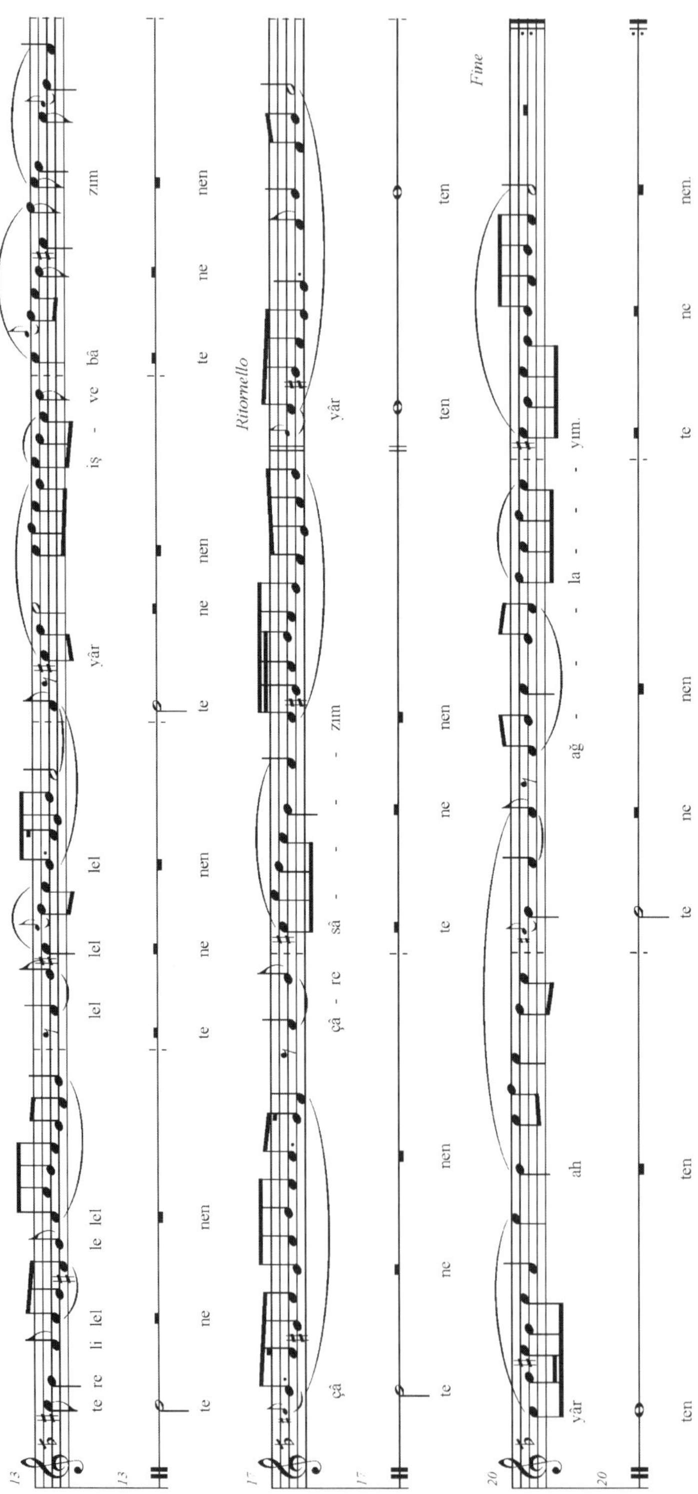
13
te re li lel le lel lel lel lel yâr iş - ve bâ zım
13
te ne nen te ne nen te ne nen te ne nen
17
Ritornello
çâ çâ - re sâ - - - - - zım yâr
17
te ne nen te ne nen ten ten
Fine
20
yâr ah ağ - - - - - la - - - - yım.
20
ten ten te ne nen te ne nen.

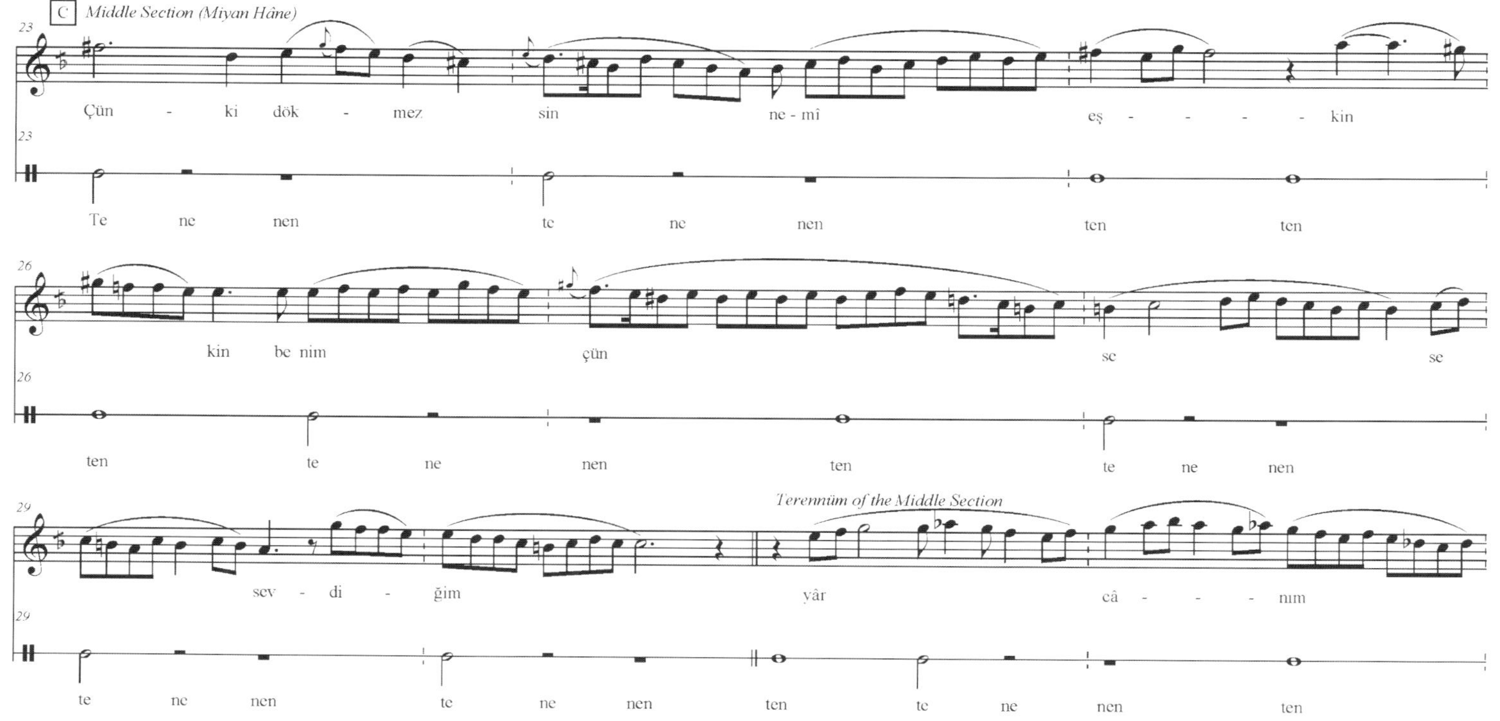
C Middle Section (Miyan Hâne)
23
Çün - ki dök - mez sin ne - mî eş - - - - - kin
23
Te ne nen te ne nen ten ten
26
kin be nim çün se se
26
ten te ne nen ten te ne nen
Terennüm of the Middle Section
29
sev - di - ğim yâr câ - - - nım
29
te ne nen te ne nen ten te ne nen ten

33
ya le lel le le lel le lel te re li yel le lel
33
te ne nen te ne nen te ne nen
36
lel lel li yâr iş - ve bâ - - - - zım
36
te ne nen te ne nen te ne nen
Ritornello
39
çâ - - - - - - çâ - re sâ zım yâr
39
te ne nen te ne nen ten ten
D.S. al Fine
42
yâr ah sev - - - di - - - ğim.
42
ten ten te ne nen te ne nen.

Fig. 3

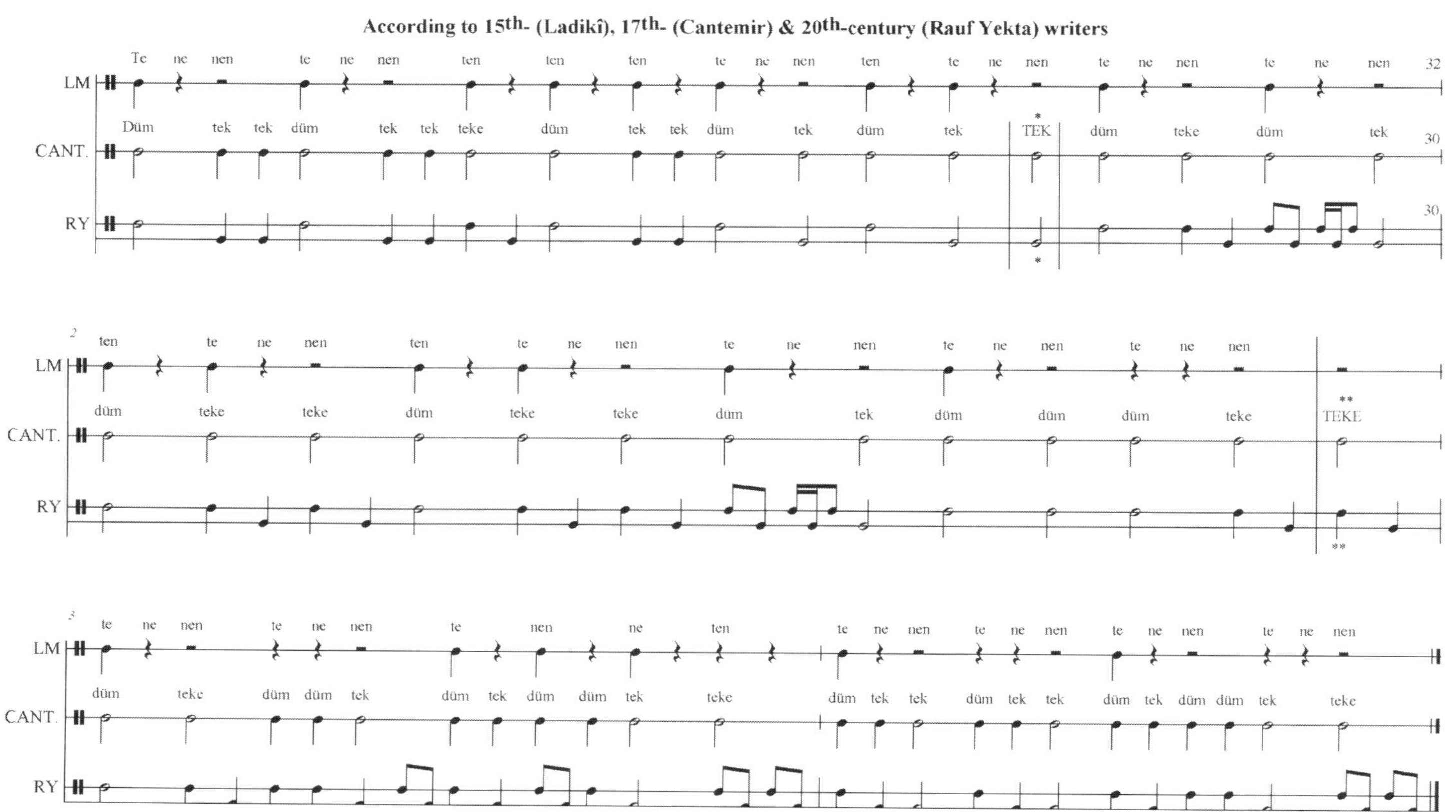

Darb-ı Fetih
According to 15th- (Ladikî), 17th- (Cantemir) & 20th-century (Rauf Yekta) writers
LM
CANT.
RY

Representations of *Uṣūl* in ʿAlī Ufuḳī's Manuscripts

Judith I. Haug

The purpose of this study[1] is to give an overview of how *uṣūl* features in the output of ʿAlī Ufuḳī. Two manuscripts are taken into consideration, one today kept in Paris under the shelfmark Turc 292[2], the other in the British Library, London, Sloane MS 3114[3]. The Psalter, Supplément Turc 472[4], is not relevant to the present study, as its melodies, which are of European origin and were transcribed without alteration, do not have an *uṣūl*-like rhythmic structure. The focus is on the Paris manuscript, the so-called compendium.

ʿAlī Ufuḳī, born around 1610 as Albert Bobowski in Lwów, which is in today's Ukraine but was then part of the Polish Commonwealth, was taken captive as a young man by raiding Crimean Tatars and sold to the Sultan's court. There, he was trained as a palace page (*içoğlan*) and later specialized as a court musician in the *meşkḫāne*. After a period of roughly twenty years, a length of time repeatedly stated by European sources, ʿAlī Ufuḳī became one of the imperial interpreters, eventually rising to the position of second dragoman of the divan. The exact date of ʿAlī Ufuḳī's death is unknown, as are many details of his life, yet sources imply that he died sometime before 1677.[5] Among his many and diverse works in the

1 This paper is part of the DFG project HA 5933/3: "Osmanische und europäische Musik im Kompendium des Alî Ufukî (um 1640): Erschließung, Analyse und (trans-) kultureller Kontext."

2 Bobowski, Albert (ʿAli Ufuḳi) [n.d.], [*Album de poésies turques [...] de la musique italienne et allemande, et la notation, quelquefois avec transcription, de chansons turques, par ʿAli Beg Bobowski, dit ʿAli Ufkî*], Paris, Bibliothèque Nationale de France, Ms Turc 292. The manuscript, which is currently being critically edited by the present author, has been made available online by the Bibliothèque Nationale de France: http://gallica.bnf.fr/ark:/12148/btv1b84150086 (accessed 2014-04-29). All subsequent citations from the source relate to this online document. See also Behar, Cem 2008, *Saklı Mecmua. Ali Ufkî'nin Bibliothèque Nationale de France'taki [Turc 292] Yazması*, İstanbul.

3 Bobowski, Albert (ʿAli Ufuḳi) [n.d.], *Hazā mecmūʿa-yı saz u söz*, London, British Library, Ms Sloane 3114. Facsimile: Elçin, Şükrü, (Ed.) 1976, *Alî Ufkî, Hayatı, eserleri ve Mecmûa-i Sâz ü Söz (tıpkıbasım)*, İstanbul. Edition: Cevher, M. Hakan (Ed.) 2003, *Hâzâ mecmûa-i sâz ü söz: çeviriyazım – inceleme*, İzmir.

4 http://gallica.bnf.fr/ark:/12148/btv1b8415002q (accessed 2014-04-28). See also Haug, Judith 2010, *Der Genfer Psalter in den Niederlanden, England, Deutschland und dem Osmanischen Reich (16.-18. Jahrhundert)*, Tutzing, p. 481ff. Behar, Cem 1990, *Ali Ufkî ve Mezmurlar*, İstanbul.

5 For the most recent summaries of ʿAli Ufuḳi's biography see Behar, Cem 2005, *Musıkiden Müziğe – Osmanlı/Türk Müziği: Gelenek ve Modernlik*, İstanbul, pp. 17-56, and Haug 2010, pp. 481-492.

fields of theology and linguistics, the translation of the Bible into Ottoman[6], the description of Islam for European readers, *De Turcarum Liturgia*[7], and his language manual *Grammatica Turcicolatina*[8] should be mentioned. All three musical manuscripts known today were taken to European libraries either shortly after ʿAlī Ufuḳī's death or even during his lifetime, so that a deeper influence on Ottoman music practice and repertoire can be excluded. Contemporaneous or later sources inspired by his notational system have also not been discovered as of yet.

As ʿAlī Ufuḳī explains in his account of Topkapı Sarayı and palace life, *Serai Enderum*, his first notations came into being relatively soon after he started his training as a court musician.[9] It seems as though some layers of the Paris manuscript, which is in fact part of an originally much larger loose-leaf collection rather carelessly bound at a later time, may be a product of those early endeavors and experiments. The two relevant sources are widely different in character, the Paris manuscript a spontaneous, personal source obviously written or assembled over a longer period of time, the London source a luxurious manuscript systematically composed for an unknown posterity.

While information about the use and interpretation of *uṣūl* in the London manuscript can only be gleaned from the analytical evaluation of internal evidence, there are a number of actual statements on the topic in the Paris source. These are not many, and they do not have much depth in terms of the speculative music theory found, for example, in Demetrius Cantemir's *Edvār* two generations later. ʿAlī Ufuḳī's comments on *uṣūl* have the character of concise lists or notes for the practitioner's and/or teacher's use.[10] But in this absence of speculative theory – which holds equally true for the representation of *maḳām* in ʿAlī Ufuḳī's manuscripts – lies the valuable possibility of an insight into the mind and working life of a practicing musician; moreover, of a bicultural musician who acquired and totally absorbed a second musical culture at an adult age[11].

Although ʿAlī Ufuḳī was not entirely unfamiliar with the speculative theory of Arabic musical tradition (see below), it was not his priority or main interest. This is in accord with Walter Feldman's observation of an "overall dearth of musical writ-

---

6 Leiden, University Library Cod.Or. 390a-e. Neudecker, Hannah 1994, *The Turkish Bible Translation by Yaḥya bin ʾIsḥaḳ, also called Ḥaki (1659)*, Leiden, p. 365ff.

7 Hyde, Thomas (Ed.) 1690, *Tractatus Alberti Bobovii Turcarum Imp. Mohammedis IVti olim Interpretis primarii, de Turcarum liturgia [...]*, Oxford.

8 Bobowski, Albert (ʿAlī Ufuḳī) 1666, *Grammatica Turcicolatna [sic] Alberti Bobovii Leopolitani Linguæ Turcicæ Professoris [...]*, Oxford, Bodleian Library, MS Hyde 47.

9 Bobowski, Albert (ʿAlī Ufuḳī) 1667, *Serai Enderum [...]*, Vienna (transl. by Nicolaus Brenner), p. 74ff.

10 Behar 2008, pp. 134-137.

11 The term "bi-musical", coined by Mantle Hood, describes the personality of ʿAlī Ufuḳī very appropriately. Hood, Mantle 1960, "The Challenge of »Bi-Musicality«", in: *Ethnomusicology 4*, 55-59.

ing" in the seventeenth century.[12] Although it cannot be ruled out that somewhere a treatise written or copied by him exists, it does not seem very probable. The Paris manuscript represents ʿAlī Ufuḳī's day-to-day life as a music page in training and later as a high-ranking court musician, and is therefore an individual and practice-oriented document. The mind and personality of ʿAlī Ufuḳī are to a certain extent open to the reader's interpretation. Theoretical notions, however, with which he must have been familiar by way of his training in the palace *meşkḫāne*, are implicitly present in the music recorded in writing and can be extracted by careful, detailed analysis as well as by comparison between different versions of the same composition in Alī Ufuḳī's two manuscripts and other available sources, such as the notation collections of Demetrius Cantemir[13] and Kevserī[14].

When Alī Ufuḳi decided to preserve in writing the repertoire he was being taught orally during his apprenticeship as a court musician, he was faced with a number of considerable difficulties arising from the fundamental differences between European and Ottoman musics, which could be metaphorically described as two distinct languages with distinct systems of grammar and syntactical functionality. Among those differences, *uṣūl*, as opposed to European concepts of measure, proportion, tempo and accentuation, is of course a fundamental issue, as it plays a pivotal role in the conception and elaboration of a composition from the very beginning of the creative process. This creative process, in Ottoman music as in all predominantly oral music cultures, extends over a period of centuries and never reaches the fixed state of a musical 'work' that is so highly valued in European music (it would be worthwhile to pursue the question of whether ʿAlī Ufuḳī was aware of this basic difference). So, when dealing with the isolated notations of the seventeenth and eighteenth centuries (prior to the more widespread use of *Hamparsum notası* and Western notation beginning in the mid-nineteenth century), it is important to bear in mind that they are snapshots taken somewhere in the course of a long stream of transmission, that they represent a frozen moment in time which is highly individual and determined by the specific theoretical and practical knowledge of the author, not forgetting such factors as the instrument he played, the school he received his training from or his personal taste and convictions.[15]

The early seventeenth century, when ʿAlī Ufuḳī acquired the foundations on which he would eventually build his system, was a period of transition in Euro-

12 Feldman, Walter 1996, *Music of the Ottoman court: Makam, composition and the early Ottoman instrumental repertoire*, Berlin (= Intercultural Music Studies 10), p. 9.

13 Tura, Yalçın (Ed.) 2001/2001b, *Kantemiroğlu: Kitābu ʿİlmi'l-Mūsīḳī ʿalā vechi'l-Ḥurufāt. Mûsikîyi Harflere Tesbît ve İcrâ İlminin Kitabı*, 2 vols., İstanbul. Wright, Owen ed. 1992b-2000, *Demetrius Cantemir: The Collection of Notations*, 2 vols., London (= SOAS Musicology Series, 1).

14 Ekinci, Mehmet Uğur 2012, "The Kevserî Mecmûası Unveiled: Exploring an Eighteenth-Century Collection of Ottoman Music", *Journal of the Royal Asiatic Society* 22, 199-225. An edition of the manuscript by Mehmet Uğur Ekinci is forthcoming.

15 The exclusive use of masculine pronouns here is due to the fact that notations by women composers or musicians have not been discovered up to now.

pean music theory, not to speak of the revolutions in compositional style. Older concepts of mensural rhythm were gradually abandoned in favor of the pulse-group measure with its patterns of accentuation that informs European notions of rhythmical organization to the present day. Further, ternary proportions ceased to exist, with the consequence that binary organization became the standard for all durational values.[16] While it is generally difficult to determine to what extent mensural concepts were still taught and considered relevant in the period and locale in which ʿAlī Ufuḳī acquired his knowledge, it may reasonably be assumed that he was still aware of them. A list of fifteenth- and sixteenth-century European theoretical works in the London manuscript gives an impression of what, in some form, he was familiar with: Franchino Gafori, Giovanni Spataro, Vincenzo Galilei and others.[17] However, at this stage of analysis it remains uncertain how he came into contact with this corpus of theory and how it may have influenced his development and use of rhythm in his notation.

Prior to the analysis of selected phenomena, some preliminary remarks are necessary. The terminology I use for note values follows seventeenth-century usage, for example "minim" instead of "half note" and "semiminim" instead of "crotchet" or "quarter note", in order not to imply the binary proportions taken for granted today. In the following examples as well as in my forthcoming edition of the manuscript, fractions as time signatures are avoided for the same reason, and only the number of basic time units in the cycle is stated at the beginning of the staff. Further, the note values of the original are not reduced, nor are the melodies transposed; that is, *rāst*, being the central pitch in ʿAlī Ufuḳī's perception of the tone system, is equivalent to c or do (in contrast to modern Turkish usage, in which *rāst* is equivalent to g or sol). In the original notations, this is represented by a C clef on the bottom line of the staff; in the following transcriptions, a standard treble or G clef is used.

Explanations of Uṣūl: *Theory, Syllables and Notations*

The longest text dealing with the basic theory of *uṣūl* with regards to systematization, terminology and execution, can be found on f.51r/205r and f.51v/205v.[18] It seems to have been taken out of a longer work, as it begins with the words "*Bab*

16 London, Justin 2001, art. "Rhythm", in: *The New Grove Dictionary of Music and Musicians*, 2nd. ed., vol. 21, New York, 277-309, p. 290ff. ("The metric revolution, *c*1600"). Houle, George 1987, *Meter in Music, 1600-1800. Performance, Perception, and Notation*, Bloomington, 1-34. Schmid, Manfred Hermann 2012, *Notationskunde. Schrift und Komposition 900-1900*, Kassel-Basel, 149-166, p. 249ff.

17 GB-Lbl Sloane MS 3114, f.9r. Elçin 1976, p. 25. The page is not part of Hakan Cevher's edition.

18 http://gallica.bnf.fr/ark:/12148/btv1b84150086/f113.item and http://gallica.bnf.fr/ark:/12148/btv1b84150086/f114.item. Behar 2008, pp. 74ff, 91ff, 95-101.

gełdik bir bab dahij" ("Chapter. Now we have come one chapter further"). Although these section headings, which are seven in total, point to a written rather than an oral source, for example a teaching manual[19], it is striking that the text is recorded in ᶜAlī Ufuḳī's system of transliteration instead of Arabic characters (or, if written from memory, instead of Italian, which he generally used for everything he formulated in his own terms).

The theory presented here seems relatively old or retrospective. Many of the rhythmic entities mentioned in the text do not appear in the collection, among them "*Czar zarb Neǵiari*", "*Hezeǵ*", "*Serendas*", "*Remlitawił*" or "*Sezarb*"[20]. A line at the bottom of f.51r/205r points to the possible source: "*Nasiredin farabi kauli deie*" ("according to the opinion of Abū Naṣr al-Fārābī", alluding to his *Kitāb al-Mūsīqī al-kabīr*, *Kitāb al-īqāᶜāt* and *Kitāb fī Iḥṣāᶜ al-īqā*[21] - or at least to a superficial understanding of their contents). The discourse on *zamān* and *ẓarb* starting at line 15 of the verso, for example, is reminiscent of al-Farabi: "*Gełdig imdi bir bab dahij Zarb nedur Vssuł nedur Vssułun ǵemi Vssuł zeman bir kaide durkim an[un] kismi ioktur zarb oldurki zemanin arasinda waki oła (Contenuto) zeman oldurki iki zarb ortasinda waki ołur Emma Vssuł ol nesne deilder ki anij bir kimse ghiore weia vgrene vssuł bir nesne dur ki Hakta ała bir ßeie Hussun werir (ghiozellik) we ia hub hawas (ghiozel) we ia latiff hulk werir (huiu Vitio costume) Meǵmui hidaietdur* [...]."[22] This kind of discourse was customary in Ottoman-Turkish music treatises of the fifteenth and sixteenth century[23], which for instance holds true in the case of Kırşehrī[24] and Seydī, the latter even stating the same *uṣūller* in the same order as ᶜAlī Ufuḳī - thus it is likely that he was trained with and/or used an Ottoman-Turkish treatise[25].

---

19 Personal communication from Eckhard Neubauer. The Italian glosses also point in this direction.

20 The London collection contains one piece in *Se ẓarb* (*Peşrev-i se ẓarb toz-ḳoparan*, f.120r/no.255; Elçin 1976, p. 232; Cevher 2003, p. 730f).

21 Neubauer, Eckhard 1968/69, "Die Theorie vom īqāᶜ: I. Übersetzung des Kitāb al-īqāᶜāt von Abū Naṣr al-Fārābī", *Oriens 21/22*, 196-232. Neubauer, Eckhard 1994, "Die Theorie vom īqāᶜ: II. Übersetzung des "Kitāb Iḥṣā' al-īqāᶜāt" von Abū Naṣr al-Fārābī", *Oriens 34*, 103-173.

22 "Now we have come one chapter further. What is «*ẓarb*»? What is «*uṣūl*»? The plural of «*uṣūl*» is «*uṣūl*». Time [«*zamān*»] is a regulation [unit of measurement] which does not have a division. Beat [«*ẓarb*»] is that which takes place [Italian gloss: is contained] in time. Time is that which takes place between two beats. But *uṣūl* is not such a thing that one could observe and learn. *Uṣūl* is such a thing like when God the Almighty ["*Ḥaḳ teᶜālā*"] gives grace [Ottoman gloss: beauty] to something, or a pleasant voice ["*avāz*"] [Ottoman gloss: beautiful], or elegant nature, [Ottoman/Italian gloss: disposition vice custom, possibly in the sense of "good and bad traits" - the passage is barely legible]. All this is a gift [from God] [...]" (author's translation). Cf. Behar 2008, p. 75ff, Neubauer 1968/69, p. 200ff.

23 Behar 2008, p. 77.

24 Doğrusöz, Nilgün 2012, *Yusuf Kırşehri'nin Müzik Teorisi*, Kırşehir, p. 88, 218.

25 Popescu-Judetz, Eugenia, and Neubauer, Eckhard (Ed.) 2004, *Seydī's Book on Music. A 15th Century Turkish Discourse*, Frankfurt/Main, p. 124f. My thanks to Eckhard Neubauer for this reference.

From the top of the verso on, short rhythmical notations consisting of note heads on single lines are added to the text, accompanying the *ten ten tenen* syllables next to which free space had been left for this purpose. The entity entitled "3 *daire Remli Tawildur*", for example, is described as "*tene ten ten tenen tenen ten*", which generally corresponds to the following notation (the 3 is original):

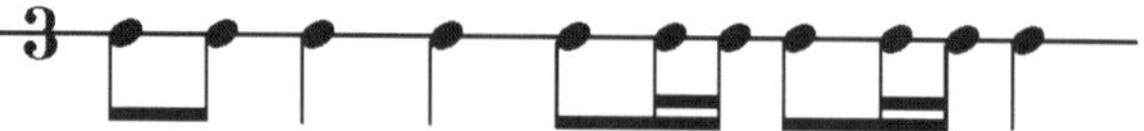

Fig. 1: *Uṣūl* notation for "*Remli Tawil*", f.51v/205v.

Furthermore, there is also an attempt at clarifying the different strokes on the frame drum for *uṣūller* "*Duwek*", "*Dewri Rewan*" and "*Semaj*". The note heads are arranged on a single line with the stems pointing downward symbolizing the right hand, the stems pointing upward the left hand. Additional letters signify the way of beating the drum, "M" for the entire hand ("*man intiera*"), "A" for the ring finger ("*dito Auriculare*", erroneous for "*anulare*") and "J" for the index finger ("*indice*").

It is interesting to note that the older, "Arabic" *ten ten tenen* syllables appear only in this text, whereas the "Ottoman-Turkish" *düm tek teke* system is employed in all other descriptions of *uṣūl* in the Paris manuscript. The two systems have the general disadvantage in common that the actual durations can only be guessed. For this reason, ᶜAlī Ufuḳī regularly added European note values for clarification: ff.149r/303r-149v/303v contain another list of descriptions with syllables, supplemented with notation, but without theoretical explanations.[26] The list was written by two or three different hands, neither of which is ᶜAlī Ufuḳī's. The main part is diligently written, largely vocalized, and organized under rubrics in red ink reminiscent of the use of red for headings and other structural purposes in the London manuscript. The form of presentation is: "*Uṣūleş Ṣōfyāne dum dum tek Uṣūleş Devr-i revān dum dum tek dum tek tek*" etc.; the rhythmic cycles named are *Ṣōfyāne*, *Devr-i revān*, *Düyek*, *Evfer*, *Devr-i kebīr*, *Çenber*, *Fāḫte*, *Berevşān*, *Muḫammes*, *Ḥafif* [sic], *Nīm devir*, *Ṣaḳīl*, *Nīm Ṣaḳīl*, *Ferᶜ*, *Evsaṭa* [sic], *Semāᶜī*, *Turkī ẓarb*, *Ḥāvī* and *Ẓarb-ı fetḥ*. More than half of the listed *uṣūller* are supplied with folio numbers on which a corresponding piece is located. *Çenber* and *Berevşān*, for example, both refer to "fol: 290" (ff.136r/290r-135v/289v), containing the *Peschrewi Zengir* (see below). Unfortunately, not all the stated folios are extant, as the manuscript in its current form is incomplete, substantial amounts of material having been lost. The text closes with an incomplete line of syllables demonstrating *uṣūl Ẓarb-ı fetḥ*, to which European note values have been added above. The section ends with a short, five-line staff drawn by hand, containing a notation for

26 http://gallica.bnf.fr/ark:/12148/btv1b84150086/f307.item and http://gallica.bnf.fr/ark:/12148/btv1b84150086/f308.item. Behar 2008, p. 122ff.

uṣūl Evfer ("*Vffer*"). In a second stage the staff was enlarged by extending the first line to the right to accommodate a notation of *Türkī ẓarb* ("*Turki zarb*"), the first two note heads being still in the five-line area.

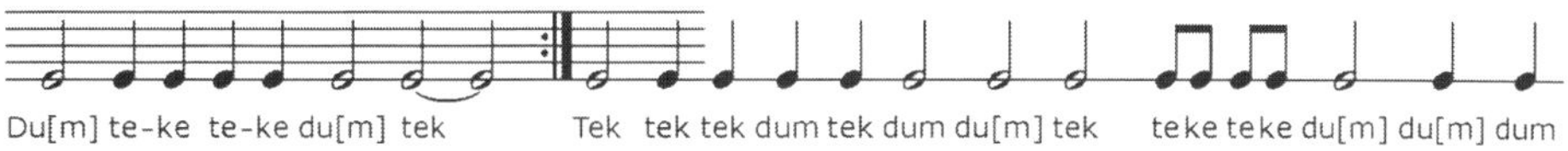

Fig. 2: *Uṣūl* notations on f.149v/303v, *Evfer* and *Turkī ẓarb*

Evfer is today familiar as a nine-beat cycle, not as a six-beat *uṣūl*.[27] But the descriptions on f.95v/249v[28] and f.191v/336v[29] also show a six-beat *uṣūl* with the same distribution of values as in Fig. 2 (except for the last note, which is in both cases one long value and not two tied shorter values), and f.95v/249v with the semiminim instead of the minim as the basic time unit. The notation has the fraction 3/2 as a designation of *uṣūl*. In the repertoire itself, *Evfer* appears once with six beats[30] and twice with the nine-beat structure[31] in use today. In the London manuscript, all eight compositions in *Evfer*, all of which are vocal, are based on a nine-beat *uṣūl*. The nine-beat *Evfer* pieces in Paris have a parallel version in London, whereas the six-beat *Murabbaʿ* does not. As usual when dealing with ʿAlī Ufuḳī's notations, this evidence can be interpreted only with the utmost caution: it may be that the six-beat structure represented an older tradition which was in the process of being replaced by a nine-beat cycle around the middle of the seventeenth century. In this context, a six-beat *Evfer* brings to mind the six-beat *Ufar* of Bukharan *Shashmaqam*.[32]

Short descriptions in European note values combined with syllables and sometimes also symbols used to designate *uṣūl* can be found attached to the notation of certain pieces in order to clarify their rhythmic structure. Unfortunately, such descriptions are not very frequent, and not all *uṣūller* occurring in the manuscript are explained in this way. Two instances can serve as examples: f.131r/285r[33] contains a demonstration of "*Fahti zarb*" following the notation of "*Der maḳām-ı Ḥüseynī / Peşrev-i külliyāt nażīresi Husta disse che si chiama Schehmurat*". The notation of the *peşrev* also includes *uṣūl* boundary lines, whereas both the description and the *peşrev* start with an inverted *tempus imperfectum diminutum* symbol as an *uṣūl* designation.

27 Özkan, İsmail Hakkı 1990, *Türk Mûsikîsi Nazariyatı ve Usûlleri. Kudüm Velveleleri*, İstanbul, p. 602. Cantemir (Tura 2001, p. 166) also gives a nine-beat structure for *Evfer*.

28 http://gallica.bnf.fr/ark:/12148/btv1b84150086/f200.item.

29 http://gallica.bnf.fr/ark:/12148/btv1b84150086/f372.item.

30 f.191v/336v, *Murabbaʿ* "*Eij dilberi ßirin dehen gionlum seni seumek ister*".

31 f.293r, *Murabbaʿ* "*Rāst pençgāh uṣūleş evfer | Yeter cevr ėdersin ben nātüvāne vāy*".

32 See Angelika Jung's contribution to the present volume.

33 http://gallica.bnf.fr/ark:/12148/btv1b84150086/f271.item. Behar 2008, p. 119f. For *uṣūl Fāḫte* see also the chapter "Ottoman *Usul* System and Its Precursors" by Owen Wright in the present volume.

Fig. 3: *Uṣūl* notation on f.131r/285r, *Fāḫte*

The description of *uṣūl* Muḫammes on f.134r/288r[34] follows the notation of the "*Peşrev-i Ramażānī uṣūl-i Muḫammes*". This is a similar case, but with some additional information: "*Ogni Cadenza e fatta a la fin di Secondo vssuł Muhammès. che saria al Decimo Vssuł de la nostra Tripla*"[35]. The calculation does not tally; furthermore, the separation lines come after every fourth beat in the notation itself, whereas in the description the beats are grouped differently (3+3+3+3+4 instead of 4+4+4+4). The description has no *uṣūl* designation, while the *peşrev* is marked "3/2".

Fig. 4: *Uṣūl* notation on f.134r/288r, *Muḫammes*

Scattered throughout the manuscript, there are five more such descriptions of *uṣūl*: *Ferᶜ* (f.103r/257r, "*ferie*"), *Ṣōfyāne* and *Evfer* ("*Sofiane*" and "*Vffer*", f.95v/249v), *Çenber* ("*czember*", f.136r/290r), again *Evfer* ("*Vffer*", f.191v/336v), and *Berevşān* ("*perewßan*", f.136v/290v).

A special and not easily interpreted case is the "*Justo Discorso de li Vssułij*" ("Proper Discourse on the *uṣūller*") on f.294r/384r[36], where ᶜAlī Ufuḳī attempts to explain certain rhythmic cycles by way of European mensural theory and a system based on the syllables "*trrr*" and "*tutiti*", faintly reminiscent of a wind-instrument tonguing pattern[37]. The page is noticeably old, worn and hardly legible due to various kinds of damage. Moreover, the descriptions on this page are somewhat problematic. For example, the "Proportion Media", which he identifies with *Düyek* ("*Duwek*"), is marked with the symbol for *tempus perfectum diminutum*, which, in the notated repertoire, is predominantly not the case: "*Proportion Media [tempus perfectum diminutum symbol] consta di quarto trrr i quali trrr deuentano qui [semiminim] Crome Et in questo si sona tutti li peschrew*".[38] This is not in agreement with the notated repertoire, in which *peşrevler* in *uṣūl Düyek* are notated with the minim as well as the semiminim as basic time units. The other rhythmic cycles mentioned on f.384r are

34 http://gallica.bnf.fr/ark:/12148/btv1b84150086/f277.item.

35 "Every cadenza is played at the end of every second *uṣūl Muhammes*, which would be in the tenth *uṣūl* of our Tripla." See also Behar 2008, p. 125.

36 http://gallica.bnf.fr/ark:/12148/btv1b84150086/f577.item. Behar 2008, p. 126ff.

37 Houle 1987, p. 97ff.

38 "*Proportio Media* consists of four *trrr*, which *trrr* here become crome [*fusae*, i.e. quavers], and in this [proportion] all the *peşrevler* are played." (author's translation).

"*Genghi harbi*", which does not appear again in the entire manuscript except for a description on f.51v/205v[39], and "*Sofiane*", both also connected to the *tempus perfectum diminutum*. As no comparable descriptions of rhythm have been found as of yet, this page remains one of ʿAlī Ufuḳī's more enigmatic creations.

Uṣūl *Designations: Verbal Statements and Symbols*

The spectrum of *uṣūl* designations is huge, and in some cases there can also be a wide spectrum of possible interpretations of each designation. There are still a number of pieces whose rhythmic structure remains unclear, as a result of unexplained (and possibly inexplicable) special signs. A substantial number of pieces – amongst which there are more vocal than instrumental compositions – have no *uṣūl* designation whatsoever. The following table gives an overview of the *uṣūller* mentioned by name in the Paris manuscript[40]:

Uṣūl	instrumental	vocal	no notation
Berevşān	4		
Çenber	3	1	1
Devr-i kebīr	5	3	1
Devr-i revān	4	4	3
"Dewri"	1		
Düyek	26	4	
Düyek-i revān			1
Evfer		3	4
Evsaṭ + Semāʿī		1	
Fāḫte	6		
Fāḫte + Devr-i kebīr		1	
Ferʿ (muḫammes)	1		1
Ḥafīf	1		1
Ḥāvī	1		
Muḫammes	2	1	
Ṣaḳīl	6		
Semāʿī	14	9	14
Ṣōfyāne	1	2	7
Türki ẓarb			

→

[39] http://gallica.bnf.fr/ark:/12148/btv1b84150086/f114.item. The London collection contains in its *Nevā* section the short instrumental "*Cengī ḥarbī*" (f.53r/no.75).

[40] The *uṣul* names are orthographically standardized, in case they appear in transliteration only.

Uṣūl	instrumental	vocal	no notation
Ẓarb-ı fetḥ	13		
"zarbi Safi"	1		
Ẓarbeyn	2		
Zencīr	1		

Table 1: *uṣūl* titling in the Paris manuscript

Those verbal statements regularly coincide with other types of designations, for example mensural-derived signs, fractions, self-invented symbols and boundary lines. What immediately leaps to the eye is the fact that vocal pieces, of which there are 254 in the Paris manuscript as opposed to 188 instrumental pieces according to current estimations, bear strikingly fewer *uṣūl* designations.

One valuable example is the "*Vssuller Peschrewi Zengir Mekam Rast*" (ff.136r/290r-135v/289v)[41], from which conclusions about other pieces can directly be drawn. The basic time value is the minim, and in addition to statements of the *uṣūl* names above their first occurrence and boundary lines after each partial *uṣūl*, the composition is marked with the symbol for *tempus imperfectum diminutum.* A sequence of five *uṣūller* corresponds with half an iteration of the 120-beat *Zencīr.* This is in agreement with Cantemir: "*Uṣūl-i Zencīr beş uṣūlden ḥāṣıl olur; yāʿnī: Düyek'den, Fāḫte'den, Çenber'den, Devr-i kebīr'den ve Berevşān'dan.*"[42] All the *uṣūller* mentioned in the *Peşrev* are used consistently throughout the manuscript and mostly coincide with Cantemir's *Edvār*, which is used as a point of reference here:[43] *Düyek* is an eight-beat *uṣūl* which is notated either based on the semiminim (in 10 cases) or the minim (in 13 cases). It appears as a verbal statement alone and in combination with mensural-derived symbols, *uṣūl* boundary lines and once with one of the self-invented signs that will become so characteristic of the London manuscript. The ten-beat cycle *Faḫte* (5 instances), always based on the minim, is likewise encountered in combination with lines and mensural symbols. These instances are corroborated by the above-mentioned *uṣūl* description on f.131r/285r. ʿAlī Ufuḳī's description of *Çenber* as a twelve-beat cycle is not supported by Cantemir, who describes it as having twenty-four beats.[44] Nonetheless, from his description of *uṣūl Zencīr* cited above, it is clear that *Çenber* must indeed have twelve beats. In the Paris

41 http://gallica.bnf.fr/ark:/12148/btv1b84150086/f281.item and http://gallica.bnf.fr/ark:/12148/btv1b84150086/f280.item. The piece also appears in the London manuscript on f.117v/no.249 (Elçin 1976, pp. 227-228, Cevher 2003, pp. 716-718).

42 "The *uṣūl Zencīr* results from five *uṣūller*, namely *Düyek*, *Fāḫte*, *Çenber*, *Devr-i Kebīr* and *Berevşān*." (Tura 2001, p.168f.).

43 It should be kept in mind that citing Cantemir as the only reference point for the study of 'Alī Ufuḳī's implicit theory is not without problems: Besides the fact that there are mistakes and contradictions in the *Edvār*, 'Alī Ufuḳī and Cantemir are two generations apart and a common background of tradition cannot be presupposed.

44 Tura 2001, p. 210.

manuscript, it occurs three times, once based on the semiminim and twice on the minim. In one of these cases, a mensural symbol – the sign for *tempus perfectum diminutum* – is added. *Devr-i kebīr* appears as a fourteen-beat *uṣūl*, six times based on the minim, of which one is also accompanied by an *uṣūl* designation based on a combination of the *tempus perfectum diminutum* symbol, a European numeral 3 and an Arabic numeral 2. One further instrumental piece is based on the semiminim and in addition bears an *uṣūl* designation that is made up of the *tempus imperfectum diminutum* symbol and a triangle. Two *peşrevler* are erroneously headed "*Düyek*", but their respective concordances in the London manuscript show that both are in fact *Devr-i kebīr*.[45] Sixteen-beat *Berevşān* is unproblematic, occurring five times based on the minim, one of which also has a designation combined from an unidentified symbol, a European 3 and a circle (which could actually be the *tempus perfectum* symbol).

As regards the matter of the basic time unit – which can be either the minim or the semiminim, as is clear from the cited examples, or in very rare cases the semibreve – there is no straightforward explanation at hand. Most importantly, it seems that the basic value does not have any influence on the actual speed of performance. For example, it would not make sense to play *Ẓarb-ı fetḥ* at double speed if it is written in smaller values.[46] Of the *uṣūller* named in the manuscript, *Çenber*, *Devr-i kebīr*, *Düyek* and *Ẓarb-ı fetḥ* are encountered in both basic values[47]; the same holds true with respect to the basic values that the various mensural and self-invented symbols can appear with. It seems that this also pertains to the vocal repertoire, although the percentage of pieces carrying a verbal or verbal-combined *uṣūl* designations is smaller by far.

The second large group is characterized by the use of European mensural symbols, fractions or various compounds based on them. The interpretation of these signs is especially difficult, as they seem to denote a broad range of different rhythmical entities. Neither do they seem to be related to the basic time unit – one might expect, for example, a *tempus diminutum* sign to correlate to a larger basic value, but that is clearly not the case. Furthermore, pieces that bear the *tempus imperfectum diminutum* sign, today known as *alla breve*, can be interpreted as three-, four-, and seven-beat structures, each with both basic unit possibilities.

---

45 Paris f.167v/311v-168r/312r (http://gallica.bnf.fr/ark:/12148/btv1b84150086/f325.item and http://gallica.bnf.fr/ark:/12148/btv1b84150086/f324.item), London f.64v/no.107 (Elçin 1976, pp. 128-129, Cevher 2003, pp. 464-466), Paris f.287r/372 (http://gallica.bnf.fr/ark:/12148/btv1b84150086/f563.item), London f.18v-19r/no.14 (Elçin 1976, pp. 34-35, Cevher 2003, pp. 190-192).

46 Personal communication from Mehmet Uğur Ekinci.

47 In the London manuscript (vocal and instrumental), *Ẓarb-ı fetḥ* appears all 13 times with the semiminim as the basic time unit; of the four *Çenber* occurrences, two are based on the semiminim and two on the minim; all 27 appearances of *Devr-i kebīr* are based on the minim; *Düyek* is divided almost evenly between those based on the minim (32 instances) and those based on the semiminim (31 instances), with an additional two occurrences, both vocal, based on the semibreve.

Combined with the verbal statement *Düyek* ("*Duwek*"), the *tempus imperfectum diminutum* can stand for eight minims to the cycle[48], or, combined with "*Ṣaḳīl*", for forty-eight semiminims[49]. In addition, the Zencir *peşrev* cited above has this symbol. The fraction 3/2, which appears frequently, especially in the vocal repertoire, poses a comparable difficulty of interpretation, as in many cases it is not immediately clear whether a three- or a six-beat structure is intended.

The self-invented symbols that will feature so prominently in the London manuscript[50] are encountered in Paris only very rarely. One of those few instances, at f.286r/371r, features a tiny illustration of the signs for *Düyek* (a circle with the Arabic number 2 inside) and *Semāʿī* ("*Semah*", a triangle pointing to the right; two triangles are found here, one empty and one with an Arabic number 4 inside, probably an error for the 3 that would be expected).[51] The right-facing triangle is regularly used in the London manuscript either alone or inside a circle, but always without a numeral. The symbols between the first two staves of a piece entitled "*Semaij rast*" appear to have been added at a later time, as the ink and pen visibly differ from those used for the musical notation. The symbol for *Düyek* is encountered only once in the manuscript, namely on f.231v[52] in the "*Peşrev-i eğlence ʿacem düyek*". The triangle for *Semāʿī* appears in the Paris manuscript in only one other instance: on f.295v/149r[53] it is combined with the *tempus imperfectum diminutum* symbol and the verbal statement "*Dewri Kebir*". This compound sign may be interpreted as "4+3 beats to the cycle", which would comply with the required seven beats. On the other hand, the *tempus imperfectum diminutum* symbol does not always and unambiguously signify four beats, as for example in the *Varṣāġı* "*Yā İlāhī mürvet eyle sen inṣāfa getür yārī*" (f.119v/273v[54]) which seems to have a seven-beat structure, or in the untitled *peşrev* on ff.47v/201v-48r/202r[55], which can be identified as *uṣūl Ẓarb-ı fetḥ* by comparison with its concordance in the London manuscript, the "*Peşrev-i Südci-zāde der maḳām-ı mezbūr uṣūleş ẓarb-ı fetḥ*"[56] (f.88v/no.165). The last occurrence of a self-invented symbol is on f.103r/257r[57], where a notation of *uṣūl* Ferʿ in syllables and Western note values is preceded by a circle with an Arabic 4 inside.

48 f.2r: http://gallica.bnf.fr/ark:/12148/btv1b84150086/f11.item.

49 f.170r/314r: http://gallica.bnf.fr/ark:/12148/btv1b84150086/f329.item.

50 An overview can be found in Cevher 2003, pp. 40-43.

51 http://gallica.bnf.fr/ark:/12148/btv1b84150086/f561.item. Behar 2008, p. 73.

52 http://gallica.bnf.fr/ark:/12148/btv1b84150086/f452.item.

53 http://gallica.bnf.fr/ark:/12148/btv1b84150086/f580.item.

54 http://gallica.bnf.fr/ark:/12148/btv1b84150086/f248.item.

55 http://gallica.bnf.fr/ark:/12148/btv1b84150086/f106.item and http://gallica.bnf.fr/ark:/12148/btv1b84150086/f107.item.

56 Elçin 1976, p. 177, Cevher 2003, pp. 588-590.

57 http://gallica.bnf.fr/ark:/12148/btv1b84150086/f215.item.

Pieces Without Information

A large number of pieces, both instrumental and vocal, lack any kind of *uṣūl* designation; in total there are 59 such instrumental pieces and 111 vocal pieces. As far as I can understand at my current stage of research, the rhythmic units which are not designated with an *uṣūl* name are broken up into the smallest discernible units, mostly 3 and 4, but also 5 and 7. The bulk of the three-beat structures also work as six-beats, but in many cases it is difficult to ascertain which interpretation was intended. As ʿAlī Ufuḳī repeatedly uses the number 3 in the context of *Semāʿī*, it is possible that he regarded *Semāʿī* as a three-beat *uṣūl*.[58]

Generally speaking, *uṣūl* boundary lines can sometimes help analysis and identification, but they rarely appear, and if so, they often coincide with statements of the *uṣūl* name in any case. Further points of reference are sections marked off by repeat signs or other lines, segni etc., but the grouping and distancing of note heads is generally also very worthy of consideration. In some cases, mainly with regards to instrumental pieces, identification of the *uṣūl* has already been possible, either by comparison with the concordances in the London manuscript, in which the intended *uṣūl* is almost invariably stated, or simply by counting and observing the features described above. In the case of the untitled *peşrev* on f.281v/360v[59], an attribution to *uṣūl Berevşān* was possible:

Fig. 5: f.281v/360v, untitled *peşrev* in *uṣūl Berevşān* (*ḫāne* 1 and *mülāzime*).

58 Öztuna describes "*Semâî*" as "3 *zamanlı ve* 3 *darblıdır*". Öztuna, Yılmaz 2006, *Türk Mûsikîsi Akademik Klasik Türk San'at Mûsikîsi'nin Ansiklopedik Sözlüğü*, İstanbul, vol.2, p. 287.

59 http://gallica.bnf.fr/ark:/12148/btv1b84150086/f552.item. Behar 2008, p. 124f.

The piece does in fact have an *uṣūl* designation, namely a *tempus perfectum diminutum* symbol seemingly overwritten with a crooked line (the *uṣūl* designation is obscured by the binding and is difficult to decipher). Another sixteen-beat option would be *Muḫammes*, but the rhythmical organization of the piece is consistent with a short description in European values and Ottoman syllables which ʿAlī Ufuḳī added to another *peşrev* in *uṣūl Berevşān*: "*Vssul perewßan due triple et cinq[ue] quadre*".[60] It is probable that he actually means two groups of three and five groups of two (not four). This would correspond exactly to the evidence of the *peşrev* shown above.

It is noteworthy that in the vocal repertoire statements of *uṣūl* by name are very rare, whereas the *peşrevler* predominantly have some kind of designation. As is obvious from Table 1, the number of vocal pieces with defined *uṣūller* is smaller, although the total number of vocal pieces is larger than that of instrumental compositions; moreover, the range of *uṣūller* employed is narrower. Many instances of *uṣūl* statements are related to song texts without musical notation, mainly towards the "end" of the manuscript in its current binding. The reason for this is that the Paris manuscript, which, as a source, is a multi-levelled combination of notation collection, commonplace book, *mecmūʿa* and scrap paper, contains sections which show features of the Ottoman-style *mecmūʿa* or *cönk* – divan poetry without musical notation, written by many different hands, accompanied by headings stating *maḳām* and/or *uṣūl.*

In any case, something is visibly different in the vocal repertoire. A question that is as important as it is complicated is whether those pieces which can be designated as "folk music" – meaning the pieces belonging to the *ʿāşıḳ* sphere, headed "*Türki*" or "Varṣāġı" in the manuscripts or attributable to those genres on account of formal criteria – are understood as having an *uṣūl* in the sense of court music, or rather something else. Some pieces, which seem to be a minority, may have been meant to be sung freely, while others – in the present author's opinion these form the largest part of the folk repertoire – have a rhythmical structure in the sense of a *kırık hava*[61] but not an *uṣūl* in the sense of Ottoman court music. In the Paris manuscript, of the 150 notated pieces attributed or clearly attributable to the folk sphere, 62 have some designation while 88 do not (41.3% versus 58.7%), whereas of the 41 notated courtly pieces 28 have a designation while 13 do not (68.3% versus 31.7%). In the London manuscript the proportion of folk pieces with designations is even smaller (30.7%).

60 f.136v/290v; http://gallica.bnf.fr/ark:/12148/btv1b84150086/f282.item.

61 For the modern theory of *kırık hava* see Markoff, Irene 2001, "Aspects of Folk Music Theory", in: *Garland Encyclopedia of World Music*, vol. 6, New York, 77-88, p. 79ff.

Conclusion

In the London manuscript, the system of *uṣūl* designation has reached a higher level of coherence and standardization, as in general have all features of the notation: it is, to use Owen Wright's wording, "much fuller, much more assured".[62] It is important to keep in mind that the Paris manuscript was not necessarily finished before the London manuscript was begun; on the contrary, the former source gives the impression of having been compiled over a longer period of time (if compilation is the correct term at all – we are dealing with an obviously incomplete loose-leaf collection consisting of various different kinds of papers, bound at a later date by somebody other than the author and without particular diligence). The only explanation for the incomplete state of ʿAlī Ufuḳī's treatment of *uṣūl* is that there were various stages of experiment, development and unification, of which we are not aware because they were never written down, or, just as probably, lost.

There is still a large amount of material to evaluate and conclusions are waiting to be drawn. Yet there is hope that at the end of this work there will be more clarity about how certain *uṣūller* were understood in mid-seventeenth century Istanbul, or at the very least about how ʿAlī Ufuḳī understood them.

62 Wright, Owen 2013, "Turning a Deaf Ear", in: *The Renaissance and the Ottoman World*, Anna Contadini and Claire Norton (Eds.), Farnham, 143-165, p. 162.

2.
Usûl in Written Tradition: Consensus and Variation, Theory and Praxis

The *Usûl* Issue in Kırşehrî According to a Fifteenth-Century Manuscript

Nilgün Doğrusöz-Dişiaçık

The fifteenth century was a very rich period in terms of the variety and abundance of writings related to music. Indeed, most of the *edvâr* (music theory) books were written during this particular period in history. Amongst the written sources concerning the history of Turkish music, clues about how music theory actually was are given in the books called *kitâb-ı edvâr* ("book of cycles"), where *makam*s and *usûl*s are explained in circular form. In the history of music theory, the *Kırşehrî Edvârı* is considered to be the first of the Anatolian *edvâr*s. This work was written by Yûsuf Kırşehrî in 1411 in Persian, though nobody knows where the autograph copy is today. In this case, the oldest and most reliable copy must be used. The work which will be the main concern of this paper is registered at the Bibliothèque Nationale de France under the catalogue number Supp. Turc 1424 (among the Oriental Manuscripts), and was written in March 1469, i.e. half a century after the original manuscript. This work was translated into Turkish by Harîrî bin Muhammed, who was requested to do so by someone in his circle, so that it could be accessed and comprehended by a greater number of people. With regards to *edvâr* books, it is a sign of greater reliability if the name of the author and the date of registration (*ferağ*) appears inside the book, as it does in this case. Therefore, based on this evidence, this copy should be considered the most reliable source for Kırşehrî's *Edvâr*.

The Content

The work primarily contains the following subjects: opening prayer and the reason why the work was written; discourse on the fact that music is a valuable science and the retelling of the camel story[1] in order to prove this argument; *makam* and

1 During the time of Safiyyüddîn, the *ulemâ* or religious scholars of the city of Baghdad prohibited the practice of (the science of) music. When Safiyyüddîn heard about this he went to the caliph and asked for permission to demonstrate the importance of this science. The caliph then asked how this demonstration could be undertaken. Safiyyüddîn first instructed them to bring a camel and keep it away from water for forty days, then offer the camel both water and music and see which the camel would prefer. If the camel were to prefer water over music, this would show that music was not a science of vital importance. When the time came for the test, they tied a rock to the camel's feet, brought water in a silver cup, and the people of Baghdad gathered to watch the camel with great curiosity. Safiyyüddîn started singing a *nevbet-i müretteb* in the *makam zengûle* as they untied the camel's feet. The thirsty camel, instead of moving towards the water, stood still and turned his head over to the passionately singing Sheikh Safiyyüddîn, with tears in his eyes. This

facts concerning *makam* (i.e. the 12 *makams*, seven *âvâzes* and four *şûbes* and the relationship of these with the 12 signs of the zodiac, seven heavenly bodies (stars and planets), and the four fundamental elements of the creation of universe); *terkîbs* (compound modes); *usûls*; musical forms; which *makams* should be performed according to the hour of the day, the physiology of human beings and the influence of connected elements; the classification of instruments.

In this paper, we will discuss how *usûl* (rhythmic cycle), which is one of the two basic elements in the *edvâr* genre, should be read in Kırşehrî's *Edvâr*. Accordingly, the following topics will be analyzed: Kırşehrî's classification of *usûl*; the classification of *usûl* according to masters of music; *usûl*, *darp* ("beat") and the definition of *zaman* ("time"); anecdotes about *usûl*; the relationship between forms and *usûls*.

At times, it can be observed that a certain obliqueness characterizes the expressions used in the translation of Kırşehrî. Unfortunately, it is not possible for the missing information to be completed from later copies of the work. For this reason, the way to understand what is meant in those expressions is to compare the manuscript with another manuscript or a manuscript dating from the same period. In this paper, we have tried to establish a relationship between the *Kitâb-ı Edvâr* of Hızır bin Abdullâh (1451) and Seydî's *El-Matlâ* (1504), based on the information gathered by Kırşehrî (1469). An important feature of the work in question is that it is a translated work, and this needs to be borne in mind while carrying out research on it.

Reading the Usûls

When we arrive at the section where Kırşehrî analyzes the *usûls* in his *Edvâr*, three phenomena have to be taken into consideration; this is also the case in the works of Seydî and Hızır:

1. *Usûls* are first ordered only according to their names.
2. *Usûls* are then expressed in prose.
3. *Usûls* are demonstrated again through circles/cycles.

The pieces of information contained in these three modes of explanation might not be compatible with each other, since sometimes an *usûl* that appears in the list is not explained or shown in cyclic form. This is why comparative research needs to be done in this field. Here we will deal only with *usûls* that are expressed by means of cycles or prose, without having been given in list form. Some symbols are placed outside the cycles in Seydî's illustration of *usûls*, whereas in Hızır's treatment of *usûls*, numbers denoting consonants have been

test was performed three times in a row and each time the result was the same. And so, on that occasion it was understood that music was vital to humanity, and appreciation for it grew day by day (see Doğrusöz, Nilgün 2012, *Yusuf Kırşehri'nin Müzik Teorisi*, Kırşehir: Kırşehir Valiliği Yay., p. 43, 57, 185-186).

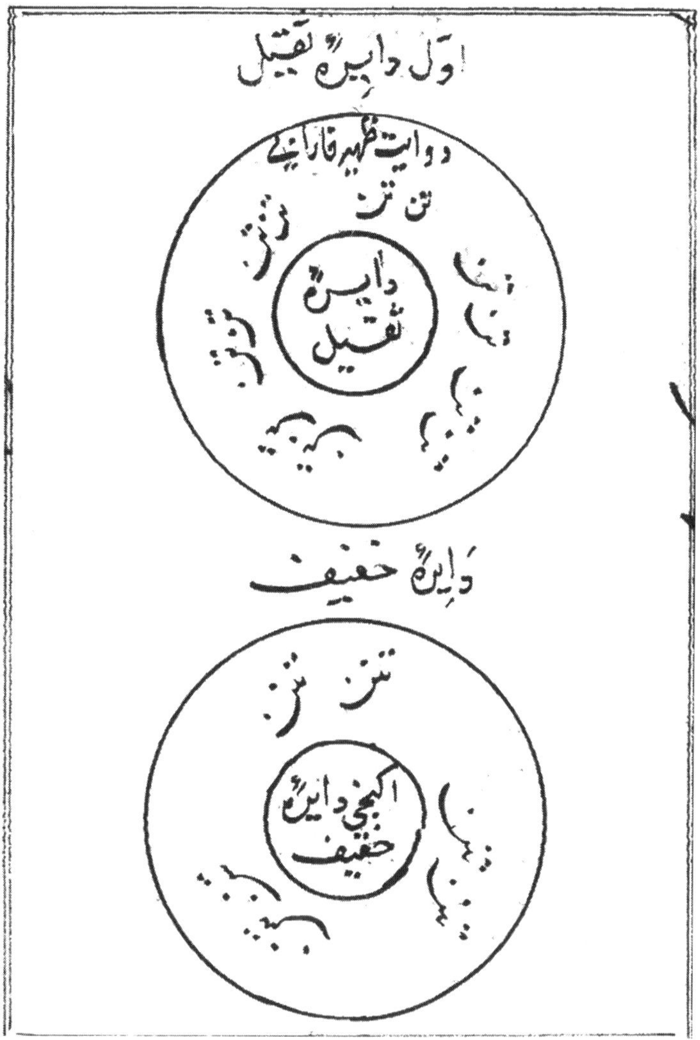

Figure 1: Cyclic form of *sakil* and *hafîf* (fol.19b)

put over each letter group to denote the vowels. There are short explanations such as *ten* = 2, *tenen* = 3, *tenenen* = 4 or special symbols.[2] These kind of symbols and numbers greatly facilitate attempts to correct those parts of the work which are incorrectly written and to verify the correctly written ones. No similar symbols are encountered in Kırşehrî.

2 Seydî: II = *tene*; IΛ = *tenen*; IIΛ = *tenenen*. Hızır: *sebeb hafîf* = *ten* (= 2); *sebeb sakil* = *tene* (1+1 = 2); *veted mecmû* = *tenen* (= 3); *veted mefrûk* = *tâna* or *tenne* (2+1=3); *fâsıla sugrâ* = *tenenen* (4); *fâsıla kübrâ* (5) (Popescu-Judetz, Eugenia and Neubauer, Eckhard 2004, *Seydî's book on music: A 15th century Turkish discourse*, Frankfurt a.M: Institute for the History of Arabic-Islamic Science, p. 201f.).

The Classification of Usûls *in Kırşehrî (fols.17a-19b)*

Usûls are divided into two according to Kırşehrî: *sakil* (heavy) and *hafîf* (light), as shown in figure 2 below.

Sakil	Hafif
1. Verşan	1. Remel
2. Revan	2. Remelikasir
3. Türkî	3. Çahardarb
4. Semai	4. Sedarb
5. Fahte	5. Rahıkerd
6. Serendazi	6. Muhammes
7. Buhariçardarb	7. Remelisengin
8. Hezec	8. Çardarbıhafif
9. Evsat	9. Darbeyn
10. Çifte	

Figure 2: Classification of *usûl* (fol.17a-17b)

While the author does not explain most of the *usûls* mentioned in fig. 2, he does explain the *usûl darbeyn*. Kırşehrî calls *darbeyn* that *usûl* which is formed by combining *sakil* and *hafîf*. He then writes: "But now we have reached the section of *nakarat*. *Nakarat* is such an object that it resembles the process whereby poets apply the *aruz* system in parts. Just as *'mefâ'ilün fe'ilâtün'* is indispensable for the poet, the elements of *darp*, *usûl* and *nakarat* are equally as important for the singer [*gûyende*]", thus relating the matter of *usûl* to singers rather than to instrumentalists. He goes on to state the number of *nakarat*, in other words the syllables which constitute the number of beats of the *usûls* which he previously mentioned. These syllables and the number of beats they represent are listed accordingly in figure 3.

Kırşehri	
Sakil (24)	Ten-ten-ten-ten-ten-ten-ten-ten-ten-ten-ten-ten
Hafif (16)	Te-nen-te-nen-ten-te-nen-te-nen-ten
Remel-i Tavil (18)	Ten-ten-te-nen-te-nen-ten-ten-ten-ten
Remel-i Kasir (14)	Ten-ten-ten-te-nen-te-nen-ten
Çardarb (30)	Te-nen-te-nen-ten-te-nen-te-nen-ten- ten-ten-ten-te-nen-te-nen-[ten]
Muhammes-i Tavil (38)	Te-ne-nen- ten- te-ne-nen-ten-te-ne-nen-ten-te-ne-nen-ten-te-ne-nen-ten-ten-te-ne-nen-ten
Vereşan (12)	Te-ne-ten-te-ne-ten-te-ne-ten
Türkidarb (10)	1 . Ten-te-nen-te-nen-ten 2. Te-nen-te-nen-ten-ten
Fahte (14)	Ten-te-nen[en]-te-nen-te-nen-ten
Sakil-i Tavil (24)	Te-ne-nen-ten-te-ne-[nen]-ten-te-ne-nen-ten-te-ne-nen-ten
Remel (12)	Te-ne-nen-ten-te-ne-nen-ten
Hezec (6)	Te-ne-ten-ten
Muhammes-i Kasir (8)	Te-nen-te-nen-ten
Hezec-i Kasir (4)	Te-ne-nen
Remel-i Sengin (7)	Ten-te-nen-ten

Figure 3: *Usûls* with syllables (fol.18a ff.)

The Display of Usûl*s in the Form of Cycles (fols. 19b-24a)*

The issue of how to read *makam*, *âvâze*, *şûbe* and *usûl* cycles in Kırşehrî was initially problematic. In the translations, it is necessary to follow the cycles showing the interconnections between *makam*, *âvâze* and *şûbe* from left to right, the *makam* cycles from right to left and the *usûl* cycles from left to right. In this section *usûl*s are shown in cyclic form but the *nakarat*s of some of them have not been written.

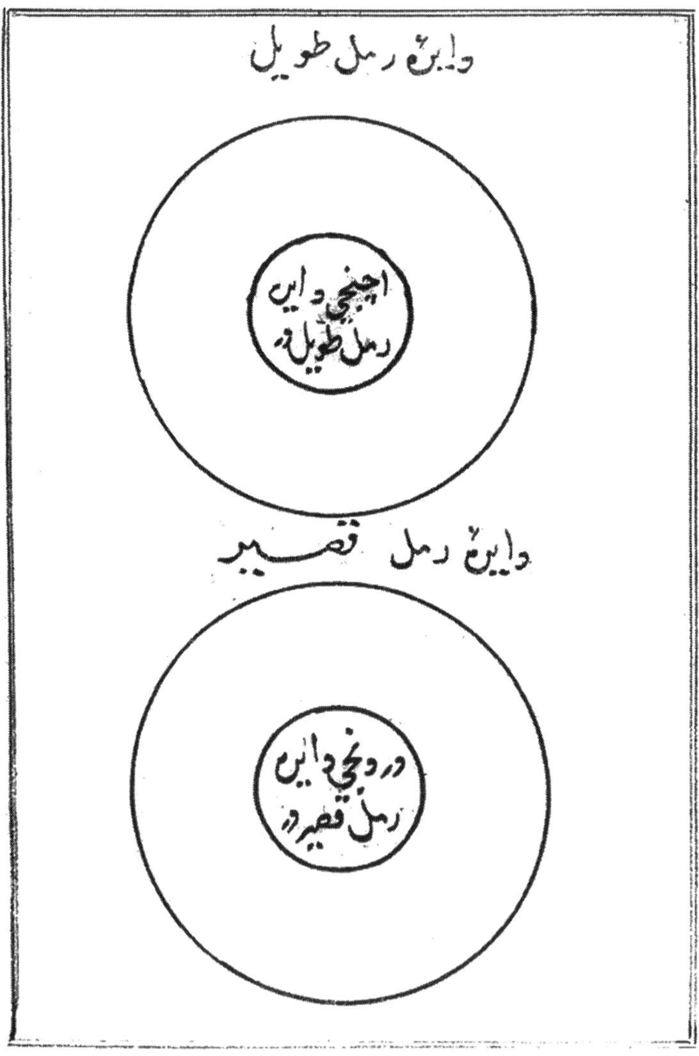

Figure 4: Empty cycles (*remel-i tavîl* and *remel-i kasîr*, fol. 20a)

The Classification of Usûl *According to Masters of Music*

In the *Kırşehrî Edvârı*, the question of who might have been meant by the expression "*bir nice üstatlar*"" ("many masters") in the sentence *"geldük bir dahı bir nice üstâdlar rivâyet eylerler ki asl-ı darb ikidür"* (fol. 19a) requires close investigation. Since they are not mentioned as "old masters" but simply as "many masters", these masters might well be thought of as contemporary figures. However, at fol. 1b-3a one of the most important names of the science of music, the learned Safiyyüddîn Abdülmümin, is stated to have formed nine *felek*s (levels of space), and nine different types of beats and *usûl*s. It is mentioned in the book that these "many masters" divided the original *darp*s or beats into six. These six *darp*s are given as follows: 1. *revân*, 2. *türkî*, 3. *semâî*, 4. *fâhte*, 5. *remel-i tîz*, 6. *remel-i sengîn*. No information is given on how many *nakarat*s these *darp*s consist of, but they are said to have been "close to each other, but not similar". Hızır[3] also seems to agree with Kırşehrî that the original number of *darp*s is six. Seydî[4], however, divides the *darp* into four types: 1. *fâhte*, 2. *semâî*, 3. *revân*, 4. *remel-i tîz* or *remel-i sengîn*. He does not include *türkî* in this classification.

In his work, Kırşehrî states that the *usûl darbeyn* belongs to Hârûn and that Muhammed Şah Rebâbî[5] and Kemal Tebrizî[6], who are in possession of *çârdarb*, have *düvanzede/düvazde*. The term *düvanzede*, which means twelve, is probably the name of an *usûl*. Furthermore, Kırşehrî mentions that the three *usûl* names which he mentions are classified as six by him.

Definitions of Darp *("Beat" or Musical Metre),* Usûl *(Rhythmic Pattern), and* Zaman *("Time") (fols. 24a-24b)*

Kırşehrî first chooses to discuss *darp* as a section and then attempts to explain what *darp*, *usûl* and *zaman* are. "You should know that *usûl* is the plural form of the word *asl* [meaning essential, authentic, real, original, genuine]. *Usûl* is a foundation that has no essence. It is a spontaneous gift of God, he gives it to whomever he pleases." From this sentence we understand that the word *usûl* – which means roots, essences, the authentic or original ones – is the plural form of the word *asl*. Kırşehrî, by stating *"Pes usûl ol nesne degüldür ki kimse ânı göre ve ögrene"*("*Usûl* is not

3 Hızır bin Abdullâh, *Kitâb-ı Edvâr* (15th century), Topkapi Palace Museum, Revân Collection, Ms. 1728, fol. 93b.

4 *Hazâ el-Matla'fi Beyanü'l-Edvar ve'l Makâmat ve fi Ilmü'l Esrâr ve'r-Riyâzat*, also known as "*Seydî'nin el Matla'ı*", Topkapi Palace Museum, Ms. A 3459, fol. 30a.

5 The musician Muhammed Şah Rebâbî from Azerbaijan lived in the period between Safiyyüddîn Urmevî (d. 1294) and Merâğî (d.1435) as recorded by the latter (for detailed information see Popescu-Judetz and Neubauer, Eckhard 2004, p. 205, 377).

6 Kemâl Tebrîzî, was the favorite court musician and companion of the Ilkhanid Sultan Ebû Said (ruled 1316-1335) (for detailed information, see ibid, p. 205, 378).

an object that is visible or physically comprehensible by anyone"), means that *usûl* is not an object to be seen, but is a gift of God and that God gives it to whomever he pleases, indicating that it is a matter of talent.

According to Kırşehrî, *darp* occurs between two *zamans* ("time"), therefore *zaman* is the period between two *darps*, i.e. two beats. Kırşehrî states that God may give someone a beautiful voice or a beautiful appearance but if he has no *usûl*, then one cannot appreciate the beauty of his voice. Thus he points out the importance of the *usûl* and knowledge of the *usûls*. He clarifies the topic with a story. According to this story, Safiyyüddîn Urmevî hears Ebû Ali Sînâ asking "Is there a science in the universe that I do not know?". In the city of Baghdad, he has six disciples that he himself educated and who had learnt the science of music very well. He asks them to go to the city of Egypt and to go to Ebû Ali Sînâ's dwelling and "make him hear what this science is and how it is". The disciples reach Egypt, where they find Ebû Ali Sînâ, kiss his hand, and sit down and start singing and performing *nevbet-i müretteb.* Ebû Ali Sînâ is mesmerized by what he hears. He has heard about them but never seen them with his own eyes. When the *nevbet* is over, he becomes very fond of this science, calling it *"hûb ve latîf ve nâzük ʿilm"* ("the gay and beautiful and pleasant science") and dedicates much of his time to understand it. He learns about the essences and details of every *makam*, and understands the *nakarat* and cycle of each one. He attempts to compose a song but cannot succeed, because he is not proficient in *vuruş* and *usûl* ("beat" and rhythmic pattern). He makes a great effort and works very hard, but cannot manage to compose a song, remaining incapable of doing so. Kırşehrî concludes, *"Pes eyle olsa usûl dahı hidâyet-imiş"* ("give up, *usûl* is a matter of talent"), by which he means that although *usûl* is supposed to be learnt through education, education is not enough. He thus ends his story by emphasizing that it is a matter of talent.[7]

Throughout the description of the *nevbet-i müretteb* form put forward in the *Edvâr*[8], the names of the two types of *usûl*, *sakil* and *hafîf*, are mentioned. In Kırşehrî's *Edvâr*, he gives individual advice to those who wish to sing and those who wish to play an instrument. The information that is given in this section is as follows. The masters determined three names for the performance of the *nevbet-i müretteb.* The

7 There are many historical inaccuracies in this story. Agayeva and Uslu explain the reasons behind the incessant mentioning of the names of Fârâbî, Urmevî and Ibn Sînâ in *edvârs* under three headings: 1. The desire to show that music is an honourable and sacred thing; 2. The desire to demonstrate that the science of music is in accord with religion; 3. The intent that the *edvâr* writers have to claim a close connection to these masters by showing affinity to them through reading their texts etc. (see Agayeva, Süreyya and Uslu, Recep 2008, *Ruhperver: Bir XVII.yy Müzik Teorisi Kitabı*, Ankara: Ürün Yayınları, p. 8; Doğrusöz, 2012, p. 25).

8 According to this description, first a *makam* is performed and a *peşrev* is played, and then a *hüsrevâni* is performed, which means another *makam* and *peşrev* are played. By choosing *sakil* ("heavy") or *hafîf* ("light") *usûls* two cycles of *nakış nakarat* are played. Then a *gazel* is sung and a *kavl* is performed. Afterwards, a *nağme* and a song containing a *kavl* is played before the *nevbet* concludes. Between the *peşrev* and the *gazel* forms, names of individual *usûls* are mentioned (fols. 25a-25b, see also Doğrusöz 2012, pp. 146-148).

first is *kabl*, the second is *maa*, the third is *ba'd*. During the *kabl* section, if someone wants to learn singing, first he is supposed to beat the *darp*s and then read/sing the lyrics of the poem. *Maa* is the case when he performs the beating of the *darp* and the reading of the poem at the same time. For *ba'd*, the performer first reads/sings the lyrics of the poem and then beats the *darp*. Now, these are symbols and beneath these symbols there are many hidden treasures. These symbols and treasures are hidden in this science. In this science, a very prominent master is required so that the student can understand the symbols. It is underlined that these modes of application, as mentioned above, need to be learnt especially from a *kavi* master (one who is highly proficient in performance and is knowledgeable).

An Example of the Usûl *Descriptions in Kırşehrî: The Description of the* Usûl-*Types* Hafîf *and* Sakil

In total, nineteen *usûl* names are given – ten *sakil* (heavy) *usûl*s and nine *hafîf* (light) *usûl*s. However, only fifteen *usûl*s are described and some of these *usûl*s do not appear in the classification of *usûl*s. The *usûl*s which do not have a description although they are in the classification are: *semâî*, *buhârîçârdarp*, *serendâz*, *revan*, *sidarb*, *evsat*, *rahıkerd* and *çifte darp*. The *usûl*s of which descriptions are given although their names are not in the classification are: *sakil-i tavîl*, *remel-i tavîl* and *muhammes-i tavîl*. In some of the descriptions of *usûl*s, there are significant misspellings and orthographic mistakes between the textual and the cyclic expression. For example, the *usûl hafîf* is described as having sixteen *zaman*s (fol. 18a): when *tenen tenen ten* is sung twice, it is correct and the calculation arrived at is faultless. But in the cyclic representation of *hafîf* it is written as *tenen tenen tenen tenen tenen tenen* (see figure 5).

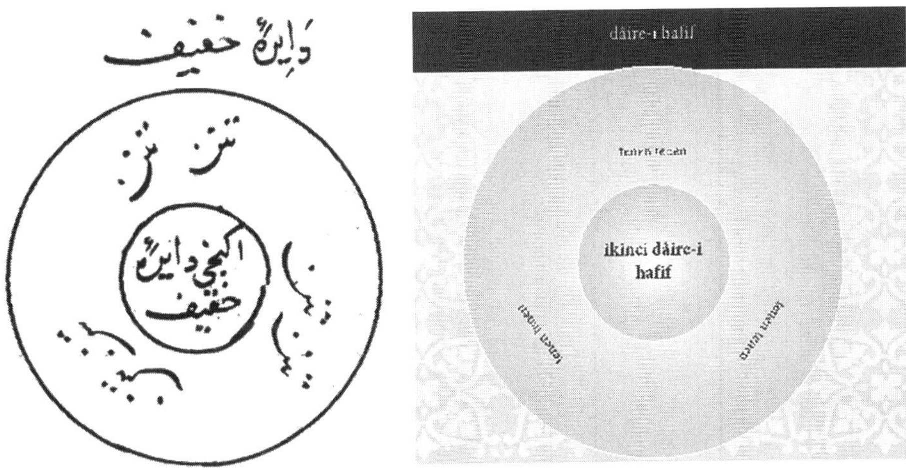

Figure 5: Cyclic description of *hafîf* (fol. 19b)

In this case we are faced with two conflicting descriptions: the number of beats in the calculation within the cyclic description amounts to eighteen, hence the calculation proves to be wrong. In this case a comparison with its contemporaries has been made (in this comparison the same method has been applied in checking against the descriptions and cycles) and it has been concluded that the first description in the text is correct. Further proof is offered by *hezec-i kasîr* (see figure 6), since a half-cycle of *hafif* corresponds to *muhammes-i kasîr* (8) and a quarter-cycle to *hezec-i kasîr* (4) .

Thus, we see that an *usûl* can be described with two different names and *nakarats* (syllables) in Kırşehrî. In Kırşehrî's work, it can also be observed that an *usûl* is sometimes described with two alternative names and *nakarats*. Thus it is stated that while the refrain of the *usûl sakil* (see figure 7) can sometimes be *ten ten ten*, it can also be written with the *aruz* meter *tenenen ten* and that this type of expression is known also as *sakil-i tavîl.*

Conclusion

Due to the errors and faults in the text – such as the case of certain *usûl* cycles being left empty, the inconsistencies observed between the cyclic and textual descriptions of *usûls*, and the text which is sometimes found outside the figures, resulting in a disorganized appearance – we have concluded that this work might be a preparatory one, a preliminary work that the author prepared before completing a later version. When the song text part of the work is considered apart from the theoretical section of the *Edvâr*, the names of forms that were used in the fifteenth century, such as *amel*, offer a further clue. The lyrics and poems that

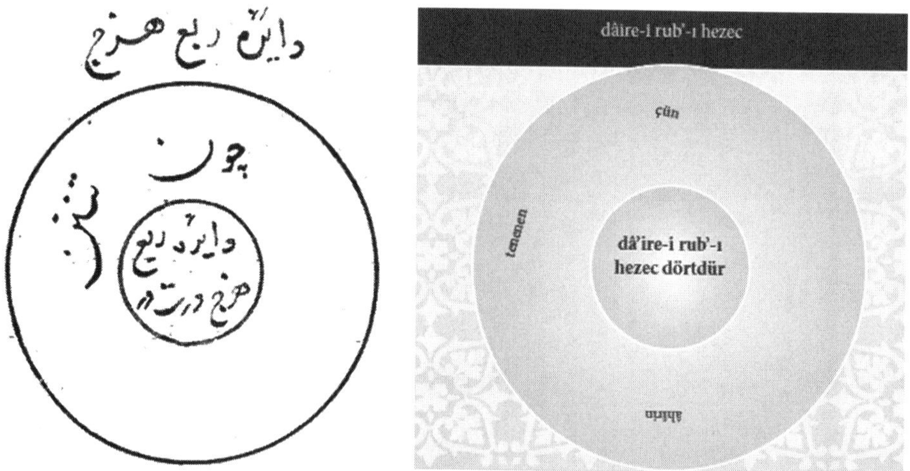

Figure 6: *Hezec-i kasîr* (quarter of the meter *hafif* (nakarat: *te ne nen*, fol. *23a)*

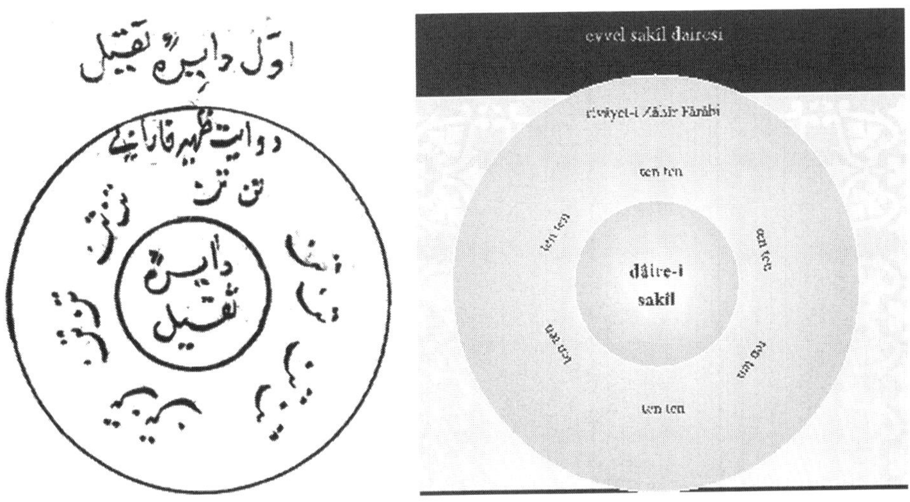

Figure 7: *Sakil* (fol. 19b)

Harîrî wrote down belong to the famous scholars of the era between the thirteenth and fifteenth centuries, such as Safiyyüddîn Urmevî, Abdülkâdir Merâğî, Kutbeddin Şirâzî and Mollâ Câmî. The fact that these poems and lyrics are in the book seems to prove once again that the entire book was written during the reign of Sultan Mehmed II. In these poems and lyrics, the most frequent *usûl*s are the following: *sidarb*, *çârdarb*, *sakil*, *hafîf*, *nîm-sakil* and *evsat*.

How to Transcribe and Analyze *Usûl* and Tempo in the Cantemir Music Collection

Ş. Şehvar Beşiroğlu / Ozan Baysal

Music is a timely art. Whether it is a simple pattern of pulses, or an organized series of pitches, or an energetic shaping of sounds, or an interaction of all, it occurs in a temporal dimension and gradually unfolds in time. The organization of such movement(s), and the characteristic shape of this organization is called rhythm. As time provides rhythm the necessary temporal space and rhythm gives time a meaningful expression, both of these concepts are intrinsically dependent upon each other. A change in the way we perceive, understand and categorize time would also change our comprehension of rhythm, which will consequently affect our listening experiences as well as the music we create and perform. In short, as Cooper and Meyer state, "to study rhythm is to study all of music."[1]

If one investigates the musical geography of the Middle East and Anatolia, it will be seen that the study of music rests on an oral tradition called "*meşk*", which affects many spheres including teaching, transmission, representation and performance. At the core of this musical tradition stands the study of rhythm, which has been shaped through the recitation and singing of religious and poetic texts. It is a fact that almost all vocal pieces of the Turkish classical repertoire were based on poetry which was written according to a rhythmic structure called "*aruz*". In order for this poetic rhythm to be in harmony with the rhythmic cycles, or *usûl*, of the music, it was necessary to be familiar with both. This also made the study of poetry an essential part of musical education.

As a result of the *meşk* tradition, the interpretation and performance of the Turkish repertoire is highly dependent on memory. This means that a work is unlikely to be preserved in its original form, since, as has been suggested by many psychologists, the memory also has a constructive nature of its own: "Remembering is not the re-excitation of innumerable fixed, lifeless and fragmentary traces. It is an imaginative reconstruction, or construction, built out of the relation of our attitude towards a whole mass of organized past reactions or experience."[2] In parallel with Bartlett's statement, this aspect of *meşk* would also leave room for improvisation, re-interpretation, re-organization, embellishment and/or simplification and paves the way for an active synthesis with each moment in

---

1 Cooper, Grosvenor and Meyer, Leonard B. 1963, *The Rhythmic Structure of Music*, Chicago: University of Chicago, p.1.

2 Bartlett, Frederic Charles 1995 [1932], *Remembering: A Study in Experimental and Social Psychology*, Cambridge: Cambridge University Press, p. 213.

which the pieces are recalled and performed. This also explains the consistent 'non-preference' (or 'rejection') of music notation as a tool, since, as Behar states, "notating a piece produces a 'standardized' version of it, and this standardization inevitably limits the freedom of interpretation enjoyed by musicians during their own rendition of the work."[3]

Due to these facts, while analyzing and interpreting a musical work from notation, one must also take into consideration the transcriber's intention with regards to exactly how much the music is to be embellished, considering the notation as a more or less accurate representation of the principal skeletal aspects of the piece and allowing interpretative space for the performers. Besides this, as notational representations reflect the conceptual frameworks of the music they are employed in, analyzing them within their cultural contexts along with their original versions becomes a crucial prerequisite for our understanding (and building) of such theoretical systems. One can argue that our 'modern' theories of *usûl* and the rhythmic structures of *makam* music may possibly be related to a misleading conceptual framework based on the 'imported' representations of Western music notation. Most important here are the implications inherent in the utilization of meter and the barline.

If we consider the pulse as the regular beat which falls at equal time intervals, meter in music can be defined as the periodic organization of such pulses grouped according to the regular patterns of recurring accents. Thus, meter implies not only the periodicity but also a hierarchy of 'strong' and 'weak' beats. Such elements of periodicity, regularity and recurrence then function as a common ground for musical figures, be they melodic or rhythmic. Due to this, meter also has an anticipatory aspect, as London states: "Meter involves our initial perception as well as subsequent anticipation of a series of beats that we abstract from the rhythmic surface."[4] However, meter in Western music is a mental construct derived from the music itself, and is generated by the attentive processes of the listeners. Once the meter is mentally established, the presence of the hierarchical distribution of the beats due to their metric accent orients the listener (as well as the analyst and the transcriber) to group the melodic/rhythmic figures in the music accordingly. By contrast, when one looks at *makam* music, the rhythmic cycles of the *usûl* present themselves as different layers of sonic activity, and within the *usûl* it is hard to find such an organized hierarchy between the beats. Thus, the 'strong-weak' beats appear as phenomenal accents rather than metric accents.[5] As Bar-Yosef writes, "The

---

3 Behar, Cem 1987, *Klasik Türk Musikisi Üzerine Denemeler*, İstanbul: Bağlam Yayınları, p. 38.

4 London, Justin 2004, *Hearing In Time: Psychological Aspects of Meter*, New York: Oxford University Press, p. 4.

5 The difference between metric and phenomenal accents is explained by Lerdahl and Jackendoff as follows: phenomenal accents are "any event at the musical surface that gives emphasis or stress to a moment in the musical flow"; metric accents are "any beat that is relatively strong in its metrical context" (Lerdahl, Fred and Jackendoff, Ray 1983, *A Generative Theory of Tonal Music*, Cambridge, MA: MIT Press, p. 17).

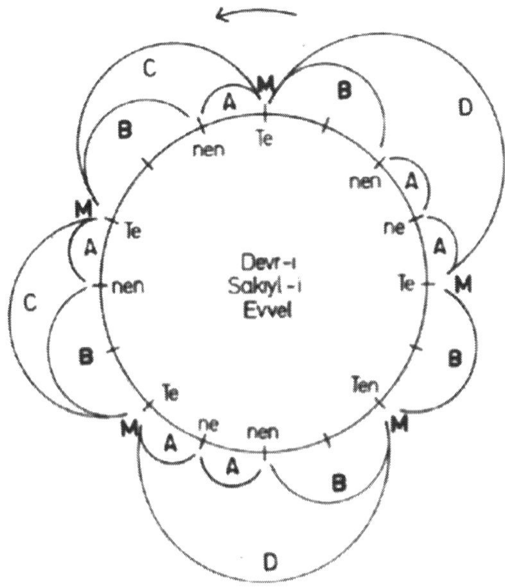

Figure 1: *Devr-i sakiyl-i evvel usûl* in Merâğî (Bardakçı's transcription)[6]

īqāʿ contains only a rhythmic phenomenal level, namely the sequence of stresses executed by the drum. There is no metric level."[7] Since Fârâbî, the concept of rhythm in the geography of the Middle East has been denoted by the term *îkāʾ* and explained in a similar way to the rhythmic modes of ancient Greece. Incorporating the views of Fârâbî, Safiüddîn Urmevî and Kutbüddîn Şîrâzî, Abdülkâdir Merâğî explains *îkāʾ* as "a group of beats that have a particular and limited time between them", and describes *îkāʾ* as rhythmic cycles that have a close relationship with poetic meter.[8] Similarly to Fârâbî, Merâğî speaks of seven fundamental *îkāʾ*s.[9] The rhythmic cycles in Abdülkâdir Merâğî's works (fourteenth to fifteenth centuries) are visually depicted as cycles. The divisions correspond to different syllables (related to prosody, or openness and closedness) having different durations and eventually providing a rhythmic framework. The name of the cycle is written at the center, around which the cycle revolves. Figure 1 is Bardakçı's transcription of the *usûl devr-i sakiyl-i evvel* as it is found in Merâğî's theoretical works.

As we approach the Ottoman period, what is understood by *îkāʾ* is a rhythmic cycle having a close relationship with poetic meter (*aruz*). Thus, the rules of *îkāʾ* originate from the principles of *aruz* and the rhythmic cycles are connected with

6 Bardakçı, Murat 1986, *Maragalı Abdülkadir*, İstanbul: Pan Yayıncılık, 84.
7 Bar-Yosef, Amatzia 2007, "A Cross Cultural Structural Analogy between Pitch & Time Constraints", *Music Perception: An Interdisciplinary Journal*, no. 24, 265-280, p. 268.
8 Bardakçı 1986, p. 78f.
9 Ibid.

the old *aruz* structures. Similarly to *aruz*, *îkā'* is formed by syllables (such as *ten, nen, te, ne*), and the accent of each beat (strength and weakness) is evaluated depending on whether the syllable has a vowel at the end or not. *Îkā'* also has elements that determine the tempo, such as *sebeb*, *vedet* and *fâsıla*.

Ali Ufkî is the first person to write the *usûl*s in a linear fashion during seventeenth century. However, as can be seen from Figures 2 and 3, although due to his linear representation the *usûl*s are 'barlined', we do not come across any internal barlines in his musical transcriptions.

Cantemir is the first person to view the *edvâr* tradition with a new and different perspective in the Ottoman period. As Feldman notes, his use of terminology and methodology while explaining the *makam*s and *usûl*s signals the beginning of an Ottomanization of music in the eighteenth century. Cantemir refers to *îkā'* as *usûl* and analyzes the rhythmic structures, including the subject of tempo, under the heading of *usûl*.[10] *Usûl* is defined in Cantemir as follows: "*Usûl* is the balance and proportion in music, such that, through the power of *usûl*, it is ensured that the rhyming of the tune is not more or less than is necessary."[11]

Cantemir speaks of two basic concepts while explaining the elements that make up *usûl*, which are the "fundamental *vezin*"' (*asıl vezin*) and the "incidental *vezin*" (*arızi vezin*).[12] Here, what is explained as the fundamental *vezin* is that which represents the original pattern of the *usûl*. This is denoted by numerals which also determine the way it is performed.

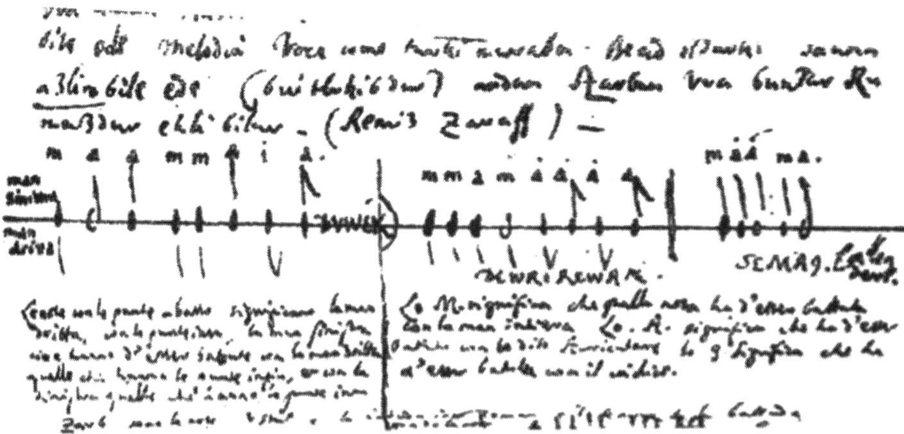

Figure 2: *Usûl* transcription in Ali Ufkî[13]

[10] Tura, Yalçın, (Ed.). 2001, *Kantemiroğlu: Kitabu 'İlmi'l-Musiki 'ala vechi'l-Hurufat / Mûsikîyi Harflerle Tesbît ve İcrâ İlminin Kitabı, I. cilt, Edvâr* (*tıpkıbasım – çevriyazı – çeviri – notlar*), İstanbul: Yapı Kredi Yayınları, p. 158ff.

[11] Ibid., p. 159.

[12] Ibid.

[13] Behar, Cem 2008, *Saklı mecmua. Ali Ufkî'nin Bibliothèque Nationale de France'taki [Turc 292] yazması*, İstanbul: Yapı Kredi Yayınları, p. 92.

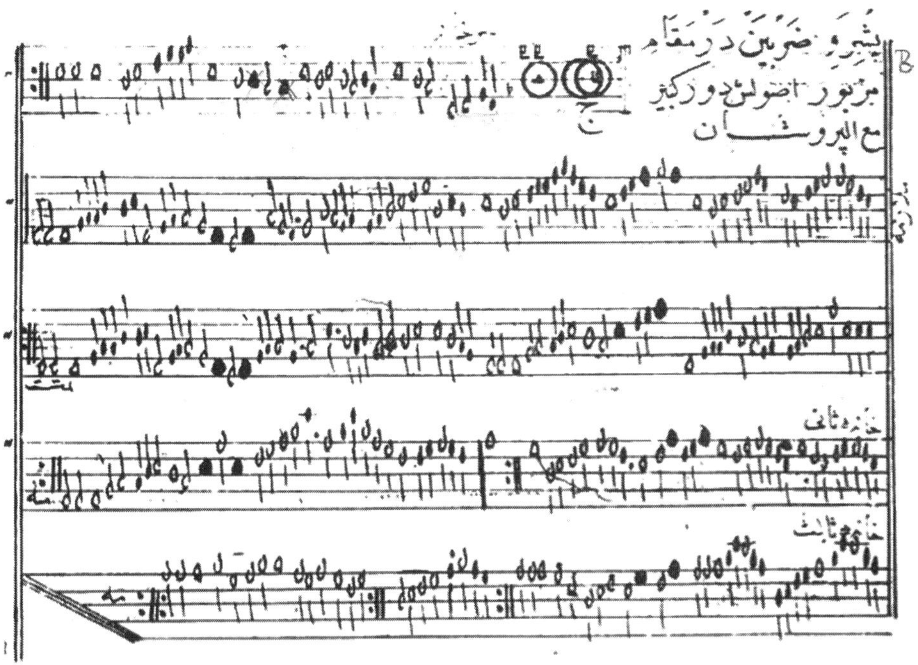

Figure 3: Musical transcription in Ali Ufkî[14]

What is most interesting in these definitions is that Cantemir expresses the theory of *usûl* and *vezin* through the utilization of the *tanbur* instead of the traditional pedagogical instrument, the *ud*. In the ancient systematist school, *îkāʾ* and the oral tradition were placed at the forefront, whereas in Cantemir the rhythmic tradition is being explained by an instrument for first time in the Ottoman period, while the tempo is explained by the strokes of the plectrum of the instrument. For example[15]:

<u>Elements forming the *usûl* in the fundamental *vezin* (*asıl vezin*):</u>

Four types:

Düm / one plectrum (playing with one stroke of the plectrum)
Tek / one plectrum (playing with one stroke of the plectrum)

Te-ke / two plectrums (playing with two strokes of the plectrum)
Te-ke te-ke / four plectrums (playing with four strokes of the plectrum)

---

14 Elçin, Şükrü (Ed.) 1976, *Alî Ufkî, Hayatı, eserleri ve Mecmûa-i Sâz ü Söz (Tıpkıbasım)*, İstanbul: Milli Eğitim Basımevi, p. 178.

15 Ibid.

Elements forming the *usûl* in the incidental *vezin* (*ârızî vezin*):

Four types:
Düm / two or four strokes of the plectrum
Tek / two or four strokes of the plectrum
Te-ke / four strokes of the plectrum
Te-ke te-ke / eight strokes of the plectrum

In this study we are going to compare various depictions of the *usûl berefşân* and the various transcriptions of *peşrev*s written in this *usûl* from different sources, including Ali Ufkî's *Mecmû'a-i Sâz ü Söz*[16], Cantemir's *Edvâr*[17], and Suphi Ezgi's work *Nazarî ve Amelî Türk Mûsikîsi*[18]. Our aim is to develop an analytical approach to the issue of rhythm in *makam* music via the subjects of *usûl* and *vezin*, and to determine the differences between pieces from the Ottoman *makam* music repertoire. These differences result from notational transcriptions that imply a Western sense of meter, and result in differences in performance, interpretation and analysis.

Although the 16-time-unit *usûl berefşân* first appears in the Cantemir manuscript as *berefşân*, it is one of the three 16-time-unit *usûl*s termed *sakiyl-i evvel* in the Arabic and Persian theory books. In these books, the 16-time-unit *berefşân* has 11 beats, whereas in Cantemir it has 14[19]:

Sakıyl-i evvel (16 time units):
Ten nen te nen te ne nen ten te ne nen

Cantemir's *berefşân* (16 time units):

Düm	*Tek*	*Düm*	*Tek*	*Düm*	*Düm*	*Tek*	*Düm*	*Düm*	*Tek*	*Te-ke*	*Te-ke*
2	1	2	1	2	1	1	1	1	2	1	1

On the other hand, one can observe that Cantemir also preferred circular depictions when explaining *usûl*s (Figure 4). However, his method was different, as he did not divide the circle according to the time units but rather according to the types of beats (not quantity, but quality), and wrote their durations below.

16 Cevher, M. Hakan, ed. 2003, *Hâzâ mecmûa-i sâz ü söz: çeviriyazım – inceleme*, İzmir; Elçin 1976.

17 Tura, Yalçın, 2001 and 2001b *Kitābu ʿilmi'l-mūsīḳī* [...], *II. cilt, Notalar* (*tıpkıbasım –çeviri – notlar*), İstanbul: Yapı Kredi Yayınları; Wright, Owen (Ed.) 1992b, *Demetrius Cantemir: The Collection of Notations, Volume 1: Text*, London: SOAS Musicology Series 1.

18 Ezgi, Subhi, 1933-1953, *Nazarî ve Amelî Türk Musikisi* (5 vols.), İstanbul: İstanbul Konservatuvarı Neşriyatından.

19 Tura 2001, p. 164.

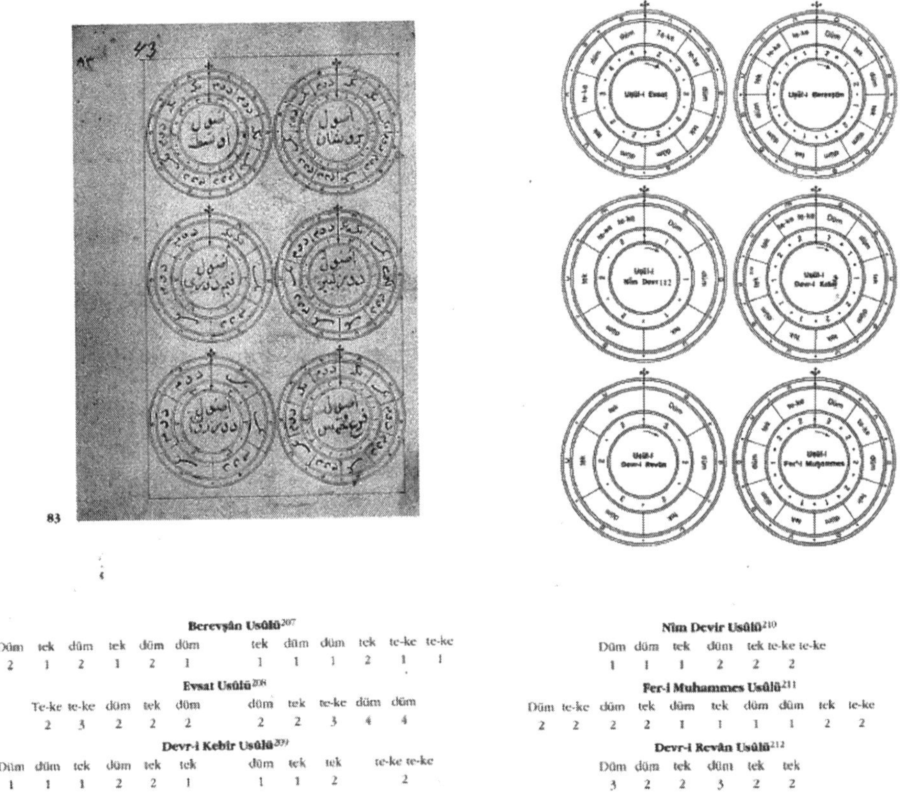

Figure 4: *Usûl* depictions in Cantemir[20]

This 16-time-unit *usûl* is depicted in the same way a century later in Abdülbâki Nâsır Dede's treatise from around the turn of the nineteenth century.[21] However, during the same century, together with the process of Westernization in the Ottoman Empire, as pieces began to be transcribed in Western notation we also start to see a change in descriptions. This is clearly observed when we come to the early twentieth century and look at the musicological studies of Raûf Yektâ Bey and Suphi Ezgi.

Suphi Ezgi describes the *usûl berefşân* by dividing it into two types.[22] *Nîm berefşân* (slow *berefşân*) is the 16-time-unit version and is depicted as 16/8 or 16/4 in the time signature. These 16 units are then divided into one *semâî* (3 time units, 2 beats), one *Türk aksağı* (5 time units, 3 beats) and two *sofyan*s (each having 4 time units, 4 and 3 beats consecutively). Thus *usûl nim berefşân* in Suphi Ezgi is 16 time

20 Ibid., p. 164f.

21 Tura, Yalçın (Ed.) 2006, *Nâsır Abdülbâkî Dede: İnceleme ve Gerçeği Araştırma (Tedkîk ü Tahkîk)*, İstanbul: Pan Yayıncılık, p. 71.

22 Ezgi 1935 (vol.2), p. 83ff.

Figure 5: *Usûl berefşân* in Suphi Ezgi[23]

units with 12 beats. Besides this, notice the change of beat at the last two time units of the *usûl* (Figure 5) – in Cantemir each one was "*te-ke te-ke*".

However, one should realize that the depictions of the *usûls semâî*, *Türk aksağı* and *sofyan* here only refer to time units, as the original beat divisions of the respective *usûls* are different from the versions we see in the example above.

Below is an updated circular representation of the *usûl berefşân*. Here the cycle is divided into 16 time units, and the relative beats (*düm* and *tek*) are presented in different circles, thus visually providing both the quantitative and qualitative aspects. Such a visualization shows the inner dynamics and the gestural character of the *usûl* more efficiently than its linear counterpart.

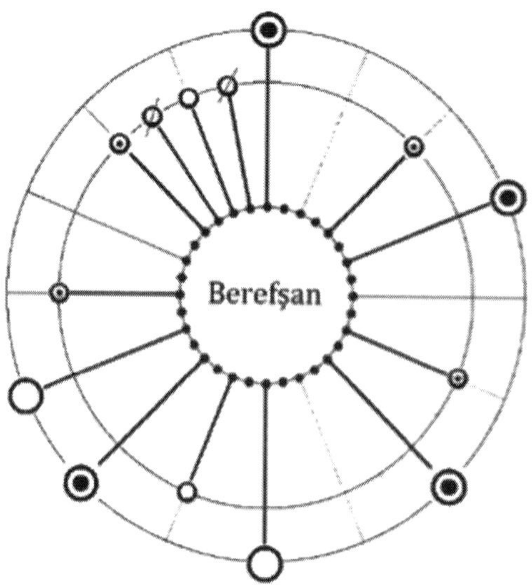

Figure 6: *Usûl berefşân*, circular representation

In the next two representations (Figure 7), the first one shows how Ezgi divides *berefşân*, each of the four circling arrows around the cycle denoting a sub-group, whereas in the second one the circling arrows are distributed according to the

23 Ibid., p. 83.

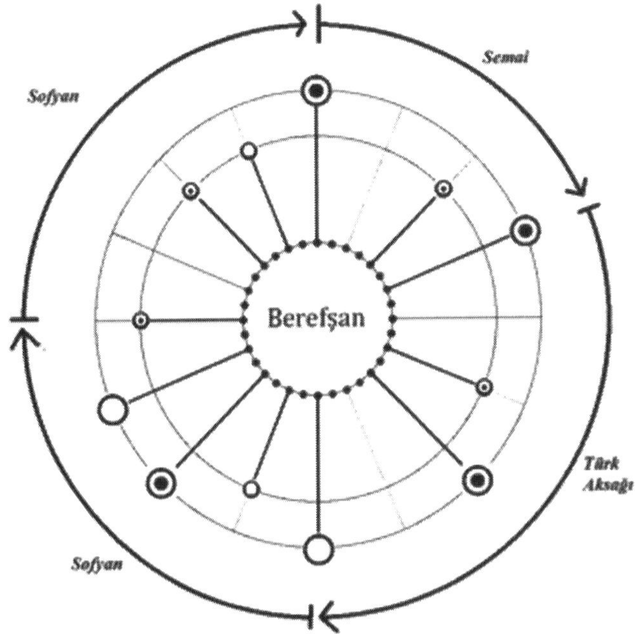

Division of Berefşan according to S.Ezgi

Figure 7: Interpreting *berefşân*

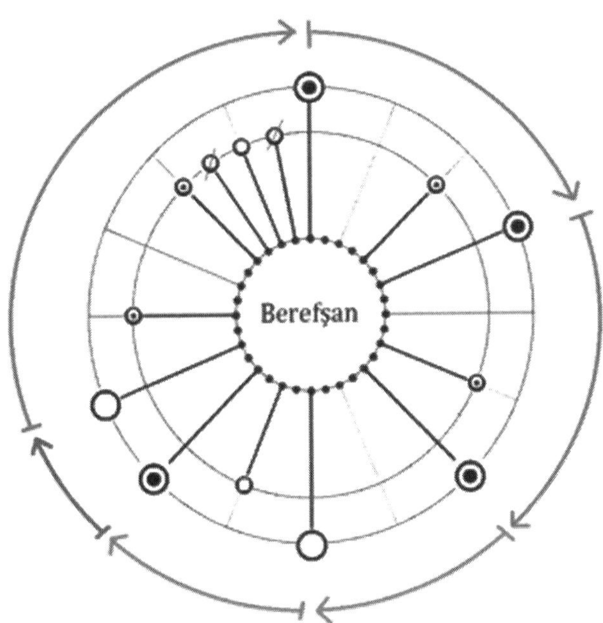

Temporal Gesture of Berefşan

Figure 8: *"Der makâm-ı nevâ usûleş berevşân"* in Cantemir[24]

phenomenal accents supplied by the *düm* strokes. Notice how the *düm* strokes start by lasting 3 time units and then gradually undergo a diminution, shrinking first to 2 time units, then to 1 time unit and finally making a resolution by finishing with 5 time units, in which the end of the rhythmic cycle is also signaled by the last *teke-teke* strokes.

As our musical example, we have selected the opening of the *peşrev* which is titled *"Der makam-ı neva usûleş berevşan"* in Cantemir and composed by Şerif. The title of the same piece appears as *"Beyati Peşrevi"* in Suphi Ezgi's book.[25] The primary source is Cantemir's transcription (Figure 8). Notice that the piece is written in letter notation while the rhythmic length of each note is denoted by numerals indicating the time units written below them.

When we compare the notated examples of this piece (Figure 9) which are taken from the transcriptions of Owen Wright and Yalçın Tura, we realize that Tura uses the quarter note as the basic note value (medium *vezin* in Cantemir), whereas Wright and Ezgi both use the eighth note (slow *vezin* in Cantemir).

Although Ezgi and Wright come closer to Cantemir's *vezin* specification by equating 126 bpm to an eighth note value, discrepancies arise due to assigning metrical characteristics to the *usûl* cycle, which would eventually alter the performance and the interpretation of the melodic *seyir* accordingly.

24 Tura 2001b, p. 92.

25 Ibid., p. 83f.

Figure 9: Comparing transcriptions (top to bottom: Tura[26], Wright[27], Ezgi[28])

26 Ibid., p. 92.
27 Wright 1992b, p. 103.
28 Ezgi 1935 (vol. 2), p. 83.

First of all, the use of dotted barlines and the division of the *usûl* into subsections not only produce a hierarchy of metrical relations among the beats, but also reinforce the sense of the barline throughout the performance. With regards to the *usûl berefşân*, the sense of ending produced while approaching the last beats of the rhythmic cycle is significantly reduced once the grouping is made as two consecutive *sofyans* (each having different beats) instead of the natural flow driven by the phenomenal accents of the *usûl*. A similar perception occurs as the last beats of the *usûl* (*te-ke te-ke*, as seen in Cantemir) – which not only strengthens the 'closing' sense of the rhythmic cycle but also signals the beginning of a new cycle – are altered to *te* – *ke*. Another important thing to note here is the change of accent relationships in the last group of *sofyans*: as the last beat of the first group (*düm*) becomes 'weaker' than the first beat of the second group (*tek*), the performer is inclined to play as if it were a syncopation.

The second discrepancy results from interpreting the melodic *seyir* according to the phenomenal accents of the *usûl*, which is also derived from the desire to assign them metrical roles. This is manifested by using beams while transcribing to staff notation, especially when connecting eighth notes together in groups by the use of beams. Naturally, this causes the performer (and the analyst) to consider some pitches (those which seem to be standing at 'stronger' areas) as structurally more important than others, which eventually alters their performance by the use of plectrum (or hammer) strokes.[29] We should keep in mind that in the Cantemir treatise these notes were written with letters with assigned numerals denoting the time unit of each pitch. What we are doing here is posing a question rather than providing an answer: what happens to music as a whole if we leave the notes as they were originally written and do not use beams at all?

Bearing this question in mind, our last example includes three different versions of the same piece, which is titled *"Der makam-ı neva 'Firaknâme' berevşan"* in the Cantemir treatise (Figure 10). The same piece – with the same title – is included in Wright's book as well as Hakan Cevher's, in which it is titled *"Pişrev-i Ali Beğ"*. Similarly to the previous example, Tura's transcription uses quarter notes as the primary rhythmic value, thus there is no use of beams, whereas Cevher and Wright use eighth notes as the primary rhythmic values, and rely on beams in their transcriptions.

29 This may not be the only result if we also consider the possibility of performers interpreting the beamings according to different performance practices and also altering their rhythmic values. To give an example: if such beaming was interpreted according to baroque performance practice, and if the relation of two beamed eighth notes were considered as *notes inégales*, the resulting difference would be even more drastic as the first eighth note –or in baroque terms the 'good' note– would not only be played as if it were more accented, but also significantly longer than the second ('bad') one.

Figure 10: Comparing transcriptions (top to bottom: Tura[30], Cevher[31], Wright[32])

30 Tura 2001b, p. 91.
31 Cevher 2003, p. 425.
32 Wright 1992b, p. 101.

Lastly, we present a cyclical analysis of the piece, based on the version with quarter note values without the use of beams (Figure 11). The cyclical analysis model is constructed by superimposing the two concepts of time on top of each other; that is, by bending the 'linear' time (which is derived from the changes in melodic movement) spirally around a time 'cycle', which is denoted by the reconstructed circular representation of the *usûl berefşân*.[33] The model is advantageous for observing how the two separate layers of melody and *usûl* are interrelated. The upper figure includes the analysis of cycles 1-2 and the lower figure the analysis of 3-4.

Notice how the melodic subblocks a1, a1 and b1 of the first cycle, and c1, c1* and c2 of the second, third and the fourth cycles begin in parallel with the first three *düm* strokes of the *usûl.* On the other hand, the initiation of the melodic subblocks b2 and b3 as seen in the same areas of cycles 1, 2 and 4 do not show such a parallelism with the *düm* strokes, although they appear at exactly the same moments in different cycles. However, recall from our observation of the temporal gesture of *berefşân* that these fall into the areas where there is a significant change in rhythmic activity, more specifically a rise in rhythmic complexity and aperiodicity. Added to this fact, the conflict observed here between the melodic and rhythmic layers results in a rise of musical tension, which is then resolved first by the signal of the last *düm* stroke followed by the whole note *nevâ* (subblock b3) that coincides with *tek.* As we have stated before, the last two beats (*te-ke te-ke*) reinforce the sense of the closing of the *usûl* while also signaling the arrival of the next cycle.

In short, this study has raised some of the questions which are encountered in the processes of transcription, interpretation and analysis of Ottoman *makam* music. We limited our scope to the issue of rhythm, with particular attention given to the elements of *usûl* and *vezin*, and aimed to develop a critical approach by comparing different transcriptions. We pointed out how 'metric' implications may alter the sense of rhythm not only in the *usûl* layer but also in the melodic layer, and most importantly in the total rhythmic activity of the music which is produced by the interaction of both layers. Finally, we proposed an alternative and complementary model of analysis for recognizing how different musical elements interrelate and operate within the music. We believe that such alternative analytical strategies –which take as their basis the representations used in the primary sources– and the aesthetic attitudes reflected in such representations are needed for revealing important events which might have gone unnoticed with current techniques of analysis.

> "Hidden inside the rhythm of music, there is a secret ... the world would turn upside down if I had revealed it..."
>
> Şems

---

[33] The cyclical analysis model is proposed by Ozan Baysal (2011) in the PhD thesis *Phrase Rhythm and Time in Beste-i Kadims: A Cyclical Approach*, supervised by Prof. Dr. Ş. Şehvar Beşiroğlu. See also Baysal, Ozan and Beşiroğlu, Şefika Şehvar 2013, "Uzatma Teorilerinin Makam Musikisine Uygulanabilirliği: Döngüsel bir Analiz Modeli", *Porte Akademik 8 (Müzikolojide Güncel Yaklaşımlar Özel Sayısı)*, 155-168.

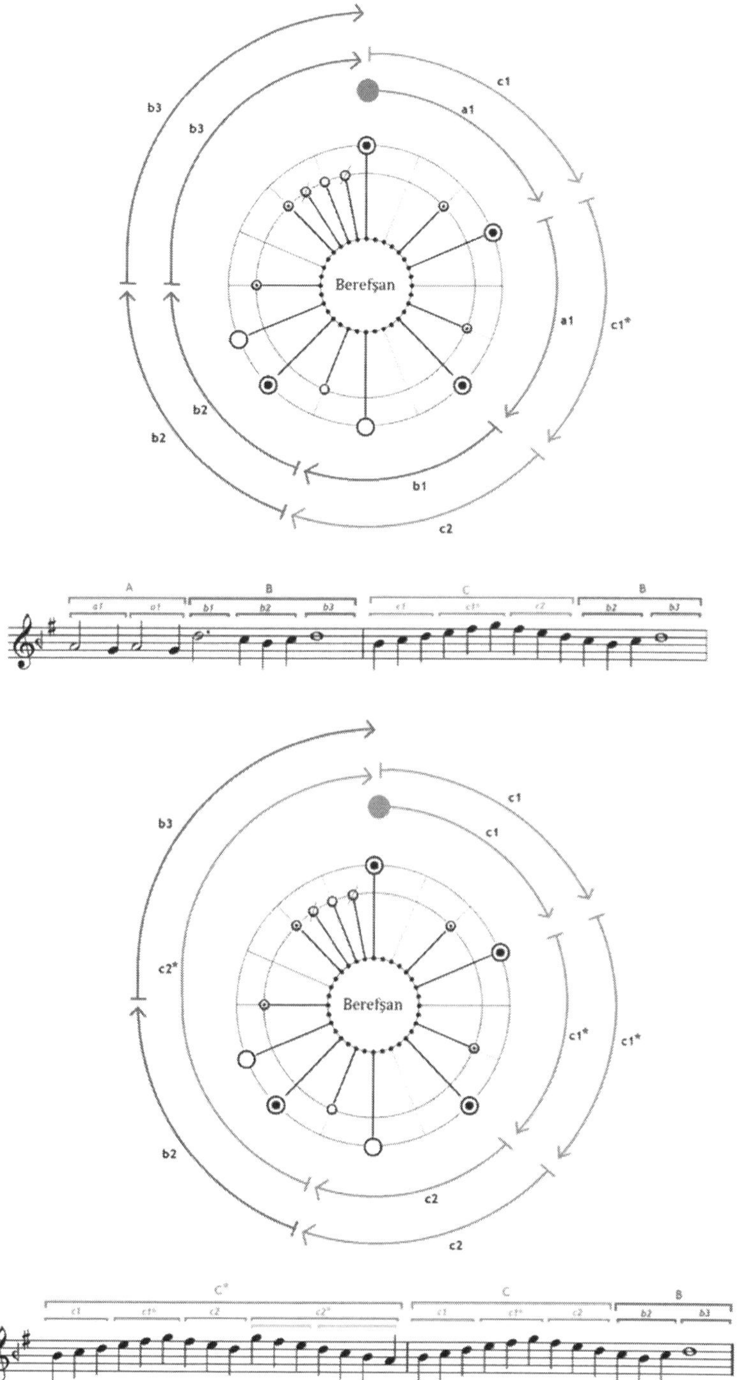

Figure 11: Cyclical analysis of *"Nevâ 'Firâknâme' berefşân"* (opening)

The Role and Importance of Periods in Understanding the *Usûl Hâvî* and *Büyük Usûl* (Large *Usûl*) Structures

Ruhi Ayangil

Introduction

Büyük usûller, literally meaning "large or long rhythmic structures", are well-thought-out combinations of rhythms. These structures are made up of various smaller *usûl* templates, which are added to each other in various ways in time.

As templates, *büyük usûl*s also played very basic and determining role both in composition, shaping and improving the melodic patterns, and in the field of educational (including the *meşk* [Ar. *mashq*] tradition), especially to help convey *makam*ic compositions by heart without the use of notation. In that sense, these structures full of mysteries functioned as a kind of coding system for centuries.

Information about the topics of *makam*ic composition and *usûl* were once termed *ilm-i te'lîf* ("the science of composition") and *ilm-i ika'* ("the science of *usûl*s or rhythms") respectively. So they were created through dynamic interaction in the hands of old masters, and as a result of their creativity, these fields of activity reached quite sophisticated points in the process of historical development.

As far as we know, the old masters used various large *usûl* templates as integrated patterns during their compositional efforts. But, the question of why they preferred some of them to others cannot easily be answered, and the question may take its place amongst the endless enigmas of creativity.

There are more than thirty *usûl* structures including compound cycles (*darbeyn*) which were used in the past, ranging from 16 beats, called *çifte düyek*, to 120 beats, called *zencîr*, which is the last and the longest one. These also continue to be used today in composing purely instrumental pieces, such as *peşrev*s, and some vocal forms, such as the *beste*. The 64-beat *usûl hâvî* is also included amongst them.

In this essay, the role and importance of "rhythmic periods" (with reference to melodic periods) in understanding the *büyük usûl*s will be discussed, and the *usûl hâvî* will be used as an example to explain the subject.

Some Elemental Issues in Regard to Larger Usûl*s*

Kantemiroğlu points out in his treatise that it is extremely difficult to understand and perform the *büyük usûl*s only by reading the meters and the rhythmic cyphers. The author goes on to advise us that *usûl*s need to be implemented with the help of a master, who knows the essence of such matters.[1] So indeed, it is inevitable that one gets into difficulties upon closer inspection of the large *usûl* structures. We must therefore clarify some issues, such as: the philosophy of the design of larger *usûls*, the rudiments of their movements (metronome values), their ratios (time and motion analyses), their components and recording formats, developments in time, structural and contextual changes, differences between their historical and present appearances, the issue of how they were termed. These seem to us to be the points which should be taken into consideration, and which need further explanation.

In the light of these elemental issues, various complexities confronted musicians in the past and they also occupy researchers today. Most of these elemental issues need to be reinterpreted, because several authors, within the frame of same subject, offer us rather different viewpoints.

As a specific example, the *usûl hâvî* is also affected by these difficulties and contains similar problems within itself.

For instance, even though Ali Ufkî recorded the *usûl hâvî* as 16 beats in his manuscript, beginning with Kantemiroğlu, most authors until today state that the *usûl hâvî* is a large 64-beat *usûl*. Successive authors later described the rhythmic values of *hâvî* as 64/2, 64/4, and even 128/4, which differ from each other. Only the following informative words were commonly shared amongst authors, which state that it is a combination of the beats of *hafîf-i sânî*, which means the speed of the *usûl* would be faster in comparison with *hafîf-i evvel*, but *ma non troppo*. Another term which was commonly shared is "*mûtedil*". As the word connotes, the tempo of *hâvî* would not be too fast or too slow, but a moderate speed would be preferred by students and performers.

Historical Context

Accompanying their musical collections, the first examples of *hâvî* may clearly be observed in two manuscripts, which are known as *Mecmu'â-i Sâz ü Söz*[2], written by Ali Ufkî, and *Kitab-ı İlm-i Mûsikî ʿalâ Vech'il Hurûfât*[3], written by Kantemiroğlu. Both can be dated to the mid-seventeenth and early eighteenth centuries.

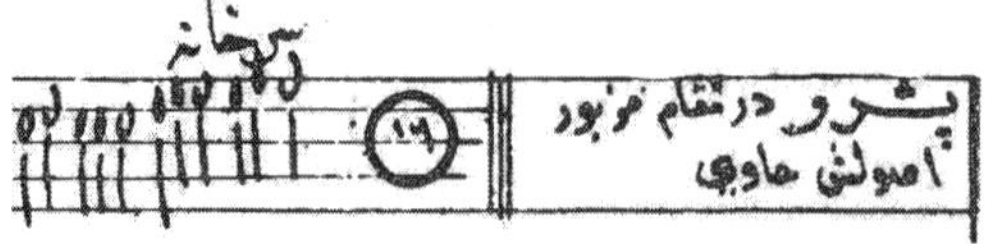

Example 1: *Hâvî usûl* in *Mecmu'â-i Sâz ü Söz*[4]

1 Tura, Yalçın (Ed.) 2001, *Kitābu ʿilmi'l-mūsiḳī ʿalā vechi'l-ḥurūfāt. Mûsikîyi harflerle tesbît ve icrâ ilminin kitabı, I. cilt, Edvâr* (*tıpkıbasım – çevriyazı – çeviri – notlar*), İstanbul: Yapı Kredi Yayınları, p. 161.

2 British Library, MS Sloane 3114.

3 Copy in İstanbul Üniversitesi Nadir Eserler Kütüphanesi, T.Y.1856.

4 British Library, MS Sloane 3114, fol.169r (nr. 358).

Example 2: *Hâvî usûl* in *Kitab-ı İlm-i Mûsikî ʿalâ Vech'il Hurûfât* [5]

When Ali Ufkî's notation is combined with Kantemir's presentation, the structure of *hâvî* can be represented together in a linear notation:

Ali Ufkî ve Kantemir'de Hâvî Usûlü

16/1

Nim Hafif usûlü

Darb-ı Kürdî usûlü

Example 3: *Hâvî usûl* according to Ali Ufkî in MS Sloane 3114 and Kantemiroğlu in T.Y.1856

---

5 İ.Ü. Nadir Eserler Kütüphanesi, T.Y.1856, fol.7r.

Additionally, while Tanbûrî Artin, a musician of the eighteenth century, describes the *usûl hâvî* solely by means of graphic representation, the composer and theoretician Seyyid Abdülbâkî Nâsır Dede does not mention *hâvî* anywhere in *Tedkîk ü Tahkîk*, which is his famous nineteenth-century treatise.

Example 4: *Hâvî usûl* in Tanbûrî Artin's treatise[6] [redesigned by author]

Later, however, Hâşim Bey informs us about the *usûl hâvî* by using circular diagrams within his *Mecmûa*, possibly transferred with some differences from a copy of Kantemiroğlu's treatise.

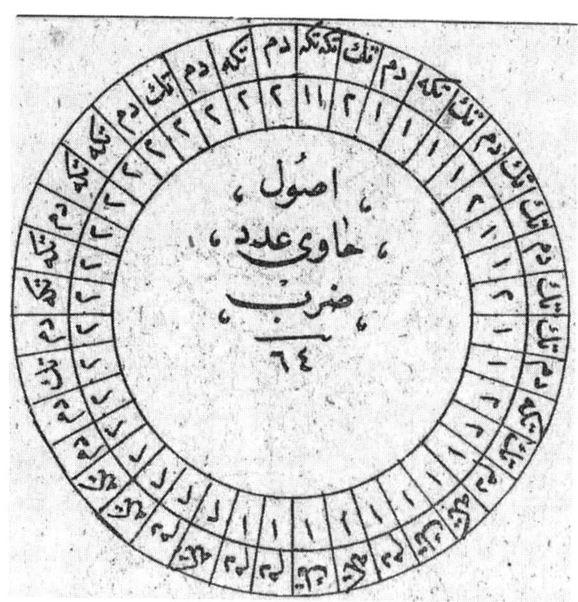

Example 5: *Hâvî usûl* circle in Hâşim Bey's treatise[7]

6 Popescu-Judetz, Eugenia 2002, *Tanburî Küçük Artin: A Musical Treatise of the Eighteenth Century*, İstanbul: Pan Yayıncılık, p. 97.

7 Hâşim Bey, Hacı Mehmed 1280/1864, *Mecmûa-i Kârhâ ve Nakışhâ ve Şarkıyât [Mûsıkî Mecmûası]*, 2nd edition, İstanbul, p. 12.

Apart from these, we find some other new and unique "*usûl terkîbs*", or complex rhythmic combinations created around *hâvî*, which focus our attention on a different matter. These rhythmic experiments most probably were not so much used by musicians, but today they can play a considerable role in making comparisons between the combined *usûls*. However, we learn that *hâvî* is the basic element of these combined structures, while *muhammes*[8] and *ferʿi*[9] constitute their secondary building stones. Despite the fact that this looks like a rather absorbing case, and deserves to have more words devoted to it, it oversteps the limits of this essay.

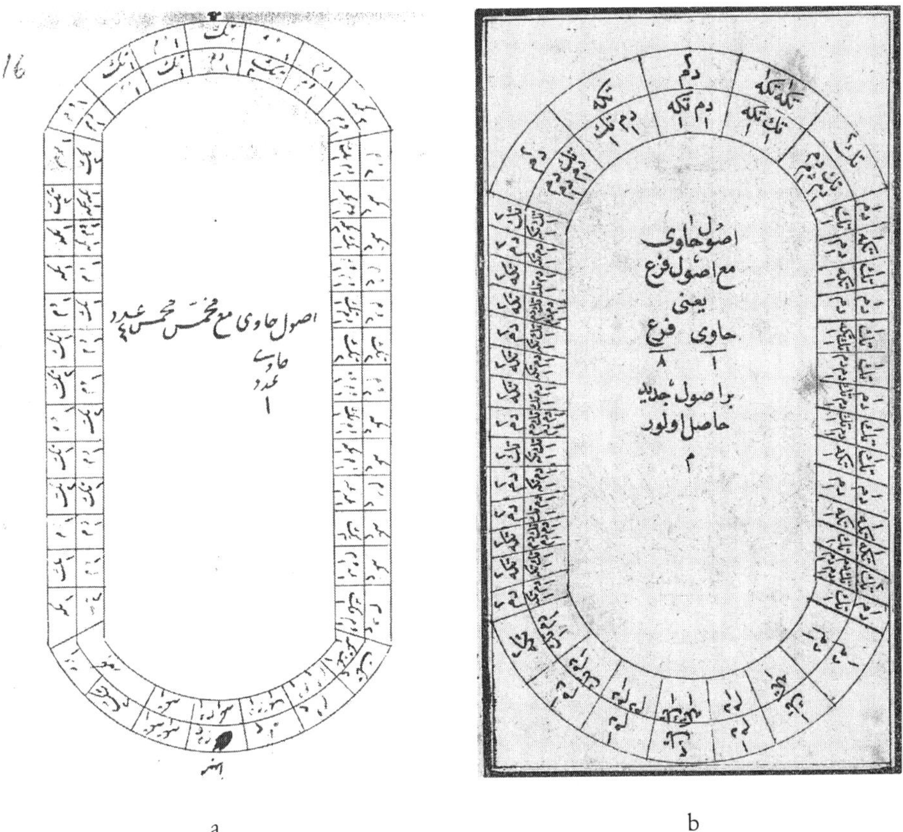

a b

Example 6: *Hâvî usûl* circles with a) *muhammes* (Kantemiroğlu) and b) *ferʿ-i* (Hâşim Bey) *usûls*

8 İ.Ü. Nadir Eserler Kütüphanesi, T.Y.1856, fol.43r.
9 Hâşim Bey 1280/1864, p.16.

Hâvî *in Modern* Usûl *Theory*

The founder of the methodology of modern Turkish *makam* music theory, Raûf Yektâ Bey, at the beginning of the twentieth century, presents the *usûl hâvî* as a large 64-beat *usûl*, which was created by removing some beats from the structure of the even larger *usûl, darb-ı fetih*. To summarise, in Yekta's own words, "This *usûl* is one of the most specific and most difficult *usûl*s of Turkish music. Because its Arabic-derived name literally means 'consisting of', the *usûl hâvî* also consists of some parts of the *usûl darb-ı fetih*, so it is descibed with this name. When 22 beats from the beginning, and two more beats from the middle part, which is 24 beats in total, are removed from the structure of *darb-ı fetih*, the *usûl hâvî* appears."[10] However, he does not express the reasons for this selective organisation; the question may find the an answer only in Yektâ's analytic observations. Yektâ continues: "Due to its difficulty, some beginners cannot perform it properly, and they beat *hafîf* twice, instead of performing the whole structure of *hâvî*. This must never be accepted, because this attitude causes the unique taste of *hâvî* to be lost."[11] Thus the author warns us to reject the inadequate practices of "untrained" performers.

Example 7: *Darb-ı fetih usûl* in Rauf Yektâ's treatise[12] [designed by author]

10 Yektâ, Rauf 1986, *Türk Musikisi*, (trans. Orhan Nasuhioğlu), İstanbul: Pan Yayıncılık, p. 131.
11 Ibid.
12 Ibid., p. 133. The beginning of *hâvî usûl* is marked with "X/ HB".

Rauf Yektâ Bey'de Hâvî Usûlü

Example 8: *Hâvî usûl* in Rauf Yektâ's treatise[13] [designed by author]

Subhî Ezgi is the first theoretician to explain in his treatise large *usûl*s through rather segmented structures, as smaller units of beats or bars, which appear as equal or non-equal sets. The basic approach of this system suggests that the structures of *büyük usûl*s are nothing other than the sum of smaller *usûl* structures. Thus, according to Ezgi's description, *hâvî* is the sum of two times *sofyân*, two times *yürük semâî*, seven times *sofyan*, and one instance of *nîm hafîf*, which also consists of four times *sofyân*. Furthermore, Ezgi also uses only a normal staff and rhythmic syllables to express the whole structure of the *usûl*, instead of using a single-line rhythmic staff.

Subhi Ezgi'de Hâvî Usûlü

[TÜMNE, C II, 165]

Example 9: *Hâvî usûl* in Ezgi's treatise[14] [designed by author]

13 Ibid., p. 131f.

14 Ezgi, Subhi 1935, *Nazarî ve Amelî Türk Mûsikîsi,* vol. II, İstanbul, p. 165.

Although Ezgi and Rauf Yektâ were contemporaries of each other, there are considerable differences between their perceptions of the *usûl hâvî.*

Ezgi ile Yektâ, Konuk, Uz, Ungay - Heper'in Hâvî Usûlü gösterişi ve vuruşu mukayesesi

Example 10: Comparison between Ezgi's and Yektâ's *hâvî usûls*[15] [designed by author]

In summary, Rauf Yektâ is the only person who derives the structure of *hâvî* from within the structure of *darb-ı fetih,* while Ezgi is the first theoretician to call our attention to the smaller elements of large *usûls*. This provides some hints which can be related to the concept of "rhythmic periods".

Dividing the Büyük Usûls *into Periods*

Dividing the *büyük usûls* into periods, as a new viewpoint or approach, helps us to understand and to convey knowledge about the *büyük usûl* structures in detail and in a simpler way. In other words, by referring to symmetrical or non-symmetrical sets of beats within a large *usûl,* we can understand how the structures of large *usûls* are designed, or what kind of relationship exists between rhythmic integrity and melodic creativity.

In addition, among the questions that need to be answered are: how does rhythmic integrity determine the melodic flow? And is there a relationship between melodic and rhythmic periods?

---

15 See footnotes 13 and 14.

Identifying the melodic and rhythmic patterns in any composition may be the easiest approach in order for melodic and rhythmic periods to become visible. For this reason, we have attempted to divide the *usûl hâvî* into periods.

At first glance, it is observed that *hâvî* can be easily divided into two equally combined parts. [CP1] and [CP2] symbolize each equal or symmetrical part of the whole *usûl* structure. Secondly, [CP2] (the second combined part of *hâvî*) can also be further divided into two equal parts, which consist of [CP2]a and [CP2]b. When the division is examined, it is seen that [CP2]b represents the *usûl nîm hafîf*, which is unanimously presented by all authors as the last component of the *usûl hâvi*. When attention is paid to the [CP2]a division, the second half is termed here as the *usûl darb-ı kürdî*, is as it is recorded in the manuscript Y.211/9 in İ.Ü. Nadir Eserler Kütüphanesi. This *usûl* is mostly seen as a final pattern in other large *usûl* structures.

Hâvî Usûlü

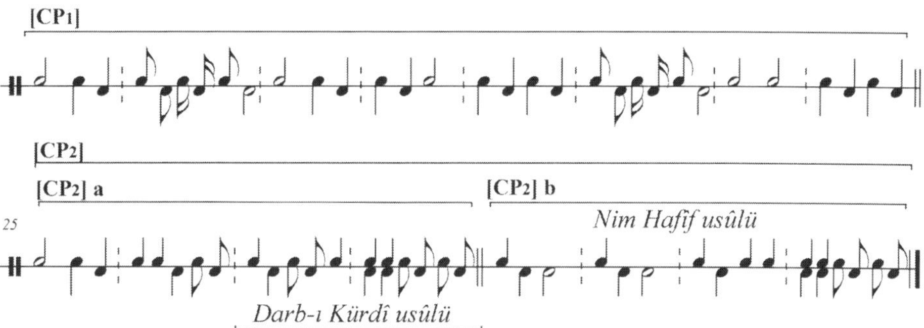

Example 11: *Hâvî usûl* in Ali Ufkî (MS Sloane 3114) and Kantemiroğlu (T.Y.1856) [designed by author]

On the other hand, if we look at the whole of the [CP2]a division, it can be recognized as the second half of the *usûl hafîf*. So the second half [CP2] of *hâvî* is actually an inversion of the *usûl hafîf*.

According to their rhythmic dynamics, the first combined period [CP1] of *hâvî* seems smoother than the second half [CP2], due to its wider distribution of beats. These rhythmic dynamics may be clearly observed in Solakzâde's *acem peşrev* by comparing Ali Ufkî's and Kantemiroğlu's texts, written together below.

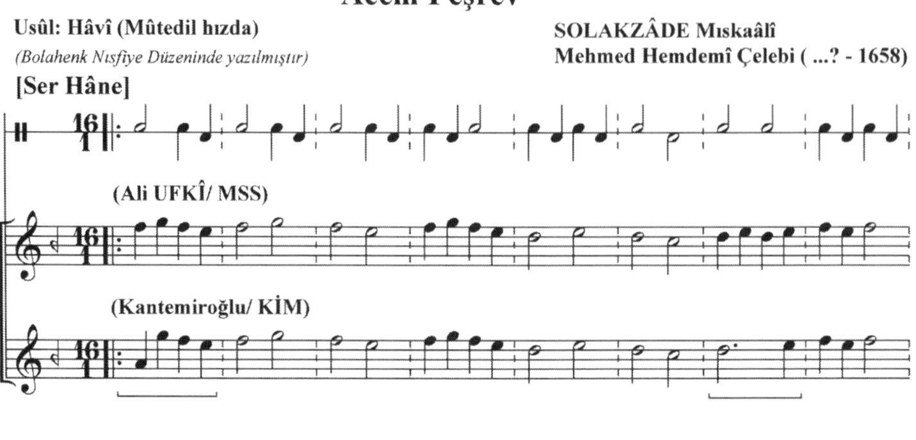

Example 12: Comparison of *acem peşrev* by Solakzâde according to Ali Ufkî[16] and Kantemiroğlu[17] [designed by author]

On the other hand, the relationship between groups of beats and melodic lines may also be examined by a further comparison of the texts, as illustrated below.

As can be seen, not only changes in pitch and note values, but also differentiation in rhythmic dynamics comprising several instances of syncopation in relation to the melodic line indicate subsequent changes in both melodic and rhythmic dimensions. Hence, beginning with the variation of certain groups of beats, until the use of rhythmic syllables and their beat patterns, most of these changes or regulations have reached the present through a historical process. As can be seen in Example 14, changes in the structure of the *usûl hâvî* have occurred in more than ten places during the course of time. However, the other large *usûl* structures also have some similarities with it.

16 British Library, MS Sloane 3114, fol.80v (nr. 153).

17 İ.Ü. Nadir Eserler Kütüphanesi, T.Y.1856, fol.82a.

Example 13: Changes, especially syncopations in Solakzâde, *acem peşrev* according to Ali Ufkî and Kantemiroğlu[18] [designed by author]

[18] See footnotes 16 and 17.

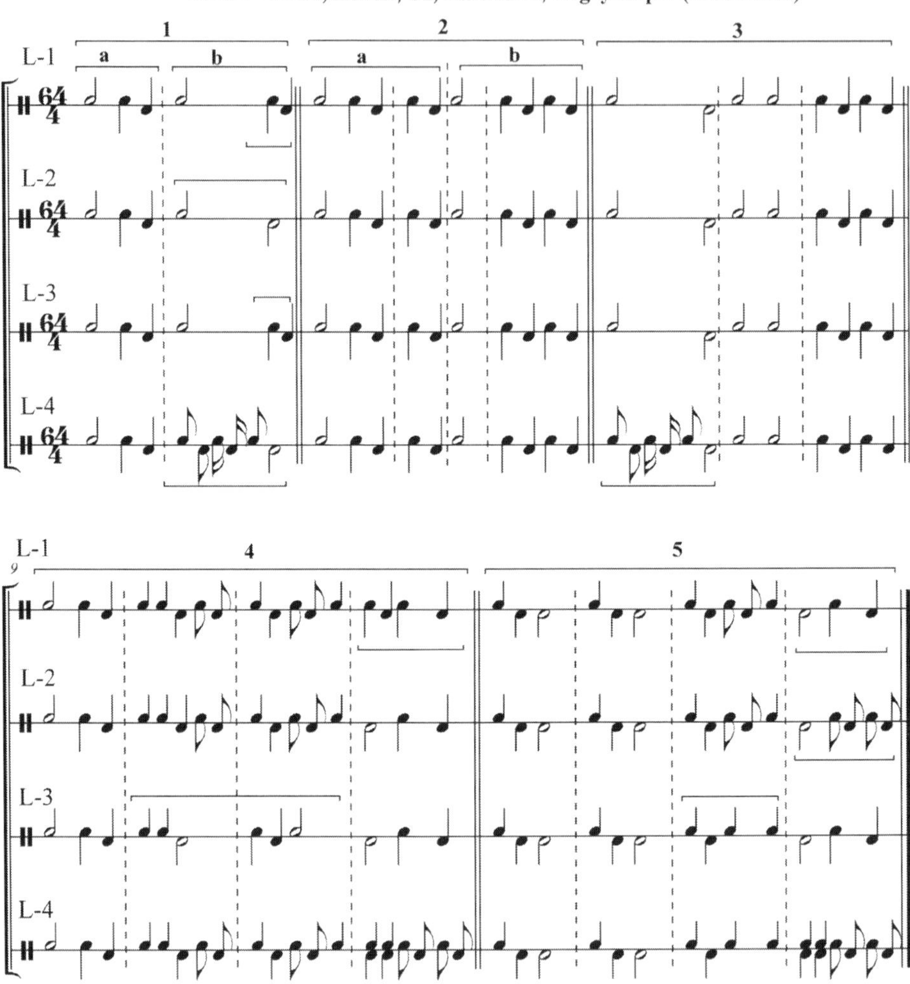

Example 14: *Hâvî usûl*, comparative chart of the periods [designed by author]

As a second stage of periodization, *hâvî* can be divided into smaller symmetrical or non-symmetrical periods. Examining these periods, they appear to be in a striking relationship with the melodic periods. However, although it may not be sufficient to establish a rule, a comparison between the *peşrev*s in *acem* and *bûselik aşîrân* will be enough to lay down some principles about symmetrical and non-symmetrical divisions.

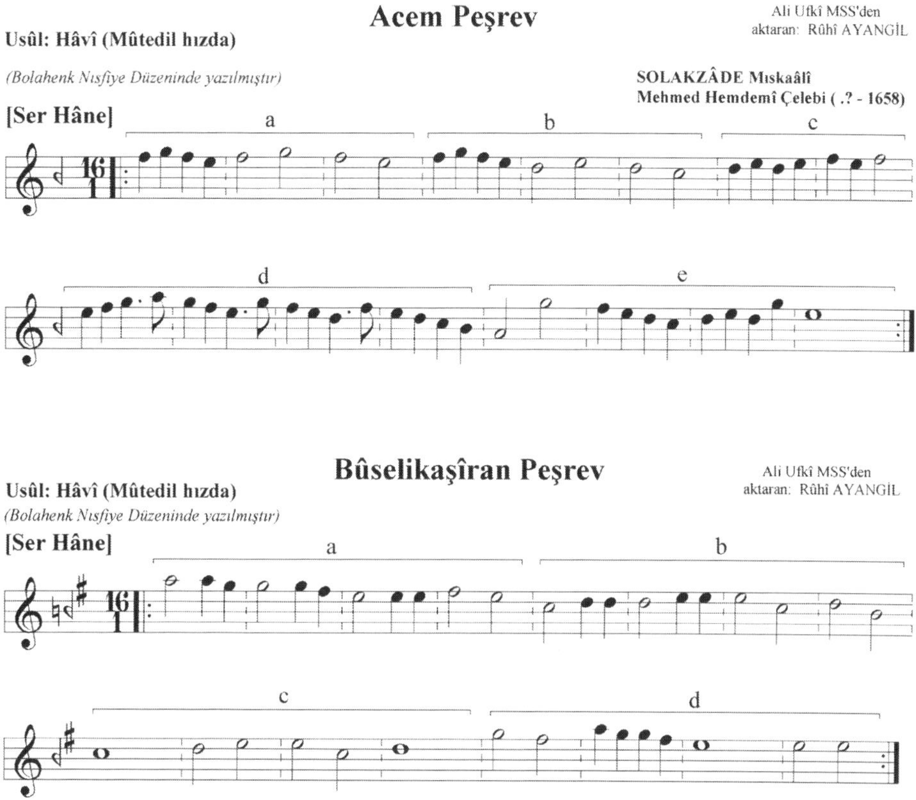

Example 15: Symmetrical and non-symmetrical divisions[19]

Consequently, these sorts of relationships between rhythm and melody or various rhythmic effects can play a role in dividing *büyük usûls* into periods, in different styles. In Example 16, five main divisions of symmetrical or non-symmetrical periods are presented, with the purpose of recognizing the probable rhythmic components of the *usûl hâvî*, which may assist multiple comparisons with melodic periods.

Conclusion

Since Plato and his pupil Aristoxenos, who called rhythm "*kineseos taxis*" ("the order of movement") and "*taxis chronon*" ("the order of time"), most masters from West to East have enthusiastically dedicated themselves to shaping and interpreting the concepts of movement and time throughout the centuries, since the fundamental elements of the science of rhythm (*ilm-i îkâ'*) are movement and time.

[19] British Library, MS Sloane 3114, fol.169r (nr. 358).

Ali Ufkî ve Kantemir'de Hâvî Usûlü

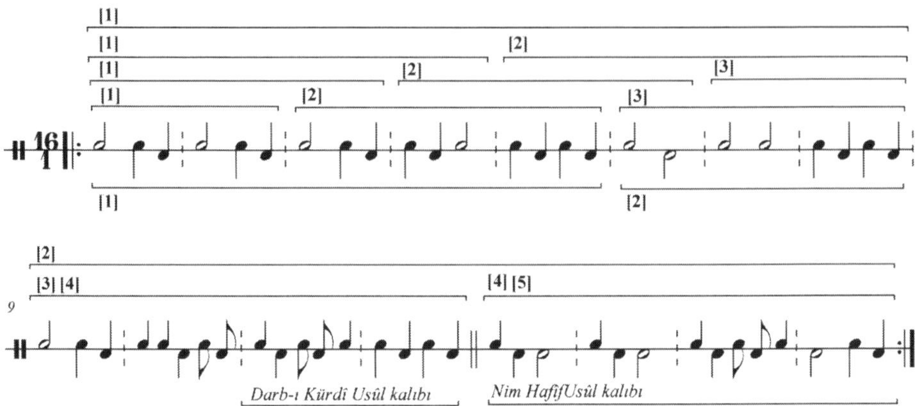

Example 16: Probable rhythmic periods in the *hâvî usûl*

As mentioned before, these complex templates functioned as a sort of coding system for centuries, especially in transferring the corpus of *makam*ic music from generation to generation by heart, due to the lack of any recording method.

At this point it should not be forgotten that even this coding system may become insufficient, as when melodies are forgotten. Because unless melodies are constantly repeated and *usûl*s regularly beaten, poor memorization causes immense losses in the repertory of *makam* music, which has already happened.

However, to be able to comprehend the larger *usûl* structures is not an easy task due to their complexities and ambiguities. Nonetheless, dividing the unified structures into smaller modules such as rhythmic periods, which is applied here to the *usûl hâvî*, implies that these changes will be able to provide us with some inner information, which will help to enlighten the path.

3.
Usûl and Musical Structure

The Art of Melodic Extension Within and Beyond the *Usûl*

Walter Feldman

Makam *and* Usûl

It is generally understood from a variety of Ottoman and modern Turkish sources that a modal system – described in seventeenth-eighteenth century sources as *makam* and *terkib* – and a system of rhythmic cycles – termed either *usûl* or *ika* – form the basis for all urban, and especially all courtly music in Turkey. But we are in a vastly different situation in describing the modal system on the one hand, and the functioning of the rhythmic system, on the other. Whereas from Prince Cantemir onward (ca. 1700), theorists showed great interest in defining final and opening pitches of *makams*, distinctions of primary, secondary or compound modal entities, distinctions of melodic progression (*hareket, seyir*) and – by the late nineteenth century – increasingly fine distinctions among adjacent pitches, the use of modulation etc., in describing *usûl*, the norm in the Ottoman period was simply to state the number of beats and their internal division. Even more recent Turkish theorists have very little to say about the relationship of *usûl* and melody. The reasons for this are not difficult to uncover, but they bring to the fore the limitations in our understanding of how Ottoman compositions were created and taught.

The difference between *makam* and *usûl* in modern Turkey can be seen in the respective positions of the *taksim* – the purest expression of *makam* – and the status of compositions in the long *usûls*, which represent the most developed manifestation of the *usûl* principle. This difference may be correlated in part with the function of notation and transcription in the *taksim*, on the one hand, and compositions in the more complex *usûls*, on the other. The adoption of staff notation for Ottoman music, gradually through the nineteenth century, and definitively by the early twentieth century, did not eliminate the oral creation of *taksim* improvisations. While some musicians (mainly in the post World War II era) created transcriptions of recorded *taksim*s – especially those of Tanburi Cemil Bey (d. 1916) – most serious musicians learned many of these *taksims* by repeated listening to the original recording, rather than from transcriptions. The learning of such a *taksim* by rote was regarded as a pedagogic exercise, not as a new piece that a musician might perform – because, in essence, a *taksim* was an original 'composition.' Unlike the Persian *gushe* or the Azerbaijani *sho'be*, there is no pedagogic model for *taksim* learning. The only model is the melodic progression, the *seyir* of the *makam*. How this learning is accomplished is part of a complex series of 'cues' that an aspiring musician picks up from many sources, including recordings, one or more teacher/models, and some musical theory. But the expression of *usûl* has no such 'pure' manifestation equivalent to the *taksim*. Unlike South Indian musical culture, for example, Turkish classical music has no tradition of solo percussion performances. The *usûl* only exists as a vehicle for a composition. And here the difference between the orality of *taksim* playing and that of the composition of either the courtly instrumental or vocal repertoire makes itself clear.

Two quotations from the eighteenth century address two aspects of the relationship of melody to rhythmic cycle. The first, by Prince Cantemir, speaks of this relationship in composition, while Charles Fonton is describing the role of the performer. Nevertheless I would claim that they are both referring to one musical conception which came to characterize Ottoman music, and underwent particular momentum during the eighteenth century, when both of these writers lived in Turkey.

Cantemir wrote: "because these [*usûls*] are so intricate, those who do not know the meter cannot play the songs at all, even though they were to hear that song a thousand times."[1]

Charles Fonton: "Frequently, however, the great masters among them disguise the meter in its execution such that it is unrecognizable to the others. It is not that they are deviating from it, for they would not be esteemed for that, rather they mix all the embellishments of the Art which go unnoticed by the Common Crowd."[2]

In this quotation Cantemir stresses the intricacy of the *usûl* system, but the implication is that the musical complexity results from the positioning of the melody over this system. Thirty years later, Fonton stresses the freedom that the "great masters" have in emphasizing or de-emphasizing the significant points where melody and "meter" (i.e. *usûl*) interconnect. However, the most recent source research[3] would suggest that Ottoman society always nurtured a variety of musical standards among several social groups and strata, which were probably correlated more with social/economic status than with ethnicity or religion. To put it another way, even within the composed and ultimately courtly repertoire (i.e. apart from rural and avowedly popular urban repertoires), musicians and music-lovers living in varying degrees of social proximity to those musicians who actually performed at and composed for the imperial court had access to more or less current, more or less sophisticated variants of this general courtly repertoire.

During the nineteenth century these musical processes continued until a major bifurcation occurred during the reign of Abdul Hamid II, under whose reign the music of the court received little support, while the more popular versions of

---

1 This statement appeared in his *System of the Mohammedan Religion*, published in Russia in 1722, whose original language may have been Greek. See Popescu-Judetz, Eugenia 1981, "Dimitrie Cantemir's Theory of Turkish Art Music", *Studies in Oriental Arts*, Pittsburgh, 99-170, p. 103.

2 Neubauer, Eckhard 1999, *Der Essai sur la musique orientale von Charles Fonton mit Zeichnungen von Adanson*, Frankfurt: Institute for the History of Arabic-Islamic Science, p. 61.

3 See the chapter in the present volume by Jacob Olley.

courtly music as well as purely popular genres were developed in the newly created *gazino* clubs of Istanbul and other major cities. Among the many musical criteria which distinguished the urban musical sub-styles, the choice of *usûl*/rhythmic cycle, and with it the choice of musical genres, were particularly crucial. Added to this were new developments in musical pedagogy by which purely oral composition and transmission co-existed with several forms of musical notation. Not surprisingly, more popular performance venues discouraged the use of the genres requiring long and complex *usûls*. The conservative 'reaction' among the musicians of the elite social groups, led by Rauf Yekta Bey and a number of other musicians, also saw the need for Western notation as a means to preserve and fix the compositions of the past. But even such a conservative master as Rauf Yekta still used simple 4/4 bar lines when writing complex *usûls*, in which the compositional unit was usually not 4/4. This was apparently an inheritance of earlier usage of staff notation from the time of Donizetti Pasha at the Ottoman court (beginning in 1828) and became solidified in the many popular publications of Ottoman music that appeared in the later nineteenth century. Thus, this kind of notational convention worked against the oral learning of the *usûls* with their melodies in *peşrevs* or *bestes*.

After a generation of official neglect and even discouragement during the Republic – in which the older courtly genres were preserved through private social gatherings and "*meşk*" – the revived 'classical' performances, particularly of Mesut Cemil on the radio, emphasized choral performance of the vocal repertoire, and deemphasized the percussion accompaniment to the *usûl*. The combination of declining visibility of the Ottoman courtly repertoire, increasing reliance on notation in pedagogy, and the widespread lack of familiarity with the relationship between percussion, *usûl* and melodic structure, has rendered a structural understanding of the role of *usûl* a fragile and obscure musical technique. Already by the turn of the century the vast majority of new vocal pieces were in the much simpler *şarkı* form, for which there was a public. After World War I rather few vocal compositions utilizing the long *usûls* were being created.

Especially since the further developments of choral performance under the State Turkish Music Chorus under Dr. Nevzad Atlığ in the 1960s the musical 'gestures' implicit within Ottoman vocal compositions have been accentuated, often obscuring any relationship with *usûl* structures. Since the late 1980s this has also led to a 'reaction' among tradition-conscious musicians to reinstate percussion, but by this late date often without much command of the *usûl* melodic relations as they had been understood by earlier Ottoman composers.

When we examine the nature of this relationship of melody and *usûl*, many of these musical 'gestures' reveal a conflict between musical phrase and formal rhythmic structure. This in itself was apparently the product of a long internal development within Ottoman music, reaching back to the beginning of the continuous creation of this music from the last third of the seventeenth century. The extent to which this internal development also implied a shared history with the post-Byzantine chant of the same period (which has no codified *usûl* system or percussion) is at present a moot point, which may perhaps be integrated at a later stage of analysis. Lacking contemporary notations for most of the vocal courtly repertoire, even the form (or variant forms) in which they were written in the early twentieth century – or at times somewhat earlier – coupled with the various records of the older instrumental repertoire in the long *usûls*, provide ample material with which to assess how such musical issues were dealt with, at least since the second half of the eighteenth century, when the current forms of the long *usûls* had crystallized.

Due to the lateness of most notated sources for the vocal repertoire, we cannot be certain of the attributions of particular musical details, or even entire pieces, to the composer whose name they bear. This is particularly true of early "masters" such as Buhurizade Itri (d. 1712). While many compositions survive in a single primary version (which is republished in many later sources with minor variants), others have more than one 'primary' source. A comparison of compositions ostensibly dating from the middle of the eighteenth century with those of the late eighteenth or the nineteenth century frequently reveal characteristic stylistic differences in the relation of *usûl* and melody that implies an evolution within the later pieces.

As a first step in stating the problem, two issues need to be addressed briefly. One is the relationship between long and short *usûls*, and the second is the relationship between melody and prosodic structures within vocal genres.

For the first question, we can state that there is an obvious tendency for items in the short *usûls* – e.g. *sofyan*, *düyek*, *semai*, *aksak semai*, *aksak* – to display a high degree of congruence between *usûl* and melody, in keeping with the ultimately dance-derived nature of these *usûls*. But even here we may note a frequent lack of total correspondence, especially in vocal items in *aksak semai*. In addition the "heavy" (*ağır*) forms of these *usûls* usually bring with them a radically different approach to this correspondence, in effect forming a separate category from both the short and the long *usûls*. The long *usûls* – beginning with *fahte* in 20 beats – function along very different principles from the short ones, which we will pursue at some length below. The *usûl evsat* in 26/8, true to its name ("intermediary"), functions a bit like both types of *usûl*.

The vocal genres using the short *usûls* – both within the secular and the *Mevlevi* repertoires – reveal a degree of awareness of the long and short patterns of the *aruz* prosodic system of Ottoman and Persian poetry. Since the *Mevlevi ayin* has retained the older *usûl* patterns *devr-i revan* (14/8), *düyek* (8/8), *evfer* (9/4) and *semai* (6/8), connections with the *aruz* may be found. This is less important in the third *selam* sections, which are usually in the newer form of *devr-i kebir* (28/4).[4] Ottoman

4 See Feldman, Walter 2001, "Structure and Evolution of the Mevlevi Ayin: the Case of the Third Selam", in: *Sufism, Music and Society in Turkey and the Middle East*, Hammarlund, Olson and Özdalga, (Ed.), Istanbul: Swedish Research Institute, 49-65.

theoretical writers from Cantemir to Rauf Yekta Bey never point to the *aruz* of poetry as having any special relevance to the vocal repertoire. It is only when the functioning of the *usûl* system was forgotten in post 1970s Turkey that this argument was put forth at all.[5] In the secular *fasıl* forms we do not find a determining influence of the *aruz* upon melody. Rather, there is a basic practice of avoiding longer musical notes corresponding to short prosodic syllables. But similar placement of syllables may be found also in the rural *âşık* music, whose texts are often in *hece vezni* – the indigenous Turkic syllabic meter, rather than *aruz* prosody. Our first vocal example below, composed by İbrahim Ağa (d. ca. 1740), to a text by the *âşık* Karacaoğlan, exemplifies this possibility.

This connection of prosody and rhythmic cycle even becomes weaker in the "heavy" (*ağır*) forms of the *usûls*, such as *ağır aksak* in 9/4 and *ağır aksak semai* in 10/4. With the long *usûls* found in the *beste*, *kar* and *nakış* forms, this influence is nonexistent. It is instructive to recall that the model for the creation of current courtly forms *beste* and *nakış* were the *peşrevs* which had retained the use of the long *usûls* even after they had been dropped from the vocal repertoire of the first half of the seventeenth century. Beginning in the last third of the seventeenth century, the courtly vocal repertoire was developed both through the 'recreation' of the Iranian *kar* form and the rapid evolution of the folkloric *murabba* songs as the new *murabba beste*, utilizing only long *usûls*.[6]

Terkib, Seyir *and* Usûl

In my earlier work on the instrumental repertoire of the seventeenth and early eighteenth century[7], I pointed out the conditions that led to the abandonment of the older system of discrete melodic sections, known as the *terkib*. In the seventeenth century each *hane* of a *peşrev* might contain several *terkibs*. Gradually, it would seem, from the middle to the last third of the eighteenth century this technique was abandoned in favor of a single flowing melody for each *hane*. It does not seem that the *terkib* was ever in use for the new courtly vocal repertoire of the eighteenth century, but most documents are lacking. I surmised that this formal change was caused primarily by the development of melodic progression (*seyir*), which demanded that each formal section of a composition express a sig-

5 See on this question Aksoy, Bülent 2008b, "Fasıl Musikisi Divan Edebiyatının Musikisi Midir?", in: *Geçmişin Musiki Mirasına Bakışlar*, Bülent Aksoy (Ed.), Istanbul: Pan Yayıncılık, 17-35.

6 See the argument in Feldman, Walter 2015, "The Musical 'Renaissance' of Late Seventeenth Century Ottoman Turkey: Reflections on the Musical Materials of Ali Ufki Bey (ca. 1610-1675), Hafiz Post (d. 1694) and the 'Maraghi' Repertoire", in: *Writing the History of "Ottoman Music"*, Martin Greve (Ed.), Istanbuler Texte und Studien, Würzburg: Ergon.

7 Feldman, Walter 1996, *Music of the Ottoman court: makam, composition and the early Ottoman instrumental repertoire*, Intercultural Music Studies 10, Berlin: VWB Verlag für Wissenschaft und Bildung, pp. 336-338.

nificant part of the *seyir*. This helped to render the division into *terkibs* irrelevant, as these *terkibs* were often paratactic, and did not imply a melodic progression. In the *peşrev* repertoire created until the late seventeenth century the essential pitches of the melody had to fall on the basic strokes of the *usûl* cycle, imparting a dance-like quality to most pieces, even to the long compound cycle *zencir*, which then had five *usûls*, resulting in a total of 60 beats. The main exception to this rule were the *peşrevs* in the longest *usûls*, especially *darb-ı fetih* in 88 beats, and to some degree the *peşrevs* in *sakil* in 48 beats. As I had demonstrated in my analysis of the single fragment of a *peşrev* in *sakil* by Itri (d. 1712), we can see the early stages of the spreading of melodic material rather unevenly over the beats of the *usûl*, giving the impression of a high degree of independence of melodic development and rhythmic cycle.[8]

Thus it would seem that the other major cause for the loss of the *terkib* concept was the change in the *usûl* system, which had already been demonstrated by Owen Wright in 1988, and all subsequent serious work on this topic. In the chapter within his "*Edvar*", "Introduction to the Science of the Letters of Music" (1700), Cantemir already refers to this new practice by noting that certain pieces were meant to be performed at a slower overall tempo. In fact he devised a separate system of notation – which he called "the smallest of the small meter" (*asğar-ı sağir vezni*): "the reason for this is that the meter of the *usûl* in some *terkibs* is taken very slowly".[9]

During the course of the eighteenth century, most *peşrevs* – and we must assume most of the *murabba bestes*, which used the same *usûls* – became increasingly slow and ponderous in performance. In time this led to the Ottoman expression "*aheste beste*" ("slow [as a] *beste*"). As Wright had shown in 1988, this rhythmic 'retardation' had as its corollary melodic 'elaboration', as there was now much more 'space' for the melody to fill. With the increasing number of notes now in use within each cycle (*devir*) of the *usûl*, new questions arose as to how these pitches should relate to the beats of the *usûl*. During the course of the eighteenth century this concept developed rapidly, and – even given the lateness of our notated documents – it would appear that each generation witnessed new experiments in this direction. These culminated in the practices enshrined, as it were, in the better preserved repertoires of the great Ottoman composers of the late eighteenth and nineteenth centuries, such as Tanburi İsak, Zeki Mehmed Ağa, İsmail Dede Efendi, Delalzade, or Zekai Dede. By this time (and even somewhat earlier) the melodic 'gestures' frequently overwhelmed the ostensible *usûl* structures that theoretically supported them. Only a careful analysis of a wide corpus of this repertoire, including both comparisons of usages within the same *usûl*, and the usages of individual compos-

8 Feldman, Walter (forthcoming), "Itri's 'Nühüft Sakil' in the Context of Ottoman Peşrevs of the Seventeenth Century", in: *Tuning the Past: Theory and Practice in the Music of the Islamic World*, Rachel Harris and Martin Stokes (Ed.), SOAS Musicology Series, Farnham: Ashgate.

9 See Feldman 1996, p.333.

ers (when the corpus may be judged at least partly reliable), can lead us to a better understanding of the compositional process that had resulted in this complex but still orally composed and transmitted courtly music.

Usûl *in Practice*

The best way to demonstrate the kinds of issues and questions presented by the existing Ottoman musical corpus is to analyze a few examples from the mid-eighteenth to the mid-nineteenth century. In the space available this can only be a short survey of different vocal and instrumental genres, utilizing a few of the short, 'medium' and long *usûls*. Such a brief analysis cannot be regarded as in any way authoritative but only points the way to tackling the problem with the use of a much larger corpus of material.

Aksak semai (10/8)

The most common short *usûl* in the Ottoman courtly *fasıl* is *aksak semai* in 10/8 – it appears twice, in the vocal *ağır semai* and in the instrumental *saz semai*. In the *ağır semai* it may also employ the "heavy" variant *ağır aksak semai* in 10/4. Even in this short pattern, Ottoman composers tried to achieve a mixture of melodic/ rhythmic correspondence and patterns of enjambment, similar to what they created in the medium and long *usûls*. These 'enjambments' are much more common in the vocal *ağır semai*, but may also make an appearance in the *saz semai*. Perhaps the locus classicus is the famous *Uşşak Semaisi* by the *Mevlevi* Neyzen Salih Dede (d. 1888). The function of the *saz semaisi* as the 'finale' of the courtly *fasıl* suite seems to have suggested a more regular connection between *usûl* and melodic 'downbeat'. But this particular item demonstrates a complexity that is more typical of other genres of the repertoire, and appears less frequently in this function.

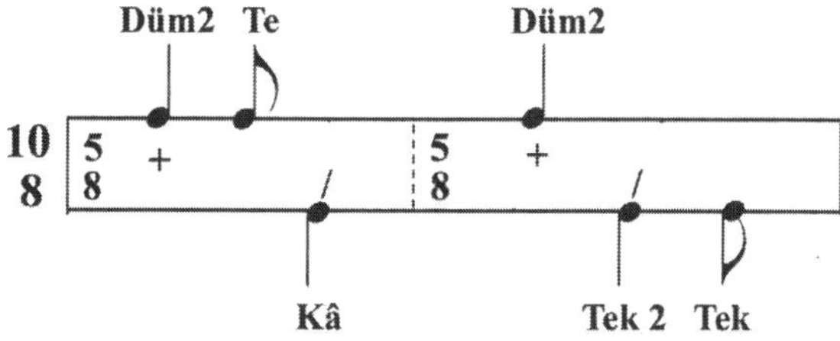

Chart 1: *Usûl aksak semai*[10]

[10] Özkan, İsmail Hakkı 2011, *Türk Musikisi Nazariyatı ve Usûlleri: Kudüm Velveleleri*, Istanbul: Ötüken, p. 661.

Ex. 1: *Uşşak Saz Semaisi*, Salih Dede.[11]

[11] Atlığ, Nevzad 1988, *Türk Musikîsi Klasikleri*, Yıl 2, Cilt 2, Sayı 8, Istanbul: Türk Dünyası Araştırmaları Vakfı, pp. 252-253.

(Ex. 1: *Uşşak Saz Semaisi*, Salih Dede.)

In the first two measures of *hane* 1 the composer confines his melody to a single *devir* (cycle) of the *usûl.* Thus the first measure reposes on G (the subtonic), while the second closes on A, the finalis. There is either a held note or a one-eighth rest at the end of each measure. Thus far we have a symmetrical antecedent/consequent structure, which, apart from the exotic 10/8 time signature and the *uşşak* modality, would appear quite European. But for the remainder of the first *hane*, the *teslim*, and the second and third *hanes*, we will leave this symmetry behind.

Measures 3 and 4 are almost variants of one another (dropping one pitch for measure 4), but the melody of measure 3 actually ends on the note c at the beginning of measure 4. Measure 4 does indeed come to an end on the tenth beat of that measure, but on the note B, the second degree of the *makam*, and hence a "suspended cadence" (*asma karar*). The following measure 5 shows a different melodic contour, but still concludes on the identical suspended cadence. Measure 6 repeats measure 4 almost verbatim, but it concludes on the *karar* A. If the measure had ended here we could have seen it as the consequent of measure 5. But instead it uses its final eighth note to leap up to the upper tonic (a), and creates a descending sequence within the upcoming *teslim* section, which only concludes in the middle of the second measure of the *teslim*, but on the suspended cadence B. This behavior is repeated in measures 2 and 3, with a ten-beat melody beginning on beat 5 of measure 2, and continuing into beat 5 or measure 3, ending on the dominant d. A new descending sequence now commences, until the end of the *teslim* in the following measure. We can follow the second and third *hanes*, and observe similar compositional techniques utilizing the lower and then the higher domains of the *makam* (in *hanes* 2 and 3 respectively). Symmetry only returns with the switch to the *usûl sengin semai* (6/4) in *hane* 4.

A generation or more earlier Sadullah Ağa utilized somewhat similar techniques in his *Ağır Semai* in *muhayyer*.

The first enjambment commences even before the first *düm* of the *usûl* cycle. The first syllable of "*hal*" is sung on the upper tonic (a) on what would be the last three beats of the previous *usûl* cycle. The drumming would commence on the second syllable of the text ("*li*"). Thus measure 1 has an 'extra' three beats (eighth notes). *Hane* 2 begins and ends on the note d. But its real function is an 'introduction' to measure 3, which extends into the opening three beats of measure 4. With the fourth beat of this measure a new melody appears, based on the upper octave of the basic *makam muhayyer*, and ending on the note a (*muhayyer*), extended into the next measure. The *zemin* melody ends on the note a ("*vay*") in the middle of the last cycle; the remaining beats are covered by an instrumental break (marked "*saz*"). The first syllable of the *terennüm* ("*ca–*") begins before the *usûl* cycle of the *terennüm* has actually been introduced – reproducing exactly the technique seen in the opening notes of the *zemin*. The *terrenüm* and the *miyan* sections of the piece reproduce similar techniques of cutting the basic *usûl* in two, and allowing a melody to commence somewhere in the 10 beat cycle and conclude at some other point toward the beginning or the middle of the succeeding 10 beat cycle. The main difference between the *miyan* and the *terennüm* is the use of the upper octave in the former, and descending melodies within the basic octave of the *makam* for the latter.

It is intriguing to note that the musical technique of starting the melody *qabl* ("before"), *maᶜ* ("with") or *baᶜd* ("after") – the first meaning "starting the composition before the beginning of the cycle, with the first attack (*iqaᶜ*) of the cycle"[12], evidently had existed in the Islamic art musics of the fourteenth century, as it was cited by both Maraghi and Ibn Kurr in Egypt.[13] But, as both Wright and the present author have attempted to prove, most of the courtly vocal repertoire utilizing complex *usûls* had been lost between the later sixteenth and later seventeenth centuries in both Safavid Iran and Ottoman Turkey.[14] Whether this technique was

---

12 Wright, Owen 2014, *Music theory in Mamluk Cairo. The ġāyat al-maṭlūb fī ᶜilm al-anġām wa-'l-ḍurūb by Ibn Kurr*, Farnham: Ashgate, p. 107.

13 Ibid.

14 Wright, Owen 1992, *Words Without Songs: A Musicological Study of an Early Ottoman Anthology and Its Precursors*, London: SOAS (SOAS Musicology Series, vol. 3) and Feldman (forthcoming).

Ex. 2: *Muhayyer Ağır Semai*, "*Hal-i Siyahi*" by Sadullah Ağa, *zemin* and *terennüm*.[15]

15 Ömürlü, Yusuf, *Türk Mûsıkîsi Klâsikleri: Muhayyer Makamı*, Cilt 9, No. 103, Istanbul: Kubbealtı Mûsıkî Enstitüsü.

simply reinvented in the later eighteenth century in Istanbul, or whether some earlier 'classic' examples had indeed been preserved – perhaps in the peripheral Safavid courts, as suggested by Pourjavadiy[16] – is impossible to determine.

Evsat (26/8)

As a medium-length usual we may take *evsat*, with 26 beats, written today either in eighth or in quarter notes. The grouping of beats in *evsat* is as follows:

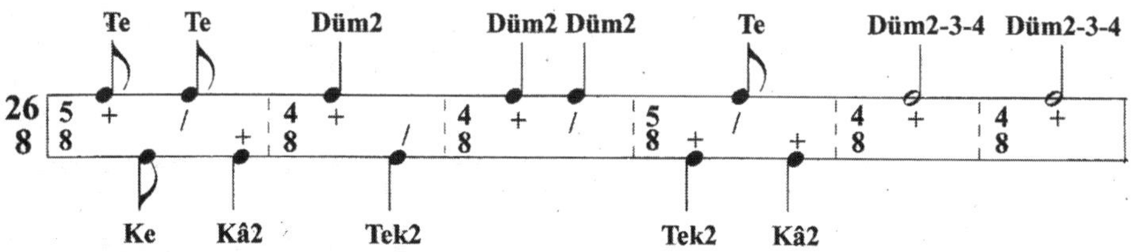

Chart 2: *Usûl Evsat* [17]

We see that the *usûl* is constructed of a unit of 5 beats, followed by two units of 4; this pattern is then repeated, giving two units of 13 beats, totaling 26. Thus a complete cycle of the *usûl* is constructed 5+4+4/5+4+4. *Evsat* is used for *şarkı* and also for the Sufi hymn termed *tevsih*. Let us look a *şarkı* in *makam mahur*, *usûl evsat*, by the mid-eighteenth century composer İbrahim Ağa.

The text of this song is taken from the *âşık* (folk bard) Karacaoğlan, and is written in the folk prosody of 11 syllables in two stanzas of five lines each; thus any reference to the metrics of classical *aruz* is rendered irrelevant. The melody repeats after two lines of the poetry, and so we have selected just these two lines and their melody:

Sabah olsun ben şu yerden gideyim
Garip bülbül gibi feryad edeyim

Let the dawn come and let me leave this place
Let me lament like a lonely nightingale

The entire melody is composed of four *usûl* cycles, totaling 104 beats, or 24 measures of the transcription. On the broadest level there are two large melodies, each comprising two *usûl* cycles, or 12 measures; on the transcription the first is marked I and the second II. On the simplest level – ignoring microtonal differences for the moment – *mahur* is the descending cousin of the *makam rast*. Both

16 Pourjavadiy, Amir Hosein 2005, *The Musical Treatise of Amir Khan Gorji (c. 1108/1697)*, Ph.D. Dissertation, University of California, Los Angeles.
17 Özkan 2011, p. 742.

Ex. 3: *Mahur Şarkı*, "*Sabah olsun ben şu yerden gideyim*" by İbrahim Ağa.[18]

have the note G (*rast*) as finalis, but *mahur* reaches this G by a long descent beginning at its octave g (*gerdaniye*). Within the two large melodies of this *şarkı* the first (I) both begins and ends on *gerdaniye*, while the second (II) shows *gerdaniye* briefly before beginning its long descent, which gradually will take it to *rast*. This much is standard for melodies in *mahur*. Melody I concludes neatly with a quarter note on g. But within both melody I and melody II the rule is for the final notes of both the half cycle and of the end of the full cycle to be extended into the beginning of the next cycle. Likewise the final cadence will begin at the end of the final measure in 4/8 of the previous half cycle. We will explain this in more detail below.

What we might term the final cadence of this song appears in two melodically nearly identical forms, but in transposition: in melody I, beginning in measures 8 and 9 starting with a leap from g to c, and in melody II, measures 8 and 9,

18 İstanbul Belediye Konservatuvarı, *Türk Musikisi Klasiklerinden: Mahur Faslı*, No: 6, Istanbul, 1954b, p. 92. The missing 5th barline in the second (II) section was added by the author.

leaping from G to C. The text has the linguistically corresponding forms: *aman gideyim canım* (I) and *aman edeyim canım* (I), ("mercy, let me go, oh my soul!"; "mercy, let me do [lament]! Oh my soul!"). Both of these melodies begin with the word "*aman*" on the last sixteenth note of the second measure of 4/8 in the half-cycle, and then go on into the next 4/8 measure. These cadential melodies are virtually mirror images of one another; where the cadence of I uses ascending phrases toward the conclusion on g, the cadence in II uses descending phrases as it approaches the finalis G. Both the first and second parts of melody I and the corresponding parts of melody II employ identical rhythmic figures.

But in *usûl evsat* this enjambment sometimes also corresponds to drum strokes within the *usûl.* Thus the first musical half-line, using the words "*Ah sabah olsun*" ("Ah let it be dawn!") extends over the first half-cycle (5+4+4) until the first note g held for one quarter note (i.e. 2 eighth notes) of the next half cycle (beginning with 5/8). The following words "*ben şu*" (d-g) take up the remaining 3 eighth notes of the 5/8 measure. Thus the internal rhythmic asymmetry of the component sections is placed within the firm architectonic symmetry of the entire song.

Zencir (120/4)

For the purposes of this short survey we will skip from the 'medium' length *usûl evsat* to the longest *usûl* in Ottoman music, the compound *usûl* known as "the chain" (*zencir*). As the chart below demonstrates, this is composed of five *usûls*, as follows:

1. *çifte düyek* (16/4)
2. *fahte* (20/4)
3. *çenber* (24/4)
4. *devr-i kebir* (28/4)
5. *berefşan* (32/4)

Heuristically, by moving to this compound *usûl* we can see something of the functioning of each of these *usûls*, and how they function together in a unified composition. As our single example we will take the *beste* in *makam sazkar* by Tabi Mustafa Efendi (d. ca. 1770), a *sermüezzin* and one of the major composers of the mid-eighteenth century. This is a relatively early example, and it allows us to view a rather 'archetypical' method of handling *usûl* and melody in *zencir.* Already in the following generation, with the *Gülizar Zencir Beste* by Tanburi İsak (d. 1814) we can see significantly more complex handling of the *usûl*/melodic relations. *Bestes* in *usûl zencir* furnish a very rich body of material, as most of the existing *makams* in Ottoman music feature one or more *bestes* in this compound *usûl.* This shows that it was not considered a rarity but rather a fairly common choice for the opening *beste* of the courtly *fasıl.*

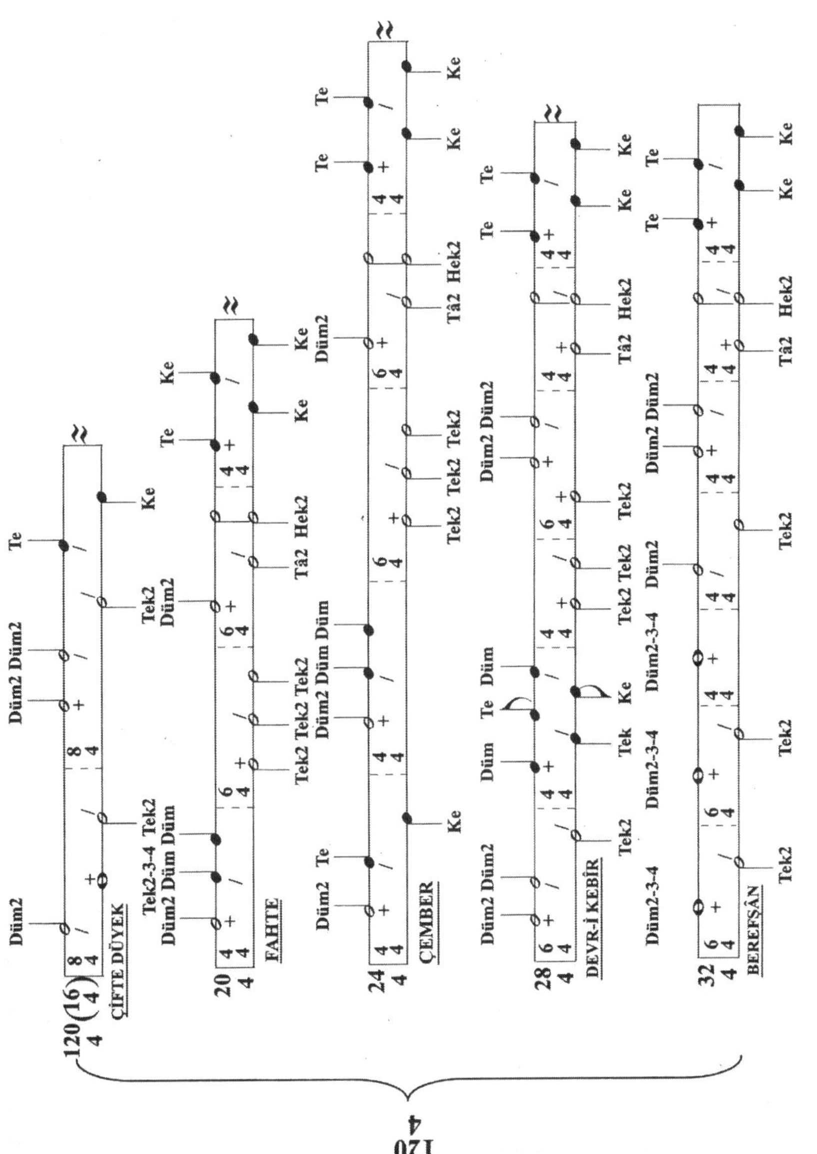

Chart 3: *Usûl Zencir*[19]

19 Özkan 2011, p. 797.

In the eighteenth century *sazkar* was regarded as a *terkib* modal entity, subordinated to *makam rast* (finalis G) but also including the *makam segah* (finalis B). The most complete and relevant description of *sazkar* was written by Kemani Hızır Ağa, a court musician who was an older contemporary of Tabi Mustafa (somewhat before 1749). It is worth quoting this description because the shifting tonal centers of this *terkib* align to a great extent with the principal subdivisions of the *usûl*, or at least help to determine how this melodic/rhythmic alignment was perceived:

> "*Sazkar* is that which commences from *dügah* [A] and demonstrates *segah* [B], and then the secondary scale degree (*nim*) between *segah* and the scale-degree *buselik* [B], and from that secondary scale degree it demonstrates *neva* [d] and *hüseyni* [e], and returning from *hüseyni* it demonstrates the aforementioned secondary scale degree and then demonstrates *segah* and *dügah* and *rast* and *aşiran* [E], and from *aşiran* it demonstrates *ırak* [F#] and *rast* [G] and *dügah* [A] and from *segah* it concludes upon *rast* without [touching] *dügah*."[20]

This *beste* by Tabi Mustafa exemplifies the melodic progression (*seyir*) of *sazkar* as given by Hızır Ağa. Even the *terennüm* and *miyan* sections, where by later generations modulations might be expected, maintain the same basic *seyir*. The piece as we have it features a passing 'modulation' to *araban* (today with the intonation of *hüzzam*) in the *çenber* portion. Likewise *dügah* is often raised by a half-step to A#, which is not mentioned by Hızır Ağa and may well not have been the practice in his generation. There are periodic fluctuations between f# and f natural in the upper tetrachord, as might be expected for both *rast* and *segah*. Hızır Ağa stresses the alternation of the pitch then called "*segah*" and one somewhat higher, which is now termed "*segah*," as the *segah* note of the earlier eighteenth century was closer to the note named "*uşşak*" in modern Turkish music.[21]

Below is the 'standard' notation for this *Sazkar Beste*, with the corresponding basic *usûl* pattern written below, and aligned with each section of the melody.[22]

This is indeed an elegant and much admired part of the Ottoman vocal repertoire. Let us briefly view the interrelations of mode, melody and *usûl*. Within the rhythmic compound of *zencir*, several of the constituent melodies appear to function independently within the boundaries of the *usûl*, while others 'bleed', as it were, into the following *usûl* section. In general the correspondence of 'downbeats' of the melody with the basic strokes of the *usûl* are intermittent, with occasional placing of the heavy "*düm*" stroke under a rest ("*es*") in the melody. However, most of the *usûls* features either a closing or transitional melody for the

20 Hızır Ağa, *Tefhîmü'l-Makamat fi Tevlîdi'n-Negamât*, Topkapı Sarayı Hazine Kütüphanesi 1793, 22, trans. Feldman 1996, p. 213.

21 On this issue see Feldman 1996, pp. 206-213.

22 I would like to acknowledge my teachers İncila Bertuğ and Fatih Salgar, then of the State Turkish Music Chorus (which Mr. Salgar now directs) from whom I learned this beste in 1984.

Zencir **Sazkâr Beste** **Tabi Mustafa Efendi**

Ex. 4a: *Sazkar Beste* of Tabi Mustafa Efendi (d. ca. 1770)[23]

---

23 İstanbul Belediye Konservatuvarı, *Türk Musikisi Klasiklerinden: Sazkâı Faslı*, No: 5, Istanbul, 1954b, p. 68.

Sazkâr Beste

Zencir

Tabi Mustafa Efendi

Zemin

Çifte Düyek

Dum
Tek

Fahte

D
T

Çenber

Terennüm

Devri Kebir

Berefşân

1.

2.

Miyan

Çifte Düyek

Fahte

Çenber

Ex. 4b: *Sazkar Beste* of Tabi Mustafa Efendi (d. ca. 1770) with sublinear *usûl* correspondence.[24]

---

24 I thank Cristobal Martinez (New York University Abu Dhabi) for the digitization.

last 4 or the last 8 beats, comprising "*teke teke*" or "*ta hek, teke teke*". No doubt the "*ta hek*" – as a change from the more common *düm* or *tek* strokes – acted as a cue to alert the singer and accompanying musicians that a transition was about to take place, at least during the learning stage of *meşk*, and possibly to the audience as well during performance.

Despite the nominal length of the constituent *usûls*, the melody of the *çifte düyek*, *fahte* and *çenber* sections is subdivided into units of 12 beats. Thus the opening melody in *çifte düyek* in both the *zemin* and *miyan* sections comprises 12 quarter notes. In the *zemin* this melody is squarely within *makam segah*, and concludes on the note *segah* (B), while in the *miyan* it is in *makam rast* and concludes on the note *rast* (G). In both cases this is followed by a 4 beat 'transition' (with the drum strokes *tek–teke*). In the *zemin* this transition ends on A (*dügah*), while in the *miyan* it hits the note A in passing, before concluding on G (*rast*), but only in the first four beats of the following *usûl–fahte*. In the *miyan* in *fahte* the essential melody commences on d (*neva*) for twelve beats, before closing with a four-beat formula, centered upon *neva*, supported by the four-beat stroke *teke-teke*. Thus, once again the essential melody comprises 12 beats; i.e. 20, minus 4 beats at the beginning and 4 beats at the end.

Both *çenber* melodies (in the *zemin* and *miyan*) are constructed out of 12-beat units. In the *zemin* the modality is prepared by the transition of fahte, ending on A. Thus the *çenber* melody enters on *hüseyni* (e), the fifth degree from A, before modulating to *hüzzam*, and ending with a "suspended cadence" (*asma karar*) on B. The second 12-beat unit erases *hüzzam* and concludes on d. The *çenber* melody in the *miyan* is squarely in *makam rast*. Its first 12-beat section commences on G and ends on d, while the second 12 beats commence on B and end likewise on d. Thus, throughout both the *zemin* and the *miyan* the most common rhythmic arrangement is 12/4, regardless of whether the nominal *usûl* is in 16/4, 20/4 or 24/4.

In addition there is a tendency toward enjambment between *çifte düyek* and *fahte*. This is somewhat implicit in the *zemin*, where the 'transitional' four beat section at the end of *çifte düyek* leaves the *segah* modality of the opening 12 beats, and appears to blend into the opening 4 beats of the fahte section, which are clearly *rast*, utilizing all the lower notes mentioned by Hızır Ağa (*rast*, *aşiran*, *ırak*). In the *miyan* section this enjambment is even more pronounced, for the four beat transition at the end of the çifte düyek only concludes on the note *rast* (G) at the very opening of the fahte section, and cannot be interpreted in any other way.

This enjambment of the çifte düyek and fahte sections of *zencir* appears to have been an established compositional practice. It appears first in the *peşrev* in *hüseyni*, called "The Great *Zencir*", by Gazi Giray Han in the Cantemir Collection. While in this earlier period the relevant *usûls* were düyek in 8 beats (not 16 beats) and *fahte* in 10 beats (instead of 20 beats), the melodic practice is similar to what we see in Tabi Mustafa's *beste*. Just as in the *miyan* of Tabi Mustafa's *beste*, here the *düyek* melody only closes upon the opening note (d) of the fahte section:

Ex. 5: *Hüseyni "Büyük Zencir"*, Tatar Han.[25]

25 Wright, Owen 1992b, *Demetrius Cantemir: The Collection of Notations, Volume 1: Text*, London: SOAS Musicology Series 1, p. 403.

M b is separated from M a not by the usual *ve leh* but by the phrase *terkīb-i s̱ānī* ('second combination'). Elsewhere *terkīb* may mean 'mode', but here seems to refer to the combination of rhythmic cycles making up *zencir*.

H2 b **3:** 12+*e* ♪.

(Ex. 5: *Hüseyni* "*Büyük Zencir*", Tatar Han.)

We can see a similar joining of the *çifte düyek* and *fahte* sections of the *Nühüft Zencir Beste* by Abu-Beki Ağa (both *zemin* and *miyan*) and in the *zemin* of the *Ferahnak Zencir Beste* by Zekai Dede (d. 1896). Thus, this type of enjambment seems to have been a compositional 'tradition', extending at least from the early eighteenth century (when Cantemir transcribed it) until the end of the nineteenth century, if not further.

In the *beste* of Tabi Mustafa the *terrenüm* – comprising *devr-i kebir* and *berefşan usûls* – is invariable, appearing the same way after the *zemin* and after the *miyan*. The 28 beats of *devr-i kebir* are divided into two broad sections of 14 beats each. But the first 14 beats is actually further subdivided into a rising melody moving from *segah* to *neva* (d), and then an 'arch' moving from G to c and back down to G (*rast*). The second melody requires a full 14 beats, and moves up through the first pentachord of *makam rast*, and then downward to the lower *pentachord*, as far as *yegah* (D). The melody in *berefşan* (32/4) travels widely, beginning with an 8/4 melody in the basic tonal area of *rast*, but then leaping upward to *muhayyer* (a) to create a descending sequence of 14 beats, before concluding with a kind of doubled cadence on *rast*, corresponding to the long *usûl*-stroke 'cadence' of "*ta hek/teke teke*," comprising 8 quarter notes. Since *berefeşan* is the *usûl* of the second section of the *terennüm* that closes the entire *beste*, this final creation of a long, continuous melody, plus the doubled final cadence, represents an emotional 'culmination' of the entire piece.

Conclusion

These four musical examples – three vocal and one instrumental – demonstrate musical techniques of relating melody and *usûl* that typify the Ottoman courtly repertoire. The 'heart', as it were, of this repertoire were the vocal compositions using the long *usûls*, that is, the *beste*, the *nakış beste* and the *kar*. This repertoire had very little presence in the *gazino*, even in the later nineteenth century, let alone the twentieth. Thus among the majority of the dwindling audience for sophisticated urban music in Turkey, this repertoire was increasingly obscure. It survived thanks to the efforts of a limited number of elite musicians who encouraged its performance at private musical sessions. Some of these men were also composers, mainly of *şarkı*, but sometimes also of *bestes*. Vocal compositions were learned at *meşk* sessions with their *usûls*, in the simple form, beaten on the knees. The divisions of "*düm*", "*tek*", "*teke*", "*ta*" and "*hek*" helped to fix specific sections and syllables of the piece with the *usûl*, even where a melody deviated quite far from the normative *usûl* pattern. Musicians who had learned the compositions in this way were in a much better position both to compose new items in these genres, and to be able to communicate the structure of older pieces. This knowledge survived at the interface of kinetic, musical and analytic understanding.

With the founding of radio choruses and then the State Turkish Classical Music Chorus, a part of the Ottoman repertoire utilizing a range of *usûls* has been preserved in public performance, albeit without the oral pedagogy and use of percussion. At the turn of the twenty-first century, traditionalist performing groups such as Lalezar and Bezmara recorded serious Ottoman courtly repertoire. Currently this repertoire is being performed by ensemble and chorus leaders, notably Ruhi Ayangil, Gönül Paçacı and Murat Salim Tokaç.

There is at present virtually no possibility of 'field-work' within the musical communities in the major Turkish cities to ascertain 'correct' or 'normative' usage of the long *usûls* in vocal compositions. Only musicians who were born early in the interwar era had the possibility of learning in this manner.[26] However, the vast surviving repertoire composed in the long *usûls* offers rich material with which to rediscover the compositional techniques employed by Ottoman composers from the eighteenth to the early twentieth centuries, and hence to better understand the full musical meaning of the *usûl* system within Ottoman music.

26 Most of the last musicians who had learned this vocal repertoire orally (at least in part) have passed away within the past thirty years. The major exception are the synagogue cantors of the *Maftirim* repertoire, whose use of orality as a pedagogic method has continued significantly until today (Jackson, Maureen 2013, *Mixing Musics: Turkish Jewry and the Urban Landscape of a Sacred Song*, Stanford: Stanford University Press). However the last active creators of this music passed away as long as fifty years ago (e.g. Moshe Cordova, d. 1964). The cantors and choristers who perform the music today – always without percussion – do not seem to have the specific knowledge of musical theory and of *usûl* in particular to enable them to recreate the compositional process of this repertoire.

Rhythmic Augmentation and the Transformation of the Ottoman *Peşrev*, 18th – 19th Centuries

Jacob Olley

The transformation of the Ottoman *peşrev* from the early notated collections of ʿAlî Ufuḳî and Demetrius Cantemir to its manifestation in the modern Turkish repertoire remains an unsolved problem in Ottoman music studies.[1] A central characteristic of this transformation is the augmentation of the rhythmic cycle, which Owen Wright has argued is linked to gradual tempo retardation and melodic elaboration.[2] This paper proposes a new hypothesis about the augmentation of the rhythmic cycle by studying a group of *peşrev*s found in several different sources from the eighteenth to nineteenth centuries. While Wright's study compared early notations with modern published versions of the same *peşrev*s, the present paper draws on two additional sources which fall between Cantemir and the contemporary period. The first is the mid-eighteenth century Kevs̱erî collection, which was until recently unavailable to researchers[3]; the second is a collection of Hamparsum notation from the early nineteenth century[4]. By comparing different versions of the same pieces as they appear in these sources and considering the impact of performance practice and theory on the transformation of the *peşrev*, the paper sheds new light on historical change in the Ottoman repertoire.

---

1 The problem was first identified by Owen Wright 1988, "Aspects of historical change in the Turkish classical repertoire", in: *Musica Asiatica* 5, Richard Widdess, ed., Cambridge: Cambridge University Press, 1-107. A further article by Wright which addresses this issue in detail is Owen Wright 2007, "Mais qui était «Le compositeur du *péchrev* dans le makam *nihavend*»?", *Studii şi cercet. Ist. Art., Teatru, Muzică, Cinematografie, serie nouă*, 1(45), 3-45. See also Ralf Martin Jäger 1998, "Die Metamorphosen des *Irak Elçi Peşrevi*", in: *Berichte aus dem ICTM-Nationalkomitee Deutschland: Berichte über die Tagungen des Nationalkomitees der Bundesrepublik Deutschland im International Council for Traditional Music (UNESCO) am 26. und 27. Januar 1996 in Münster und am 07. und 08. Februar 1997 in Berlin*, Marianne Bröcker, ed., Bamberg: Universitätsbibliothek Bamberg, 31-57; N. Doğrusöz Dişiaçık and D. Uruş 2012, "Meşk ile intikalde müzik eseri: III. Selim'in Suzdilara Mevlevi Ayini", *International Journal of Human Sciences* [online], 9(2), 427-445; Mehmet Uğur Ekinci 2012, "The *Kevserî Mecmûası* Unveiled: Exploring an Eighteenth-Century Collection of Ottoman Music", *Journal of the Royal Asiatic Society*, Series 3, 22(2), 199-225.

2 Wright 1988.

3 Milli Kütüphane (Ankara), Mf1994 A 4941. For a description of the manuscript and its contents see Ekinci 2012.

4 İstanbul Üniversitesi Nadir Eserler Kütüphanesi, Y 203-1. The manuscript was originally housed in the archive of Istanbul University Conservatory Library and is the first item to appear in Jäger's catalogue of Hamparsum manuscripts. See Ralf Martin Jäger 1996b, *Katalog der hamparsum-notası-Manuskripte im Archiv des Konservatoriums der Universität Istanbul*, Eisenach: K.D. Wagner, xxi-xxii.

The collection of Hamparsum notation, Y 203-1, is a manuscript of 18 closely written pages divided into two columns; headings are in Armeno-Turkish (i.e. Turkish in Armenian characters) with later annotations in Arabic and Latin script. The manuscript contains a note written by Suphi Ezgi in 1941, which states that the handwriting is identical to other collections believed to have been written by Hamparsum Limoncyan (1768-1839) himself.[5] Although there is no internal evidence which confirms the attribution to Limoncyan, on the basis of musical style and the composers included in the manuscript, it may at least be assumed to date from the first half of the nineteenth century. The latest composer represented in the collection is Nû'mân Ağa, who died in 1834. The manuscript contains 69 instrumental pieces: 41 *peşrev*s and 28 *semâî*s, though the present paper is concerned only with the *peşrev*s. In terms of the distribution of rhythmic cycles (not including *semâî*), the most popular is *devr-i kebîr* (10 pieces), followed by *darb-ı fetih* and *düyek* (6 pieces each), *berefşân* (5 pieces), *fâhte* (3 pieces), *sakîl*, *hafîf*, *muhammes* and *darbeyn* (2 pieces each) and *zencîr*, *remel* and *çenber* (1 piece each).[6]

Out of a total of 41 *peşrev*s in the collection, 19 (or 46%) appear in eighteenth-century sources (table 1). This should be taken as a mimimum, however, since there may well be other pieces which I failed to identify. 14 of the pieces were notated by Cantemir, of which 3 pieces also appear (in a different version) in the Kevs̱erî collection. A further 4 pieces appear in Kevs̱erî but not in Cantemir. One piece (*uzzâl, devr-i kebîr*) appears twice (in a slightly different form) in Y 203-1, the first time attributed to Ahmed Ağa and the second time to Nâyî Osmân Efendi. The comparison of the different versions of this group of *peşrev*s offers great potential for understanding the process of transformation in the Ottoman instrumental repertoire in terms of formal structure, melodic elaboration, modal usage and rhythmic-melodic congruence. However, I will focus here on the augmentation of the rhythmic cycle.

The augmentation of the rhythmic cycle (ex. 1) consists in the doubling of the number of time units (e.g. from 14/4 to 28/4) and the performance of two cycles of the rhythmic pattern (in the newer version of the piece) within the time period of one cycle (in the older version).[7] Rhythmic augmentation has been iden-

---

5 *"Bu defterde 64 parça peşrev ve semâî yazılıdır, Necib paşadan aldığımız defterlerdeki yazının aynı hat olduğu ve bu defterinde Hamparsum tarafından Koca Reşid paşaya verilmiş olduğunu onun Torunu B. Necmeddin Koca Reşid tarafından beyan edilmiş olduğundan, bu defterin Hamparsum tarafından yazılmış olduğunu kabul ettik 9/12/[1]941 Dr. Suphi Ezgi"* (p. 18). It is presumably on this basis that Jäger supposes the manuscript is an autograph of Hamparsum Limoncyan (Jäger 1996, xxii).

6 For the sake of simplicity, names of rhythms, modes, composers and pieces are spelled according to modern Turkish conventions, rather than the original Armeno-Turkish or Ottoman orthography. Thus, *uzzâl*, rather than *iwzal*, *ʿuzzâl* etc.

7 See Wright 1988. The number of time units may in fact appear to be quadrupled, as when a half-cycle of the original *devr-i kebîr* is notated as 28/4 (ibid., p. 7); but I am concerned here with the comparative length of the underlying rhythmic pattern, rather than representational differences in time signature.

Usûl	**Makâm**	**Title**	**Composer**[8]	**Y 203-1**[9]	**Cant.**[10]	**Kev.**[11]
Devr-i kebîr	*Sultânî ırâk*			2	290	
Devr-i kebîr	*Acem aşîrân*	*ʿEskiʾ*		4		357
Devr-i kebîr	*Beyâtî*		Behrâm Ağa	51	54	434
Devr-i kebîr	*Acem*		Sultân Veled	53		470
Devr-i kebîr	*Uzzâl*		Ahmed Ağa	55	118	414
Devr-i kebîr	*Uzzâl*		Nâyî Osmân Efendi	65	118	414
Devr-i kebîr	*Sabâ*	*Nâz ü niyâz*	Şeyh Osmân Efendi	69	95	
Düyek	*Râst*	*Menekşezâr*		9	169	
Düyek	*Segâh*	*Zülf-i nigâr*		15	318	
Düyek	*Pencgâh*	*Gülistân*		60	27	
Düyek	*Rast*		Ahmed Bey	63	107	
Darb-ı fetih	*Sırf Bûselik*			1		396
Darb-ı fetih	*Eviç*			6	9	480
Darb-ı fetih	*Hüseynî*		Muzaffer	29	10	
Sakîl	*Nişâbûr*		Solakzâde	13	160	
Sakîl	*Bûselik aşîrân*	*'Küçük'*		56	113	
Berefşân	*Uşşâk*			8	99	
Hafîf	*Şehnâz*		Arabzâde	16		490
Remel	*Isfahân*		Kantemiroğlu	43	278	

Table 1: Correspondences between *peşrevs* in Y 203-1, Cantemir and Kevs̱erî collections

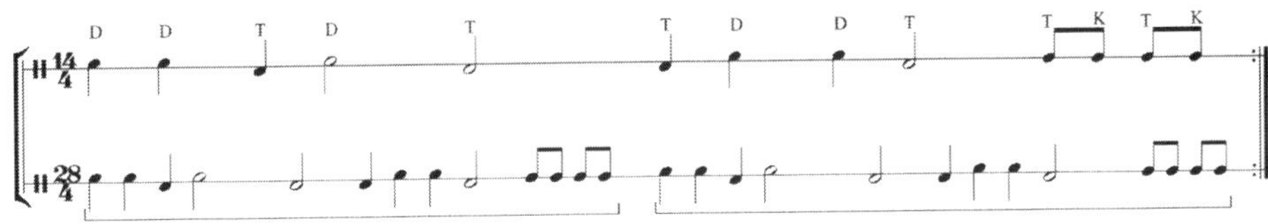

Ex. 1: Rhythmic augmentation in *devr-i kebîr*[12]

8 Rhythm, mode, title and composer are those contained in Y 203-1; divergences from the information given in Cantemir or Kevs̱erî are not indicated here.

9 Number of piece in collection (*not* page number) as determined by the present author.

10 Numbering of pieces follows Owen Wright 1992b, *Demetrius Cantemir: The Collection of Notations. Vol.1: Text*, London: Ashgate.

11 Number of piece in collection as determined by the present author (verified by Mehmet Uğur Ekinci [e-mail communication, 10th January 2013]). Since most pieces in the Cantemir collection were simply copied out by the author(s) of the Kevs̱erî collection, I have indicated here only variants of these pieces and those pieces which exist in Kevs̱erî but not in Cantemir. The 195 original or variant pieces in the Kevs̱erî collection, which are found on fols. 115v-118r and 125r-180v, appear to have been added later, probably by a different author (see Ekinci 2012, pp. 211-212).

12 The basic beat pattern represented here, consisting of 'heavy' (*D[üm]*) and 'light' (*T[ek], K[a]*) sounds, is based on Cantemir's c. 1700 treatise *Kitâb-ı ʿİlmü'l-Mûsiḳî ʿalâ Vechi'l-Ḥurûfât* (İs-

tified as an aspect of historical change in the Ottoman repertoire by a number of scholars, and is particularly associated with the cycle *devr-i kebîr*, a fact which is reflected in modern Turkish theory by the occasional addition of the adjective *muzaaf* ("doubled").[13]

Rhythmic augmentation is thus a characteristic of certain *usûl*s, and occurs in only some of the *peşrev*s found in Y 203-1. It does not occur in the pieces in *darb-ı fetih, sakîl, berefşân* or *hafîf*. Pieces in *düyek* do display this feature, but in any case this is already observable in the Cantemir collection.[14] Of the four pieces in *düyek* in table 1, two (Y 203-1 nos. 9 and 60) display an augmented cycle in relation to their predecessors in Cantemir. Rhythmic augmentation does not seem to have occurred in nos. 63 and 15, but in the case of the latter this may be due to a mistake in Cantemir's notation.[15] The *peşrev*s in *düyek* also display greater melodic divergence from their earlier versions, to the extent that there is little or no correspondence between them in later sections. This may be connected with the brevity of the rhythmic cycle, which, since it entails smaller-scale melodic phrasing, may allow for more variation when memorising the piece according to the *meşk* system.[16] It could also indicate a wide range of contemporaneous performance tempi for this cycle (perhaps connected with different functions or contexts); the simultaneous existence of pieces with both normal and augmented cycles in *düyek*, dating back to the late seventeenth century, would support this argument.

The *peşrev* in *remel*, a rare cycle of 28 time units, shows straightforward rhythmic augmentation throughout the piece. The Cantemir version has a total of 11 cycles (plus a repetition, labelled "*eyḍan*"), while the version in Y 203-1 has 22 cycles i.e. exactly double. The structural relationship between the two versions, in which there is a redistribution of sectional boundaries but no change in overall length, can be seen below (fig. 1). The case of *devr-i kebîr*, however, is far more complex. Firstly, only three out of the seven pieces in *devr-i kebîr* display rhythmic augmenta-

---

tanbul Üniversitesi Türkiyat Araştırmaları Enstitüsü Kütüphanesi, Y 100), p. 83. Rhythmic ornamentations (*velvele*) and later variants on the pattern are not included in this example.

13 Ibid., pp. 8-9; See also Heinz-Peter Seidel 1972/3, "Studien zum Usul 'Devri kebîr' in den Peşrev der Mevlevi", *Mitteilungen der deutschen Gesellschaft für Musik des Orients 11*, 7-69, pp. 38-49.

14 A case in point is Cantemir's version of the *peşrev* in *segâh ('Zülf-i nigâr'*, no. 318), in which the rhythmic cycle is doubled in relation to the version notated by ʿAlî Ufuḳî in *Mecmûʿa-yı Sâz u Söz* (British Library, MS Sloane 3114, fol. 98v). No. 84 (*hüseynî, düyek*) also has an uncertain relationship between melody and rhythmic cycle, which Wright understands (as in the case of no. 318) as a notational error (where Cantemir's ١ should equal not 1 time unit but 1/2). But the presence of such errors, which are also to be observed in the case of another duple metre, *muhammes* (e.g. nos. 72 and 292), itself suggests that these *usûl*s were subject to different interpretations in performance. See Wright 1992; cf. Jäger 1998, pp. 37-39, where the augmentation of the cycle is explicitly labelled as "*çifte düyek*" ("double *düyek*").

15 See previous footnote.

16 On the importance of the rhythmic cycle in oral transmission and memorisation, see Cem Behar 1998, *Aşk Olmayınca Meşk Olmaz*, İstanbul: Yapı Kredi Yayınları, pp. 16-20.

Cantemir no. 278

H1		M [+ eyḍan]			H2			H3		
1:	2:	3:	4	5:	6	7:	8:	9:	10:	11:

H1		H2								H3										H4	
1	2:	3	4:	5	6:	7	8	9	10	11	12	13	14:	15	16	17	18:	19	20:	21	22:

Y 203-1 no. 43

Figure 1: Rhythmic augmentation in Y 203-1 no. 43 (*ısfahân, remel,* Kantemiroğlu)[17]

No.	Makâm/title/composer	Rhythmic augmentation
2	*Sultânî ırâk*	Augmentation in H1-3 only
4	*Acem aşîrân/ᶜEskiʾ*	No augmentation
51	*Beyâtî*/Behrâm Ağa	Augmentation in H1-3 only
53	*Acem*/Sultân Veled	Augmentation in H1-4
55	*Uzzâl*/Ahmed Ağa	No augmentation
65	*Uzzâl*/ Nâyî Osmân Efendi	No augmentation
69	*Sabâ/Nâz ü niyâz*/Şeyh Osmân Efendi	No augmentation

Table 2: Rhythmic augmentation in pieces in *devr-i kebîr*, Y 203-1

tion (table 2). This demonstrates that the process which led to the augmentation of the rhythmic cycle was not complete by the first half of the nineteenth century, and furthermore that it did not affect all pieces in *devr-i kebîr*.[18]

To complicate matters further, however, in two of these pieces (nos. 2 and 51) the rhythmic cycle is *not* doubled in the fourth *hâne*. An identical phenomenon is observed by Owen Wright in the case of a Mevlevî *peşrev* in *çargâh* which appears in a later Hamparsum collection.[19] Wright states that the piece "juxtaposes material from two distinct phases, the final *hâne* being a survival from a period prior to the augmentation of the rhythmic cycle".[20] However, since this is evidently not an isolated phenomenon, it would seem useful to consider other interpretations. It is important to remember that the augmentation of the rhythmic cycle is an aspect of musical praxis – that is, notated sources reflect the decisions of performers. Rather than representing distinct historical phases, the peculiar way in which pieces in *devr-i kebîr* are notated in Y 203-1 may reflect a practice of

17 Cycles are numbered continuously; H = *hâne*; M = *mülâzime*; repetitions are indicated by a colon (:).

18 It should be acknowledged that Wright 1988 emphasises that his analysis of the process of tempo retardation/melodic elaboration is applicable only to "a very precise and circumscribed part of the twentieth-century instrumental repertoire" (37) i.e. the *peşrevs* connected with the Mevlevî rite.

19 Wright 1988, pp. 65-69.

20 Ibid., p. 67.

Example 2: *Devr-i kebîr* as usually written in Hamparsum notation[21]

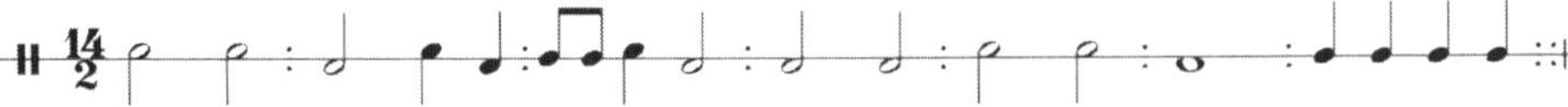

Example 3: *Devr-i kebîr* as written in Y 203-1 (nos. 2 and 4)

doubling or halving the rhythmic cycle in performance. There are two possible ways to understand this – firstly, that the rhythmic cycle was doubled or halved without altering the tempo of the melody, or, alternatively, that the augmentation of the rhythmic cycle coincided with a change in tempo.

The piece in *sultânî ırâk* displays another unusual feature which may support the first interpretation. The cycle *devr-i kebîr* is usually expressed in Hamparsum notation as 4+4+4+2, where each subdivision is marked by two dots (:) and the end of the cycle by four dots (::) (ex. 2). However, the first two *hâne*s of the piece in *sultânî ırâk* are written instead as 4+4+4+4+4+4+4 (ex. 3). Initially, this would simply suggest that the rhythmic cycle has not been augmented. But the third *hâne* is then notated in the usual manner (4+4+4+2), with two cycles corresponding to one cycle of the original. This could be understood to mean that the cycle was augmented only in the third *hâne*. The apparent alternation of normal and doubled cycles also occurs in the piece in *acem aşîrân*, but this time within the duration of a single *hâne*, in which case the tempo of the melody must have remained constant.

Yet it seems more likely that, in both of these cases, the scribe was simply mistaken: it would appear that the first two *hâne*s of the piece in *sultânî ırâk* were in fact played with an augmented cycle, but the author failed to represent this in the notation. Furthermore, whereas in *sultânî ırâk* seven subdivisions of Hamparsum notation (4+4+4+4+4+4+4) correspond to one cycle in Cantemir, in the case of *acem aşîrân* they correspond to two cycles (in Kevs̱erî). It seems improbable that two cycles in Kevs̱erî could have corresponded to only one cycle of *devr-i kebîr* (which would imply rhythmic diminution) in the nineteenth-century version. The irregular occurrence of the seven-subdivision cycles in the piece also makes it unlikely that the rhythm could have alternated between normal and doubled cycles. It is worth noting that both of these pieces appear in the earliest pages of the manuscript, while other pieces in *devr-i kebîr*, which appear later, use only the "correct" or standard notation of the cycle. It may be that the scribe was

21 The articulation of the beat pattern (for timbral values, see ex. 1 above), which cannot be specified in Hamparsum notation, is taken from an Armenian treatise written during roughly the same period as Y 203-1. See H. Minas Bžškean 1997 [1815], *Eražštutʿiwn or ē hamaṙōt tełekutʿiwn eražštakan skzbancʿ elewējutʿeancʿ ełanakacʿ ew nšanagracʿ xazicʿ*, Aram Kʿerovbean (Ed.), Erewan: Girkʿ Hratarakčʿutʿiwn, p. 166.

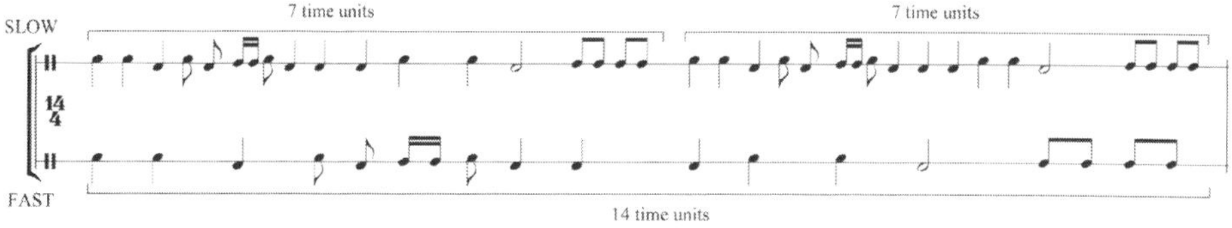

Example 4: First and second levels of tempo in *devr-i kebîr*

initially experimenting with the notation of the cycle. At the very least, then, the author's decisions (as in the case of *düyek*) reflect his uncertainty about how the rhythmic cycle should be performed. This is not surprising if we imagine that these *peşrev*s could have been played without rhythmic accompaniment, and it demonstrates that the relationship between the rhythmic cycle and the melody was becoming increasingly distant. Furthermore, the peculiarities of the written record should remind us that, like most historical processes, the augmentation of the rhythmic cycle happened neither overnight nor in an orderly sequence, but occurred gradually and in a somewhat random fashion.

Nevertheless, we are still faced with the unambiguous fact that the cycle is not augmented in the final *hâne* of the *peşrev*s in *sultânî ırâk* and *beyâtî*. To explain this, we might now turn to eighteenth-century writing on music and the theoretical understanding of rhythmic augmentation during this period. In his mid-eighteenth-century treatise, Ḥızır Aġa states that two levels of rhythm exist, which he designates as "*mertebe-yi żarb-i evvel*" and "*mertebe-yi żarb-i s̱ânî*".[22] In the case of *devr-i kebîr*, the first level (*mertebe*) is given as 7, the second as 14. This initially seems somewhat puzzling: if it indicates an augmentation of the rhythmic cycle, we might expect the first level to be 14 and the second 28.[23] However, it may be interpreted to mean that the first level represents a slower tempo than the second level. If the rhythmic cycle is augmented (i.e. played at a slower tempo), one doubled cycle of *devr-i kebîr* is equal to seven time units of the non-augmented cycle (ex. 4). This interpretation is supported by Tanbûrî Küçük Artin, writing around the same period, who gives two versions of the rhythmic cycle *darb-ı fetih*, where the slower version is said to have half the number of beats ("*Darb-ı fetih – yürüyüşü seksen sekiz darbdır, ağırı kırk dört darbdır*").[24]

Therefore, if it cannot be shown that the rhythmic cycle was doubled or halved while maintaining the same tempo, the case of the fourth *hâne* may indicate two different levels of tempo. The use of a different tempo for the final *hâne* would not

22 *Edvâr-ı Ḥızır Aġa*, Süleymaniye Kütüphanesi, Hafid Efendi 291, fols. 19a-20a. Ekinci 2012 suggests a slightly earlier date for the treatise – see his discussion of the relevant sources at 208.

23 It should be noted that this is the case for some rhythmic cycles e.g. *nîm devir*, where the corresponding values are 9 and 18, *frenkçîn* (12 and 24) and *muhammes* (16 and 32).

24 Eugenia Popescu-Judetz 2002, *Tanburî Küçük Artin: A Musical Treatise of the Eighteenth Century*, İstanbul: Pan Yayıncılık, p. 97.

be without precedent, of course, since it occurs in the *semâî*. The fourth *hâne* may be transformed in other ways too: in the piece in *acem* (no. 53), while the rhythmic cycle is augmented throughout the piece, the fourth *hâne* is based on new melodic material unrelated to the original. In the case of the "*Elçi*" *peşrev* in *düyek* discussed by Jäger, a newly composed fourth *hâne* is attributed to a recently deceased performer, Tanbûrî İsak.[25] The fourth *hâne* may therefore have allowed for more creative input from the performer, and for this reason its manner of performance was more flexible – flexibility here encompassing modulation, the creation of new melodic material, and the display of virtuosity through a faster tempo. The special status of the fourth *hâne* also meant that it may have been considered optional and was more likely to be omitted. In Jäger's study, a later nineteenth-century version of the "*Elçi*" *peşrev* includes only three *hâne*s.[26]

Of course, it might simply be that the fourth *hâne* was accidently omitted by the author or that it had been forgotten in the intervening years. Alternatively, Wright's hypothesis of gradual tempo retardation would suggest that the final *hâne* was left out due to the increasing duration of the piece.[27] But there is one final example from the group of *peşrev*s under consideration which demonstrates that this was not necessarily the case. The *peşrev* by Behrâm Ağa in *beyâtî* (no. 51) also appears in Suphi Ezgi's *Nazarî ve Amelî Türk Mûsıkîsi* (published between 1933 and 1953).[28] It is evident that the piece is transcribed from Y 203-1, since the manuscript was in Ezgi's possession and contains many of his annotations. Ezgi's transcription follows the original closely, but inexplicably omits the fourth *hâne*. Rather than attributing this to carelessness on the part of the author, I would argue that Ezgi may have regarded the fourth *hâne* as a corrupted, later interpolation.

The fact that the rhythmic cycle is not augmented means that there is a higher degree of melodic density in the fourth *hâne*. While the previous *hâne*s have a density of between 19 and 25 attacks per cycle, the figure for the fourth *hâne* is 39 attacks per cycle (a similar relationship is seen in the piece in *sultânî ırâk*) (table 3).

Section	**Attacks per cycle**
1st *hâne* + *teslîm*	25
2nd *hâne*	20
3rd *hâne*	19
4th *hâne*	39

Table 3: Melodic density in Y203-1 no. 51

25 Jäger 1998.
26 Ibid., p. 33. The entire *peşrev* is, however, attributed to Tanbûrî İsak.
27 See Wright 1988, pp. 17-18.
28 Suphi Ezgi 1933-53, *Nazarî ve Amelî Türk Mûsıkîsi*, vol. 3, İstanbul: Millî Mecmua Matbaası, pp. 33-34.

Although higher melodic density is usually associated with a slower tempo, if the aim was the display of virtuosity, in this case it may have coincided with a faster tempo. But even if the tempo of the fourth *hâne* was not increased, the high degree of melodic density creates the impression of increased tempo (i.e. there are more sixteenth notes) and reflects a highly embellished performance style – what might nowadays be termed "*piyasa tavrı*" or a "commercial style". The increase in melodic density from the *teslîm* to the fourth *hâne* is shown in ex. 5 below (the rhythmic cycle has been added for the purpose of analysis).

Ezgi's subtle editing of the rest of the *beyâtî peşrev* (in which he smooths out the melody by omitting rests, integrating ornamental notes into the main melody line, and replacing sixteenth notes with eighth notes) illustrates his editorial policy, which was to purge the music of impurities and to establish a "classical" style (ex. 6 below).[29] The highly embellished fourth *hâne* would therefore have been inimical to Ezgi's aims. The omission of the fourth *hâne* by Ezgi shows that the apparent loss of material due to gradual tempo retardation and the attempt to counter expanding performance times is in fact the result of modern editorial practices. One obvious conclusion to be drawn from this is that researchers need to be wary when using modern published editions to understand historical change in the Ottoman repertoire. But a larger analytical point can be made: if the loss of melodic material in the *peşrev* is less extensive than hitherto assumed – and there is no substantial loss of material in any of the other *peşrev*s from Y 203-1 – then it is also necessary to reconsider the theory of gradual tempo retardation itself.

[29] See Wright 1988, pp. 91-100 for a detailed analysis of Ezgi's editorial procedures.

Example 5: Y 203-1 no. 51 (*beyâtî*, *devr-i kebîr*, Behrâm Ağa)[30]

30 Y 203-1, p. 13. Subdivisions of the rhythmic cycle in the original notation are marked here by dotted bar lines, ends of cycles by double bar lines (or repeat signs where applicable); beaming reflects the grouping of notes within each subdivision. The interpretation of signs for ornaments and articulation follows Bžškean 1997 [1815], p. 125.

Example 6: Ezgi's transcription of Y 203-1 no. 51[31]

[31] Ezgi 1933 53, vol. 3, pp. 33-34 Ezgi's alterations to the original notation are indicated by asterisks (*).

Aspects of Formal Structure and Melodic Time Organization in the Early 19th-Century *Peşrev*: Some Conclusions on Zekî Mehmed Ağa's (1776-1846) "*Şehnâz Bûselik Peşrevi*" and its Contemporary Versions

Ralf Martin Jäger

Preliminary Thoughts

Over the last 25 years, several studies, each one important in its own way, have explored and discussed the instrumental repertoire of Ottoman music based on primary sources and in its historical dimension for the first time. Based primarily on Kantemiroğlu's collection of notations written in the early eighteenth century, it has been possible to track the development of important works across several centuries and to show how they were continuously re-composed in order to be preserved in the repertoire. During this process, not only was the realization of *makam* steadily refined, but musical time was also adapted to the prevailing aesthetic requirements, and thus the rhythmic structures of the melodic line and the musical form were subjected to quite fundamental changes.[1]

A significant result of these studies was the recognition that the instrumental repertoire of Ottoman music was never a historical one until well into the nineteenth century, although a significant part of the work-clusters[2] that were passed on was brought into the transmission process initially by historical composers. A

1 These phenomena have been described by a number of scholars, independently from each other and with partly different research results. See Wright, Owen 1998, "Aspects of Historical Change in the Turkish Classical Repertoire", in: Richard Widdess (Ed.), *Musica Asiatica* 5, Cambridge, 1-108; Feldman, Walter 1996, *Music of the Ottoman Court. Makam, Composition and the Early Ottoman Instrumental Repertoire* (=*Intercultural Music Studies* 10, ed. Max Peter Baumann), Berlin, esp. pp. 330-338, and also Jäger, Ralf Martin 1998, "Die Metamorphosen des Irak Elçi Peşrevi", in: Marianne Bröcker (Ed.), *Berichte aus dem ICTM-Nationalkomitee* VI/VII, Bamberg, 31-57, and 2004, "The Aesthetic of Time in Traditional Ottoman Art Music", in: Panikos Giorgoudes (Ed.), *Proceedings of the 1st International Conference of the Cyprus Musicological Society*, Nicosia, 75-96.

2 The concept describes here a composition which, on the basis of specific requirements intrinsic to culture and period, is brought into transmission and subjected to a continuous transformation process within the community of this tradition. According to existing observations, a musical piece may endure in a community's mainly oral-tradition-based repertoire as long as it takes part in the process of continuous adaptation. I therefore find this description more appropriate than "composition", which is, nevertheless, henceforth used for the sake of convenience, although referring to a "work-cluster".

comparison of the *Kitâb* of Kantemiroğlu with the "London" manuscript of Ali Ufukî suggests that the pieces were probably written down as edited versions, possibly also as instrument-specific variants.[3] However, the question remains unanswered whether the diachronic variation of individual pieces can be attributed entirely to the transmission process, or if it possibly already occurred on the synchronic level, and the sources from the nineteenth century simply document a different transmission context from Kantemiroğlu (and Mustafa Kevserî). The quality of the rare manuscripts from the early eighteenth century that contain musical notation is assured by Kantemiroğlu's excellence in music theory and performance, as well as his recognized authority; but due to the lack and unavailability of other sources, further verification is currently not possible.

The early Hamparsum-notation manuscripts provide sources that allow a differentiated study of synchronic repertoires for the first time, and they also contain "words with songs" again, for the first time after Ali Ufukî, starting from at least the 1840s.[4] Although single manuscripts constitute only a selected part of the repertoire, they complement each other's content and quite often contain at least partially parallel transmissions, which, fortunately for historical ethnomusicology, enable research on almost synchronic time periods. For the analysis and understanding of formal structure and melodic time organization in the early nineteenth-century *peşrev*, this fact is significant.

In the first part, the present paper will examine a particular section of the instrumental *peşrev* repertoire of the earlier nineteenth century: the pieces composed by the generation of musicians that passed away between 1805 and 1846, and that are notated in more or less contemporary music manuscripts. Of interest are not only the names of the composers who were included in the written tradition, but especially the *usûl-ler* they used.

The second part offers a case study of special interest: the versions of Zekî Mehmed Ağa's (1776-1846) "*Şehnâz Bûselik Peşrevi*". The process of the emergence of these variants will be examined on the basis of selected early nineteenth-century manuscript sources. The results of the case study are of general importance for understanding the relations between *usûl* and musical form, *usûl* and rhythmic progression of the melodic line, and *usûl* and composition.

---

3 This is clear, for instance, from a comparison of different versions of Küçük Ahmed Bey's (d. ca. 1650) *Râst Peşrevi, Usûl Düyek*, as recorded by Kantemiroğlu [Dimitri Kantemir], *Kitâb-ı 'İlmü'l-Mûsıkî 'alâ Vechi'l-Hurûfât*, İstanbul Üniversitesi Türkiyat Araştırmaları Enstitüsü, Arel Kütüphanesi Y 100 (former signature: Nr. 2768), p. 59 (fol. 96r), and by Ali Ufukî [Albert Bobovsky], *Mecmua-i Saz ü Söz*, British Library, Sloane 3114, fol. 110r (Nr. 221). Ali Ufukî's version includes, unlike Kantemiroğlu's, phrases characteristic of *santur* playing.

4 See Seidel, Heinz-Peter 1973/74, *Die Notenschrift des Hamparsum Limonciyan. Ein Schlüssel, Mitteilungen der Deutschen Gesellschaft für Musik des Orients* 12, 72-124, and Jäger, Ralf Martin 1996, *Türkische Kunstmusik und ihre handschriftlichen Quellen aus dem 19. Jahrhundert* (=*Schriften zur Musikwissenschaft aus Münster* 7, ed. Klaus Hortschansky), Eisenach, pp. 235-270.

Observations on the Peşrev-*Repertoire of the Early 19th Century, Composed by Contemporary Musicians (d. 1805-1846)*

On the Manuscripts

So far it is possible in only a few cases to plausibly date the available manuscripts from the nineteenth century or to attribute them to particular scribes. A significant number of manuscripts appear to have been written over the course of a relatively long time period and with the contributions of several persons. Earlier notations have been corrected and complemented, more often than not, by later hands. In addition, the paper and various types of Hamparsum notation used give no more than general indications of date.[5]

For this paper, five manuscripts were selected, most likely written between 1815 and 1850 and which, on the basis of their reception history, seem to have been especially influential. The manuscripts İstanbul Üniversitesi Nadir Eserler Kütüphânesi (İÜko) Y.203/1 (Hamparsum autograph), Y.211/9 (possible Hamparsum autograph according to Suphi Ezgi) and – related to but written earlier than the latter – Y.205/3, which originally belonged to Mustafa Reşid Paşa's library, all come from the collection of *Darü'l-Elhân*, known today as İstanbul Belediye Konservatuvarı. The hitherto uninvestigated Hamparsum autograph manuscript that was previously owned by Sadettin Arel and is currently held in the collection of İstanbul Üniversitesi Türkiyat Araştırmaları Enstitüsü, and the Hamparsum-notation manuscript from the Istanbul Archaeological Museums Library were also taken into account. Dating of the latter manuscript is based on the repertoire it includes and the fact that at least one of the scribes used an earlier version of the notation system. A further clue is provided by the addition of "*Merḥûm*" to the name Hammâmî-zâde İsmâîl Dede Efendî in the last third of the manuscript, a part that was not arranged according to a plan; this evidence suggests a date close to the year of his death in 1846.

Together, the manuscripts allow a relatively differentiated examination of the instrumental repertoire from 1815 to 1850. However, it should be noted that the sources cover only a selection of the pieces that existed in the performance practice of the time. It cannot yet be evaluated how precisely the manuscripts illustrate the instrumental music culture of the period.

Thoughts on the Repertoire

In the five manuscripts, a total of 496 instrumental compositions are found. 317 of these include names of the composers. It is remarkable in several respects that among these, only less than half (147) of the pieces belong to composers who

5 For a comprehensive overview, see Jäger 1996.

died between 1805 and 1846 and thus could be considered contemporary composers. The focus of the manuscripts' contents can be related to the primary intention of the scribes to collect old works in order to save them from oblivion.

	Number of *Peşrevs* by 'Contemporary' Composers (d. 1800 – 1846)	Number of Pieces by 'Contemporary' Composers (d. 1805 – 1846)[6]	Composers known (overall)	Notations (overall)
İÜko Y.203/1	08	10	31	72
Arel 110	20	32	88	166
İÜko Y.211/9	28	47	93	114
İÜko Y.205/3	23	36	71	91
İAM 1537	20	22	34	53
Total	99	147	317	496

According to current knowledge, all notations discussed here transmit revisions of historical works in the style of the late eighteenth and early nineteenth centuries. Considering this fact, it is thus conceivable that the content of the manuscripts actually represents the historical process of repertoire formation to a certain extent. This applies to the Hamparsum manuscripts Y.203/1 and Arel 110 to a lesser degree, each of which include only ca. 30% contemporary works, compared to Y.211/9 and Y.205/3, with a share of ca. 50%, or İAM 1537 with almost 65% of contemporary compositions.

Notably, Hamparsum autographs Y.203/1 and Arel 110 include the smallest proportion of named composers with 43% and 53% respectively. The percentages from later manuscripts, namely İAM 1537 (64%), Y.205/3 (78%) and Y.211/9 (81%), are significantly higher. The information on the originator of a work-cluster thus seems to have become increasingly important with time.

On the whole, a total of 15 contemporary composers were recorded in the manuscripts. By far the most often transmitted composer, Tanbûrî İsak Ağa (ca. 1745-1814) is named in all of the manuscripts. He is followed by Kemâni Corci (d. ca. 1805), Sultân Selîm III. (1761-1808) and Tanbûri Emin Ağa (ca. 1750-1814). In the following generation of composers active up to the mid-1830s, Nâyî Ali Dede (d. ca. 1820), Kemâni Ali Ağa (ca. 1770-1830) and Nûmân Ağa (ca. 1750-1834) are among the most significant persons. The last generation is represented partly by Hammâmî-zâde İsmâîl Dede Efendi (1778-1846), but even more by Nûmân Ağa-zâde Zeki Mehmed Ağa (1776-1846), who shares the fate of passing away in the same year.

65% of the instrumental pieces attributed to contemporary composers belong to the *peşrev* form. The *usûl* repertoire of the instrumental composers who died be-

6 Including the composers who are named in the manuscripts, as well as those to whom certain pieces can be ascribed.

tween 1805 and 1846 and are transmitted in all five manuscripts contains the entire spectrum that is usually represented in the *peşrev* form. Almost all of the larger *usûl-ler* are used, though unevenly distributed; only *evsat* (26 *żarb*) and *remel* (28 *żarb*) are not included. Especially often represented *usûl-ler* are *devri kebîr* (14 *żarb*), *usûl* of the *mevlevî-ler*; *düyek* (4 *żarb*)[7], which is short and comparatively simple to compose upon; *darb-ı fetih* (88 *żarb*), an *usûl* favored by Tanbûrî İsak Ağa; *fahte* (10 *żarb*), which is also quite short; and finally *sakîl* (48 *żarb*). On the diachronic level, there is no tendency towards an increasing usage of shorter *usûl-ler* in this time period, as could be expected considering the musical change from 1828 onwards. On the contrary, we observe once more an increasing variety after 1820, and new compositions appear based not only on the *usûl devri kebîr*, which is always strongly represented, but also again on *sakîl*, *darb-ı fetih* and even *zencir*. Especially interesting is the diversity of the percentage occurrence of *usûl-ler* in the consulted manuscripts. Here, the individuality of single manuscripts becomes obvious again. While the short *usûl düyek* does not appear at all in Y.203/1, it ranks first in İAM 1537. *Sakîl* is particularly present in the three later manuscripts, *darb-ı fetih* appears frequently and *hâvî* only in Y.211/9 and 205/3.

On the whole, the statistical data are meaningful. They provide a multifaceted overview of the composers transmitted in the manuscripts and the consistence of the repertoire, as well as revealing information about details such as the usage of *usûl-ler*. But most of all, they show the perhaps unexpected individuality of single manuscripts, which makes music-historical conclusions concerning overall contexts seem possible only after an evaluation of most of the available sources.

Formal Structure and Melodic Time Organization in the Early 19th-Century Peşrev: Some Conclusions on Zekî Mehmed Ağa's (1776-1846) "Şehnâz Bûselik Peşrevi" *and its Contemporary Versions*

The unity of *usûl-* and *makam*-realization is a primary criterion that characterizes each and every piece of Ottoman art music. Franz Joseph Sulzer, writing in 1781, already pointed to the significance of *usûl-ler* in this regard:

> »[Turkish] rhythms contain beats that serve for them as rests or caesura, dots, ties, staccato marks, slurs and repeat signs; in short, their rhythms are for them what notation and written marks are for us, and by means of these they can more or less do without the art of composing[8], which is indispensable for European music with its few rhythms.«[9]

7 The index of İAM 1537 specifies the variant of the *usûl* as *tek düyek*.

8 Ger. *Setzkunst*

9 Sulzer, Franz Joseph 1781, *Geschichte des transalpinischen Daciens, das ist: der Walachey, Moldau und Bessarabiens, im Zusammenhange mit der Geschichte des übrigen Daciens als ein Versuch einer allgemeinen dacischen Geschichte mit kritischer Freyheit entworfen von Franz Joseph Sulzer, ehemaligem k. k. Hauptmann und Auditor*, vol. 2, Vienna, p. 442.

It was possible for trained musicians to quickly remember a piece they had studied only once, based on the parameters of *makam* and *usûl*, with addition of a composer's name or, in case of vocal pieces, the first line of the lyrics. Titles usually including these data in numerous anthologies are sufficient evidence: "words without songs".[10]

Change of the underlying *usûl* during the historical transmission of a work can be observed in only a few instances, and even these changes, on the whole, aim merely at a deceleration of the elapsing musical time. A good example is the "*Irak 'Elçi' peşrevi*" written by Kantemiroğlu in *usûl düyek*, which, according to Haydar Sanal, originates from the realm of the *mehterhâne*. The work was substantially revised as it was transferred to the *ince sâz* repertoire, probably by Tanbûrî İsak, who added the fourth *hâne*, if not more. *Usûl* decelerates here to *çifte düyek*, only to accelerate again to *düyek* in a source from the late nineteenth century.[11] Even though the *usûl* remains ultimately in the domain of *düyek*, the effects on the formal structure of *peşrev* and the design of the melodic line are significant.

Considering this, the possibility of transmitting a piece by applying different *usûl-ler* seems conceivable. More precise knowledge concerning this is in the first place to be expected when enough sources are made available through future research for investigation and verification of parallel transmission of different variants, or even versions, of a piece. It will then also be possible to reach new conclusions regarding the usage of *usûl-ler* and their metamorphoses between the variants emerging from different patterns of transmission.[12]

The Versions of Zekî Mehmed Ağa's (1776-1846) "Şehnâz Bûselik Peşrevi"

In 1943, a collection of traditional Ottoman art music edited by Ahmed Irsoy (1869 – 1943) and Suphi Ezgi (1869 – 1962) with selected works of "Dede [...], Dellalzade [...], Hâfiz Abdullâh [...], Itri [...], Kara İsmâîl Ağa [...], Nazîm [...]" and "Mehmed Bey", appeared in the publication series *İstanbul Konservatuarı Neşri-*

---

10 Cf. Wright, Owen 1992, *Words without Songs. A Musicological Study of an Early Ottoman Anthology and its Precursors*, London: SOAS Musicology Series: 3.

11 Cf. Jäger 1998.

12 The Institute for Musicology of Westfälische Wilhelms University Münster will launch a project in October 2015 in cooperation with Orient-Institut Istanbul (Max Weber Foundation) and together with leading international experts, entitled "Corpus Musicae Ottomanicae (CMO): Critical Editions of Near Eastern Music Manuscripts." The aim of the long-term project, funded by the German Research Foundation for 12 years, is first to prepare critical editions of manuscripts from the nineteenth century written in Hamparsum notation, then, in a second phase, to begin with the transnotation and edition of important manuscripts that are exemplary for this time period and written in Western notation, thus making the nineteenth-century repertoire available for future research for the first time in the form of reliable critical editions.

yatından, which also included Zeki Mehmed Ağa's (1776-1846) "*Şehnaz puselik makamında ve sakil usulünde Peşrev*".[13]

Yılmaz Öztuna mentions this piece in his list of composers' works, but in *usûl muhammes*.[14] Two contemporary notations of the *peşrev* in İÜko Y.2011/9 confirm this indication, while a third – and also contemporary – record of the work in İAM 1537 does not state the *usûl*.[15] Could this attribution of *usûl* be a mistake on the part of the experienced editors, or does the *peşrev* exist in at least two variants with different *usûl-ler*? If the latter should be the case, the results of the case study would be of general importance for understanding the relations between *usûl* and musical form, *usûl* and rhythmic progression of the melodic line, and *usûl* and composition.

Ahmed Irsoy's and Suphi Ezgi's Print Version and its Sources

Zeki Mehmed Ağa's "*Şehnaz puselik makamında ve sakil usulünde Peşrev*" formally corresponds to the type of *peşrev* consisting of 4 *hâne* with *mülâzime* (also called *teslîm*). Here, each *hâne* comprises only one *usûl*-cycle, and is therefore relatively short. In historical works recorded in the sources used for this research, some of the individual movements are significantly longer, for instance in Buhûrî-zâde Mustafa Itri's (ca. 1683 – 1712) "*Nühüft* [*Peşrevi*], *Usûlî* [*Ağır*] *Sakîl*" in the version of Arel 110, where usual lengths cover two (first *hâne*), three (second and third *hâne*) and four (fourth *hâne*) *usûl*-cycles.[16]

In Zeki Mehmed Ağa's *peşrev*, the main part of the *hâne* is shortened further by the integration of the *mülâzime* – which, due to the short duration of the piece as a whole, does not have its own *usûl*-cycle, in contrast to the historical works – into the span of *sakîl*, occupying exactly one third of the cycle.

We will address the question of whether the combinations of the melodic line suit the requirements of *sakîl* below. First, it is necessary to clarify which sources the edition of Irsoy and Ezgi is based on. Among the sources included in this study, only İAM 1537 comes into question, since the other manuscripts use *usûl muhammes*.

---

13 Irsoy, Hafız Ahmed and Dr. Suphi Ezgi (Ed.) 1943, *Türk Musikisi Klasiklerinden*, İstanbul: İstanbul Konservatuarı, pp. 48-49. For a facsimile of the first *hâne*, see Example 1.

14 Öztuna, Yılmaz 2006, *Türk Mûsikîsi – Akademik Klasik Türk San'at Mûsikîsi'nin Ansiklopedik Sözlüğü*, 2 vols., Ankara: Orient Yayınları vol 2., p. 521.

15 The manuscript İAM 1537 belongs to the collection of İstanbul Arkeoloji Müzeleri Kütüphanesi. Manuscripts of İstanbul Üniversitesi Devlet Konservatuvarı (İÜko) are held in the Nadir Eserler Department of İstanbul Üniversitesi Kütüphanesi today. This *peşrev* was recorded with a third rhythmic cycle, namely *usûl hafîf*, on page 164 of the manuscript İÜko Y.212/10b, which is now lost, but would have been another approximately contemporary source. This source, which would be quite conclusive for the context of this research, is unfortunately not available today.

16 Ms. Arel 110, pp. 22-23.

Example 1: Formal division (*hâne* and *mülâzime*) of the representation of *usûl sakîl* in Zeki Mehmed Ağa's *"Şehnaz puselik makamında ve sakil usulünde Peşrev"*

Example 2 presents the transcription of the beginning of the notation from İAM 1537 on page 55. A comparison of the first *hâne* up to the beginning of the *mülâzime* alone shows the remarkable similarity of both notations. Aside from a few rhythmic details that can be traced back to an imprecise transnotation, the melodic phrases shown in the examples correspond exactly with each other. In all probability, the manuscript İAM 1537 was the direct source of the print version; at any rate, both of them document the same pattern of transmission.

(1) The length of the note is doubled in the manuscript.
(2) In the manuscript the pitch *tîz buselîk* is given.

Example 2: Possible source (İAM 1537, p. 55 ff.) for the print version of Zeki Mehmed Ağa's *"Şehnaz puselik makamında ve sakil usulünde Peşrev"*

This also becomes evident when the matter of *usûl* is investigated.

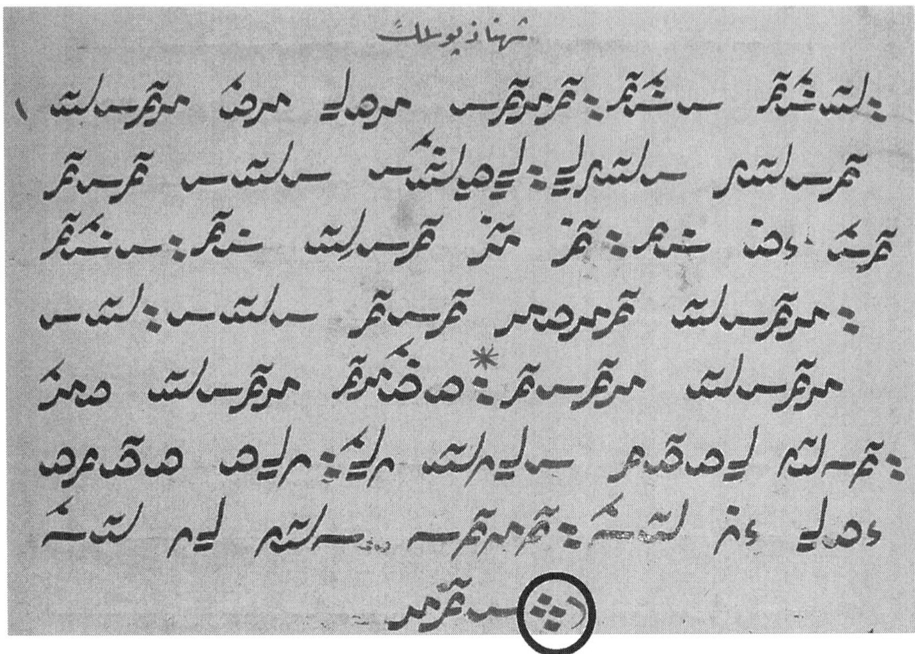

Example 3: Facsimile of Zeki Mehmed Ağa's *"Şehnaz Buselîk [Peşrevi]"*. Detail marked: Mensural character marking the end of the *usûl*-period. Ms. İstanbul Arkeoloji Müzesi Kütüphânesi 1537, p. 55.

The fact that the duration of one *hâne* with *teslîm* corresponds exactly to one cycle of *usûl sakîl* suggests that this is in fact the intended *usûl* here. Moreover, a technical detail concerning the writing of Hamparsum notation in this source is also revealing: The four-dot mensural sign used to mark the end of cycles in *büyük usûl-ler* is placed only at the end of the *teslîm*, where the first *sakîl*-cycle finishes. Since all signs of rhythmical groupings, including the asterisk at the beginning of the *teslîm*, are applied carefully and correctly, it can be assumed that this mensural sign, too, was placed intentionally.

Finally, there are purely musical reasons pointing to *sakîl*. These can be illustrated with a comparison of the third *hâne-ler* of Zeki Mehmed Ağa's *peşrev* and Buhûrîzâde Mustafa Itri's (ca. 1683 – 1712) "*Nühüft [Peşrevi], Usûlî [Ağır] Sakîl*" in the version of Arel 110. The third *hâne* is especially suitable for such a comparison, as musical time usually slows down in this section.

A *büyük usûl* consists of several periods, each with its specific sequence of beats to accelerate or decelerate musical time. These periods constitute spheres of tension and relaxation, which are utilized during the rhythmization of the melodic line and applied in various ways, e.g. by using interlocking techniques, where a direct interaction between the rhythmic structure of the melodic line and the

Example 4a: Buhûrîzâde Mustafa Itri (ca. 1683 – 1712), "*Nühüft [Peşrevi], Usûlî [Ağır] Sakîl*" (Version Arel 110, pp. 22-23). Detail of third *hâne*.

Example 4b: Zekî Mehmed Ağa (1776-1846), "*Şehnâz Bûselik Peşrevi [Sakîl]*" (Version İAM 1537, pp. 55-56). Detail of third *hâne*.

usûl takes place (marked with a dotted line in example 4). Another possibility is the division of a rhythmic *usûl*-stroke into shorter time values (marked with a dashed line in example 4). The example reveals that the rhythmic structures of the melodic lines in both versions realize the specifications of *usûl sakîl* exactly and with a significant frequency. This phenomenon is already observable on the level of notational technique, i.e. the formation of rhythmic groupings.

The details summarized above verify that the version of Zekî Mehmed Ağa's "*Şehnâz Bûselik Peşrevi*" found in İAM 1537 most probably represents the transmission pattern which attributes the piece to *usûl sakîl.* Ahmed Irsoy and Suphi Ezgi based their edition in their publication of classics on this version, and it cannot be ruled out that they were aware of or even used the manuscript held in the library of Istanbul Archaeological Museums today.

The Muhammes *Versions in Y.211/9: Aspects of* Usûl-*Change in Zekî Mehmed Ağa's* "Şehnâz Bûselik Peşrevi"

This finding is of major importance, since it would imply there must have been a second pattern of transmission, which was contemporary, i.e. existed already during the lifetime of the composer. The variants of the piece in Y.211/9 suggest this as well:

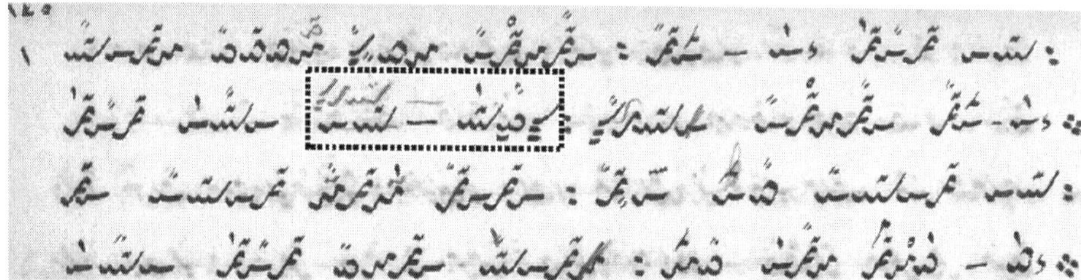

Example 5a: Zekî Mehmed Ağa (1776-1846), "*Şehnâz Bûselik [Peşrevi], Muhammes*", first *hâne*. Version 1. İstanbul Üniversitesi, Nadir Eserler Kütüphânesi, İÜko Y.211/9, 134-137, here: p. 134 (bottom)-135.

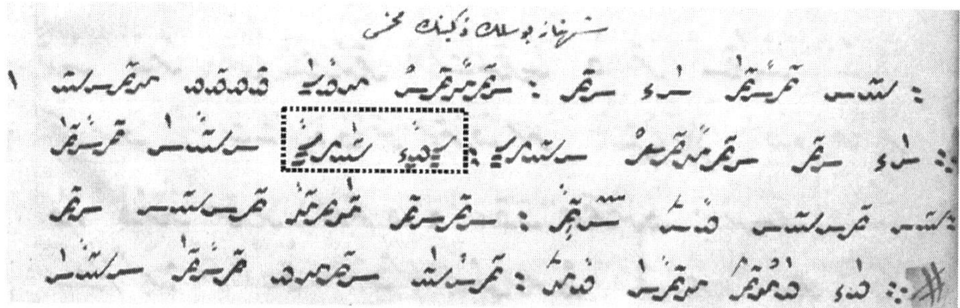

Example 5b: Zekî Mehmed Ağa (1776-1846), "*Şehnâz Bûselik [Peşrevi], Muhammes*", first *hâne*. Version 2. İstanbul Üniversitesi, Nadir Eserler Kütüphânesi, İÜko Y.211/9, 240-242, here: p. 240.

Both of these variants are written by the same hand, which is different from the hand that begins the manuscript and which, according to Ezgi, could belong to Hamparsum Limonciyan. Even a cursory comparison shows that a number of corrections to the earlier version were fully implemented in the latter. Characteristic examples can be seen at the very beginning of the first *hâne* (marked with a dotted line in example 5).

A detailed analysis of the two variants reveals that the first version constitutes a preliminary stage of the second, which is a product of considerable revision. Most profound are the changes in the third *hâne*, i.e. in the section where the influence of the *usûl*'s characteristics on the rhythmization of the melodic line is particularly obvious, as exhibited by the analysis of the variant in *sakîl*. There is reason to believe that the revisions, which primarily concerned the rhythmic structure of the melodic line, were motivated by the presumed change in *usûl*. The entire *hâne* is affected by the changes, whereas the *teslîm* remains unchanged:

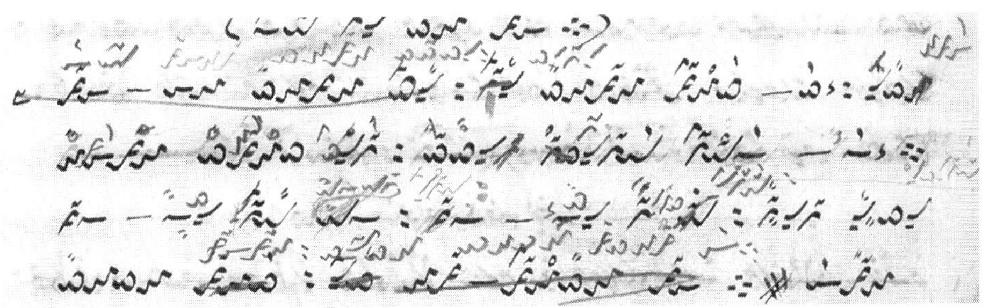

Example 6: Zekî Mehmed Ağa (1776-1846), "*Şehnâz Bûselik [Peşrevi], Muhammes*". Substantial revision of third *hâne*. Version 1. İstanbul Üniversitesi, Nadir Eserler Kütüphânesi, İÜko Y.211/9, 134-137, here: p. 136 (middle).

Before pursuing these considerations further, it should be clarified whether a transition from *sakîl* to *muhammes* is arithmetically possible at all. Since each *hâne* with *teslîm* corresponds *exactly* to one cycle of *sakîl*, the number of primary metrical units (*żarb*) in *sakîl* must be divisible by that of *muhammes*. This can be problematical according to current theory, as represented, for instance, by İsmail Hakkı Özkan, since here *sakîl* is described in all its variants as a 48-time-unit rhythm[17], while *muhammes* consists of 32 time units.[18] Establishing a mathematical relation without complication is not possible.

The situation is different when the contemporary variants of the *usûl-ler* are taken into account, as recorded in a foldout affixed to Y.211/9.[19] Here, *muhammes* is intentionally described as a 16-time-unit rhythm and not, as is common today, a 32-time-unit rhythm. Thereby a numerical relation is possible, since three cycles of *muhammes* correspond *exactly* to one cycle of *sakîl*. A comparison of both variants with *velvele* (embellishments) reveals further correlations (see example 7).

There are only a few matching beats between the first cycle of *muhammes* (marked with a continuous line in example 7) and *sakîl*, and none at all in the second (marked with a dotted line in example 7). As the example illustrates, *muhammes* represents here a musical time structure accelerated by a factor of 2 compared with *sakîl*. This is demonstrated, for example, by the time structures in the second cycle of *muhammes*, where beats of quite long duration are set against short ones. This changes with the third *muhammes*-cycle (marked with a dashed line in example 7), where there is an almost exact correspondence between se-

17 Özkan, İsmail Hakkı 1990, *Türk Mûsikîsi Nazariyatı ve Usulleri. Kudüm Velveleri*, İstanbul, pp. 678-680.

18 Cf. ibid., pp. 670-671.

19 A facsimile of this – still unique – source and its transcription are published in: Jäger 1996, pp. 186-187.

Example 7: *sakîl* and *muhammes* – Comparison of the versions given in Y.211/9

quences of beats. İsmail Hakkı Özkan describes such a variant of *sakîl* too, which he distinguishes from the "*eski şekil*", i.e. "the old form".[20]

Considering the transition from *sakîl* to *muhammes*, the comparison of these two *usûl-ler* delivers the following results:

1. A change of *usûl* in the case of Zekî Mehmed Ağa's "*Şehnâz Bûselik Peşrevi*" is, in a purely arithmetical sense, possible.
2. The change of *usûl* would have no necessary consequences for the rhythmization of the melodic line in the *teslîm*. In Zekî Mehmed Ağa's "*Şehnâz Bûselik Peşrevi*", this section is located in each *hâne* exactly at the position of the third

20 Özkan 1990, p. 680.

muhammes-cycle, which corresponds to the final part of *sakîl* in contemporary variants.

3. The *usûl-ler* clearly differ from each other in the first two *muhammes*-cycles. Changes in the rhythmization of the melodic line are expected principally in the second cycle of *muhammes*, as it otherwise would not correspond to the *usûl*'s character.

The third consequence is of particular interest, since the analytical comparison of the third *hâne-ler* of Zeki Mehmed Ağa's *peşrev* and Buhûrîzâde Mustafa Itri's "*Nühüft [Peşrevi], Usûlî [Ağır] Sakîl*" in Arel 110 proved precisely the middle section of the *sakîl*-cycle to be particularly characteristic for this *usûl*. This probably confirms the assumption, also derived from the examination of corrections in the first variant Y.211/9, that the revisions concerning primarily the rhythmic structure of the melodic line are motivated by the change of *usûl*.

It is worthwhile to analytically compare particularly the middle sections of the third *hâne-ler* in all three versions.

Analytical Comparison of the Sakîl *and* Muhammes *Versions*

First of all, there are differences to be noted in the upper staves of examples 8a and 8b, which can be interpreted as performance variants (marked with dotted lines). Changes in the lower staves on the other hand, alter the substance of the *peşrev* (marked with dashed lines). In Version 1 from İÜko Y.211/9, the legato sequence consisting of beats with longer values is dissolved into a chain of sequences accentuated with rests, which interacts with the corresponding beats of *muhammes* (marked by arrows). Especially conclusive are the revisions of *hâne*'s ending. Here, *usûl muhammes* requires a conclusion by means of the final sequence of beats *teke teke*, which does not occur in the version in *usûl sakîl*. The *muhammes* version meets these requirements in two ways: It accelerates the rhythmization and interconnects with the *usûl*, while at the same time cadencing to *muhayyer* in the final phrase (marked by dotted arrows).

The rhythmic conception of the melodic line originally related to *usûl sakîl* is in the lower system mostly abandoned and adapted extensively to *muhammes*. The remnants are eliminated in the second version in Y.211/9 (see example 8c).

Only the melodic segments that are already consistently adapted to *usûl muhammes* are taken over from the first version (lower system, marked with dashed lines). All other parts are either revised or, as in the case of the conclusion (lower system, marked with solid lines) modified again by cadencing to *muhayyer*, which is moved forward to the heavy *tek*-beat and whose note value is doubled (marked by dotted arrow). Rhythmic structure in the upper system is most strongly affected (marked with dotted lines). The melodic line as a whole is, in comparison to the first *muhammes* version, greatly accelerated and, moreover, interacts subtly

Example 8a: Zekî Mehmed Ağa, "*Şehnâz Bûselik Peşrevi*" [*Sakîl*] (Version İAM 1537, 55-56). Detail of third *hâne*, pp. 55-56.

Example 8b: Zekî Mehmed Ağa, "*Şehnâz Bûselik [Peşrevi], Muhammes*", (Version 1, İÜko Y.211/9, 134-137). Detail of third *hâne*, p. 136.

with the *usûl*, so that an *interlocking* occurs (upper system, marked by arrows) at several points. There is also an acceleration in the middle section of the lower system preceding the conclusion, which is motivated by the *usûl* (marked with dotted lines).

Only in the second revised version in Y.211/9 does the *sakîl peşrevi* become an outright *muhammes peşrevi*. The melodic material, incidentally, remains generally untouched by the revisions.

Example 8c: Zekî Mehmed Ağa, "*Şehnâz Bûselik [Peşrevi], Muhammes*", (Version 2, İÜko Y.211/9, 240-242). Detail of third hâne, p. 241.

Conclusion

It is surprising to learn that even a parameter such as the *usûl*, which, like *makam*, is very closely connected with each individual piece, can in principle be changed, and at least in some cases actually has been changed. Regardless of whether the change of *usûl* is caused by a misunderstanding in the transmission or based on an intentional revision, it is bounded by music-theoretical preconditions and "systemic rules", which can also be of an aesthetical nature.

If we want to tentatively generalize the results of the individual analyses, the primary requirement is a numerical relation between the durations of the source *usûl* and target *usûl*. This can be provided by a transformation from *düyek* to *çifte düyek*, i.e. doubling the time of a rhythmic cycle from 4 to 8 *żarb-lar*, as in the case of "*Irak Elçi Peşrevi*"'s revision, ascribed to Tanbûrî İsak. However, this is not merely an augmentation but a change in the sequence of beats itself, which, in turn, requires a rhythmic adaptation of the melodic line. On the other hand, the numeric relation of *usûl* durations can also consist in one of the cycles merging several times into the other. In the example analyzed, the presumably original *usûl sakîl* corresponds exactly to the three cycles of *usûl muhammes* obtained through the transformation, in its variant generally used in the early nineteenth century.

Structural similarities or partial correspondences between source and target *usûl-ler* generally facilitate *usûl* change. In the example analyzed this is provided by the equivalence of *sakîl*'s last third with a complete cycle of *muhammes*. This consistency enables an exact transfer of the formal structure as well, without having to change the original conception of the *teslîm*.

The analyzed versions of Zekî Mehmed Ağa's "*Şehnâz Bûselik* [*Peşrevi*]" illustrate the substantial relations between *usûl* and work, which Franz Joseph Sulzer pointed out as early as 1781, in an exemplary fashion.[21] They affect at least three parameters, which are outlined here, though only as postulations due to the insufficient amount of material analyzed so far:

1. *Usûl* and rhythmic progression of the melodic line: The rhythmic course of the *usûl* underlying the piece has a decisive impact on the rhythmization of the melodic line. The comparison of excerpts from the third *hâne-ler* of Buhûrîzâde Mustafa Itri's "*Nühüft* [*Peşrevi*], *Usûlî* [*Ağır*] *Sakîl*" and Zekî Mehmed Ağa's "*Şehnâz Bûselik Peşrevi* [*Sakîl*]" demonstrates that the rhythmical prerequisites of *usûl* progression are almost identically applied in both works. Yet it is not impossible for a work to switch from the initial *usûl* to another *usûl*. In this case, the rhythmic conception of the melodic line will be gradually adapted to the new *usûl* until it fulfills its requirements, as three versions or variants of Zekî Mehmed Ağa's "*Şehnâz Bûselik* [*Peşrevi*]" exemplify. This allows an objective insight into the synchronic transmission mechanisms of Ottoman art music culture for the first time. As the examples illustrate, types of interaction between these two rhythmic parameters of the work vary from rhythmic unison to complex interlocking structures. However, according to the results of the analyses, it is in any case intentional.
2. *Usûl*, overall musical time structure and musical form: *Usûl* determines the formal conception of a "work" to a great extent. Although it is subordinate to the preselected type of form used by the composer, which, in the abovementioned *peşrev* of Zeki Mehmed Ağa consists of 4 *hâne-ler* with *mülâzime* or *teslîm*, it still influences the course of formal progress substantially. In this respect, the composer utilizes *usûl* in an individual manner to structure the form. As the analyzed examples show, the work-cluster initiated by Buhûrîzâde Mustafa Itri arrives at solutions different from the work of Zekî Mehmed Ağa in its version in İAM 1537 regarding the realization of *sakîl* during its more than 100 years of transmission. They differ significantly, for instance, in terms of overall duration. An important parameter, namely the amount of musical time designated to the whole work, proves to be dependent on the composer's intention as well as on aesthetic premises determined by period and context.
3. *Usûl* and composition: The underlying *usûl* is an essential design principle for all compositions of Ottoman art music and is not any less important than *makam*. It is the central parameter shaping overall rhythmic structures for the composer, which, however, first emerges during performance through the heterophonic interaction between the melodic line and *usûl* with *velvele*. At the same time, it constitutes the framework of the form for the performing musi-

21 See above, footnote 9.

cian, providing the central point of orientation for the performance of the work in ensemble. Although the significance of *usûl-ler* for the composition of art music is barely studied, the analyses of selected pieces show how fundamental it may be, especially for instrumental works. Presumably, in a similar way to the *usûl*-bound *sâz semâî* that, from a purely formal perspective, constitutes a special kind of *peşrev*, *peşrev-ler* represent various formal models depending on their *usûl*, from which the composer can select. The selective analyses here provide only indications of certain formal criteria, for instance those of *sakîl peşrevi*, though they differ significantly from those of *muhammes peşrevi*. Clarification of the importance of *usûl* for the structure of form and the overall design of musical time should be seen as one of the most urgent desiderata for research on the Ottoman instrumental repertoire.

* * *

The manuscript Y.211/9 allows a rare glimpse in the workshop of a reviser of traditional Ottoman art music. The example of Zekî Mehmed Ağa's "*Şehnâz Bûselik Peşrevi*" demonstrates with a high degree of probability how a new transmission pattern is derived from an existing work. Here, we have a double peculiarity: firstly, the revision concerns a change of *usûl*, which is rarely observed; secondly, it occurs in temporal proximity to Zekî Mehmed Ağa's lifetime.

4.
Regional Traditions and Neighbouring Cultures

How Turkish are "*al-uṣūlāt al-turkiyya*" in Kubaysī's *Safīna*?

Salah Eddin Maraqa

This paper should be understood as a tiny contribution to the methodology applied in the field of historical musical research. It does not intend to provide a definite answer to the question posed in its title, namely how Turkish "*al-uṣūlāt al-turkiyya*" in Kubaysī's *Safīna* are; rather, the paper proposes a method to obtain a convincing answer, not only to this, but also to similar questions.

To begin, I will outline some general facts about the *Safīna*, the song text collection under study, and its compiler, Ḥusayn ibn Aḥmad al-Kubaysī. There are two known exemplars of the *Safīna*; the first is in Damascus, preserved at al-Assad National Library (previously kept at al-Ẓāhiriyya Library), and bears the shelf mark ʿāmm 4725 (198 folios). The second one, on which the current investigation is based, is preserved at the Staatsbibliothek in Berlin with the shelf mark or. oct. 1088 (192 folios). This Berlin manuscript, undoubtedly an autograph, was completed at the end of Shaʿbān of the year 1200 of the Hiğra, i.e. the end of June 1786 and not 1785, the date mistakenly given by Amnon Shiloah in the first volume of his *Theory of Music in Arabic Writings*.[1] The *Safīna* in fact bears no title. The word *safīna* (lit.: ship) means a large collection or anthology of literary texts, primarily poems and songs. Amnon Shiloah gave Kubaysī's work the title *Safīna bi-fann al-mūsīqā wa-l-anghām* (An Anthology in the Art of Music and Modes), a title that refers to the exordium of the work, which is written, as is often the case, in rhymed prose. The passage in question actually reads: "*hāḏihī safīnatun jamaʿtuhā bi-fanni 'l-mūysīqā*[2] *wa-'l-anghām wa-'l-uṣūl muḥtawiyatun ʿalā kalāmi ahli 'l-adabi wa-'l-qabūl*"[3] (This is an anthology I compiled in the art of music, modes, and metres containing the words of the literati and people of acceptance) (Fig. 1).

1 Shiloah, Amnon 1979, *The Theory of Music in Arabic Writings (c. 900-1900) – Descriptive Catalogue of Manuscripts in Libraries of Europe and the U.S.A.*, Répertoire International des Sources Musicales B/X, Munich, no. 158, p. 238.

2 The most widespread version of the word "music" in Arabic music literature throughout the seventeenth and eighteenth centuries is in fact, for an as yet unknown reason, the version *mūysīqī* or, as in the present case, *mūysīqā*.

3 MS Berlin, Staatsbibliothek, or. oct. 1088, fol. 3v.

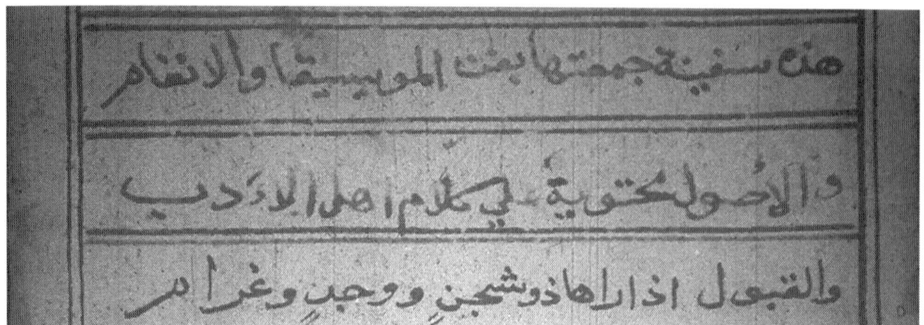

هذه سفينة جمعتها بين الموسيقا والانغام
والاصول المكتوبة في كلام اهل الادب
والقبول اذا راها ذو شجن ووجد وغرام

Fig. 1: MS Berlin, Staatsbibliothek, or. oct. 1088, fol. 3v.

If we are to accept the title given by Shiloah the word "*wa-'l-uṣūlāt*" (and Metres) might be added, given the *Safīna*'s significant contribution to the study of musical metres.

The *Safīna* contains 739 songs and is made up of six sections (Table 1).[4] The first and longest section contains twenty-nine *nawbāt*. Each *nawba* is dedicated to a single *nagham* and in a few cases, songs in related *anghām* were interpolated.[5] The songs are mainly of the genres *muwashshaḥ* and *zajal*, though some songs are in the *qaṣīda* form. The *nawbāt* are given in ascending order, corresponding to the way ʿAskar al-Ḥalabī ordered the *anghām* in *Rāḥ al-jām* near the end of the seventeenth century.[6] In ten of the *nawbāt* the song texts are divided into two categories. First, those performed with "Turkish" metres, and second, those performed with "Arabic" metres (however, "Arabic" metres are not entirely excluded from the "Turkish" *nawbāt* and vice versa). Of the remaining unspecified nineteen *nawbāt* some can, due to their content, be easily added to one or the other category; others contain mixed material. Section two of the collection (139v-142r) lists the seven "Arabic" and twenty-five "Turkish" metres, recorded with the Persian-Turkish onomatopoeic syllables *dum* and *tak*, which indicate only the quality, not the quantity, of a stroke. The third section of the collection (fol. 142v-149r) is made up of five *nāṭiq*-compositions. Section four (150v-158r) is composed of five *bashrāwāt*, followed by four new songs, which can be added to *nawbat bayātī*. Section five of the *safīna* (158r-168v) reproduces a shorter version of a treatise on music falsely attributed to an unknown author, Ṣafadī. The last section of the collection (173v to the end) contains *ashghāl*, also organised in *nawbāt* (this time not systematically) and attrib-

4 The Berlin MS was at some point bound incorrectly. The right order of the folios is: 1r-6v, 7'r-7'v (two folios bear the no. 7, hence fol. 7 precedes 7'), 9r-9v, 7r-8v, 190r-190v, 10r-189v, 191r-192v.

5 *zarkulā* and *nikrīz* in the case of *raṣd*, *nahāwand* in the case of *nawā*, and *ruhāwī* in the case of *awj*.

6 Al-Ḥalabī, ʿAskar al-Ḥanafī al-Qādirī 1083/1672, *Rāḥ al-jām fī shajarat al-anghām*, MS Paris, Bibliothèque Nationale, Arabe 3250, fol. 36v-42v, here fol. 41r.

Sect. 1	(fol.3r-139v):	twenty-nine *nawba*
Sect. 2	(fol. 139v-142r):	list of seven "Arabic" and twenty-five "Turkish" metres
	(fol. 149v):	miscellaneous material 1
Sect. 3	(fol. 142v-149v):	five *nāṭiq*-compositions
	(fol. 149r-150v):	miscellaneous material 2
Sect. 4	(fol. 150v-155v):	five *bashrāwāt*
	(fol. 155v-158r):	addenda to *nawbat bayātī*
Sect. 5	(fol. 158r-168v):	a shorter version of a *risāla* attributed to an unidentified author (Ṣafadī)
	(fol. 169r-173v):	miscellaneous material 3
Sect. 6	(fol. 173v-End):	*ashghāl al-Shushtarī*

Table 1: The content of Kubaysī's *Safīna*

uted to the mystic and *ṣūfī* poet al-Shushtarī (610-668/1213-1269). Sections two to four as well as five and six are separated by miscellaneous material such as attributions and addenda to former *nawbāt*.[7]

As to the compiler of the *Safīna*, we unfortunately know almost nothing about Ḥusayn ibn Aḥmad al-Kubaysī (Fig. 2).

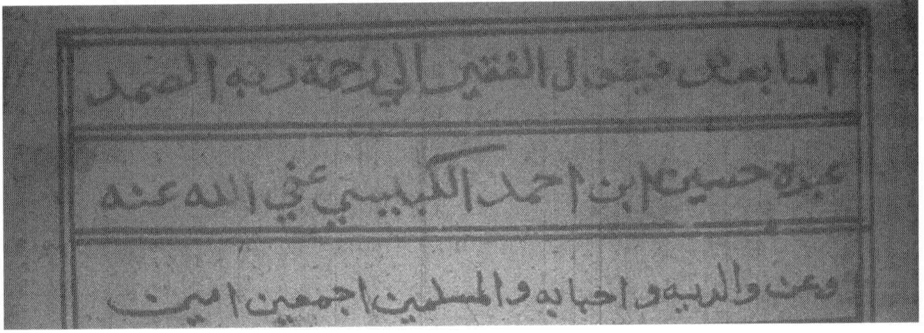
اما بعد فيقول الفقير الى رحمة ربه الصمد
عبده حسين ابن احمد الكبيسي عفي الله عنه
وعن والديه واحبابه والمسلمين اجمعين امين

Fig. 2: MS Berlin, Staatsbibliothek, or. oct. 1088, fol. 3v

The compiler is not to be confused with the identically named Shaykh Ḥusayn ibn Aḥmad al-Kubaysī al-Baghdādī al-Dimashqī (d. 1252/1836), the *Ḥanafī Muftī* of Damascus mentioned by al-Bīṭār in *Ḥilyat al-bashar* and by Jamīl al-Shaṭṭī in *Aʿyān Dimashq*.[8] According to his own statement, al-Kubaysī was a *Ḥanafī* and *Shādhilī* (Fig. 3).

7 For additional details regarding the *Safīna* and a comparison with previous and later song text collections, see Neubauer, Eckhard 1999/2000, "Glimpses of Arab Music in Ottoman Times from Syrian and Egyptian Sources", *Zeitschrift für Geschichte der arabisch-islamischen Wissenschaften 13*, 317-365.

8 Al-Bīṭār, ʿAbd al-Razzāq 1993, *Ḥilyat al-bashar fī tārīkh al-qarn al-thālith ʿashar*, Muḥammad Bahjat al-Bīṭār, ed., vol. 1, 2nd ed., Beirut: Dār Ṣādir, pp. 552-553; al-Shaṭṭī, Jamīl 1994,

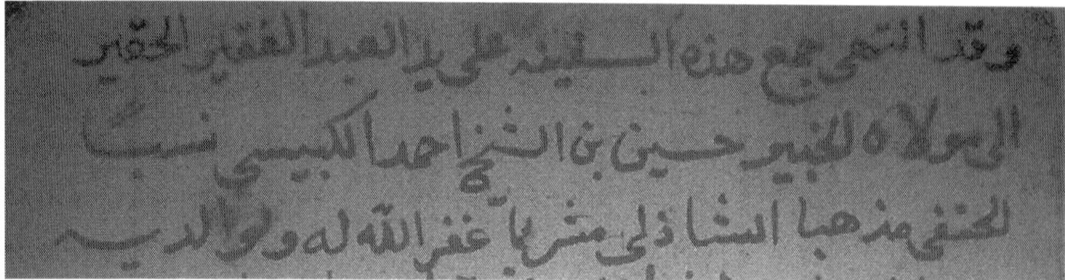
وقد انتهى جمع هذه السفينة على يد العبد الفقير الحقير
الى مولاه الخبير حسين بن الشيخ احمد الكبيسي نسبا
الحنفي مذهبا الشاذلي مشربا غفر الله له ولوالديه

Fig. 3: MS Berlin, Staatsbibliothek, or. oct. 1088, fol. 192v

This, together with the fact that he recorded works by al-Shushtarī (610-688/1212-1269), led Amnon Shiloah to assume that al-Kubaysī might be of Maghrebian descent.[9] But this was certainly not the case: being a *Shadhilī* was not unusual for a Syrian at that time. According to al-Murādī, when the Maghrebian *shaykh* and *imām* of the *Shadhilī ṭarīqa* Muḥammad al-Muzṭārī (d. 1107/1695)[10] came to Damascus in 1096/1685, the *Shadhilī ṭarīqa* became very famous there and the number of its followers and devotees grew (*wa-min dhālika 'l-waqt ishtahart al-ṭarīqa al-shādhiliyya bi-Dimashq wa-kathura atbāʿuhā wa-'l-ākhidhūna bihā*).[11] Additionally, the *Safīna* contains at least two *ashghal* by *al-Shushtarī*, in which al-Muzṭārī and his famous *shaykh* Qāsim b. Aḥmad al-Sufyānī are mentioned by name.[12] In addition, al-Kubaysī reveals himself to be a song writer (Fig. 4).

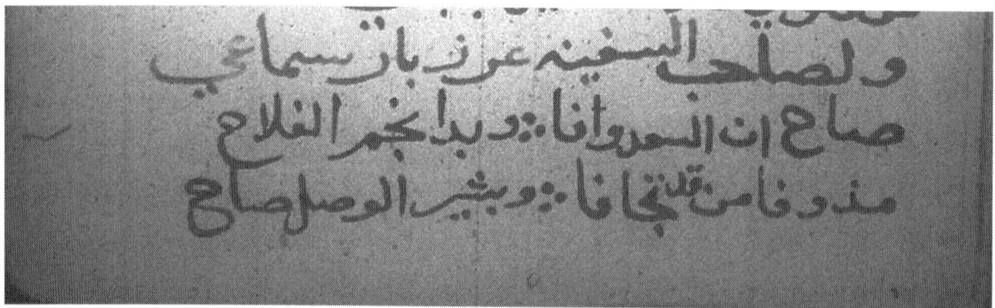
ولصاحب السفينة عرزبار سماعي
صاح ان السعد وافا ؛ وبدا نجم الفلاح
مذ وفا من قد تجافا ؛ وبشير الوصل صاح

Fig. 4: MS Berlin, Staatsbibliothek, or. oct. 1088, fol. 132r

He also immortalised himself in the *Safīna* with a *zajal* in modeʿ*arazbār* and metre *samāʿī*, in which he even reveals his forename (Fig. 5).

Aʿyān Dimashq fī al-qarn al-thālith ʿashar wa-nisf al-qarn al-rābiʿ ʿashar Min 1201-1350 H., Damascus: Dār al-Bashāʾir, p. 92.

9 Shiloah 1979, no. 158, p. 238.

10 Also spelled al-Muṣṭārī, see Trimingham, John Spencer 1998, *The Sufi Orders in Islam*, 2nd ed., Oxford [i.a.]: Oxford Univ. Press, p. 278.

11 Al-Murādī, Abū al-Faḍl Muḥammad Khalil ibn ʿAlī ibn Muḥammad 1301/1883, *Silk al-Durar Fī Aʿyān al-Qarn al-Thānī ʿAshar*, ʿĀrif Bāshā und Aḥmad Beg Asʿad (Ed.), vol. 4, Cairo: al-Maṭbaʿa al-Mīriyya, pp. 33-34.

12 MS Berlin, Staatsbibliothek, or. oct. 1088, fol. 179v,182r, and 186r.

خانه
من محسن صلوات • تترى نضيها وسلام
ما دعا داع ووافا • او افل نجم الصباح

Fig. 5: MS Berlin, Staatsbibliothek, or. oct. 1088, fol. 132v

Finally, we find al-Kubaysī mentioned as a scribe of *Ḥanafī* literature, as in this work on inheritance law (Fig. 6) by Aḥmad al-Ḥarastī (d. 1115/1703), the famous jurisprudent. This would mean that al-Kubaysī must have died after 1210/1796, the date of completion of this copy of Ḥarastī's work, which is at least ten years after the completion of the *Safīna*.

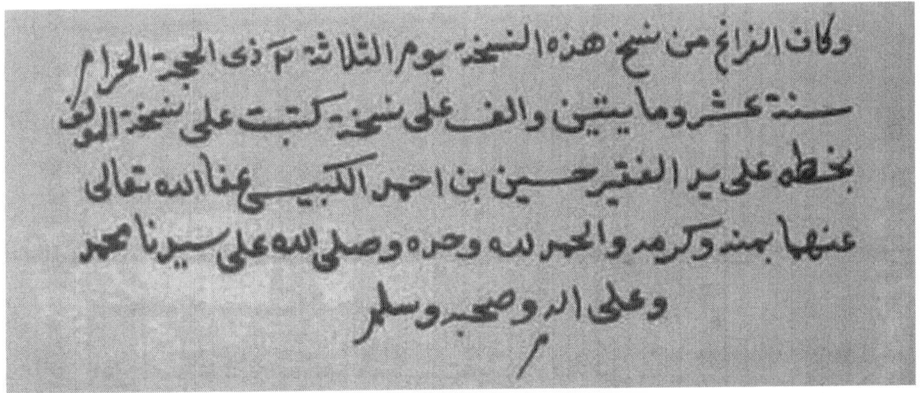

وكان الفراغ من نسخ هذه النسخة يوم الثلاثاء ٢٣ ذي الحجة الحرام
سنة عشر ومايتين والف على نسخة كتبت على نسخة المولف
بخطه على يد الفقير حسين بن احمد الكبيسي عفا الله تعالى
عنهما بمنه وكرمه والحمد لله وحده وصلى الله على سيدنا محمد
وعلى اله وصحبه وسلم

Fig. 6: MS Mecca, Library of Umm Al-Qura University, no. 20754, fol. 48r

To turn to the main issue of the paper: al-Kubaysī recorded, as already mentioned, twenty-five "Turkish" metres. Table 2 shows all metres which appear in the *Safīna*.

Metres followed by an asterisk are the ones notated by al-Kubaysī. In the order of their notation these are: *shanbar*, *zarb fatḥ*, *hazaj*, *khafīf*, *janzīr turkī*, *jifta dūyak*, *fākhita*, *dawr kabīr*, *thaqīl*, *mārūshān*, *nīm dawr*, *nīm thaqīl*, *ramal*, *turk zarb*, *nawakht*, *uyūn hawasī*, *ṣūfiyān*, *samāʿī*, *awsaṭ*, *mukhammas turkī*, *rawān*, *aqṣaq samāʿī*, *yukruk*, and *jank ḥarbī*. The check mark designates metres that – based on a thorough study of all available Arabic song text collections previous to the *Safīna* – here appear for the first time in a practical music source. As to the nomenclature of the "Turkish" metres, we see that two of these metres have never appeared in Turkish music literature. The first is *nawakht*, which Öztuna and Kāẓım Uz confirm is an Arabic metre.[13] The second is *uyūn hawasī*. As a metre, *uyūn hawasī* is known only in Syria,

13 Öztuna, Yılmaz 2006, *Türk Mûsikîsi – Akademik Klasik Türk San'at Mûsikîsi'nin Ansiklopedik Sözlüğü*, vol. 2, Ankara: Orient Yayınları, p. 107; Uz, Kāẓım 1964, *al-Iṣṭilāḥāt al-Mūsīqiyya*,

"Arabic" metres	"Turkish" metres	song captions + interior
--------	--------	51
	aqṣaq samāʿī *	7
	aqṣaq ḥuzzām ✓	2
arbaʿa wa-ʿishrūn *		9 + 5
	awsaṭ * ✓	24
dārij		4
	dawr kabīr * ✓	5
	fākhita * ✓	6 + 1
	fatḥ zarb also *zarb fatḥ* * ✓	4
	jank ḥarbī * ✓	1
	jifta also *shift dūyak* * ✓	2
	jifta samāʿī ✓	1
	khafīf (*turkī*) * ✓	9
	ḥāwī * ✓	2
	hazaj * ✓	1
iskandarānī *		6
	mārūshān *	6 + 2
maṣmūdah		2
mudawwar ʿarabī *		47 + 2
mudawwar ḥuzām ✓		1
muḥajjar ʿarabī *		45 + 1
muḥajjar ḥuzām ✓		1
mukhammas ʿarabī *		27 + 2
	mukhammas turkī * ✓	3
	nawakht *	79 + 1
	nawakht hindī	1
	nawakht khafīf	1
	nawkht thaqīl	3
	nīm dawr also *nim dawr* * ✓	5
	nīm thaqīl * ✓	0
niṣf arbaʿa wa-ʿishrīn *		0 + 2
	ramal * ✓	5
	rawān * ✓	1
	samāʿī * ✓	92 + 2
sāyib wa-marbūṭ ✓		1

translated from Turkish into Arabic by Ibrāhīm al-Dāqūqī, Baghdad: Maṭbaʿat Dār al-Jumhūriyya, p. 97.

"Arabic" metres	"Turkish" metres	song captions + interior
	shanbar (*turkī*) * ✓	38
sittata ʿashar *		55 + 5
	ṣūfiyān * ✓	84
	thaqīl (*turkī*) * ✓	4
	turk zarb * ✓	1
	uyūn hawasī * ✓	23
	yukruk *	68 + 2
	zanjīr or *janzīr* (*turkī*) * ✓	6
janzīr ʿarabī		1
janzīr ḥuzzām ✓		1
	zarbayn	9

* Metres notated by al-Kubaysī

✓ Metres appear for the first time in a song text collection

Table 2: All metres which appear in Kubaysī's *Safīna*

from where it was later imported to Egypt. Just as there are metres mentioned in the song captions but not notated,[14] there is also one metre which is notated but never appears in the song text collection, namely *nīm thaqīl.* This metre, however, was later notated again, first in *Sulāfat al-ḥān*[15], and then in *al-Safīna al-adabiyya*[16] by Aḥmad al-Safarjalānī (1311-1234/1818-1893), two very important Damascene sources, which will be referred to again shortly.

By first examining the metres notated by al-Kubaysī, especially the "Turkish" ones, and by then comparing them to their namesakes recorded in contemporaneous Turkish-Ottoman music sources, one could easily be tempted to claim that the metres were inaccurately recorded. On closer examination, and in comparison with later song text collections and sources on Arab music theory, one comes to the conclusion that this might indeed be the earliest evidence of the emergence of a solid local or regional Arabo-Ottoman or Syrio-Egyptian music tradition under prevailing Turkish-Ottoman influence. The first notated "Turkish" metre *shanbar* (Fig. 7) serves here as an example for how such a comparison unfolds.

14 For example *aqṣaq ḥuzzām, jifta samāʿī,* the three *nawakhts* (*hindī, khafīf* and *thaqīl*) and *zarbayn.*

15 Anonymous 1860, *Sulāfat al-ḥān fī 'l-alḥān*, MS Damascus, al-Asad Library (previously at al-Ẓāhiriyya Library), ʿāmm 4013, p. 2.

16 Al-Safarjalānī, Aḥmad Afandī 1308/1890-1, *al Safīna al adabiyya fī 'l-mūsīqa al-ʿarabiyya*, Damascus: Maṭbaʿat Wilāyat Sūriyya al-Jalīla, pp. 3-4.

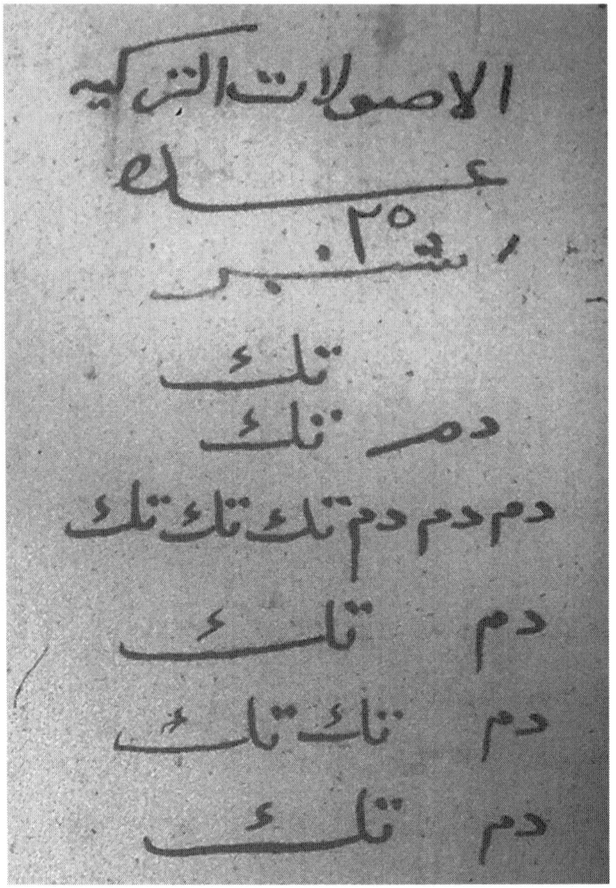

Fig. 7: *shanbar* by al-Kubaysī; MS Berlin, Staatsbibliothek, or. oct. 1088, fol. 130v

Figure 8 contains the notations of the metre *shanbar* by al-Kubaysī in comparison with the single twelve-unit *čember* handed down in Turkish-Ottoman sources, as determined and summarised by Eckhard Neubauer.[17]

A quick look at the above notations suggests that there is no relation or similarity between them. Our conclusion could be that Kubaysī's notation is wrong. This would be a conclusion drawn from "synchronic", trans-regional comparison. But what if we attempted a "diachronic", intra-regional comparison – that is, to find notations of the same metre in later Syrian sources? Indeed, we have at least

17 Cf. appendix no. 1 in Neubauer, Eckhard 1999, *Der Essai sur la musique orientale von Charles Fonton mit Zeichnungen von Adanson*, Frankfurt: Institute for the History of Arabic-Islamic Science at the Johann Wolfgang Goethe University, p. 277. Now and hereafter, whenever the metres found in contemporaneous Turkish sources are mentioned, the reference will always be the aforementioned study by Neubauer.

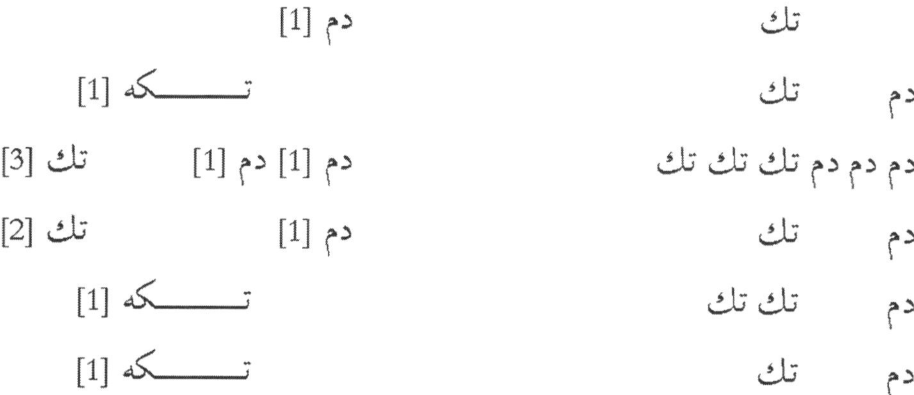

Fig. 8: *čember* in Turkish-Ottoman Sources (left) and *shanbar* by al-Kubaysi (right)

Fig. 9: *shanbar* by al-Safarjalānī (above) and in *Sulāfat al-ḥān* (below)

two sources, both from the nineteenth century, which might help us further. These are the previously mentioned anonymous *Sulāfat al-ḥān* (1860) and *al-Safina al-adabiyya* by al-Safarjalānī (1308/1890-1). Figure 9 shows the notations of al-Safarjalānī and the compiler of *Sulāfat al-ḥān*.

The circle in the notation indicates a *dum*, the vertical bar a *tak*, and the dot a rest.[18] All have the same value, usually transcribed as a crotchet. The three-circle sign (*qafla*) represents a *dum* followed by two *dum* strokes, each with half the value of the first *dum* (a crotchet followed by two quavers). Both versions above are identical, though the version of *Sulāfat al-ḥān* starts with the last *dum* of that by al-Safarjalānī. The consistent use of rest dots by al-Safarjalānī allows for a reliable transcription of the metre *shanbar* into a modern, two-line staff-notation. The result is a twenty-four-unit metre (Fig. 10):

Fig. 10: *shanbar* by al-Safarjalānī in modern notation

18 The compiler of *Sulāfat al-ḥān* does not use the dot in his subsequent notations, as in the case of *shanbar* (fig. 9).

If we place the formula of al-Kubaysī underneath the Western notation, we obtain the following result (Fig. 11):

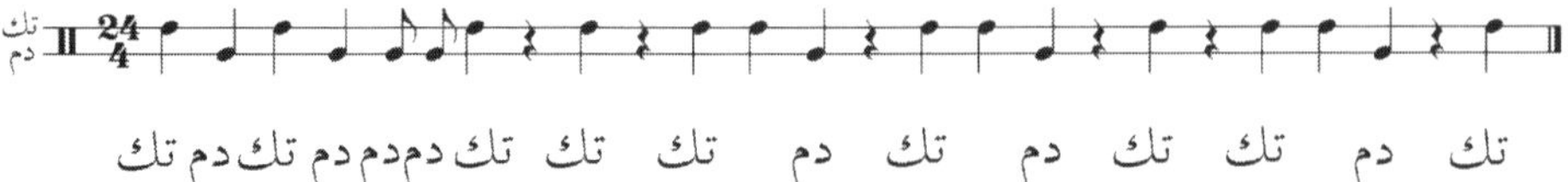

Fig. 11: *shanbar* by al-Safarjalānī with underlying syllables of al-Kubaysī

Thus, we see that, apart from the negligible halving of some *tak* strokes, Kubaysī's version matches exactly the two later Syrian versions of the same metre. The music literature of the twentieth century (for example *Kitāb al-muʾtamar*, and of course D'Erlanger's *La musique arabe*) distinguishes between two metres by the name of *shanbar*, though both have the same durational value (twenty-four units). One is *shanbar turkī* and the other is *shanbar ḥalabī* (Aleppine). It is clear that the *shanbar* in circulation since the time of al-Kubaysī and used throughout the nineteenth century is *shanbar ḥalabī*.

Yet even with this knowledge, a legitimate question remains unanswered: namely, how much does the Aleppine version differ from the Turkish one? The Western, two-line staff-notation helps us answer this question. If we double the values of the units of the Turkish-Ottoman formula and place it underneath the Aleppine one starting with its last *dum*, we obtain the following result (Fig. 12):

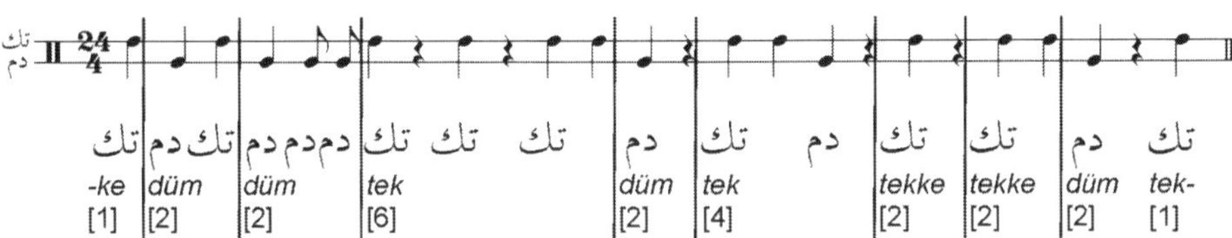

Fig. 12: *shanbar ḥalabī* in relation to *čember* in Turkish-Ottoman Sources

The congruence of the two formulas is quite obvious, and if we recall the fact that the formula written down by the compiler of *Sulāfat al-ḥān* also starts with the last *dum* of the formula notated by al-Safarjalānī (Fig. 9), it becomes even more so. Additionally, if we consider the recent Turkish formula (as notated by Öztuna[19]) we can note that it is even closer to the *ḥalabī* one (Fig. 13).

---

[19] Öztuna 2006, vol. 1, p. 206.

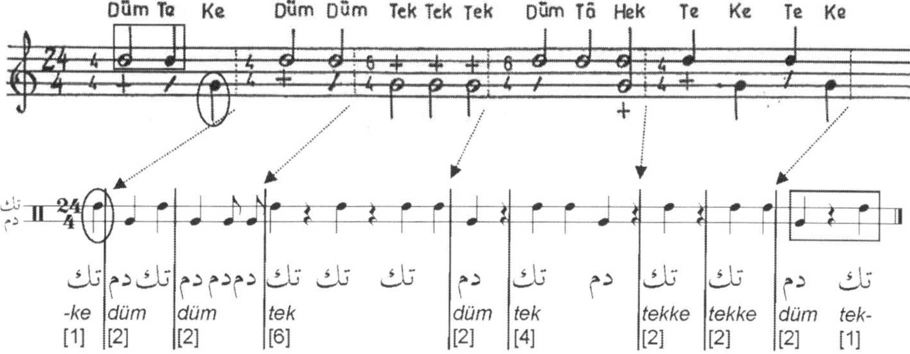

Fig. 13: *shanbar ḥalabī* in relation to Turkish-Ottoman *čember* in old and recent practice

First conclusion: This comparative method can be applied to almost all metres notated by al-Kubaysī, for they have parallels in later sources. The decisive step is to expand the scope of research and work synchronically as well as diachronically.

However, one sometimes encounters more intricate cases, such as the metre *uyūn hawasī*, recorded thus by al-Kubaysī (Fig. 14):

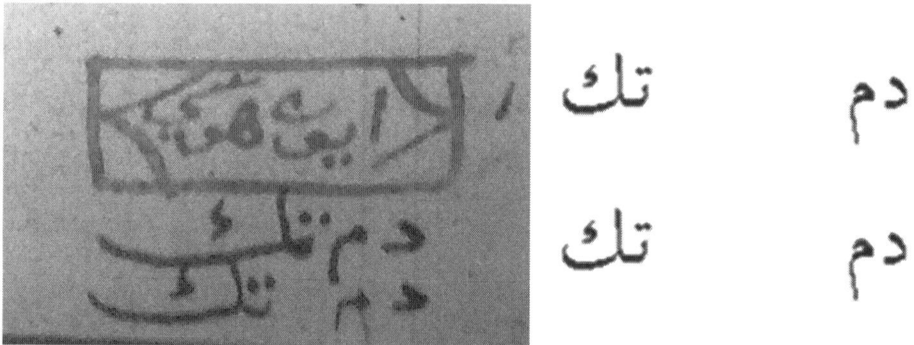

Fig. 14: *uyūn hawasī* by al-Kubaysi; MS Berlin, Staatsbibliothek, or. oct. 1088, fol. 132v

We are quite certain that a metre by the name of *uyūn hawasī* has never existed in Turkish-Ottoman music: a comparison on this basis is therefore impossible. All later Arabic sources give *uyūn hawasī* as an eleven-unit metre, and the attempt to align Kubaysī's formula with the later ones is anything but convincing. The question raised here, then, is how to proceed. The answer is by examining the repertoire itself and tracing the songs in Kubaysī's *Safīna* to which the metre *uyūn hawasī* is ascribed in previous and later collections. al-Kubaysī handed down 23 songs in this metre, seven of which appear in later song text collections (Table 3).

Song	Kubaysi	Ḥijāzī[20]	*Sulāfat al-ḥān*	Khulaʿī[21]	Ḥulw[22]
bi-abī bāhi 'l-jamāl	fol. 120r: *awj/uyūn hawasī*	p. 191: *awj/ifranjī*	p. 349: *awj/aqṣaq*	p. 133: *awj/aqṣāq*	
bayna qaysūn wa-rabwī	fol. 53r: *rakb/uyūn hawasī*		p. 72: *ṣabā/aqṣaq*		
ṣāḥi khabbir fātira 'l-ajfāni ʿan wajdī	fol. 113v: *rāḥat al-arwāḥ/uyūn hawasī*	p. 47: *rāst/ifranjī*	p. 182: *iṣfahān/aqṣaq*	p. 98: *kardān/aqṣāq*	p. 44: (*māhūr/aqṣāq*)
ṭāliʿu l-afrāḥi ḥayyānā	fol. 115r: *ʿajam/uyūn hawasī*		p. 331 *ʿajam/aqṣaq*		
layyinu 'l-aʿṭāfi wa-'l-mayli	fol. 142r: *ramal/uyūn hawasī*		p. 164: *nawā/aqṣaq*		
mutaḥajjibun zāhi 'l-maʿnā	fol. 64v: *sīkāh/uyūn hawasī*		p. 100: *sīkāh/aqṣaq*		
yā badri daʿ qawla 'l-lawāḥī ʿannā	fol. 156v: *bayātī/uyūn hawasī*		p. 268: *bayāt/aqṣaq*		

Table 3: Concordances in later collections of songs handed down by al-Kubaysī in the metre *uyūn hawasī*

On examining the locations of these seven songs in later song collections we may note that all are ascribed to the nine-unit metre *aqṣaq/aqṣāq* or *ifranjī* (as it is called in some sources). Figure 15 shows the notation of *aqṣaq* according to the compiler of *Sulāfat al-ḥān*.

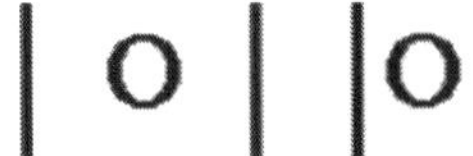

Fig. 15: *aqṣaq* in *Sulāfat al-ḥān*

20 Al-Ḥijāzī, Muḥammad Shihāb al-Dīn ibn Ismāʿīl 1311/1893, *Safīnat al-mulk wa-nafīsat al-fulk* [1273/1856 or 1857], Kairo: al-Maṭbaʿa al-Jāmiʿa.

21 Al-Khulaʿī, Muḥammad Kāmil 2000, *Kitāb al-mūsīqā al-sharqī* [1322/1904], Kairo: Maktabat Madbūlī.

22 Al-Ḥulw, Salīm 1965, *al-Muwashshaḥāt al-andalusiyya nash'atuhā wa-taṭawwuruhā,* Beirut: Dār Maktabat al-Ḥayāt.

In Kubaysī's case *uyūn hawasī* is a nine-unit metre, equivalent to the metre *aqṣaq* which appears in later song collections and works on music theory, and should be transcribed as such (Fig. 16).

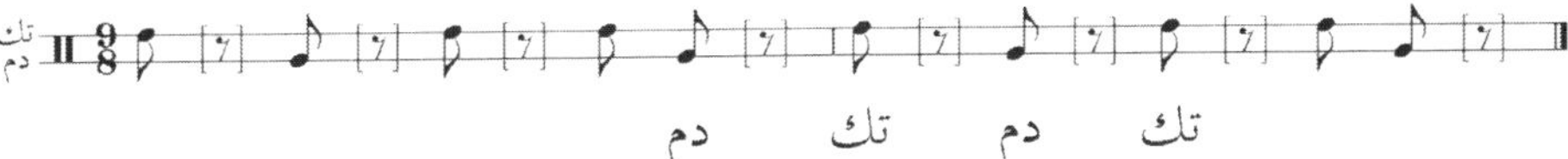

Fig. 16: Correspondence between *uyūn hawasī* by al-Kubaysī and *aqṣaq* in later sources

Second conclusion: The key to resolving similar problems is to examine the song text collections; in other words, to trace all the available concordances of a song – both earlier and later – and compare all details concerning melody, metre, and other parameters. This approach enables us to locate changes in tradition and nomenclature where they occur and therefore to draw more precise conclusions and formulate better judgements.

Some Reflections About the Pulsating, Limping, Striding, and Dance-like Movement Patterns (*Usūl*) in the Shashmaqam in the Context of the Sufi Path of Truth[1]

Angelika Jung

Preface: the Mystical Context

It is my intention to point out in this paper one aspect of the *Shashmaqam* that has so far not had a place of its own in Western research, nor in my own investigations. This may be due to the fact that we got to know the *Shashmaqam* only during the Soviet period. At that time, the focus was not on Sufi ideas and the *Shashmaqam* was interpreted and performed as a great national epic that contained love stories. On the other hand, the focus in Western research was on the analysis of the tonal system, mainly compared to the Arab, and more rarely the Turkish, tradition.

But considering the fact that the *Shashmaqam* reached its climax in a place (Bukhara) and at a time (nineteenth to twentieth centuries) when Sufi ideas and practices were widespread, it is high time we started focusing on this obvious connection.[2] Bukhara was the centre of the *Naqshbandi* order; and although, or even because, this order preferred the silent worship of God (*dhikr*) in its daily practice, the *Shashmaqam* as a whole seems to be an expression of the very ideas and principles of this mystical trend. This is not only reflected in the sung texts (*ghazals* and others) but also in the structure of the music itself.[3]

What the task of the musician and the singer who created and performed the *Shashmaqam* was and what the deeper meaning of the *Shashmaqam* consists of can be understood from the "*Mughannī-nāma*", written in the *mesnevi* form and preceding many of the manuscripts of *Shashmaqam* texts from the nineteenth century:[4]

---

1 The translation from the German original was made by Dr. Gerhard Hartmann.

2 In his book *The hundred thousand fools of God, Musical travels in Central Asia* (Bloomington 1996) Theodore Levin – as far as I can see – does not associate the *Shashmaqam* with Sufism. Rather, he analyses the conditions under which it became a "moribund classical repertoire" in Soviet Uzbekistan (pp. 46ff, 89-91, 113-115); and emphasises the important contribution of Jewish musicians to the emergence and survival of the *Shashmaqam* (p. 92, 263).

3 This is described in detail in my forthcoming publication (2015) *Der Shashmaqam aus Buchara. Beiträge zum Verständnis der klassischen Musik Mittelasiens*, Berlin, especially in chapter 5.

4 See for example manuscript no. 5734 of the Institute of Oriental Studies of the Academy of Uzbek Sciences, Tashkent, entitled *dar bayān-i Shashmaqām*. This *mesnevi* is also translated into Russian by Matyakubov (2011, *Bucharskij šašmakom*, Tashkent, pp. 208-209).

1. Singer, it is time for the melody to flare up – (or: singer, delve into the sound of the melody [*nawā*]),
   For, the whole of being rests on sound (*sadā*).
   Or (another version): For, the whole of being rests on Nothingness (*fanā*).
2. Play the melody of ecstasy, passion and joy (may also be interpreted as: create the way of ecstasy, passion and joy).
   Open, through your voice, the reception hall of my heart.
3. Play the melody of the way which has no melody[5],
   That means: tune into the cosmic order.
4. Why does the lamenting melody of the flute (*nay*) come out of a staff?[6]
   Why is the secret noise in the rose garden jubilation?
5. Is there no melody (*naghma*) in the frets (*parda*) of a harp (*chang*)?
   Is its heavenly wine not the murmur of a melody?
6. Why is the tambourine (*daf*) the mirror of the "House of Astonishment"?
   Why is the arrival of joy without tone (still)?
7. How long will the pegs (lit. "ears") of the Tanbur (*tanbūr*) be stretched?
   How long will the strings have knots on their tongues?[7]

As we can see, this is a way of achieving harmony with oneself and thereby with the whole universe and finally, when the time is ripe, emerging into perfect stillness. The mystic knows that motion and life emerged from perfect quietude and motionlessness and will return to them. In this way, in the *Shashmaqam* the path leads to various stages (*maqām*)[8]: From recognizing the comprehensive greatness of God (*Buzruk*, i.e. *buzurg* = "great") and from discovering what is "right, true and authentic" (*Rāst*) and from the infiltration of the divine melody into existence (*Nawā*), from perceiving the polarity of the world and the seeming separateness of the lover and beloved (*Dū-gāh*) and discovering the third party behind it which is invisible completeness (*Se-gāh*) – to that "shore" (*'Irāq*) and place in the heart where pain and happiness unite and pure serenity appears.

5 This topos is used frequently, e.g. in a *ghazal* by Nawā'ī sung in the *Talqīn-i Mughulcha-i Buzruk*: "There was only the song of distress; no other melody among the lovers. So I am after all your prisoner like Nawā'ī [which means: "person rich in melodies"] and have come to lose the melodies (*bī nawā*)". Sigrid Kleinmichel interprets *bī-nawā* as "sad and worried", cf. Kleinmichel, Sigrid 2003, "Nawā'ī-i bī nawā" in: *Mīr ʿAlīšīr Nawā'ī. Akten des Symposiums aus Anlaß des 560. Geburtstages und des 500. Jahres des Todes von Mīr ʿAlīšīr Nawā'ī am 23. April 2001*, Barbara Kellner-Heinkele and Sigrid Kleinmichel (Ed.), Würzburg 2003, 97-118.

6 Here, the Arabic word *ʿasā* refers to the staff of Moses.

7 The knot on the strings of the *tanbur* seems to indicate that the string for this reason cannot freely vibrate and thus is not able to sound. It seems to be also a symbolic expression for a person who, due to his or her conditioned mind and behavior, is not flowing with the stream of the universe. The expression "*tā ba kay*?" (until when?, yet how long?) is to be found in various contexts, but mostly expresses impatience and longing in striving for unification with the beloved or longing for enlightenment or truth. Saʿdi for instance says: "How long must one yearn in this narrow cage? Imagine, one day the cage will break and the bird will fly away (translated from a Persian calligraphy in: Hickmann, Regina (Ed.) 1979, *Indische Albumblätter, Miniaturen und Kalligraphien aus der Zeit der Moghul-Kaiser*, Leipzig und Weimar, image 44).

8 The *Shashmaqam* cycle, i.e. the cycle of the six *maqāms*, consists of the *maqām* cycles *Buzruk, Rāst, Nawā, Dūgāh, Segāh* and *ʿIrāq*.

But the real secret which is somehow hidden in the *Shashmaqam* is the mini cycle of the 7th *maqām*, which is not referred to as a *maqām* and is called *Ārāmijān* (lit. "peace of the soul"). This cycle, which consists of three parts (*Sarakhbār-i Ārāmijān, Ārāmijān* and *Ufar-i Ārāmijān*), can obviously be sung in different modes.[9] This may point to the fact that one need not proceed necessarily through all six stages (*maqāms*) one by one to find that deep quietude or emptiness and peace, but that one can obviously depart from any stage (*maqām*) into the "quietness of the soul" (*Ārāmijān*). Many musicians themselves were on the "path of love" (*rāh-i 'ishq*) in order to recognise and experience the inexpressible secret of life, giving up performing music once they had reached it.[10]

The aim of the mystic is to unite with the beloved being – which may be called "God" or "Nature" or the Self – so there will no longer be two things, no object and no subject, but only one that does not even know the concept of one. Lover, beloved and love will become one. There is no longer a separation, and this is real *tawhīd.* As Junayd puts it, the mystic wants to reach the state when "he is as he was before he was."[11]

I will now try to approach the rhythmic-metric structure of a *maqām* cycle by adopting the Sufi way of looking at things. The Sufi endeavours to recognise what is hidden behind the surface, behind the "curtain" (*parda, hijāb*) of the external forms of appearance. What matters in this context is to find out the hidden meaning that points to something that cannot be discerned with the outer senses, but of which you can sometimes experience a subtle fragrance or a breeze or an inner impulse.

One step in this direction is to look deeply at the meanings, the denotations of the terms used. Often in one single term a broad field of meanings opens up,

---

9 In previous notations (cf. Beljaev, Viktor M. [Ed.] 1950-1967, *Shashmaqom* Vol. I-V [transcribed in Western notation by Fajzullaev, Sahibov and Shahobov], Moscow; Karomatov, Fayzullah and I. Rajabov [Ed.] 1966-1975, *Shashmaqom* Vol. I-VI [transcribed in Western notation by Junus Rajabi], Tashkent) the mini cycle of *Ārāmijān* was formally assigned to the *maqām Dūgāh*, which in my opinion happened accidentally. Uspenskij does not mention it at all because it was associated with the so called second group of *shu'bāt.* When I asked Ari Babakhanov to prepare *Ārāmijān* for recording, he did this with a small group of musicians from Bukhara and we recorded this small cycle in the mode *Rāst* (this recording was made in 2008). But when he prepared the notation of the whole *Shashmaqam* he decided to change it into a mode with an augmented second which is nowhere else contained in the melodic material of the *Shashmaqam* and is usually referred to as *Hijāz*, which he also assigned to maqām *Dūgāh.* Ilyaz Malaev, too, contemplated *Ārāmijān* a great deal. He would have liked to enlarge *Ārāmijān* and to make a complete seventh *maqām* by adding some suitable parts composed by himself. This is, however, rejected by Ari Babakhanov. He argues that it must be a mini cycle; the musicians must have intended it to be so. My hypothesis is that we have here the symbolic clue for the abandonment of the world of forms in order to achieve infinite stillness.

10 Examples for this are Nawā'ī, Jāmī and Hazrat Inayat Khan, amongst others.

11 Cf. Schimmel, Annemarie 1992, *Mystische Dimenisonen des Islam*, 2nd edition, München, p. 213.

although we tend to reduce a word or term to only one meaning. As I will later show in detail, the terms used in the *Shashmaqam* never have only one meaning, but often have several, which, according to our understanding, are sometimes even contradictory.[12] Moreover, we will discover still another, hidden meaning which can be found and interpreted with the so-called *abjad* system, according to the method used by the Sufis.[13] I will also use this method here in order to probe more deeply into the semantic field of *Shashmaqam* terminology, epecially its various *usūls*. This attempt to reconstruct different levels of meaning does not claim absolute validity, but simply tries to broaden the so far narrow perspective on the *Shashmaqam*.[14]

The four major usūl*s in each* maqām *cycle:* Sar-akhbar, Talqin, Nasr *and* Ufar[15]

The basic meanings of the plural word *usūl*[16] are:

- Roots, fundamentals, origins
- Source and origin of something (of things) without additions (supplements)
- Fundamentals, pillars
- Something important, fundamental, imperative and essential
- Method, system

The major elements of all *usūls* consist of two types of beat of different sound quality (high and deep: *bak* and *bum*). They are produced either in the middle (*bum*) or at the edge (*bak*) of the frame drum *doira*. It seems that this shows in an elementary manner the basic quality of human perception, which is polar, which discerns high and deep, heaven and earth, day and night, breathing in and breathing out, but both qualities are determined by each other; one cannot exist without the other.

12 This still applies to many Persian words and was a frequent phenomenon in the ancient languages. Cf. Abel, Carl 1884, *Über den Gegensinn der Urworte*, Leipzig.

13 In this method the numbers assigned to the alphabetic characters of a certain word are used to create a new word which points to the hidden meaning. Idries Shah has made interesting references to this in his book *Die Sufis. Botschaft der Derwische, Weisheit der Magier* (1996, 10th edition, München, pp.155ff.).

14 This perspective on the *Shashmaqam* will shed some light upon the still unknown and undiscovered musical and spiritual wealth of the Bukharan tradition so that we do not merely believe what Levin writes in summarising the *Shashmaqam*: "When the lengthy and complex *Shash maqâm* [sic] suites are reduced to their constituent items, these items are essentially a series of urban songs with texts by local poets, some current in the nineteenth century and some historical figures." (cf. Levin 1996, p. 104).

15 I will not consider in this paper the *usūls* of the various *tarānas* which are sung in between the major sections analysed.

16 I want to point out that in the written sources on the *Shashmaqam* the term *dharb* (lit. "beat") is also used as a synonym for the term *usūl*.

Sar-akhbār. Usūl-i qadīm (ʻumm-ul adwār)

This *usūl* consisting of these two types of beat (*bak – bum*) is not an *usūl* in the sense of a rhythmic formula, but is a continuous pulsating character underlying the melody. We can find it in the first and most important piece of each vocal maqām cycle, the *Sar-akhbār*. This term is composed of a Persian and an Arabic word.

Sar means:

- Head, top, peak
- Beginning, end
- Desire, intention, plan
- Life

The plural word *akhbār* also has various meanings in the Persian language:

- Insights
- Consciousness
- News, information
- Fairy tales, legends

Thus, *sar-akhbār* could be interpreted as "supreme consciousness"[17] but also as "principal information" or "initial insights". As a matter of fact, this vocal part constitutes the beginning of each vocal cycle but could also be regarded as the origin, for it already contains the most important tonal-melodic figures occurring later on in the other sections of the *maqām* cycle. Moreover, the pulsating *usūl* of this vocal part, consisting of a high- and a low-pitched beat, is the oldest and most fundamental rhythm, because it represents the natural forms in which life expresses itself, such as breathing, pulse or heartbeat. It is called *usūl-i qadīm* or *dharb-i qadīm* (which means old *usūl*, old beat) or *ʿumm-ul adwār* (i.e. mother or source of the rhythmic periods). Here the pulse of life itself is embodied, because when breathing or the heartbeat stops, life is gone. Based on the conscious certainty of "I am", "I exist", the mystic journey can begin. Thereby the quality of the two poles *bak* and *bum* implies the third item lying behind them, which is stillness.

[17] It might also be regarded as possible that *sar-akhbār* is a Persian adaptation of the Arabic *ra's al-fuhmat*, i.e. the "principal head of cognition", which means the spiritual activity of man after his purification, or changed consciousness (cf. Shah 1996, p. 198).

Fig. 1: Beginning of the *Sarakhbār-i Nawā* in the *Maqām Nawā*.[18]

The text[19] is a *ghazal* by Hāfiz (ca. 1320-1390):

1. *Saqi*, illuminate my glass through the bright clarity of wine
   Singer, sing that the course of the world is in accordance with wishes mine
2. In the glass I saw the picture of my beloved's face
   Oh you, who has no idea of the bliss of the rapture divine...

Nawā, we could say, has been the most favored *maqām* cycle of the *Shashmaqam* for almost the last one hundred years. As early as Darwīsh 'Alī (and later in several *Shashmaqam* manuscripts), it is noted that the *maqām Nawā* dates back to the prophet David. And tradition has it that each musical tone (*āwāz*) emerging from David's throat while he was singing transmuted into 70 melodies (*lahn*). In order to hear this singing, wild beasts appeared and birds also came flying down to enjoy it,

18 The musical examples which I presented during the conference were taken from a recording published as a CD supplement to the notated edition of Ari Babakhanov's rendition of the *Shashmaqam* (cf. Jung, Angelika [Ed.] 2010, *Der Shashmaqam aus Buchara. Überliefert von den alten Meistern, notiert von Ari Babakhanov*, Berlin: Schiler-Verlag). Instead of the sound examples, I will quote here and in the following figures notated examples from the same publication.

19 The complete texts of the poetry of *Maqām Nawā* in my German translation are to be found in the 3rd chapter, paragraph 3.5 of my forthcoming book (Jung 2015).

being so enchanted that they fell down (from the trees) having lost their consciousness, i.e. they found what the Sufis search for – the unio mystica.[20]

The semantic field of the word *Nawā* is surprisingly large.[21] It means:

- Victuals, food. One's daily bread. Everything that is necessary for life such as food, clothing, instruments and other things. Food for traveling, food for the way
- Fortune, wealth, large amount of property, welfare, glamour, beauty, liveliness, benefit
- Fate, destiny, power, custom, law
- Chants of the magicians (followers of Zarathustra) and their tunes; singing of birds. Musical tone. *Maqām*. Melody. One of the famous twelve *maqāmāt* which are today also known as *dastgāh*
- Tone, melody. Voice, song. Any tone that can be produced from stringed instruments either with a plectrum or a bow. Singing
- Lament either of humans or birds
- Present. Vow
- Grandson. Son
- Gratitude, praising
- Imitation. Parrot
- Statement, expression
- Berry and seed. Seed of fruits
- Name of a musical instrument
- The greatest and best of each
- Dancing. Jumping up and down, hopping
- Happiness. Joy, satisfaction
- Burden, trouble, sorrow
- Insult, reproach
- The top of something
- Being separated; separation from the beloved
- Being conscious of something, being informed, being wise, reasonable, circumspective, and cautious
- Fate, destiny, oracle, good luck

20 Cf. Semėnov, Anton A. 1946, *Sredneaziatskij traktat po muzyke Darviša Ali* (summarised translation from Persian into Russian, introduction and commentaries), Tashkent, p. 8. This story is also to be found at the beginning of manuscript No. 5734 of the Uzbek Academy of Sciences Tashkent with the title "*dar bayān-i Shashmaqām*" dated 1285/1868.

21 Here and in other instances I refer to the two-volume Persian dictionary *Farhang-e motawasset-e Dehkhoda* (Dehkhoda, Ali Akbar et al. [Ed.], Tehran) as well as the Persian-German dictionary by Heinrich Junker and B. Alavi (2002, *Persisch-Deutsch Wörterbuch*, 9th edition, Wiesbaden).

- Line, dash/line, strip, trace, track
- Something written, document, spelling

It is extremely interesting to look at the variety and partial contrast of these meanings and to realise that they are all contained in the first meaning (victuals). All that constitutes life is contained in this single word. And, indeed, the rhythmic and melodic forms of expression in *maqām Nawā* are extraordinarily multifarious, on which, however, I cannot enlarge here. In addition, looking for the hidden meaning of *Nawā* we find the Persian word *zan* (woman). So it seems that this *maqām* contains and points to feminine qualities.

Usūl Talqīn

Talqīn means:

- To explain, to make somebody understand
- Instruction, teaching
- Persuasion, suggestion
- Reading the creed to the ears of a dying person
- In the Sufi tradition it means the initiation by a master into a particular *dhikr* until the disciple can constantly repeat it, thus keeping it in his memory.
- There is also the *talqīn-i nafas*: the instruction to acquire a particular kind of breathing, i.e. by stopping breathing an artificial delay occurs, a break, in which something new and unexpected may reach consciousness. (Such kinds of "breathing *dhikrs*" were widespread in Uzbekistan until the early Soviet period).

The *usūl* of the *Talqīn* in the *Shashmaqam* expressed in the traditional syllable language has the following structure: *bum bak īst bum bak.*

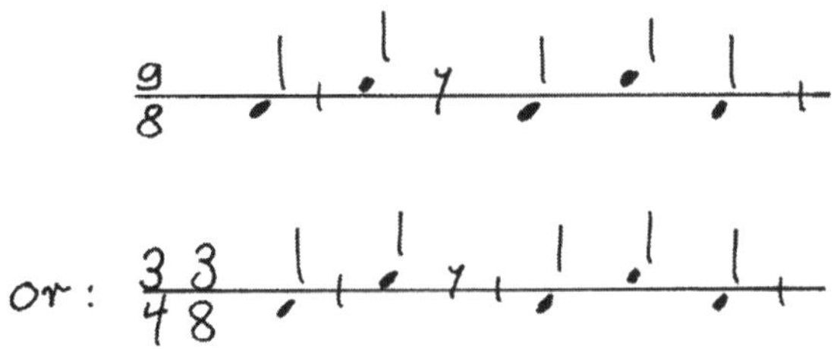

Fig. 2: The same *usūl* in Western notation

This kind of notation has been familiar for decades, but it reflects the special impulse of motion only to a certain extent. V. A. Uspenskij, who first documented the *Shashmaqam* in Western notation[22], had difficulties with this "stum-

[22] Cf. Uspenskim, V. A. 1924, *Šest' muzykal'nych poėm, zapisannych v Bucharе,* Moskau.

bling" *usūl*, for this stumbling or limping *usūl* (*usūl-i lang*) prevents an automated mechanical movement. Moreover, it is actually impossible to transcribe this *usūl* adequately into Western notation, because it cannot be counted nor measured by a metronome, not even with modern techniques; rather, one must feel it. This was a real challenge for those musicians who wanted to study the *Shashmaqam* in Soviet times without knowing the tradition from personal experience.[23]

It is obvious that the *usūl* of the *Talqīn* in the *Shashmaqam* was connected with the practice of *dhikr*. *Dhikr* is to bring back man to the moment when "God" addressed him: before the creation of world and man, "God" is said to have asked the future mankind (Koran, Sura 7/171): "Am I not your Lord?" (*alastu bi-rabbikum*?) And they answered: "Yes, we testify to it" (*balā shahidna*).

Contemplating the structure of the *usūl Talqīn* we notice that the rhythmic interval *īst* in this *usūl* is of enormous significance.[24] *Īst* is derived form *īstādan*, meaning "to stop", but also "to be". At the very moment when movement stops and stillness begins, the state of being can be felt. Leading to a delay in the movement process, this stop is of the utmost decisiveness for the process of suggestion infused by the Sufi master (see the meaning of *talqīn* above). By means of this stopping of movement, by this quietness, the memory of the primordial covenant with "God" can be activated. "Man answers with his *dhikr* the eternal words which in the true sense made him into man. Thus the *dhikr* which is now executed in time and space brings him back to the moment of the divine address, when he was given spiritual food at the "banquet of *alast*" (as Persian poets call it). Man now answers with words of praise in constant remembrance, until he may reach the point when he, the subject, is lost in the object of memory, when memory, the remembering person and the person remembered unite, as was the case before the "day of *alastu*". All that has been created will disappear, and the only true subject, the eternal God, will be as He always was and will always be."[25] It is the timeless and spaceless absolute Nothing, potentially containing everything.

23 Ari Babakhanov told me how long it took until those singers from Bukhara who did not grow up in this tradition and who learned the *Shashmaqam* from him after the independence of Uzbekistan could grasp this *usūl*.

24 Unfortunately, in the *Talqīn-i Nawā*, recorded on the CD which was released together with Ari Babakhanov's notation of the *Shashmaqam* (Jung 2010), this pause is filled with another beat of "*bak*". I asked Ari Babakhanov why this is so and he said that the *doira* player did this out of habit and for convenience, and he himself, as the teacher, did not insist on respecting this *īst* of the *usūl*, because there were so many other things which he had to be aware of in this recording. It seems to me that musicians have forgotten the importance of the pause *īst* since pieces of the *Shashmaqam* are no longer related to the Sufi context but are performed in worldly contexts like weddings and other festivities.

25 Translated into English from Schimmel 1992, p. 245.

Fig. 3: Beginning of the *Talqīn-i Bayāt* of the *Maqām Nawā*

The text is a *ghazal* by ʿAwadh (1884-1919 in Khwarizm)

1. Yesterday a drunken narcissus came to my mind;
   So the thought of the wine's intoxication disappeared from my memory.
2. I wished to put my head on the foot of the beloved.
   He said, "grow, flourish, you ignorant, foolish being".

Interestingly, the poem begins with a reference to the drunken eyes (narcissus) of the beloved, which make the lover drunk too, so that he can even abstain from wine. This corresponds aptly to the limping and stumbling *usūl*, the staggering step of a drunken person.

In the *maqām* cycle of *Nawā,* after the principal part *Sar-akhbār* and quite a number of songs (called *Tarāna*), with the vocal part *Talqīn* a new melodic mode called *Bayāt* is introduced.

Bayāt means (according to Dehkhoda):

- To turn night into day, night originating life, nighttime, dwelling of a shepherd.
- Bread which is one night old. Conservation of bread or food.
- Smoking or freezing of meat (in snow) until it is thin and tender.
- Name of a *shu'ba* in music

According to Junker/Alavi:

- Hard, dry, stale
- Worries, sorrow
- Kind of melody

Like *Nawā*, *Bayāt* is a traditional name in Arabic–Persian musical theory. While *Nawā* belonged to the 12 principal *maqāmāt*, in systematist musical theory *Bayāt* was among the 24 *shu'bāt*. And here too in the *Shashmaqam* the relation of principal *maqām* (*Nawā*) to branch *maqām* (*shu'ba*) is still maintained. The mode *Bayāt* is embedded in the larger context of *Nawā*. It is by means of this mode that the proper transformation of body and consciousness can occur. The Sufi poets often describe how so much happens at night that they cannot and do not want to sleep, because they are waiting for the visitation of the beloved, and how sometimes the desired unification happens at night. All nuances of the meaning of the word *Bayāt* are true of the state of a person who is searching for love and truth. If a person cannot sleep at night, night is turned into day. This also has a symbolic meaning: the light of consciousness forces its way into man and enlivens him, leading him to his true nature; so it is "night giving life". In the dictionary by Junker/ Alavi, however, this is profanely translated as "worries and sorrow", since a man who remains stuck in his everyday consciousness cannot sleep because of his brooding over past and future. The Sufi, however, searches for and experiences what exists here and now, i.e. the moment constituting the gate to eternity. And in the state of drunkenness and ecstasy the unification of lover, love and beloved can occur. "Smoking or freezing of meat until it has become quite tender" signifies physical transformation, which is what the Sufi poets mean when they write that they feel as if they were smoked or even fried in the presence of the beloved, while even the opposite, freezing into ice, happens. So in the melodic mode *Bayāt* a transformation of the body occurs, in preparation for the transformation of consciousness.

Nasr

A few years ago, I still believed that the spelling *Nasr* (with *sād*), which can be found in text manuscripts of the Bukharan *Shashmaqam* from the nineteenth century, was an error by the copyists.[26] The correct spelling seemed to my mind *nathr* (= prose) which can indeed also be found, but merely in manuscripts of the tablature notation that was used for recording the Khwarizmian *maqām* cycles.[27] However, I have to acknowledge that in the tradition of the Bukharan *Shashmaqam* nothing is called as it is called accidentally, but that every term is meant to indicate something, penetrating in this way to a deeper level. Every term is chosen deliberately and with a certain intention and consequence.

26 Cf. Jung, Angelika 1995, "Prosaische oder Poetische Melodien? Zu den Begriffen nathr und nazm in der Musik", in: *Iran und Turfan. Werner Sundermann zum 60. Geburtstag gewidmet*, Ch. Reck and P. Zieme (Ed.), Wiesbaden, pp. 127ff.

27 Interestingly, in the manuscript of the Khwarizmian *maqāms* published in Matyakubov, Otanazar et al. (Ed.) 2009, *Khorazm Tanbur chisighi*, Tashkent we find both spellings.

Nasr means:

- Help, helper, assistance, support, protection
- Victory, triumph. Overcoming
- Sura 110 of the Koran "The Help" (*al-Nasr*). There it says: "When the help of God comes (*al-nasr*) and the victory (*al-fath*) / and when you see people joining God's religion in masses / then praise your Lord, asking him to forgive, as he likes to forgive".[28]
- To give away. To give away something to somebody and to give one's daily bread
- To remember the punishment of God, to follow His order and to fulfill His commandment
- The whole earth is receiving rain
- To produce rain and the growth of plants

The hidden meaning is also interesting, for when applying the *abjad* method we get the word *sham*, meaning horror, fear, flight, rejection, disgust, fraud, hocus-pocus, cheating. It is in a way the opposite of *nasr* and this must also be kept in mind: when, in the process of "awakening", fear of losing the basis of one's imagined existence arises, help will come from the divine being. If the seeker sincerely wants that the mind programmed and conditioned for many years, centuries or even millennia will transfer its authority to the heart, then help will appear to bring this about and to surrender completely to Nothingness or eternal divinity without fear. This, however, requires inner maturity. So it is probably for this reason that the vocal parts with the *usūl Nasr* constitute the centre of the whole vocal *maqām* cycle, which itself is called *Nasr.* In each *maqām* cycle there are usually three vocal parts of *Nasr* which use different tonal-melodic accents, meaning that they have different modes but the same *usūl.*

The *usūl* of the vocal parts called *Nasr* consists of six beats and shows two halves, divided by the break (pause) *īst*. In traditional mnemonic notation this is rendered as: *ba-ka bum bak īst bum-bak-ko*.

It begins with the double high-pitched beat *ba-ka*, followed by *bum bak.* After this there is the important silence of the stop *īst*, in which appears true being. After the interval the answer *bum-bak-ko* follows. Perhaps the first part constitutes the request (for "help"), while the second contains the answer, or rather the "help". It would also be possible to assume that the first part symbolizes the address of God "Am I not your Lord?" and that the second part shows the answer of man who takes the responsibility: "Yes, I testify to it".

---

28 On the internet site http://quran.com/110 we can read the rather peculiar English translation emphasising victory and conquest: "When the victory of Allah has come and the conquest / and you see the people entering into the religion of Allah in multitudes / Then exalt [Him] with praise of your Lord and ask forgiveness of Him. Indeed, He is ever accepting of repentance."

So after the "stumbling" of the *Talqīn*, in the *Nasr* something reaches equilibrium. The movement stabilizes, expressing a harmonious up and down between "heaven and earth", a measured and effortless, almost dance-like movement.

Fig. 4: The rhythmic formula in Western notation and the beginning of *Nasr-i Bayāt*

The *ghazal* is by the Sufi poet Badr al-Dīn Hilālī (hanged in 1529), who is very popular in Central Asia, and begins with the words:

Nasr-i Bayāt – *ghazal* by Hilālī (in Persian)

1. Do come, come! My heart and my soul may be sacrificed to you –
   That head on my body may be in the dust of your feet.
2. In your glamour my heart shall break into 100 parts, and each part
   Into 1000 atoms and each atom shall be in your atmosphere…

This poetic text expresses the fact that man is ready to let go of everything and to surrender himself completely to the divine truth, without retention and reservations, without hypocrisy and arrogance.

After this *Nasr-i Bayāt* and two additional songs (*tarāna*), the second *Nasr* occurs – the vocal part *Āradh-i Nawā* (i.e. "help/victory of the face of life"). Here too, in the text the melting of the lover in the face of the beloved is expressed.

Nasr-i Āradh-i Nawā – ghazal by Hilālī (in Persian)

1. By the worries in my breast I am burnt, destroyed by the waterfall from my eyes
   You are the candle of everybody's feast, I am fire and water
2. For me the torture of your care is better than any joy
   Be peace for others, so that I am there for torture…

After three more *tarānas* the third *Nasr* appears, which is called *Husaynī-i Nawā.*

Nasr-i Husaynī-i Nawā – ghazal by Midhrāb (in Persian)

1. The melody of my narrow heart is like the creaking of the gate.[29]
   I am the flower, the garden, the spring and the bowl of wine, of the same colour as the wine cup.
2. I am distressed about the impossibility of recognising the sense of my existence.
   I am a tender vessel, a dress of silk, glass and the stone thrown…

After melting in fire and dissolving in water, that is, after giving up one's personal ego, the new quality can be recognised, the transformation can already be seen: The "gate to paradise" opens as man, from the position of the witness (*shāhed*), realises that the opposite poles have dissolved and duality is no longer perceived.

Ufar

Finally, at the end of each *maqām* cycle the vocal parts with the *usūl Ufar* are played and sung, which traditionally were also danced. The *usūl Ufar* used in the *Shashmaqam* belongs to the dance-like *usūls*. Spelled *Awfar*, it can already be found in the treatises of Kawkabī and Darwīsh 'Alī, but also in those of Arutin and Cantemir[30], so that one of the few relationships between the Central Asian and Ottoman-Turkish traditions can be noted. However, the Bukharan and Khwarizmian *usūl Ufar* does not resemble the Turkish *usūl Evfer*, but rather the Turkish *usūl Semâ'î*.[31]

---

29 This reminds me of an anecdote about the rejection of music by orthodox Islamic clerics, which was translated by Friedrich Rückert: "Once our Master Jalaluddin said: 'Music is the creaking of the gates to paradise.' Then one of the stupid and impudent fools said 'I do not like gates creaking.' Then our Master Jalaluddin said: 'I can hear the gates opening, but what you hear is how the gates are closing!'" (translated here into English from the German text in Schimmel, Annemarie 1995, *Rumi. Ich bin Wind und du bist Feuer. Leben und Werk des großen Mystikers*, 8th edition, München, p. 203.).

30 Cf. Jung, Angelika 1984, *Quellen der traditionellen Kunstmusik der Usbeken und Tadshiken Mittelasiens*, Hamburg, pp. 135-136.

31 Cf. ibid., p. 179.

The *usūl Ufar* as it is used in the *Shashmaqam* can appear in many concrete forms. This is due to the fact that there is not only one dance-like vocal part called *Ufar*, but a whole cycle, in the truest sense, of vocal parts which become faster and faster and more and more ecstatic. As we learn from the earliest *Shashmaqam* researchers of Soviet times (Uspenskij and Fitrat), each *maqām* of the *Shashmaqam* consisted of three large sections or three independent cycles: first, the instrumental cycle *Mushkilāt*, second, the vocal cycle *Nasr* and third, the dance cycle *Ufar*.[32] But since only one vocal part was written down under the name *Ufar*, the division into three parts was abolished later on, and the single part *Ufar* was assigned to the vocal section *Nasr*. In this way the originally intended ternary form of a *maqām* cycle, which expressed an enhancement of the components involved, was lost. The cumulation of the components brought about a heightening of energetic tension: while in the instrumental cycle (*Mushkilāt*) only instruments perform, in the vocal cycle *Nasr* singers singing poetic texts appear and are accompanied by the instruments. Finally, in the dance cycle (*Ufar*) all these components are enhanced by dancers and their special forms of expression. Thus the way led from "difficulties" (*Mushkilāt*)[33], through "help" and "victory" (*Nasr*), to the total surrendering (*Ufar*) of body, mind and soul to "God" which is the Supreme Essence and the only being.

In his version of the *Shashmaqam* Ari Babakhanov usually wrote down two vocal parts named *Ufar* (*Ufar* and *Ufar-i chiligi*), which at least points to the fact that there was and should be a whole cycle. The main form of the *usūl Ufar* is *bum ba-ka bak bum bak īst*. In Western notation the 6/8 rhythm is used, which, however, is performed rather slowly.

Fig. 5: Rhythmic description in Western notation

32 Cf. Uspenskim 1924. Uspenskij too wrote down only one *Ufar*. Most probably, at that time the musicians did not consider it necessary to inform him in a more detailed way about the many *Ufars*, because they could play and sing the ensuing *Ufars* "off the cuff", without relying on notations. But Fitrat, who received his information from the court musician and last master of the old time, Ota Jalol, explicitly states that there can be innumerable *Ufars* (Fitrat, Abdura'uf 1993 [1927], *Özbek klassik musiqasi wa uning tarixi*, Tashkent, p. 16). This is also confirmed by Ari Babakhanov.

33 Infact, the term *mushkilāt* has a deeper meaning than we might imagine from the direct translation, "difficulties".

The word *Ufar* is spelt quite differently, referring for this reason to different etymologies:

- In old treatises (Kawkabī and Darwīsh ʿAlī) the spelling is *Awfar* (alif, wāf, fe, re). This Arabic word means "numerous, affluent, most frequently". This naturally fits into the traditional practice of the performance described above. Furthermore, the hidden meaning is – according to the *abjad* method – "green"[34] or "quick, nimble, light footed, alert, fast". This makes sense with respect to the character of the *usūl* and the vocal parts named after it.
- Interestingly, in later manuscripts such as the textual sources of the *Shashmaqam* from the middle of the nineteenth century onwards *Ufar* is mostly spelled without wāf (i.e. *alif, fe, re*). According to the Dekhoda Dictionary, this word should be pronounced as *Afar* and would simply be an exclamation of agreement or applause, as in "bravo!" The verb *afarīdan* would mean "bringing about miracles, surprising".[35]

If the letters of this word are inverted – as is permissible in the *abjad* method- we get the word *fār* (light house, flare) or the word *rāf* (mace). Both meanings point to something special: to the flare, which illuminates the way to enlightenment, and to the scent of mace (the blossom smelling of musk) which, when it is used for producing smoke, for instance, has been a well-known means for heightening one's awareness since ancient times. Razia Sultanova translates *Ufar* as "fragrant".[36]

But in both cases we have no explanation for why the *usūl* and the vocal part *Ufar* in the *Shashmaqam* are pronounced neither as *Awfar* nor as *Afar*, but as *Ufar*. Could it be a peculiar Bukharan pronounciation, or is it perhaps related to another word which we do not know? Incidentally, in Tashkent and the Ferghana region it is called *Ufor.*

- Strangely enough, there is even another spelling of the same *usūl*, which is to be found in the manuscripts of the Khwarizmian tablature notation for the *tanbur*.[37] Instead of *Ufar* we read *Īfar* (alif, ye, fe, re), for which I cannot find any meaning or etymology. The local pronounciation is *Uyfar*. However, by using the abjad method for finding out the hidden meaning of *Īfar* we get *sabr* (patience) or *rabs* (waiting). And although this seems to be the opposite of "quick, nimble, light-footed, alert" (cf. above), in a Sufi context it is obviously the personal trait which is necessary for "walking on the path of love" and reaching one's goal *–tawhīd.*

34 Green could point to the prophet Khizr or the "water of life" he is said to possess.
35 There is again no explanation as to why it is pronounced *Ufar* by Uzbeks and Tajiks.
36 Sultanova, Razia 2011, *From Shamanism to Sufism*, London, p. 78. In answer to my question about where she took this interpretation or translation from, she replied that the musicians had told her so. Ari Babakhanov does not know a special translation for it and told me it denotes only "dance-like *usūl*".
37 See Matyakubov et al., 2009, p. 293, 253,177.

Fig. 6: Beginning of the *Ufar-i Bayāt*

The *ghazal* is by Badr al-Dīn Hilālī (hanged 1529) and begins with the words:

Look at the belted waist and the sword pulled out!
Look at the usefulness of diligent effort!
How he/she/it looks from the tender head at my weeping,
So he/she/it sends the look at another one's laughing.
My rogue[38] got drunk throwing the cup of wine at my head.
Look at the drunken rogue and the throwing of the cup…

38 "*šūkh-i man*" (my rogue) can be the beloved, revealing himself as the highest consciousness by which everything was created and which is paradoxical, playful and full of humour, which is always playing with itself, so to speak. The perspective from which the poet looks at things surrounding him and at himself is that of a witness, not that of an identified person.

The second *Ufar* which Ari Babakhanov quotes in his version of the *Maqām Nawā* is performed much quicker than the first *Ufar*, but is also notated as a 6/8 rhythm: bum ba-ka bum bak bum.

Fig. 7: The rhythmic formula in Western notation and the beginning of the *Ufar-i Bayāt* 2

The text is anonymous and popular and begins with the lines:

1. Oh my beloved – the one who is my moon[39], tell me, what is my fault?
   Intimate of my pain and grief, say, what is my fault?

---

39 The moon is the symbol of the beloved. But it is at the same time also the symbol of illusion as it receives its light only from the sun. This means that the beloved, who seems to exist outside the lover, is an illusion. For in the truest sense the beloved is not outside but within him; realising or experiencing this is the goal of the Sufi's "path of love".

2. From worries I fell into one hundred misfortunes, was caught and despairing.
   Why are you far from me? Say, what is my fault?
3. I sob because of heartache about you; I am conscious[40] of this world.
   I turn my face towards heaven. Tell me, what is my fault?...

It is only the complete helplessness of the seeker, aptly expressed in the text, which makes possible what in German is called "*Hingabe*" (surrender). It is quite obvious that the last section of the *maqām* cycle (*Ufar*) is intended as the surrender of the egotistical mind. At the end of these *Ufars* the fastest possible movement, i.e. the last stage of any movement, is achieved. In the dance it reaches devotion to the invisible beloved, which in its true sense is the uncreated primordial ground of any phenomenon and traditionally given the name "God", but recognised as the Highest Self or Truth or Supreme Subject. Here the highest possible drunkenness can reveal itself, which is at the same time the deepest sobriety.

The different spelling and pronunciation of the term *Ufar* could point to the fact that the Arabic origin of this word was not so deeply rooted in the memory of the musicians of this area and has not been recognised since the eighteenth/nineteenth centuries.

Even if a direct relationship[41] to the German words *Opfer* (engl. offer)[42] and/or *Ufer* (engl. banks, shore) cannot be proved, it is obvious in the context of the *Shashmaqam* that the *Ufar* section is intended to support the surrender to "God" and an opening to unconditioned love and auspiciousness. Being the last section of a *maqām* cycle, the *Ufar* dance may lead to something which we refer to in our terminology – a little erroneously – as "ecstasy": the separate, personal consciousness of the dancer/singer can melt and even disappear during the performance by dissolving in the process of dancing and singing and flowing in total awareness of the moment.

Thus, the "work" of music seems to be a sacrificial offering[43], and the musical performance appears as an act of surrendering one's ego, which is not a personal act of volition but happens by grace. By this offering, which is experienced as a kind of death, one will reach the "shore" (in German: *Ufer*) constituting the silent and omnipresent "basis" (in Russian: *opor*) from which everything arises. By giving up one's ego in "ecstasy", perception will open up and will go beyond the artificial

40 The original has the Persian word *hūsh*, which also means spirit, soul and heart, intellect, reason, insight, sense, feeling, sensation.

41 However, I would like to point out that there is a literature about language lines and relationships which in most instances we have lost sight of, e.g. Wadler, Arnold 1997 [1935], *Der Turm von Babel – Urgemeinschaft der Sprachen*, Wiesbaden.

42 Old High German: *opphar, ophar, offar, ophir, ofir* (cf. *Deutsches Wörterbuch von Jacob Grimm und Wilhelm Grimm*, accessible online at http://woerterbuchnetz.de/DWB/).

43 The "*Musicalische Opfer*" by Joh. Seb. Bach, which was erroneously only interpreted as a dedication to Frederic II, has a much deeper meaning: cf. Dentler, Hans-Eberhard 2008, *Johann Sebastian Bachs "Musicalisches Opfer". Musik als Abbild der Spharenharmonie*, Mainz: Schott-Verlag.

limits created by personality. This is what most Sufi poetry sings about and what the dervishes and Sufis call *fanā*, i.e. giving up one's false existence, coming into non-existence (*ʿadam*) and remaining in Oneness (*tawhīd*). We should be aware of the fact that in the centre of this "ecstasy" it is quiet like in the centre of a hurricane. Pir Vilayat Khan expressed it in the following way: "the highest exhilaration is sobriety, peace and quietude, a state in which everything has been overcome."[44]

These four major vocal pieces (*Sarakhbār, Talqīn, Nasr* and *Ufar*) in the vocal *maqām* cycle of the *Shashmaqam* can be compared to some extent with the four *selâms* in the *Âyîn* ritual of the *Mevlevi* dervishes.[45] And there also in the *Âyîn* cycle, it is the dance to music and words which can bring about the same complete surrender. However, unlike the *Âyîn*, the *Shashmaqam* was not performed as a ritual, but – as far as we know – as a spiritual concert (*samāʿ*) at the court of the last three emirs of Bukhara.

Finally, after the end of the last *Ufar* and at the very end of each vocal *maqām* cycle, there is a return to the very beginning of the *Sarakhbār*, called *Supārish* (i.e. "handing over").

44 Khan, Pir Vilayat Inayat 1982, *Der Ruf des Derwisch*, Essen, p. 45.

45 According to Walter Feldman (1996, *Music of the Ottoman court: makam, composition and the early Ottoman instrumental repertoire* [Intercultural Music Studies: 10, ed. Max Peter Baumann], Berlin: VWB, pp. 187ff.) the vocal parts in the *Âyîn* of the *Mevlevis* – except the introductory hymn *Na'at-ı şerîf* – consist of the first *selâm* in *usūl devri revân* or *düyek* (14/8 or 8/4), the second *selâm* in *usūl evfer* (9/4), the third *selâm* beginning in *usūl devri kebir* (28/4) and ending in *usūl semâ'î* (6/8) and the fourth *selâm* in *usūl evfer* (9/4).

Fig. 8: *Supārish-i Nawā*

The text of the *Supārish* in *maqām Nawā* is:

Nawā-yi rah-i khushnawā'ī bisāz – pur āhang-ū pur shūr-u shirīn nawāz
Play the melody (*nawā*) of the path of the beautiful melody (*khush-nawā'ī*)
Play (*nawāz*) melodiously and with fervour (also means "salt") and sweetness.

In the *Supārish* the motion slows down, returns to the rhythm of the pulse and deliberate breathing, and finally ends in the silence which the whole cycle arose from. So, mysteriously, from a higher perspective nothing seems to have happened. Musicians, instruments, music, i.e. everything, returns "to what it was before it was"... until the next cycle begins.

Conclusion

By different kinds of *usūls* and impulses, by certain words and exclamations (*ey yār, jānam āh, jān-i mā, o yāra, hay jānim, yār yallalā dūst* and others) and by intensifying the flow of melodic motions, the connection to the beloved may finally be experienced: From deliberate breathing (*usūl-i qadīm – Sarakhbār*) to teaching, learning and remembering (*Talqīn*), from asking for help and success (*Nasr*) to finally surrendering one's own ego and melting into the One Essence (*Ufar*)[46], it might be possible for a musician and listener (*shunawanda*) to reach his goal and to recognise his true nature – if grace comes, *inshā'allāh*.[47]

46 Metaphorically expressed, when the drop of water mixes with the ocean.

47 Sultanova (2011, p. 78) expresses the development taking place in a *maqām* cycle in a somewhat different way: "every single *Maqam* is identified with development from the wisdom of the first part of the *Maqam*, *Sarahbor* (main message), to a quiet *Interpretation* or the second stage – *Talkin*; observation of *Nasr* (third stage), and then the optimistic finale, conclusion to the fourth stage – *Ufar* (fragrant) [sic]."

5.
Subsequent Developments: *Usûl* in the Music of the Republic

Usûlsüz: Meter in the Concerts of Münir Nurettin Selçuk (1923-1938)

John Morgan O'Connell

During the early-Republican era (1923-1938), the renowned Turkish vocalist Münir Nurettin Selçuk (1899-1981) developed a new 'classical' style in the context of an old 'classical' venue, the concert hall.[1] Performing as a soloist (*solist*) in imitation of a recital (*resital*), he viewed himself as a 'concertiste' (*konsertist*) who had revolutionized Turkish music by adopting 'western' techniques in vocal production and by adapting 'western' conventions in vocal performance. Here, his trip to Paris was seminal (1928). Although the artist had an established career in the recording studio and the radio station, Selçuk drew upon his experience of public performances in the French capital to develop his own version of a national music (*millî musiki*), a style that assuaged the ideological prejudices of the period. To this end, he sought to create a concert program which involved the synthesis of an 'eastern' style (*alaturka*) with a 'western' idiom (*alafranga*). That is, he aimed to 'alafrangize' *alaturka* by creating a 'classical' style of Turkish music that is still performed today.

In this chapter, I examine the metric organisation of concert programs presented by Selçuk.[2] In particular, I look at his unique arrangement of musical rep-

1 In this chapter, I adopt a number of academic conventions. Where not detailed, all technical terms and institutional names use modern Turkish spellings found in Redhouse (Redhouse, Sir James 1990, *İngilizce – Türkçe Redhouse Sözlüğü*. Istanbul: Redhouse Yayınevi). When not applying Turkish equivalents, words in Arabic and Persian employ spellings found in Wehr (Wehr, Hans 1994, *A Dictionary of Modern Written Arabic*, J. Milton Cowan, ed., Wiesbaden: Otto Harrassowitz) and Haim (Haim, S. 2004, *The New Persian-English Dictionary*, Tehran: Moaser Farhang) respectively. Generally speaking, personal names are rendered in their modern form, dates (where possible) are given and surnames (where appropriate) are added. For the sake of simplicity, the plural forms of all non-English terms are represented by appending the English suffix (-s). In those instances where words are contested (such as 'western') or problematic (such as 'classical'), these are represented using inverted commas (' '). As is usual in publications concerning the Turkish Republic (see Shaw, Stanford 1977, *History of the Ottoman Empire and Modern Turkey*, 2 vols., Cambridge: Cambridge University Press, vol. 2, p. ix), the scientific transliteration of Ottoman terms is not provided.

2 In this chapter, I adopt a number of musical conventions. With respect to *usûl*, a time signature is provided as it is found in a particular source. Where appropriate, the relevant numbers are appended in parenthesis. With respect to *fasıl*, the terms 'classical' (today called: "*geleneksel fasıl*") and 'popular' (today simply called: "*fasıl*") are used to represent two types of repertoire in a *fasıl* format, the former being performed in a formal context and the latter being featured in an informal setting. See Feldman, Walter 1996, *Music of the Ottoman court: makam, composition and the early Ottoman instrumental repertoire* (Intercultural Music Studies: 10, ed. Max Peter Baumann), Berlin: VWB and Hall, Leslie 1989, *The Turkish Fasıl: Selected Repertoire*, PhD. Dissertation, University of Toronto, respectively (amongst others) for a historical overview and an ethnographic study of the Turkish *fasıl*. With respect to *güfte*, I source all song texts with

Plate 1: Representing *Usûl* – Münir Nurettin Selçuk (c. 1939)

ertoire, a concert format that deviated significantly from the standard organization of traditional suites (*fasıl*-s). Although criticized by contemporary critics for the irregular character (*usûlsüz*) of his concert presentations, I argue that Selçuk advanced an alternative conceptualization of musical meter that can be found in published collections of song texts (*güfte mecmuası*-s) and musical notations. In this matter, I suggest that his mentors Refik Fersan (1893-1965) and İsmail Hakkı Bey (1866-1927) were critical. Although unrecognized in the standard accounts of the vocalist's life, both artists played a significant role in the unique configuration of a 'classical' program that was more suited to a recording studio than to a concert hall. Widely vilified in the contemporary media for his choice and rendition of a 'classical' repertoire, Selçuk had to develop a methodical (*usûllü*) approach to Turkish music, creating a concert format that is still found today.

In Turkish, *usûl* has 2 meanings. First, *usûl* could mean method, usually a method for learning an instrument. With the expansion of music schools following the Young Turk Revolution (1908), music specialists responded to an amateur interest in *alaturka*. For example, Abdülkadir Töre (1873-1946) wrote a musical

reference to Üngör, Edhem R. 1980, *Türk Musikisi Güfteler Antolojisi*, Istanbul: Eren Yayınları. With respect to programs, a detailed analysis of the concert programs considered here can be found in my recent monograph (O'Connell, John 2013, *Alaturka: Style in Turkish Music (1923-1938)*, SOAS Musicology Series, Farnham: Ashgate).

method for violin instruction.[3] Organized into a graded series of musical exercises (181 in total), the music educator at first represented the rudiments of musical notation (lessons 1-7), before introducing a simple *usûl* (in this instance *sengin semaî*) with its characteristic beats (here called "*ika*") and a common *makam* (in this instance *makam Rast*) with a simple song (here written as "*ben seni hep özlerim*"). Mode by mode, meter by meter common *makam*-s and small *usûl*-s are introduced. 'Popular' meters like *katikofti* (8/8) and *mandıra* (7/16) are described, common meters like *sofyan* (4/4) and *devri hindi* (7/8) are detailed. After *curcuna* (10/16) is explained, an important theoretical discussion on Turkish music is appended.

Second, *usûl* could mean meter, a cyclical meter that is common in Turkish and Arab musics (amongst others). Here, the Arabic term *īqāʿ* was sometimes used interchangeably with the Turkish word *usûl*, the academic publications *Darül'elhan Külliyatı* and the *İstanbul Konservatuarı Neşriyatı* preferring to use the word *ika* rather than *usûl*. Interestingly, Tanburî Cemil Bey (1871-1916) in his musical directory entitled "*Rehber-i Mûsikî*"[4] uses both the designations *ika* and *usûl*, the former (broadly speaking) used to represent large cycles (such as *zencir*) and the latter employed to illustrate small meters (such as *curuna*). Some theorists even looked to older sources where the term *vezin* was employed. Although Cantemir[5] used the word *vezin* both to describe the metric pattern of an *usûl* (*vezn-i usûl*) and different representations of an *usûl* (such as *vezn-i sagir*), İsmail Hakkı Bey employs the word *vezin* interchangeably with *usûl*, utilizing the first in his schematic representation of *makam*-s[6] and the second in his didactic representation of *solfej*[7].

Of course, *vezin* has another meaning in Turkish music. In contrast to *usûl*, *vezin* means poetic meter in most sources. In this respect, song texts are usually composed according to the rules of prosody. Two types exist, one based on qualitative syllabic meter, the other based on quantitative syllabic meter. The first, called "*aruz vezni*" draws upon the literary rules of an Arabic-Persian tradition in 'classical' contexts, being used to set a poetic line in a regular series of long and short syllables. While sometimes overstated[8], certain musical meters are suited to particular poetic meters. As I discuss below, setting *usûl* to *aruz* in a *güfte taksimi* was a significant task in musical examinations.[9] The second, called "*hece vezni*" draws upon the oral principles of a Turkic tradition in folk contexts, being used to structure poems or

---

3 Töre, Abdülkadir [1913], *Usûl-i Talim-i Keman*, Istanbul.

4 Cemil Bey, Tanburî 1989 [1902], *Rehber-i Mûsikî*, M. Hakan Cevher, ed., Izmir: Ege Üniversitesi Basımevi.

5 Tura, Yalçın (Ed.) 2001, *Kitābu ʿilmi'l-mūsīḳī ʿalā vechi'l-ḥurūfāt. Mûsikîyi harflerle tesbît ve icrâ ilminin kitabı, I. cilt, Edvâr* (*tıpkıbasım – çevriyazı – çeviri – notlar*), Istanbul: Yapı Kredi Yayınları, pp. 158-161.

6 Hakkı Bey, İsmail 1926, *Mûsıkî Tekâmül Dersleri*, 2nd Book, Istanbul: Feniks Matbaası.

7 Hakkı Bey, İsmail 1925 [1919], *Solfej yahûd Nota Dersleri*, Istanbul: Haşim Matbaası.

8 Tanrıkorur, Cinuçen 1990, "Concordance of Prosodic and Musical Meters in Turkish Classical Music", *Turkish Musical Quarterly*, 3(1), 1-7.

9 Bardakçı, Murat (Ed.) 1995, *Refik Bey: Refik Bey ve Hatırları*, Istanbul: Pan Yayınları, p. 141.

songs in a regular number of syllables. As I also discuss below, the incorrect realization of a poetic meter in musical performance was severely criticised.[10]

In contrast to *vezin*, *usûl* means musical meter in most sources. *Usûl*-s are often explained in published anthologies (*güfte mecmua*-s). In 'classical' sources, *usûl*-s are defined and classified, their metric structure explained in terms of four beats (*darb*-s): *düm*, *tek*, *teke* and *tekâ*. Interestingly, the syllables *tâ hek* are not included.[11] As in equivalent sources, the *usûl*-s of *şarkı*-s are not provided. In Haşim Bey, only the metric cycles of major works (such as *kâr*-s and *beste*-s) are evidenced. However, in 'popular' sources, a more detailed overview of light-'classical' songs are mentioned.[12] Here, the author presents a clear method for beating an *usûl* (*usûl vurmak*). Diagrams are supplied. Where Haşim Bey gives limited information for the metric realisation of *şarkı*-s, Tahsin does not. In the latter publication, *ağır aksak* is followed by *aksak*, *çifte sofyan* progresses to *curcuna*. The meters *mandıra* and *katikofti* add a 'popular' register, the meters *vals* and *marş* add a 'western' resonance to the genres represented.

At the time, *usûl*-s are detailed in published scores. In the representation of a 'popular' *fasıl*, a particular meter is often mentioned in connection with an individual genre. Information on the composer and the mode is usually provided. The *fasıl* in the *makam kürdîli hicazkâr* is representative.[13] Following a selection of *peşrev*-s (in *ağır düyek* and *devri kebir*), a *beste* in *zencir* and a *beste* in *çenber* are both represented with the time signature "C". After a *nakış semaî* in *sengin semaî* (6/4), a string of light-classical songs (mostly *şarkı*-s) follows (42 in total); starting with the slowest and longest *usûl*-s (*ağır aksak* [10/4]) through the quicker and shorter *usûl*-s (such as *aksak* [9/8] and *düyek* [2/4]) and ending with the fastest and smallest *usûl*-s (such as *türk aksağı* [5/8] and *curcuna* [10/16]). As is usual, the cycle ends with a *saz semaîsi* (10/8) in this instance by Tatyos Efendi. As in some sources, the fourth section (*hane*) is represented idiosyncratically with the time signature 18/8.

Although not always consistent, this *fasıl* illustrates the metric character of the *fasıl* format, acceleration and diminution. In a 'classical' *fasıl* (called "*geleneksel fasıl*" today), a program would begin with the most serious works (a *kâr* or a *beste*) composed in the longest *usûl*-s. Following a second *beste* in a shorter *usûl*, a typical performance might feature a couple of *semaî*-s (an *ağır semaî* [10/4 or 6/4] and a *yürük semaî* [6/4]). As in the 'popular' *fasıl*, a graded series of *şarkı*-s would follow, getting livelier towards the end of the cycle. Even in those publications 'written in a commercial style' ('*piyasa tarzında yazılmış*'), the principal of acceleration and diminution is maintained. In a 'popular' medley of dance songs in the *makam gerdaniye*, the publisher İbrahim Efendi (1898) represents the collec-

---

10 See O'Connell 2013, pp. 153-169.

11 Such as Hâşim Bey, Hacı Mehmed 1280/1864, *Mecmûa-i Kârhâ ve Nakışhâ ve Şarkıyât [Mûsıkî Mecmûası]*, 2nd edition, Istanbul, pp. 3-18.

12 Such as Tahsin, Hasan 1906, *Gülzar-ı Musiki*, Istanbul: Şirket-i Mürettibiye Matbaası.

13 Şamlı İskender [Kutmani] [c.1923], *Kürdîli Hicazkâr Faslı*, Istanbul.

tion in an accelerating pattern by starting with 3 songs in *ağırlama* (9/8), graduating to 4 songs in *aydın* (4/8+5/8) and ending with a *koşma*, 2 *dağî*-s and 2 Rumeli *şarkı*-s in *ağır düyek* (4/4), *düyek* (2/4) and "*yürük*" *devri hindi* (7/8) respectively.

Given the widespread representation of metric cycles in published sources, Selçuk surprisingly gives little information on his use of *usûl*-s in relevant publications. In concert programs, the *usûl* of an item is rarely mentioned; that is, with the exception of metric cycles linked to a specific genre such as the 'classical' work *yürük semaî* or the folk dance *zeybek*. In addition, an unmetered improvisation (simply *gazel*) and a metered improvisation (as in *şarkı gazelli*) can be inferred from the title. In record catalogues too, the *usûl* of an item is rarely mentioned; that is again, where there is no direct connection between genre and meter as in the mystical form *durak* or the 'popular' dance tango. Even on musical scores, Selçuk hardly ever inserted the name of an *usûl* (as was conventional) above a time signature. In contrast to his contemporaries, he took the name of an *usûl* for granted having learned his craft orally, using music notation merely as an aide-mémoire during lessons and rehearsals.[14]

However, Selçuk does provide information on tempo in musical scores. Words like "*ağırlaşır*" in Turkish and "*rall[entando]*" in Italian are inserted to indicate temporal retardation. Terms like "*ağırca*" and "*yürükçe*" are employed to signify degrees of heaviness and lightness in musical performance. Interestingly, such terms appear in published scores[15] where metric acceleration in a *fasıl* format is prescribed. Selçuk sometimes designates the entry of percussion instruments (such as *davul* and *kudüm*) in his arrangement of an overture for the film entitled "*Üçüncü Selim'in Gözdesi*". However, this film was screened (1950) well after the period in question. By this time, Selçuk was a choral director and music instructor, the vocalist being required to represent Turkish music in a written format. Even then, only time signatures are used to represent metric cycles. As with other musical symbols indicating stylistic interpretation, these are not consistently detailed. Clearly, Selçuk was more comfortable with an oral manner of musical transmission (called "*meşk*") that involved memorizing a composition while beating an *usûl*.

Selçuk received a traditional education. After taking music lessons at home, he was invited to join a musical society called "*Darü'l-Feyz-i Mûsikî*", one of the many musical groups that appeared in Turkey after 1908. Founded by Üsküdarlı Edhem Nuri Bey (d. [1919]) and held in the mansion (*konak*) of Ali Şâmil Paşa (in Kadıköy), Selçuk is believed to have learned and performed around 10 *fasıl*-s with

---

14 After the early-Republican period, Selçuk sometimes did insert the name of the *usûl* in manuscript copies of musical notations. These scores are dated after 1950, probably being used in performance or for teaching. At the time, Selçuk sometimes adopted the established convention in concert programs of naming an *usûl* with the name of a genre as in "*muhammes beste*" or "*murabba çenber*".

15 Like İbrahim Efendi (1898).

the group. By way of his first teacher Edhem Bey, Selçuk could trace a musical lineage back to Yeniköylü Hasan Efendi (1823-1905), a *Mevlevî* adept who 'profited by' his association with [İsmail] Dede Efendi (1778-1846), amongst other accolades of the tradition.[16] While the date of his musical induction is usually recognized as 1915[17], a photograph (see Plate 2) and an article[18] suggest otherwise, Selçuk as a boy of around 13 (c. 1913) being celebrated by a group of distinguished musicians.

The date of his début with the Society is equally problematic. Usually represented as taking place 1917 (that is, two years after his apprenticeship with the group), Selçuk gave his first solo performance in the *Apollon Sineması* (in Kadıköy) in aid of the Ottoman navy.[19,20] The following memoir by the distin-

16 O'Connell 2013, p. 83.

17 Özalp, Nazmi 1986, *Türk Musikisi Tarihi*, 2 vols., Ankara: TRT Müzik Dairesi Başkanlığı, vol 1., p. 130; Öztuna, Yılmaz 1990, *Büyük Türk Mûsikîsi Ansiklopedisi*, 2 vols., Istanbul: Millî Eğitim Basımevi, vol.1, p. 275.

18 Sait provides a creditable schedule of Selçuk's early career. In an interview with Selçuk for the weekly magazine called "*Yedigün*", the journalist published the artist's own account of his musical career in the following manner: "I enrolled in the *Darü'l-Feyz-i* music school. After that I did not ignore my musical development while continuing my [high school] education in the Kadıköy Lisesi. First, I worked with Ahmet Efendi the son of Zekâi Dede. Then I studied with Hoca Ziya Bey. During the Great War, I went to Hungary. On my return, I first joined the *Darül'elhan*. A little while later, I worked as a founding member in the *Şark Musiki Cemiyeti*. We gave public concerts for 2 or 3 years. In all of these activities, I participated as an amateur." Selçuk continues by recounting his success as a recording artist (the start date given here is 1928). He also talks about his visit to Paris where he worked on his voice (in his words: "*vokale çalıştım*"). Upon returning from Paris, Selçuk concludes: "Upon the advice and the guidance of my friends, I gave a concert for the first time in the *Fransız Tiyatrosu*." Significantly, Sait provides a caption under a published copy of Plate 2. It reads: "Münir Nurettin was a boy of 12 or 13 years of age when he gave his first concert" (Sait, Mekki 1933, "Münir Nurettinin Yuvasında", *Yedigün* 30, 10-12, pp. 11-12).

19 According to Gökmen, the *Apollon Sineması* was opened during the summer of 1915 (Gökmen, Mustafa 1991, *Eski İstanbul Sinemaları*. Istanbul: İstanbul Kitaplığı Yayınları, p. 25). This would imply that the début performance by Selçuk cannot have occurred before that date. However, the *Apollon Sineması* had long existed as a performance venue, being owned by Greek entrepreneurs. Called: "*Halkidona* Theatre" after the Greek name for Kadıköy, it had a large auditorium consisting of boxes arranged in three tiers. After its construction (c. 1873), it hosted a number of Greek and Turkish performances. Later, it was renamed: [Kadıköy] *Kışlık Apollon Tiyatrosu* and was still staging dramatic productions at the outset of the War. As the oldest theatre in Kadıköy, it was considered to be a chic venue. As such, it was an obvious location for a concert by the *Darü'l-Feyz-i Mûsiki*. Significantly, Selçuk continued to perform in this venue when it was later called "*Hale Sineması*". He also presented concerts in the nearby Süriyye Sineması (founded in 1927).

20 A special association was set up in 1909 to develop the Ottoman navy. Subsequently called the "*Osmanlı Donanma Cemiyeti*", it sought to finance the Ottoman navy in an effort to counteract the growing threat from rival fleets in the Mediterranean. It received popular support by way of fundraising events and voluntary donations, eventually taking the form of an involuntary tax deducted from individual salaries. Initially purchasing warships from Germany, two battleships were ordered in secret from Britain. When completed, the ships were sequestered by the British Government just prior to the declaration of war (August 1914). Following popular indignation in Turkey, two German cruisers were sheltered in and transferred to Turkey, a move that undermined Ottoman neutrality (Shaw 1977, vol. 2,

Plate 2: Beating *Usûl* – Münir Nurettin Selçuk (c. 1913)

pp. 310-312). In the contemporary spirit of patriotic fervor, the concert by Selçuk in the *Appollon Tiyatrosu* must be understood as a typical fundraising event for the Ottoman navy. Like other musical performances and theatrical shows, it probably occurred before the outset of war. Significantly, the gentlemen portrayed in Plate 2 seem to be wearing a medallion (the *Donanma İane Madalyası*) especially minted for such occasions.

guished medic and music enthusiast Osman Şevki Uludağ (1889-1964) is noteworthy: "Although just a boy, Münir demonstrated the tasteful feeling of a great man. ... This youth, who was sitting in front and on the right-hand side of the ensemble, sang alone the *Kâr-ı Nev* by İsmail Dede (Efendi). The moment he began to perform '*gözümde dâim ...*' [the first words of the piece], his voice was manly yet fresh. He did not alter the contours of his face as is normal. Without wrinkling his expression, he reached the highest octave without difficulty."[21] Interestingly, Uludağ does not mention whether Selçuk embellished the meter with a tambourine (*def*) or beat the meter on his knees (*usûl vurmak*).

However, the usual date given for this concert seems improbable. First, the author highlights the youthful age of the artist, noting his clear yet manly voice. The implication here is that Uludağ considers Selçuk to be a young adolescent. Second, the concert was held in aid of the navy. Like similar fundraising events, it probably occurred prior to the declaration of war (in November 1914) when the Ottoman government received popular support in a campaign to rebuild the Ottoman navy. This issue is complicated by the performance apparently of two works by the vocalist, the first by Dede Efendi (see above) and the second by Sadullah Ağa (during a *fasıl* in the *makam bayatî araban*)[22]. Although Selçuk celebrated significant anniversaries of his début in 1951 (after 35 years) and 1966 (after 50 years), it is possible that he actually performed as a soloist at two separate events, the first in 1914, the second in 1916.

An account by the renowned violinist Cevdet Çağla (1900-1988) clarifies the issue. As a school mate of Selçuk in the *Kadıköy Sultanesi*, he described an encounter with the vocalist in front of the school. He recollected 35 years later: "On that day, I heard for the first time Münir Nurettin perform a *şarkı* in *bayatî araban* entitled '*Nimeti vaslın ...* '.[23] He also learned then that I played the violin. The following week, he invited me to a lesson ['*meşke beni çağırdı'*] ... in Kadıköy. When I entered the room, I found a number of our music experts seated on cushions all around the place." These included the composers Rahmi Bey (1864-

21 Cited in Kulin, Ayşe 1996, *Bir Tatlı Huzur: Fotoğraflarla Münir Nureddin Selçuk'un Yaşam Öyküsü*, Istanbul: Sel Yayıncılık, p. 18.

22 See Özalp 1986, vol. 2, p. 133.

23 Of course, the famous piece here entitled "*Nimeti vaslın*" was composed by Haşim Bey (1815-1868) and not by Sadullah Ağa (d. [1801]). The full title of this *şarkı* is as follows: "*Nimet-i vaslın için ey gonca leb*". It is composed in the *usûl ağır aksak* (9/4). Since the *fasıl* in *bayatî araban* by Sadullah Ağa then only contained four vocal works (two *beste*-s and two *semaî*-s), it was not unusual to supplement the relevant *fasıl* with compositions by other composers in different *usûl*-s but in the same *makam*. In this respect, it is possible (although not mentioned) that Selçuk performed this *şarkı* by Haşim Bey in his solo presentation during the *fasıl* in question. Interestingly, the vocalist rarely performed works by Sadullah Ağa or sung compositions in *bayatî araban* during his concerts or on his recordings [before 1950]. However, there is one exception. In the film entitled "*Üçüncü Selimin Gözdesi*", Selçuk performed the two *beste*-s mentioned above by Sadullah Ağa. Released in 1950, the film was not a major success for the artist.

1924) and Ali Rıfat Çağatay (1867-1935) and the teachers Zekâizade Ahmet Efendi (1869-1943) and Üsküdarlı Ziya Bey (1877-1923). He continued: "In the middle of the big room, a cushion and a table were placed. After uttering a '*Bismillâh*', Münir Nurettin knelt down on the cushion. Beating the *usûl*, he began to perform a composition whose name I was unable to remember."[24, 25]

The meeting probably occurred in 1916 (before Çağla left to study in Berlin for two years). It is interesting for three reasons. First, it shows Selçuk performing in a traditional manner beating the *usûl* of a composition kneeling down before a critical audience. Second, it indicates that Selçuk was not only performing for but was also being examined by a select group of Turkish masters. Çağla confirms this to be so in the following manner: "At a suitable moment in the composition, time was allowed for a discussion among the experts who were listening. Every master individually explained and demonstrated how this composition had been transmitted by his own teacher. Münir Nurettin listened with patience and attention to this advice which lasted some time. He imprinted it on his memory. In reality, this lesson [*meşk*] functioned at the same time as an examination [*imtihan*]." Third, it suggests that Selçuk began his formal instruction in Turkish music before his audition for the new conservatory and his instruction in a venerable ensemble.

According to the received history, Selçuk auditioned for a position in the conservatory (*Darül'elhan*) apparently in 1917. As a member of the jury, the *tanbur* master (*tanburî*) Refik Fersan heard and met Selçuk for the first time. He recalled: "A boy entered the examination room where I was present as an official assessor. When he started to sing a *beste* in the *makam yegâh* by Dellâlzade İsmail Efendi, I was in ecstasy. He performed with such style that [Muallim] İsmail Hakkı Bey ... took out his handkerchief and started to cry."[26] In another account, Fersan noted that Selçuk realized correctly the large *usûl* of the same *beste* (in *zencir*).[27] He

24 Cited in Özalp 1986, vol. 2, p. 130.

25 The anecdote by Cevdet Çağla is interesting. At the time, the violinist was especially concerned with 'western' music, taking lessons from a local teacher (Antonyadis or Andonyades), a music instructor who later supported the westernizing innovations in vocal performance advanced by Selçuk (see O'Connell 2013, pp. 190-192). Although Çağla took lessons in *usûl* and *makam* from the *Mevlevî* adept Musullu Hâfiz Osman Efendi (1840-1918), he seemed unfamiliar with the traditional manner of musical transmission (*meşk*) in Turkish music as described here. Unusual for a connoisseur, he could not remember the piece being performed. As Özalp recounts (1986, vol. 2, p. 144), he also made a number of errors with respect to stylistic convention in Turkish music when he returned from Germany to Turkey after the War.

26 Cited in Bardakçı (Ed.) 1995, p. 139.

27 Cited in Özalp 1986, vol. 2, p.129. Fersan is referring here to the relevant *beste* in the *makam yegâh* entitled "*Gönül ki aşk ile pür sînede hazîne bulur*". Today, *zencir* is recognized as the longest *usûl* in Turkish music. It is represented as a cycle of 120 beats, which is broken down into five distinctive meters: *çifte düyek* (16/4), *fâhte* (20/4), *çenber* (24/4), *devr-i kebir* (28/4) and *berefşan* (32/4). As Feldman explains (1995:316-317), two versions of this compound *usûl* existed, an older version with 48 beats, and a newer version with 60 beats. In music anthologies circulating at the time of Selçuk's audition (see for example Tahsin 1906, pp. 9-10), *zencir* is represented as a compound *usûl* consisting of 60 beats which are divided into the 5 metric cycles

noted also how Selçuk embellished the composition like embroidery with a superb manner (*edâ*) and a wonderful style (*uslûb*). In this instance, the director of the conservatory Ziya Paşa (1849-1929) burst into tears. In both narratives, the examiners foresaw an exceptional future for the artist.

The received history continues. Leaving for Hungary to study agriculture upon completing his schooling, Selçuk returned to Turkey after the Armistice of Mundros (31 October 1918). The following year he was a founding member of the *Şark Musiki[si] Cemiyeti*, a music society that emerged from the remnants of the *Darü'l-Feyz-i Mûsiki*, possibly following the death of its founder Edhem Bey. As Behar shows, the Society gave its first concert in Kadıköy, at the event advertising music lessons for men and women in music literacy (especially *nota* and *solfej*) and music transmission (especially in individual [*meşk*] and group [*fasl-ı umumî*] contexts).[28] That is, the Society fostered both a modern and a traditional approach to musical instruction. As a performer, the vocalist participated in the regular series of concerts organized by the Society in the *Apollon Tiyatrosu*.[29] As a student, he also took lessons from two distinguished members of the Society.

First, Zekâizade Ahmet Efendi taught Selçuk the essential repertoire. Here, the former functioned as the principal instructor (*esas hocası*) of the latter. Four years of musical instruction ensued, the pupil "learning several *fasıllar*" ("*müteaddid fasıllar meşketmiş*") from the teacher.[30] Second, "Bestenigâr" or Üsküdarlı Hoca Ziya Bey gave Selçuk a stylistic training. Generally referred to in the tradition as "a teacher of style" ("*üslûp hocası*"), Hoca Ziya Bey inherited a profound interest in the use of Western techniques in Turkish performance from Nedim Bey (d. [1910]), a court artist who was commonly remembered as "the nightingale of the Bosphorus" ("*Boğaziçi bülbülü*"). Emulating Nedim Bey's concern for 'western' taste and aristocratic privilege, Hoca Ziya Bey was a natural choice. In retrospect, Selçuk remembered this intensive period of musical instruction (*meşk*) as an essential basis for learning correctly a traditional style (*tavır*) and a performance manner (*edâ*) from the "mouth of a benefactor" ("*fem-i muhsin*")[31].

---

mentioned above. However, in 'popular' publications at the time, the *usûl zencir* is often represented as a cycle of 15 bars with a time signature in common time ("C") (15 x 4 = 60). For example, the *usûl zencir* is represented in such away at the beginning of a *fasıl* in the *makam kürdilîli hicazkâr* by Udî Arşak (c. 1925). In the *beste* entitled "[*Yâr*] *Ne kadar yareledi gamzelerin bak bedenim*" by Kanunî [Hacı] Ârif Bey (1862-1911), each line of the *güfte* encompasses one cycle of the *usûl*. Here, the relevant 15 bars are unconventionally broken down into a 4-bar, a 5-bar and a 6-bar phrase. Clearly, this is not the populist realization of the *usûl* that was performed by Selçuk in his ground-breaking audition.

28 Behar, Cem 1993, *Zaman, Mekân, Müzik: Klâsik Türk Musıkisinde Eğitim (Meşk), İcra ve Aktarım*, Istanbul: AFA Yayınları, p. 72, n. 89.

29 See O'Connell 2013, p. 84, n. 10.

30 İnal, İbnülemin Mahmut Kemal 1958, *Hoş Sadâ: Son Asır Türk Musikişinasları*, Istanbul: Maarif, p. 223.

31 See Selçuk, Münir Nureddin 1947, "Ses Musikimiz", *Türk Musikisi Dergisi*, 1(2), Istanbul, p. 3; also cited in Behar 1993, p. 46.

The standard account of Selçuk's musical education appears in a number of sources. When the vocalist signed a recording contract with "His Master's Voice" ("*Sahibinin Sesi*"), record catalogues emphasize his musical credentials, Selçuk "for a long time acquiring [*tehsil*] and studying [*tetebbu*] the refinements of 'eastern' music from some of the renowned masters (of the musical tradition), at first from Zekâizade Ahmet Efendi and later from 'the late' ['*merhum*'] Üsküdarlı Hoca Ziya Bey."[32] In these sources, Selçuk is also acknowledged as the founder of a new school (here spelt "*école*") in Turkish music by adapting Western techniques to traditional practice. To achieve this, he went to Paris (ostensibly to study at the "*Paris Konservatuvar[ı]*") with the aim of developing his interest in 'western' music. While there are a minor number of variants in this narrative, they show that Selçuk undertook a logical progression from an old reading to a new understanding of Turkish music.[33]

However, there is one name that is missing in this usual account of music instruction. That name is Refik Fersan. While it was professionally advantageous for Turkish performers to advertise the musical imprint of significant teachers, sometimes this occurred as a matter of convention rather than as a consequence of practice. This was the case with Selçuk. After his audition in the *Darül'elhan* (see above), Fersan chose voluntarily to instruct Selçuk in music notation and music theory so that he could pass the examination to be accepted into the imperial band as an officer. As a teacher, Fersan's assistance (*delâlet*) was solicited by Rahmi Bey and Mehmet Nurettin Bey (1867-1928), Selçuk's father. Specifically, Fersan gave Selçuk lessons in *usûl* and *makam*, teaching the elements of musical literacy using Hamparsum *notası* and 'western' notation. The didactic imprint of Fersan's tutelage is evident in Selçuk's archive.[34] There musical compositions written down in Fersan's clear hand form a significant part of the manuscript collection.

Fersan took great pride when Selçuk passed his exam.[35] He was especially pleased that he was granted a commission as a second lieutenant (*mülazim-i sani*), his duties being to work as a muezzin for the Sultan (*müezzin-i hazret-i şehriyârî*) and to perform as a vocalist (*hanende*) in the (imperial) instrumental ensemble (here called simply "*ince saz takımı*"). Although Fersan gives no details of this exam, he recounts his own gruelling examination for a position in the "*Mabeyn Mızıkası*" (another name for the Imperial Band or *Muzıkay-ı Hümayun*). After performing 5 short *taksim*-s (on his *tanbur*) and after passing an oral test (to test music literacy), he was asked a number of questions with respect to *usûl*. Starting from the beginning, he easily identified the shortest *usûl*-s. Sequentially he was interrogated about

32 See Sahibinin Sesi 1934-1935, *Marconi Radyoları: Sahibinin Sesi'ne Mensuptur* [Istanbul], p. 9.

33 See O'Connell 2013, pp. 79-108.

34 Ibid., p. 86

35 See Bardakçı (Ed.) 1995, p. 145.

the longer *usûl*-s, ending with *darb-ı fetih* (88/4). In particular, he was required to set individual metric cycles to particular prosodic structures.[36]

From the narrative, it is clear that Selçuk did not have to pass such a gruelling test. After all, he was a vocalist and Fersan was an instrumentalist. Further, Selçuk was appointed a lowly lieutenant and Fersan was appointed an elevated captain. What is evident, Fersan instructed Selçuk for about four years "since he had limited knowledge of notation and music".[37] While the sequence of events is not accurately represented, he stated that he first met Selçuk at his audition in the *Darül'elhan* (probably in 1918) and that his pupil was called up for military service (he gives the date erroneously as 1913 [1329]). Since he was at the time the principal instrumentalist (*sersazende*) in the imperial band (appointed in 1919 after the examination described above), he was in a position to instruct the vocalist and to facilitate his employment in a preferred military occupation (in 1923 [1339]). As his wife Fahire Fersan stated emphatically, Selçuk: "learned everything from Refik" ("*Refik'ten öğrendi hepsini*").[38]

With respect to *usûl*, Fersan profoundly influenced Selçuk in two ways. First, Fersan informed Selçuk's conceptualization of *usûl*. The instrumentalist taught the vocalist an older taxonomy of metric cycles. Here, the *usûl*-s *katikofti* (8/8) and *mandıra* (7/16) and the genres *aydın* (in 9/8) and *ağırlama* (in 9/8) are often referenced in record catalogues and concert programs. While certain *usûl*-s like *çifte sofyan* and genres like *dağî* were also itemized, they are now rare since certain scholars believe them to be inappropriate or redundant.[39] Here, Fersan's connection with the Turkish instrumentalist Tanburî Cemil Bey and the Armenian educator Levon Hancıyan ([1851]-1947) is very important. In the first instance, Fersan adopted the musical terminology employed by the Muslim practitioner in his definitions of *usûl*-s (such as *katikofti*) and in his conceptualization of *usûl*-s (using the term *ika*) (see Cemil Bey 1902 [1989]). In the second instance, Fersan employed the notational conventions of his Christian mentor, being proficient in his use of Hamparsum *notası*.

---

36 Ibid., p. 141.

37 Ibid., p. 145.

38 Interview in March 1994, see Plate 8.

39 See Öztuna 1990, vol. 1, p. 203, 205. In contrast to Öztuna, Özkan in his extended study of *usûl* is not so dismissive (Özkan, İsmail Hakkı 1987, *Türk Mûsikîsi Nazariyati ve Usûlleri. Kudüm Velveleleri*, Istanbul: Ötüken, p. 593). Like other music scholars, he does recognize the significance of the *usûl katikofti* (8/8) as another name for the *usûl müsemmen*. However, he does argue that the latter name is more accurate and accepted. Interestingly, Fersan is also ambivalent. In a music score (of his own composition) published with his memoirs (Bardakçı (Ed.) 1995, p. 79), the instrumentalist writes in Ottoman: "*usûl: müsemmen = (kat[i]kofti)*" at the beginning of a *şarkı* in the *makam acemaşiran* entitled "*Düşme gör, sevdâ belâ gözlerdedir*". Further, Özkan (1987, p. 596) recognizes the *usûl çifte sofyan* (9/8) as a fast (*yürük*) version of the *usûl aksak*. In song anthologies too, some scholars acknowledge the *usûl çifte sofyan* without comment (see for example Üngör 1980).

Plate 3: Learning *Usûl – Darütta'limi Musiki Cemiyeti*

Second, Fersan transmitted his knowledge of *usûl* to Selçuk in performance. As a leading member of the *fasıl heyeti* in the *Darül'elhan*, he guided his student in the correct use of the tambourine (*def*) to mark and to embellish the metric cycle in ensemble practice. A photograph of Selçuk in this role is reproduced in Kulin.[40] The use of a *def* was especially common in 'popular' contexts where the chief vocalist (*serhanende*) controlled the accelerating trajectory of the vocal medley that was traditional in *fasıl* performances (see Plate 3). There are no equivalent images of Selçuk performing in such a capacity. However, a number of accounts reveal that Selçuk did perform with a *def* in a 'popular' context. As Okur recounts, the vocalist accompanied a *fasıl* performance with a *def* when playing for Mustafa Kemal Atatürk (1881-1938) at one of the presidential "drinking sessions" ("*rakı âlemleri*").[41] In that instance, Atatürk apparently shot at Selçuk for his indolence.[42]

Interestingly, a *def* features prominently in the artist's archive. Yet, there are few visual representations of the vocalist playing a *def*. Even when he performed a *fasıl* selection in different *makam*-s during his tour of Egypt with Refik Fersan and Fahire Fersan (January 1929), he is not pictured in the relevant programs

---

40 Kulin 1996, p. 19.

41 See Cengiz, Halil E. (Ed.) 1993, *Yaşanmış Olaylarla Atatürk ve Müzik: Riyâset-i Cumhûr İnce Saz Hey'eti Şefi Binbaşı Hâfız Yaşar Okur'un Anıları (1924-1938)*, Ankara: Müzik Ansiklopedisi Yayınları, pp. 97-99.

42 See O'Connell 2013, pp. 88-90.

Plate 4: Transmitting *Usûl* – Concert in Cairo (1929)

playing a *def* (see Plate 4). Why was this so? During the early-Republican period, the *def* became synonymous with the *hanende*. Sometimes called '*hanende defi*', the *def* had become the musical instrument of a commercial musician.[43] Intimately associated with drinking houses (*meyhane*-s), the *def* like the *hanende* was not consistent with Selçuk's vision of a 'classical' music performed in a 'classical' setting. Adopting now the Arabic title "*mugannî*" (Ar. "*muğannin*") and abandoning the Persian title "*hanende*" (Pr. "*khanandeh*"), Selçuk wished to project himself onto the concert stage performing as a soloist like his Arab counterparts rather than as a chorister like his Turkish contemporaries. That is, he did not wish to be a *hanende* who played *def* in a *fasıl* setting.

Was this the reason for the failure of Selçuk to acknowledge Fersan? The concert programs published during the concert tour of Egypt are indeed revealing. Selçuk is called in Arabic "the great Turkish vocalist". However, Fersan is named simply "the tanburist" ("ṭumbūrji"). He is not even accorded the title: "*tanburî*" ("*ṭumbūrī*"). Of course, Fahire Fersan is given in French the title "*La célèbre violoniste*", her public appearance as a female instrumentalist attracting some attention. However, her title in Arabic "*kamānjiya*" (Eng. "the female violinist") is not

[43] Özalp 1986, vol.1, p. 51.

so exalted. Simply put, the elevated position of the vocalist takes precedence over the diminished status of the instrumentalists. As Selçuk would later state: "Turkish music is a singer's music" ("*Türk musıkisi hânende musıkisidir*"), the oral transmission of a vocal work while beating *usûl* taking precedent over other modes of musical instruction.[44] This is why Selçuk mentions the educator Ahmet Efendi and the vocalist Ziya Bey in his professional résumé. Here, Fersan had limited cache for professional advancement.

Yet, Selçuk was not alone in the reinvention of his past. Fersan too emphasized certain significant artists and omitted other important figures in the musical tradition. According to the received history, the instrumentalist studied with Cemil Bey for 7 years, starting at the age of 12 in 1905 and ending in 1912. In his memoirs, he nostalgically reflects upon his encounters with the master, noting how Cemil Bey inserted 'western' melodies during a *taksim* on the *kemençe* or how he embellished the fourth *hane* of a *peşrev* on the *tanbur* during one of the regular soirées hosted by his family in a waterside residence (*yalı*).[45] Later, he remembers taking lessons with the master, at first studying to read and subsequently learning to perform, eventually managing to play around 25 *fasıl*-s over a 2-year period. Interestingly, he emphasized his proficiency in musical transcription using Hamparsum *notası* to learn and to remember the musical knowledge transmitted from teacher to pupil.[46]

However, the received history is not entirely accurate. During the period, Fersan had to flee with his family to Egypt for an extended period following the Young Turk Revolution in 1908. Returning to Istanbul (probably in 1910), he continued his lessons with Cemil Bey. At this time, he also took specialist lessons in music theory with Hanciyan, learning (now accompanied by his fiancé, Fahire Fersan) uncommon works with their *usûl*-s. These pieces included *kâr*-s, *beste*-s and *ayin*-s.[47] Fersan actually states: "even *ayin*-s". Perhaps, he wished to indicate that the musical transmission of a mystical genre in a secular context by a non-Muslim educator was somewhat unorthodox. Here, Hanciyan's own colorful background is of interest. A pupil of a great master (Dellâlzade İsmail Efendi [1797-1869]), he was famed in royal circles both as a teacher and a composer, using Hamparsum *notası* to transmit 'his version' (to quote Özuna)[48] of a classical canon. Significantly, Fersan rewrote these transcriptions using 'western' notation.[49]

Yet, Fersan fails to mention adequately one important figure. This person is "*Muallim*" İsmail Hakkı Bey. Like Hanciyan, Hakkı Bey was a teacher and a composer, famed (some have suggested infamous) for his transcriptions of Turkish mu-

44 Cited in Behar 1993, p. 46, 74.
45 Cited in Bardakçı (Ed.) 1995, pp. 102-104.
46 Ibid., pp. 106-108.
47 Ibid., p. 109.
48 Öztuna 1990, vol. 1, p. 327.
49 See Bardakçı (Ed.) 1995, p. 61.

sic using 'western' notation. Like Hanciyan too, Hakkı Bey had a military career, the former as a medic in the Turkish-Russian wars (1877-1879), the latter as a musician in the *Muzıkay-ı Hümayun*. Indeed, Hanciyan and Hakkı Bey were both founding members of the *Darül'elhan*. As in other contexts, Hakkı taught solfa (*solfej*) and notation (*nota*), having taken lessons in 'western' music from his colleague in the imperial band, Mehmet Zâti (Arca) Bey (1865-1951). He also directed the large *fasıl* ensemble (called "*küme faslı heyeti*" by Fersan). There, as elsewhere, he was the first to insist on musical literacy in choral practice. He also experimented with mixed choirs (initially discontinued on the grounds of moral sensibility) and with choral conducting (using a baton [*baget*] to direct an ensemble).

In his memoirs, Fersan mentions Hakkı Bey only a few times. First, he lists Hakkı Bey in an inventory of artists in his musical circle as "the master who collects without tiring [music] written in his own hand ... ", noting that the teacher exceeded all human expectation by devoting half a century to Turkish music without any concern for commercial gain.[50] Second, he mentions Hakkı Bey during Selçuk's audition for the *Darül'elhan*.[51] Third, he cites Hakkı Bey as an examiner in his difficult audition for the *Muzıkay-ı Hümayun*.[52] Fourth, he references Hakkı Bey at his début performance in the Ferah Tiyatrosu.[53] No date is given. He states that the female audience had specifically requested that Hakkı Bey ask Fersan to play a *taksim* during the second *fasıl* of the evening. An encore was demanded, the instrumentalist playing the second *hane* of his own composition, the *peşrev* in the *makam sultanî yegâh*.

What was the reason for this limited recognition by Fersan of Hakkı Bey?[54] Fersan and Hakkı Bey worked together as teachers in the *Darül'elhan*. Fersan performed with Hakkı Bey in the *fasıl heyeti* in the conservatory. Fersan followed Hakkı Bey as an officer into the *Muzıkay-ı Hümayun*, Fersan becoming the "chief instrumentalist" ("*sersazende*"), Hakkı Bey having been a "principal vocalist" ("*serhanende*"). In Fersan's narrative, there is no sense of enmity between the two art-

50 Cited in Bardakçı (Ed.) 1995, pp. 134-135.

51 Ibid., p. 139.

52 Ibid., pp. 139-140.

53 Ibid., pp. 142-143.

54 In his memoirs, Fersan hints at Hakkı Bey's opinion of his musical ability. When enticed by his friends to apply for the most difficult exam (so that he could be appointed a captain in the *Muzıkay-ı Hümayun*), Fersan applied for an audition. When interviewed by a representative of the imperial band - a colonel (*miralay*) Salih Bey - prior to the examination, Fersan was told that he was too young and that should apply for a more junior position. Fersan replied: "Did not İsmail Hakkı Bey say anything about me?" Salih Bey responded: "He did, but not that you should apply for the highest rank." Salih Bey stated that the relevant examination required a profound knowledge of music theory, a knowledge that even the most distinguished teachers might find challenging. When Salih Bey suggested that Fersan would be ashamed on failing the audition, the instrumentalist immediately signed up, passing with distinction every part of the test. Here, the narrative suggests a certain degree of impudence on the part of Fersan. However, it also demonstrates a certain degree of disdain for the judgment of Hakkı Bey (cited in Bardakçı [Ed.] 1995, pp. 139-140).

ists. Rather, the silence of the instrumentalist might indicate a certain disdain for the vocalist. In fact, Hakkı Bey was not part of the Fersan's musical network or social circle. He is not mentioned in the musical evenings at home or the musical gatherings outside (such as the *Şark Musiki[si] Cemiyeti*). Indeed, Öztuna suggests that Hakkı Bey was lacking in general culture, both musical and social. He also criticizes Hakkı Bey for the many mistakes that appear in his musical transcriptions and in his musical publications.[55]

I wanted to find out more about the relationship between Fersan and Hakkı Bey. During my interview with Fahire Fersan (March 1994), I asked her about [İsmail] Hakkı Bey. She replied (since there are many with that name in Turkish music): "which İsmail Hakkı Bey?" I said, "'Muallim' İsmail Hakkı Bey". She retorted dismissively: "Oh that one, huh ... ". The pause in speech is reminiscent of the pause in writing, Fersan ending his reference to Hakkı Bey with the following punctuation [...]. Perhaps, it was not just an issue of class and authority. During the War, the Fersans lost their fortune, Fersan's father (Mabeyinci Faik Bey [1870-1937]) making unfortunate investments in German and Russian war bonds. Thrust into poverty, the Fersans had to consider a music profession, an unedifying solution to an unedifying circumstance. Since Hakkı Bey was involved in facilitating Fersan's professional advancement, the educator may have unwittingly become the symbol of the instrumentalist's financial impoverishment and social relegation.

Yet, the musical imprint of Hakkı Bey is apparent in the musical output of Fersan. In this matter, two musical methods are especially pertinent. Entitled: *Solfej yahûd Nota Dersleri* (1925 [1919]) and *Mûsıkî Tekâmül Dersleri* (1926), they were published by Hakkı Bey during his residence in the *Darül'elhan*.[56] Significantly, these books list a number of *usûl*-s that are no longer performed or are no longer recognized. Among these, the *usûl*-s *ağırlama* and *aydın* are listed, their time signatures (9/8) detailed and their musical realization (in terms of *usûl vurmak*) explained. Other *usûl*-s like *çifte sofyan* (9/8) and *katikofti* (8/8) have been severely criticized in retrospect by some scholars[57]. Since they appear in other sources, such criticisms seem unfair. While a number of *usûl*-s were clearly invented by "the teacher" (such as *kazancılar düyeği* [2/4] and *devr-i kürdî* [14/8]),

---

55 Öztuna 1990, vol 1., pp. 402-403. Öztuna was not alone in his criticism of Hakkı Bey. At the beginning of the twentieth century, the music theorist Rauf Yekta Bey (1871-1935) publicly criticized Hakkı Bey for his uncritical approach to transcription and attribution. So much so that Hakkı Bey was obliged to publish an open letter to Yekta Bey in *Şehbal* (1910, 1 June, p. 2). That being said, Hakkı Bey did influence the public reception of Turkish music in a number of ways. For example, he published (in 1925 [1919]) musical methods (such as *Solfej yahûd Nota Dersleri*) and collated (in 1925) musical scores (such as the *fasıl* [No. 38] in the *makam neveser*) with the commercial publisher Şamlı İskender, amongst others. See also Özalp 1986, vol. 2, pp. 34-36; Kaygusuz, Nermin 2006, *Muallim İsmail Hakkı Bey ve Mûsıkî Tekâmül Dersleri*, Istanbul: İTÜ Vakfı Yayınları.

56 *Solfej yahûd Nota Dersleri* (1925 [1919]) and *Mûsıkî Tekâmül Dersleri* (1926).

57 See Öztuna 1990, vol. 1, p., 203, 434.

many of the *usûl*-s detailed in the musical publications by Hakkı Bey appear in the musical compositions and the musical programs of Fersan.

I suggest that there are two reasons for this. First, Fersan used Hamparsum *notası* from an early age to transcribe music. With his employment first in the conservatory and later in the army, he was obliged to use 'western' notation. Accordingly, Hakkı Bey had set an important precedent in both contexts. Significantly, being able to read 'western' notation (*nota*) was an essential part of the examination process. Second (and related to the first), the regulations for the *Darül'elhan* explicitly state that teachers and students have knowledge of notation (*nota*) and solfa (*solfej*). To ensure the required standards, Hakkı Bey was appointed teacher of music theory (*nazariyat*) as well as *fasıl* music. While Fersan was bound by these strict rules of musical instruction, he was also asked to write a method for the *tanbur*.[58] While this was lost, Bardakçı reproduces some unpublished fragments from a musical treatise (probably written in 1944) that concerns simple and compound *usûl*-s.[59]

"Muallim" İsmail Hakkı Bey was a significant influence in the realm of concert convention. He was not only the first music director to expand the number of choristers in a *fasıl* ensemble, he was also the first to insist that each performer wear the same attire. For example, a picture reproduced in the journal *Şehbal* (1913) shows the entire cadre of *Mûsikî-i Osmanî* dressed in formal dress. Hakkı Bey as director is seated prominently in the center of the troupe. Further, Hakkı Bey required his singers to stand (rather than sit) during a performance. Here, he organized the musicians into a semicircle, at first directing the ensemble with a *def* and later conducting the ensemble with a baton. In contrast to traditional practice, he required all musicians to read music during a concert performance. In this respect, he is credited with singlehandedly destroying an older system of musical transmission, where beating a line (*dizi dövmek*) was central to memorizing and performing a musical canon.[60]

Hakkı Bey was also a significant influence in the realm of concert repertoire. Responsible for organizing a regular series of public performances, he endeavored to introduce his audiences to a wider range of musical modes (*makam*-s) in a structured format, in this way expanding the number of *fasıl*-s that could be performed in a classical setting. A typical program is reproduced in the *Darül'elhan Mecmuası* (1 April 1924). Following a traditional *fasıl* in the *makam acemaşiran* that included 2 instrumental pieces (a *peşrev* and a *saz semâisi*) and 4 choral works (2 *beste*-s, 2 *semaî*-s), the program featured a 'popular' medley, a *köçekçe takımı* in the *makam gerdaniye*. After the instrumental introduction (here called "*küşad*" [Pr. *goshad*]), a selection of folk genres (such as *dağî* and *ağırlama*)

58 See Bardakçı (Ed.) 1995, p. 36, 138.
59 Ibid., pp. 36-39.
60 See Özalp 1986, vol. 2, pp. 34-36.

and dance numbers (such as *aydın* and *raks*) were presented. As was usual, the medley was to be conducted by Hakkı Bey, on the program stating "*Muallim İsmail Hakkı Bey tarafından idare edilecektir*".[61]

Hakkı Bey directly informed the form and content of concerts presented by Fersan and Selçuk. In terms of convention, the vocalist stood (rather than sat) on the concert stage wearing formal dress. Although Fersan and Selçuk did not use musical scores during concert performances, they also did not employ the traditional manner of musical presentation, either beating the *usûl* by hand or with a *def*. Significantly, Hakkı Bey set a precedent with respect to concert repertoire, dividing his concerts into 'classical', 'folk' and 'contemporary' sections. Such designations like "*eski musiki eserleri*" (directed by Ziya Paşa), "*millî Anadolu havaları*" (directed by Hakkı Bey) and "*yeni eserler*" (directed by Sedâd Öztoprak [1890-1942]) mapped three distinctive parts of a 'classical' program. Although there are a number of distinctive programs represented in the *Darül'elhan Mecmuası*, the principal of modal variety and *fasıl* integrity remained paramount, folk medleys and 'popular' assortments introducing an eclectic variety of vocal forms (such as *koşma*-s and *türkü*-s) and dance genres (such as *sirto*-s and *zeybek*-s).

A concert by Hakkı Bey in Istanbul is remarkably similar to a concert by Fersan and Selçuk in Ankara. Presented in the Union Française on Friday, 23 January (1925), the concert by Hakkı Bey with the *Şark Musiki[si] Şubesi* (of the *Darül'elhan*) is divided into five sections. In the first, 3 *fasıl*-s in the *makam*-s *mâhur*, *kürdî* and *Eviç* are detailed. While the first and third *fasıl* were traditional in terms of modal integrity and metric organization, the second features a number of folk songs performed by a female soloist. In the second section, Hakkı Bey directed a medley of folksongs, 7 *türkü*-s framed by an opening *medhal* and a closing dance (called "*zeybek havası*"). In the third section, a fourth *fasıl* in the *makam rûhnevâz* featured contemporary compositions. With the exception of a *fantezi* in the *makam suznâk* by H. Sadettin Arel (1880-1955), the medley was composed by Öztoprak and consisted of 2 *şarkı*-s and 2 *longa*-s. A *küşad* and a *zeybek* were also included.

The concert by Fersan and Selçuk in Ankara (see Plate 5) shows many similarities with the program described above. Presented at the *Türk Ocağı* on Monday, 16 March (1925), it is also divided into five parts. The first features a traditional *fasıl* in the *makam acemaşiran*.[62] Although a number of related *makam*-s are featured, the *fasıl* presents a traditional scheme of genres and meters, starting with a *beste* in the *usûl muhammes* and ending with a *şarkı* in the *usûl semaî*. The second and fifth section features an instrumental duet and a vocal solo respectively. The third features a collection of *şarkı*-s in the *makam*-s *uşşak* and *hüseynî*. The fourth features a medley of folksongs (here called "*dağîlar*") that include a *divan* and a *koşma*. It ends

---

[61] See also Paçacı, Gönül (Ed.) 1999, *Cumhuriyet'in Sesleri*, Istanbul: Türkiye İş Bankası, p. 14; O'Connell 2013, pp. 116 117.

[62] Ibid., p. 117.

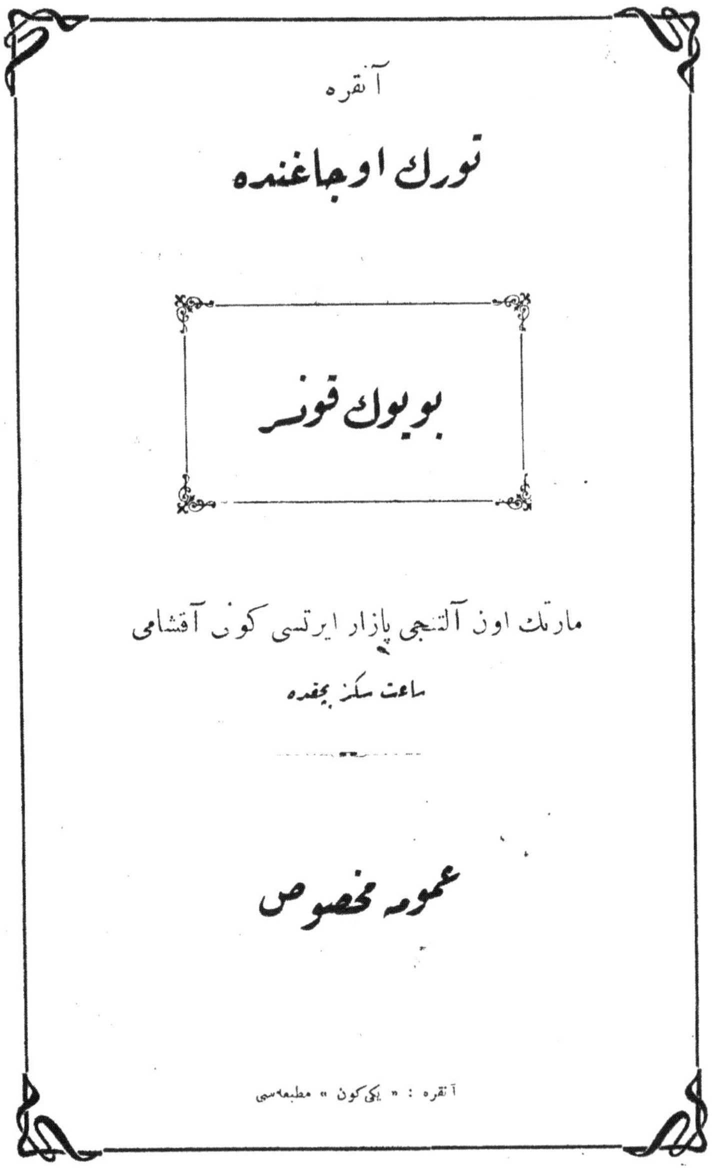

آنقره

تورك اوجاغنده

بويوك قونسر

مارتك اون آلتنجى بازار ايرتسى كونى آقشامى

ساعت سكز بچقده

عمومه مخصوص

آنقره : « يكى كون » مطبعه‌سى

Plate 5: Performing *Usûl* – Concert in Ankara (1925)

with an instrumental number entitled "*Mandıra Havası*". Like the concert by Hakkı Bey, the program included a solo performance, an instrumental improvisation and a vocal improvisation, each operating as an *ara taksimi* when graduating from one piece to another.

The programs share a number of idiosyncratic elements. Although each is broadly divided into a 'classical', a 'folk' and a 'contemporary' section, both con-

Programme du Premier Concert – برنجی قونسرك بروغرامی

PREMIERE PARTIE – فصل الاول

SOULTANI YEGAH: سلطانی یکاه

1. Pechrev : Refik Bey — ١ بیشرو : رفیق بك
2. Besté : Dédé effendi — ٢ بسته : دده أفندی
3. Agir Semaï : Dédé effendi — ٣ آغیر سماعی : دده أفندی
4. Charki : Lemi Bey — ٤ شرقی : لمعی بك
5. Charki : Dédé effendi — ٥ شرقی : دده أفندی
6. Yuruk Semaï : Dédé effendi — ٦ یوروك سماعی : دده أفندی
7. Saz Semaïsi : Cherif Mouhiddin Bey — ٧ ساز سماعی : شریف محی الدین

DEUXIEME PARTIE – فصل الثانی

RAST ET HUZAM فصل الراست والهزام

1. Pechrev : Gémil Bey — ١ بیشرو : جمیل بك
2. Rast Kar nev : Dédé effendi — ٢ راست کارنو : دده أفندی
3. Rast Charki : Dédé effendi — ٣ راست شرقی : دده أفندی
4. Rast Charki : Rassim Bey — ٤ راست شرقی : راسم بك
5. Taxim et Gazel — ٥ تقسیم و غزل
6. Huzam Charki : Bimen effendi — ٦ هزام شرقی : بمن أفندی
7. Huzam Semaï : Dédé effendi — ٧ هزام سماعی : دده أفندی
8. Huzam Saz Sémaï : Rélik Bey — ٨ هزام ساز سماعی : طنبوری رفیق بك

TROISIEME PARTIE – فصل الثالث

"FANTAISIE" فانته زی

LEYLA ! لیـلا

QUATRIEME PARTIE – فصل الرابع

HIDJAZKAR ET KURDILI فصل الحجازکار الکردی وحجازکار

1. Hidjazkar Kurdi Pechrev — ١ بیشرو : حجازکار الـکردی
2. Charki : Hadji Arif Bey — ٢ شرقی : حاجی عارف بك
3. Charki : Rifat Bey — ٣ شرقی : رفعت بك
4. Charki : Lemi Bey — ٤ شرقی : لمعی بك
5. Charki : Hadji Arif Bey — ٥ شرقی : حاجی عارف بك
6. Charki : Hadji Arif Bey — ٦ شرقی : حاجی عارف بك
7. Charki : Nicoose Aga — ٧ شرقی : نیکوغوص آغا
8. Charki : Hadji Rifat Bey — ٨ شرقی : رفعت بك
9. Charki : . . . . . . — ٩ شرقی :
10. Saz Semaïsi : Kemal Bey — ١٠ ساز سماعی : کمال بك

اطلبوا اسطوانات شرکة الجراموفون لیمتد

"HIS MASTER'S VOICE"

م.مصر ٢٢٦/٢٩/٥٠٠٠

Plate 6: Recording *Usûl* – Program in Cairo (1929)

certs are somewhat unorthodox. First, they mix a number of *makam*-s, in the first juxtaposing short *fasıl*-s in distinctive *makam*-s, in the second including different *makam*-s in a single *fasıl.* Second, the sequence of sections is somewhat irregular. In the earlier program, a selection of folk songs interrupts the progression of a traditional *fasıl*, 'popular' *şarkı*-s coming after a *kâr* but coming before a *beste.* In the later program, an instrumental interlude interrupts the usual progression from a 'classical' *fasıl* (in the *makam acemaşiran*) to a light-'classical' *fasıl* (in the *makam uşşak*). Third, the number of sections is somewhat unconventional. In contemporary performances, 3 rather than 5 sections were usual in concert programs. In short, the arrangement of the concerts in Istanbul and Ankara was eclectic, presenting a potpourri of musical modes and a variety of musical genres in an unconventional manner.

Of course, Fersan and Selçuk still offered a more traditional program (see Plate 6). During their concert tour of Egypt (1928-1929), they gave 2 concerts in Cairo. These took place in the *Azbakeya* Gardens (a theatrical venue much beloved by Umm Kulthūm [1898-1975]) on Friday, 25 January (1929) and Monday, 28 January (1929). Each performance consisted of 4 sections, each section representing a particular *fasıl* (for the most part) in an individual *makam.* Although 2 'classical' *fasıl*-s (in the *makam*-s *sultanî yegâh* and *acemaşiran*) were offered at the beginning of each evening, the other sections were devoted to *fasıl*-s consisting of light-'classical' *şarkı*-s, most of which had been composed by contemporary artists (including Fersan and Selçuk). Although the full details of the works performed are not mentioned, it is clear that the musicians wished to offer a standard program that would appeal to a local audience familiar with Arab (the *waṣlah*) and Turkish (the *fasıl*) cyclical forms. Significantly, both programs feature a vocal *gazel* and an instrumental *taksim*.

By 1929, Hakkı Bey was dead. Yet, Hakkı Bey left an indelible imprint upon both artists. In terms of musical terminology, Hakkı transmitted to the musicians a contemporary taxonomy with respect to genre and meter, in particular his classification of folk genres (such as "*halk şarkısı*") and his representation of 'classical' *usûl*-s (such as "*murabba çenber*") finding expression in the concert programs of his progeny. While the didactic legacy of the teacher is evident, it important that Hakkı Bey himself represented a particular line of musical transmission (*meşk silsilesi*), a 'western' version of Turkish music that was inculcated in the imperial band. Here, his teacher of 'western' music (Zâti Bey) and his teacher of Turkish music (Latîf Ağa [1815-1885]) informed his unique approach to musical literacy in an oral tradition. This approach was transmitted in the schools and the ensembles that flourished in Istanbul during Hakkı Bey's life. It was also transmitted in the scores and books that were published before Hakkı Bey's death.

By 1929, Fersan and Selçuk had burgeoning careers in the recording studio. Leaving Ankara (1927), both artists were approached by *Pathé Frères*. Fersan signed a contract with the company, the instrumentalist bemoaning in retrospect the quality of sound recordings.[63] Selçuk did not. However, it is clear that he intended to do so since the extant contract details 20 discs. These included *gazel*-s (both metric and non-metric) and songs (such as *kanto*-s and *fantezi*-s), the 'popular' pieces often being composed in simple meters (such as *semaî* and *düyek*). Although he recorded more serious works for Orfeon and Polydor, it is clear that his vocal style still emulated the highly melismatic character (*titrek*) of a commercial vocalist (*hanende*). Further, the schedule of items shows the juxtaposition of unrelated genres and distinctive modes, the commodification of music resulting in the dislocation of music making. In this context, the 'popular' took precedent over the 'classical' since (for the most art) only short works could be recorded.

By 1929, Fersan and Selçuk also had flourishing careers in the radio station. Founded around 1927, radio broadcasts provided an ideal medium for advertising sound recordings. Although Fersan accompanied Selçuk on a number occasions, his role as a tenured instrumentalist in the studio musical ensemble (*stüdyo musiki heyeti*) is more representative.[64] In this context, he regularly performed 'popular' *fasıl*-s, a string of *şarkı*-s in a particular *makam* which was often punctuated by improvisations (both instrumental and vocal) and which was usually

63 See Bardakçı (Ed.) 1995, pp. 150-152.

64 Ibid., p. 103.

framed by 2 instrumental work, a *peşrev* at the beginning and sometimes a *saz semaîsi* at the end.[65] Unlike sound recordings, radio broadcasts could transmit extended performances. However, these were decidedly commercial in character. Reminiscent of 'popular' venues (such as *meyhane*-s), a representative performance rarely featured 'classical' works (such *beste*-s) but often presented vernacular pieces (such as *şarkı*-s). Musical medleys entitled "musician's corner" ("*kerizgâh*") seemed to underscore the low-brow character of these early broadcasts.

Indeed, the radio studio and the recording industry informed the character of two concerts. In Cairo, the programs at the Azbakiye Gardens are remarkably similar to the musical slots in the radio station. In both instances, a number of 'popular' *fasıl*-s were performed, each usually containing a medley of *şarkı*-s in a principal *makam*. In both instances too, 'classical' works were rarely foregrounded but 'popular' pieces were frequently inserted, be they folk numbers (such as *dağî*-s) or contemporary compositions (such as *fantezi*-s).[66] In Ankara, the program in the *Türk Ocağı* anticipated the repertoire of the record studio. In both instances, the organization of meter and mode is idiosyncratic. In both instances too, the musical genres are not clearly organized into a *fasıl* structure. Indeed, the classification of genres in the concert program found their equivalent in record catalogues, old designations like *müstezat* and new genres like *millî şarkı* being found in both contexts. However, in the concerts as in the studios a *taksim* and a *gazel* were always included.

In 1927, Fersan and Selçuk signed a new contract with "His Master's Voice" (Tr. "*Sahibinin Sesi*"). Being freed from his contractual obligations to *Pathé Frères* by *Sahibinin Sesi*, Fersan recorded a selection of compositions and improvisation on ten discs. He also accompanied Selçuk, who recorded a further ten discs[67], two of which were devoted to partially-metric religious genres (*durak*-s) and four others featuring non-metric secular improvisations (*gazel*-s). In recognition of their artistic status, both artists were accorded a special black label (the FE series). With the development of electric recording, Selçuk in particular took the opportunity to experiment with a new style of vocal performance by adapting 'western' techniques to Turkish music. In addition to the correct articulation of song texts, he experimented with distinctive vocal registers and breathing techniques to develop a 'classical' style, an 'alafrangized' version of *alaturka* which addressed in his own way a contemporary debate about the correct constitution of a national music (*millî musiki*).

---

65 Ibid., pp. 101-102.

66 Here, it is worth mentioning that not all genres performed by the Fersans and Selçuk were 'classical' in nature. On the first evening, the artists presented an extended *fantezi* entitled "*Leylâ*", a number that had previously been offered at the *Türk Ocağı* in Ankara (see O'Connell 2013, p. 119). On the second evening, the musicians played a number of folk-songs, two of which had previously been performed in Ankara and were entitled "*Memo*" and "*Şehnaz Divan*".

67 Ibid., pp. 92-99.

In this matter, two moments involving *Sahibinin Sesi* are noteworthy. The first (in 1927), Selçuk and Fersan recorded an extended improvisation with *Sahibinin Sesi* on a special disc (FE 6). Entitled "Bahar olsa, çemenzâr olsa", the *gazel* (in the *makam acemaşiran*) highlighted the results of the vocalist's stylistic innovations, with the text (especially with respect to prosodic structure) and the melody (especially with respect to ornamental figures) being neatly crafted. Conceived by Selçuk as the first example of his new approach to vocal improvisation, he decorates the text with programmatic embellishment and dynamic variation.[68] In contrast to a previous recording (Artistic Orfeon 13.817) of the same poem (this time, in the *makam nihavend*), each syllable is now clearly articulated, each breath is now judiciously considered. Critical here is his abandonment of a melismatic type of vocal execution (*titrek*) favored by commercial singers (*hanende*-s). Critical here too is his application of a 'western' method in musical performance, a systematic approach to vocal production and vocal rendition in Turkish music.

At this crossroads between the 'east' and the 'west', Fersan and Selçuk now parted. This was the second moment. The following year (1928), Selçuk left for Paris ostensibly to study vocal performance for 2 years at the *Conservatoire de Paris*. Sponsored by *Sahibinin Sesi*, he attended a few concerts and took a few lessons. As I show elsewhere, he probably only stayed in France for 3 months, family obligations and professional commitments requiring his return to Istanbul.[69] Yet, it is easy to discount this trip abroad as a publicity stunt. Although Fahire Fersan (and probably Fersan himself) dismissed this sojourn in the French capital as a narcissistic whim[70], his son Timur Selçuk (b. 1946) believed otherwise[71]. According to him (interview March 1994), his father needed to go abroad to develop a new understanding of a national music (*millî musiki*) at home, using 'western' techniques and 'western' conventions to transform Turkish music at a critical moment in Turkish history.

To showcase this new style of vocal performance, Selçuk staged his 'first' concert as a 'classical' soloist (*solist*) in the manner of a 'classical' recital (*resital*). Presented at the French Theatre (*Fransız Tiyatrosu*) in Istanbul (on Saturday, 22 February 1930), Selçuk explicitly selected an established venue for operas and recitals. Here, the vocalist adopted the performance conventions of a concert artist (*konsertist*) by standing (rather than sitting) in front of (rather than behind) a select group of instrumentalists. Significantly, Fersan was not included. Dressed in tails (*frak*), Selçuk employed the musical techniques of a 'western' vocalist to project his voice from the stage to the auditorium. Unusually, Selçuk did not require a choral backing or use a percussion instrument (such as a *def*). Rather, he sang by himself without technical assistance for more than two hours. This was excep-

68 Ibid., p. 49.
69 Ibid., p. 109.
70 Ibid., pp. 106-107.
71 Ibid., pp. 48-49.

tional. For those present, it was considered to be courageous.[72] For those not present (including Fahire Fersan), it was considered to be foolhardy.

In retrospect, Selçuk considered that his 'first' concert was completely new.[73] Although a precedent did exist (see above), Selçuk eschewed the modal organization and the temporal acceleration characteristic of the traditional *fasıl*. That is, he juxtaposed unconventionally *makam*-s (such as *rast* followed by *kürdili hicazkâr*) and he sequenced inappropriately *usûl*-s (such as *semaî* coming before *çifte sofyan*). Like his concert in Ankara (1925), the potpourri was organized into five sections. Like the concert in Ankara too, one section was devoted entirely to *alafranga* compositions, 2 *fantezi*-s which featured a cellist and a pianist as accompanists. Significantly, the program did not include any religious genre (such as a *durak*) or a vocal improvisation (such as a *gazel*). Although he had previously recorded representative examples of these musical forms, he was responding to a contemporary ambivalence towards certain sacred pieces (especially mystical works) and particular secular styles (especially vocal improvisations) that were considered to be inappropriate or vulgar respectively.[74]

The 'classical' concert was in fact a 'popular' concert. Backed by *Sahibinin Sesi*, the program featured 17 pieces that had been (or would be) recorded by Selçuk for the company.[75] Only one of these was a 'classical' composition, the *Kâr-ı Nev* by Dede Efendi. The other recordings included 11 light-'classical' songs (*şarkı*-s) and 3 'folk' songs (a *divan*, a *dağî* and a "*halk şarkısı*"). In addition, the 2 *fantezi* numbers entitled "*Ne olur*" by Fersan and "*Tereddüt*" by Çağatay were available for purchase. Only the *şarkı* in the *makam nikriz* entitled "*Gönül ne için*" by the female composer Fâize Hanım (Ergin) (1892-1954) was not recorded by the vocalist. In the program, it is attributed to her husband, Ruhi Bey. *Sahibinin Sesi* also benefitted from advertising. As sponsors of the 'first' concert, the commercial concern organized ticket sales and collated ticket receipts. This was not always done efficiently or accurately. In particular, the logo of the company was prominently displayed on concert programs.

The 'first' concert was not entirely successful. From an artistic perspective, music critics were ambivalent about the 'alafrangized' style of *alaturka*, especially when performing 'classical' works by Dede Efendi. One critic (Ahmet Vâlâ Nurettin or Vâ Nû Bey [1901-1967]) even suggested that Selçuk sounded hoarse, perhaps straining from the pressure of projecting his voice across a large auditorium for two hours. As I show elsewhere, the concert venue suffered from poor

---

72 See for example Karabey, Lâika 1966, "Münirin Cesareti", in: *Üstad Münir Nurettin Selçuk'un 50. San'at Yılı Jübilesi* (Anon.), Istanbul: Nebioğlu Yayınevi, p. 14.

73 See O'Connell 2013, pp. 153-154.

74 See O'Connell, John M. 2003, "Song Cycle: The Life and Death of the Turkish Gazel: Review Essay", *Ethnomusicology 47(3)*, pp. 399-414.

75 See O'Connell 2013, pp. 109-139.

FRANSIZ TİYATROSUNDA

Münir Nurettin

Beyin

Konser Programı

Refakat edecek hey'eti musikiye :

MES'UT CEMİL Bey, RUŞEN Bey, NUBAR Ef.

ARTAKİ Ef. ve Mösyö VASİLİEF

22 ŞUBAT CUMARTESİ GÜNÜ

akşam saat tam 21½ ta

Konsere on yaşından aşağı çocuklar kabul olunmaz.

Plate 7a: Programing *Usûl* - Concert and Program in Istanbul (1930)

Konser Programı

Birinci Kısım

Kemençe, Tambur refakatile

1.— **Rast kârı nev** *(klasik)* . . . DEDE EFENDİ
2.— **Suzinak şarkı** *(pek revadır)* AHMET RASİM BEY
3.— **Uşşak** *(neden hiç durmadan)* SUPHİ ZİYA BEY
4.— **Huseyni** *(feryad idiyor)* . . . SUPHİ ZİYA BEY
5.— **Şehnaz divan** *(vardımki yurdundan)*

ikinci Kısım

Tambur, kemençe, kanun refakatile

1.— **Hüzzam** *(Durmasın aksın)* . BİMEN EFENDİ
2.— **Segâh** *(benim sen nemsin)* . AHMET RASİM BEY
3.— **Nehavent** *(süzüp süzüp)* . . RAHMİ BEY
4.— **Mahur** *(dün yine günümüz)* . REFİK BEY

Üçüncü Kısım

Tambur refakatile

1.— **Rast şarkı** *(senin aşkınla)* . ABDİ EFENDİ
2.— **Kürdili Hicaskâr** *(sana eycanımın canı)* RAHMİ BEY
3.— **Nigriz** *(gönül ne için)* . . . RUHİ BEY

ONBEŞ DAKİKA İSTİRAHAT

Dördüncü Kısım

Fantaziler, keman, violonsel, piano refakatile

1.— **Ne olur** . . . . REFİK BEY
2.— **Tereddüt** . . . . ALİ RİFAT BEY

ON DAKİKA İSTİRAHAT

Beşinci Kısım

Keman, tambur, kanun refakatile

1.— **Hüzzam** *(Kirpiklerinin)* . . . ARTAKİ EFENDİ
2.— **Ferahnak** *(ruhumda bahar)* ARTAKİ EFENDİ
3.— **Daği** *(akşam olur)*
4.— **Halk şarkısı** *(allı yemeni)*

SON

MÜNİR NURETTİN Beyin eserleri
münhasıran
"Sahibinin Sesi" Plâklarında zaptedilmiştir.

Plate 7b: Programing *Usûl* - Concert and Program in Istanbul (1930)

acoustics.[76] Another critic (Peyami Safa [1899-1961]) was concerned about the repertoire. In particular, he condemned the *alafranga* compositions or *fantezi* numbers in the fourth section. He considered these to be "gaudily ornamented like a woman's shoe manufactured by a cheap cobbler". He concluded: "Let us save our music from melodies that are adulterated and from a synthesis of styles." As a commercial initiative, ticket sales were disappointing. Only 333 seats out of a possible 536 were sold. Since the most expensive boxes were not filled, profits were minimal especially when costs were deducted.

The 'first' concert was not the last. Over the next three years, Selçuk developed a concert style that continues to inform 'classical' performances of Turkish music today. Here, critics played a role. They censured Selçuk for his mistaken rendition of song texts, the artist failing to realize the correct scansion of particular lyrics (especially in folk songs) or to present the correct articulation of specific words (especially in 'classical' numbers).[77] Although Selçuk was not always to blame, the public debate demonstrated that the artist was sometimes careless with his choice of texts and in his representation of genres. Especially irksome for his detractors, concert programs were resplendent with errors and inconsistencies, be they the incorrect spelling of musical modes or the inappropriate classification of musical forms. The same critics censured Selçuk for his innovative approach to vocal performance. In particular, they criticized him for inserting "unrelated melodies" and for imposing "inappropriate caesuras" in the manner of an *alafranga* artist.

Selçuk engaged actively in this debate. He defended robustly his representation of individual genres, arguing that mistakes in a song text were the responsibility of the composer. For him, the task of an artist was one of interpretation and not one of creation. Here, Selçuk invoked a 'western' precedent by recognizing the fixity of a musical work and by acknowledging the distinction between a creator and an interpreter. Similar to an *alafranga* artist, he believed that it was his duty to infuse a work with the appropriate spirit (*ruh*) and meaning (*ma'na*), his use of melodic extension and metric variation being entirely consistent with the compositions performed. Selçuk even adopted the language of 'western' music, referring to an embellishment as "vocalize" and to a pause as "*un point d'orgue*". To validate his argument, he emphasized his traditional background in *alaturka* and his contemporary interest in *alafranga*, his studies at the *Paris Konservatuvarı* being employed (somewhat incredulously) to underscore his credentials as a 'virtuose'.

The debate about Selçuk had a wider significance. It erupted at time of increased acrimony against *alaturka* both at an institutional level and at an executive level. In the former, the performance of *alaturka* had been excluded from the

---

76 O'Connell, John M. (forthcoming), "Concert Platform: A Space for a Style in Turkish Music", in: *Music and Architecture in Islam*, Michael Frishkopf and Federico Spinetti (Eds.), Austin: University of Texas Press.

77 See O'Connell 2013, pp. 253-268.

İstanbul Konservatuvarı after 1926[78] and would be banned from *İstanbul Radyosu* during 1934[79]. In the latter, a proclamation against *alaturka* was announced by Mustafa Kemal Atatürk (1881-1938) in the National Assembly (*Millet Meclisi*) in 1934. At both levels, *alaturka* was not consistent with a contemporary aspiration towards a national music (*millî musiki*). Two issues were especially pressing. First, *alaturka* was viewed as the symbolic capital of the Ottoman Empire. It had no place as the musical expression of the Turkish Republic. Second, *alaturka* was performed in 'popular' venues such as nightclubs (*gazino*-s) and drinking houses (*meyhane*-s). The fact that it was patronized by non-Muslims and non-Turks made it especially repugnant to nationalist sensibilities in the new state.

Selçuk had to combat such prejudices. Instead of *alaturka*, he advocated a 'classical' style of Turkish music. Now called "Turkish classical music" ("*Türk klâsik musikisi*"), he hoped to acquire for 'eastern' music (*şark musikisi*) the same respect accorded to 'western' music (*garb musikisi*). This is why he donned the formal attire of a 'western' tradition, emulating the concert convention and the concert format of a 'classical' recital. Here, he had to challenge some nagging uncertainties. On the one hand, he had to address the *alaturka* stereotype (*alaturkacı*), the inebriated musician who bellowed and grimaced (as Safa would have it) with drunken abandon in insalubrious locales. On the other hand, he had to address his *alafranga* detractors, either composers or folklorists who wished to develop a national idiom by arranging folk song in a contemporary setting. Selçuk presented an alternative solution. By melding *alaturka* with *alafranga*, he was able to fashion a new style of Turkish music that was both morally respectable yet politically acceptable.

Selçuk chose select platforms to stage his 'classical' style. After the *Fransız Tiyatrosu*, he moved (in 1931) to the *Melek Sineması*, a modern construction with excellent acoustics. Here, the issue of projection was not problematic. However, the issue of articulation was. Music critics could now hear mistakes made by Selçuk with respect to scansion and diction. And so, the debate about Selçuk erupted. In actual fact, the *Melek Sineması* was not a fashionable venue. That is, it did not suit the 'classical' pretensions of a 'classical' artist. Accordingly, Selçuk moved again (in 1932) to the *Glorya Sineması*, a nearby setting that fulfilled the musical requirements and the social aspirations of a 'concertiste'. By 1933, the concert programs were also distinctive. Now organized into three sections each consisting of four works, the repertoire covered 'classical', light-'classical' and folk genres. This organized approach to programing encompassed mode and meter, each section now demonstrating integrity (with respect to *makam*) and acceleration (with respect to *usûl*).

---

78 See O'Connell, John M. 2000, "Fine Art, Fine Music: Controlling Turkish Taste at the Fine Arts Academy", *Yearbook for Traditional Music 33*, pp. 117-142.

79 See O'Connell 2013, p. 65-67.

Plate 8: *Usûllü* – Fahire Fersan (1994)

In the *Glorya Sineması*, Selçuk developed a systematic (*usûllü*) approach to concert performance. Not only was the program carefully configured (with respect to mode and meter) but it was also judiciously constructed (with respect to genre and style). He even included annotated texts in (some) concert programs, thereby sidestepping any potential criticism concerning his literary erudition and his musical expertise. Of course, there were still mistakes in type setting and errors in musical representation. However, these were not always the fault of the artist. Although the concert series was sponsored by *Sahibinin Sesi*, much of the repertoire performed had not been (and would not be) recorded by the record company. In addition, the cost of tickets was less but the sale of tickets was more. Here was a new collaboration between the local artist and the foreign enterprise, a new way of advertising musical products that was both aesthetically challenging yet ideologically astute. As I show elsewhere, it was also financially lucrative.[80]

80 Ibid., pp. 219-226.

In this chapter, I have traced the development of a 'classical' style in Turkish music. With reference to Münir Nurettin Selçuk, I show how an artist melded his traditional education in *alaturka* with a non-traditional interest in *alafranga* to forge an 'alafrangized' *alaturka* in a concert setting. While the vocalist emphasized his qualifications in 'eastern' music (by way of an established line of oral transmission [*meşk silsilesi*]) and highlighted his credentials in 'western' music (by way of an apparent training at an eminent institution [the *Conservatoire de Paris*]), he was in fact indebted to two major figures in Turkish music, the instrumentalist Tanburî Refik Fersan and the teacher "Muallim" İsmail Hakkı Bey. In different ways, both men taught Selçuk how to design and how to present a concert program, a contemporary format that was more suited to a recording studio than to a radio station. It was this model that informed his 'first' concert in the *Fransız Tiyatrosu*. It was this model that provoked the scorn of his contemporary critics.

To address his detractors, Selçuk developed a systematic approach to concert programing, a modernized version of the traditional *fasıl* that was organized around the central principles of modal integrity and metric acceleration. This 'classical' program was first presented in the *Glorya Sineması* and not in the *Fransız Tiyatrosu*. Of course, Selçuk would revert to a vulgar populism in subsequent concerts. Again, he would suffer the contempt of critics, some of whom represented *alaturka* pejoratively as "*düm tek*" with respect to music or "*hoppa*" with respect to genre. Here, onomatopoeic syllables (such as "*hey hey*" or "*vay vay da vay vay*") were creatively yet damagingly deployed against him. Yet, Selçuk was able to maintain his status as a concert artist even when performing repertoire principally derived from drinking establishments. Here, his sartorial sense and his social standing provided a tangible and a symbolic frame for validating the commercial rewards that came with musical production. For Selçuk, the 'alafrangization' of *alaturka* was both politically judicious and economically advantageous.

Fantezi/Fantasy and *Usûl*

Martin Stokes

For those whose experience of Turkish music began with the troubled years of the early 1980s, the word *fantezi* will summon to mind an experimental moment in the career of *arabesk* star Orhan Gencebay. The defiant and politically loaded slogans of Orhan Gencebay's mid-1970s style, of which "*Batsın Bu Dünya*" is perhaps the best remembered, seemed to disappear. It was replaced, at least in his post 1980 work, by an *arabesk* that was concerned with instrumental artistry, which was ornate and virtuosic, and which involved a play of 'eastern' and 'western' musical tropes. '*Fantezi*' signified Gencebay's difference from his rivals in the *arabesk* world – Müslüm Gürses, Ferdi Tayfur and others. For his fans, it was what made his *arabesk* emotionally sophisticated, formally adventurous and stylistically cosmopolitan. It was what distanced his work from the emotionally monochromatic pain (*acı*) of mainstream *arabesk*, and its associations with the folk music of the south east of the country.

The term seemed to loose its currency in the 1990s, but by then new styles of popular music were emerging anyway. It would be easy, in retrospect, to dismiss Gencebay's aestheticism as brief distraction, a welcome one perhaps, at a moment of political and economic privation for the vast majority of Turkish citizens. But the term *fantezi* has a long and complex history in the Turkish popular domain. It is a history that both poses and raises some significant questions about the relationship between art and popular music, between formal play and emotional expression, and between ideas about 'east' and 'west' in Turkey. Far from being a momentary distraction, Gencebay's *fantezi* is part of a wider story.

Yılmaz Öztuna connects the word *fantezi* with the Turkish music provided for Egyptian cinema in Turkey in the 1930s, and hence the origins of *arabesk*.[1] It goes without saying that for Öztuna, and for others following in his footsteps, this is not a good thing. Consider Yahya Kemal Taştan's comment in *Köprü Dergisi*, for example, as recently as 2006:

> *"...bidayetinde popüler olan şarkıları klasik bir mahiyet kazanırken, onu taklit eden müziklerin giderek soysuz bir duygusallığı, hafif usûllere yer vermesi ve buna paralel olarak büyük temalardan kaçması, şarkı formunu da dejenere etmiş ve 1930'larda popüler olan, şarkının başka bir türü ve hafif müziğe yakın olan 'fantezi' tarzının doğuşuna zemin hazırlamıştır..."*
>
> "Whilst these once popular songs have now gained an aura of classicism, the inauthentic emotionality, the simplification of meters and, parallel to this, the avoidance of major themes in the music that imitated them degraded the *şarkı* form and prepared the

---

1 See Öztuna, Yılmaz 1987, *Türk Musikisi: Teknik ve Tarihi*, Istanbul: Türk Petrol Vakfi Lale Mecmuası Neşriyatı, pp. 50-54.

ground for the birth of the *fantezi* style, which was another kind of *şarkı* form, close to light popular music."[2]

It is worth considering these characterizations with some concrete examples in mind. Consider, for example, Sadettin Kaynak's famous *Kürdilihicazkar Fantezi*, "*Bir Esmer Dilberin Vuruldum Hüsnüne*", with words by Ercüment Er. This was one of Sadettin Kaynak's compositions for the 1940 Umm Kulthum film *Dananir*, circulated in Turkey as *Harun Reşid Gözdesi*, with a new soundtrack sung by Müzeyyen Senar. The song, you will recall, starts in *curcuna*, and shifts to *düyek* (with the words "*kalbime gün doğdu güzel yüzünden…*"). This section is followed by a *gazel*-like section; the first vocal section, in *curcuna*, then comes back as a brief refrain. The song is full of quirky and lyrical moments, stoppings and startings, and shifts of mood. It is not – as I discovered, in performance with an ensemble comprising both Egyptian and Turkish musicians, in a concert exploring shared repertory – at all easy to perform. Our Egyptian percussionist had immense difficulty coping with the rapid shifts of tempo and *usûl*. It is odd, to say the least, that Taştan should decide to blame *fantezi* – songs such as this – for degrading Turkish art music's rhythmic and metrical sensibility. It would seem to demonstrate rather the opposite.

'Degraded' or not, how might we understand this rhythmic and metrical sensibility? One might start where Öztuna and Taştan start, with its origins as a film song. The action in the original Umm Kulthum song sections, and the odd parcels of time supplied by the film narrative to those dubbing it and providing the Turkish-language music, may well have stimulated the kinds of formal play on display in this song, of which Sadettin Kaynak's song composition is full. Conventional *şarkı* form could, of course, have been extended or contracted, but these formal conventions might not have sat easily with the images on screen. Something more fragmented, involving constant stopping and starting, may well have permitted the necessary flexibility in duration, and some kind of loose articulation with the camera work. Unfortunately, at the present time it is difficult to know. The Turkish soundtracks of the Egyptian films are not at the moment available for consultation, and the situation resembles one of a crazy jigsaw, comprising, on the one hand, a number of Turkish songs still sung today in the classical tradition and known at least by some to be associated with particular Egyptian films, and, on the other, the films of Abd al-Wahhab and Umm Kulthum, available in their Egyptian Arabic versions. Quite how well 'quilted' the Turkish versions were into the original Egyptian films, or whether, indeed, such a quilting was actively sought for, is, at the moment, hard to know.

Film musicals in Turkey, as elsewhere, were inspired by *The Jazz Singer* of 1927. Movies from the rapidly modernizing, cosmopolitan and (later) state-supported

---

2 Taştan, Yahya Kemal, 2006, "Teganni'den Irlamak'a Musikinin Serencamı", *Köprü Dergisi* 99 no. 67, http://www.koprudergisi.com/index.asp?Bolum=EskiSayilar&Goster=Yazi&YaziNo=446 (accessed 27 March 2015).

film industry in Cairo in subsequent decades proved highly attractive in Turkey, as in many other parts of the world. Umm Kulthum's *Widad* and Abd al-Wahhab's *Dumu'a al-Hubb* both created a sensation on the streets around Şehzadebaşı in 1938. New songs and Turkish vocals were attached to the sung portions, by composers, musicians and vocalists like Sadettin Kaynak, Salahattin Pınar, Şükrü Tunar, Haydar Tatlıyay, Hafız Burhan, and Sadi Işılay. This passed without much comment, other than a palpable degree of popular excitement, until the early 1940s. As Murat Özyıldırım suggests in a recent article, the annexation of the Hatay in 1938 generated a climate of anxiety about how to turn the Arabic-speaking populations of Antakya, Adana, Mersin and Urfa into Turkish nationals. This sparked efforts to de-Arabize the media.[3] A ban on Arabic language films in the south in 1942 was followed by a blanket ban across the country in 1948. It seems to have been ignored – 8 Egyptian films were shown in 1949 alone, apparently.

The Turkish language additions to and dubbings of the Egyptian films and the post-1949 imitations, seem, then, to have flourished in an atmosphere of cosmopolitan cultural creativity. Sadettin Kaynak (1865-1961) was perhaps the most significant contributor to it. He was a religious functionary in the Ottoman state – in which capacity he got to know the Anatolian and Arab eastern provinces during the First World War. He travelled widely as a recording artist in Europe. On his return he threw himself into the film industry, providing the music for some 85 films for İpekci Kardeşler, over roughly a 20 year period, from 1933 to 1952.

Whatever their rationale in relation to the original Egyptian film narratives, the multi-*usûl*, multi-sectional nature of Sadettin Kaynak's *fantezi*-s clearly became an independent stylistic feature during these years. Consider, by way of a second example, his *Nihavent Fantezi*, "*Menekşelendi Sular*".[4] As is well known, Safiye Ayla recorded the song and made it famous. Zeki Müren then appropriated it. A note on a concert programme on display in the Zeki Müren museum in Bodrum comments that he always used to perform this song at the end of concerts. It starts with a brief instrumental in *sofyan*; the opening verse in *düyek*; a *semai* chorus; there is a brief return of *düyek*, followed by a *gazel*-like section; then back to the beginning for the instrumental introduction, and the *semai*/waltz chorus. There seem to be various different performance traditions of this song, one stemming from Safiye Ayla herself, the other apparently initiated by Zeki Müren, with a much longer and more extended *gazel* section, and different practices of locating the repeats of the instrumental introduction. One can see why Zeki Müren might have liked the song, one that he was clearly able to make 'his own'. The sentimental tone, the changes in mood and poetic perspective, the opportunities it afforded for vocal

---

3 Özyıldırım, Murat 2011, "Türkiye'de Arap Müziği üzerine Düşünceler", *Musiki Dergisi*, http://www.musikidergisi.net/?p=1821 (accessed 27 March 2015).

4 For a more thorough discussion and contextualization of this song, see Stokes, Martin 2010, *The Republic of Love: Cultural Intimacy in Turkish Popular Music*, Chicago: University of Chicago Press, pp. 48-58.

improvisation, the hybrid, east-west feel of the song imparted by its *nihavent* tonalities were in tune with *gazino*-oriented commercial song practice (shaped, to a significant extent, by Zeki Müren himself), and, more broadly, the liberalism of the Menderes years in Turkey.

"*Menekşelendi Sular*" raises the possibility that the multi-*usûl*, multi-sectional nature of *fantezi* songs was motivated not just by the demands of dubbing for Egyptian cinema translations, or a spirit of play and experimentation, but by *expressive* considerations. There is, at least in this song, a relationship between the shifting moods of the various sections of this song and their *usûl*. The opening *düyek* verse depicts the poet in melancholic, contemplative mode ("*Menekşelendi sular, sular menekşelendi/esmer yüzlü akşamı dinledim yine sensiz*", "Violet went the waters, the waters went violet/I listened to the dark-complexioned evening once again without you…"). The *semai* chorus, addressing the beloved, expresses resolve by turning the last line of the verse on its head. All roses may indeed have thorns, and all nightingales be tormented. But that doesn't have to be us! ("*Her kuş bülbül olmazmış/her çicek de gül, Ayşe*!"). The *serbest* section reverts to self-pity, and the more predictable consolations of fantasy ("*İçli bir özleyişle bırak beni yanayım/Gözlerinde gördüğüm rüyama inanayım*", "Leave me to my inner longing, for I am burning/Allow me to believe in the dream I saw in your eyes").

"*Bir Esmer Dilberin Vuruldum Hüsnüne*" and "*Menekşelendi Sular*" continue to be sung today. So the history of *fantezi* cannot be relegated in any simple sense to a stage in the development of modern *arabesk*, or seen as a stylistic degeneration or emotional trivialization. In particular, the charge of rhythmical and metrical simplification seems wide of the mark. Sadettin Kaynak's *fantezi* songs of the 1930s and 40s seem, by contrast, to be remarkably intricate in this particular regard. And they raise questions when one tries to think of them in conventional music historical terms.

Let me try to characterize these patterns a little more broadly. If one surveys the obvious sources like the TRT archives, or online sources like neyzen.com, for all of their problems, one discovers many of these multi-sectional songs are labeled *fantezi*, but not all.[5] One also encounters songs that are labeled *fantezi* but which have no *usûl* shifts, in Sadettin Kaynak's oeuvre as well as others. (I am excluding from my field of inquiry, at least for present purposes, songs from the 1960s, when the term '*fantezi*' starts to refer to almost any light waltz-time piece, usually in *nihavent*). A few feature, instead, a play on multiple *makam*-s, rather than multiple *usûl*-s, like, for example, Sadettin Kaynak's "*Filiz oldum büküldüm uzandım kollarına*" which shifts from *şedaraban* to *nikriz* to *mahur*. And one encounters multisectional,

5 My sources in what follows are primarily the following websites: turksanatmuzigi.org, neyzen.com, trt.notaarsivleri, sarkilarnotalar.com. See also the entry and list of songs under Sadettin Kaynak's name in İnal, İbnülemin Mahmut Kemal 1958, *Hoş Sadâ: Son Asır Türk Musikişinasları*, Istanbul: Maarif.

multi-*usûl*-ed songs by composers other than Sadettin Kaynak, for example, Mutlu Torun, Fahri Kopuz and others. But Sadettin Kaynak greatly exceeds any other contemporary composer, or composer of film music, in number of multi-sectioned *fantezi*. Some 275 songs are attributed to him on lists of works available on these websites. Of these, 65 are labeled '*fantezi*'. Even if we bear in mind that some multi-sectional songs are not included in this category, and some *fantezi* are not multi-sectional, we are still talking about a large proportion.

Of these I have located around 30, in various different notations, and recordings of the songs in older or newer versions. The process of gathering a field here is a little haphazard, but I think I have a cross section, and a useful vantage point. A few quick generalizations are possible – firstly, by looking, simply, at a list of songs and song types of the kind given in the biographical studies. The largest number of *fantezi* seems to be concentrated in *nihavent*: 12 (out of 25 in total in *nihavent*) are *Nihavent Fantezi-s*; after that 7 (out of 26) are in *muhayyer*; 7 (out of 23) are in *hicaz*; 6 (out of 28) in *hüzzam*; 5 (out of 11) in *segah*; 4 (out of 9) in *muhayyer-kürdi*; 4 (out of 10) in *acemaşiran*; 2 (out of 5) in *beyati-araban*; 1 (out of 3) in *kürdilihicazkar*. Not only are there more *Nihavent Fantezi*-s than *fantezi*-s in other *makam*-s, but there is a higher proportion. However one looks at it, there is some kind of connection between the *makam nihavent* and *fantezi* form.

Secondly, thinking about my smaller sample of 30, the *usûl* multi-sectioning processes fall into some observable patterns. In some, a section is marked, or performed, or indicated by pauses, as *usûl*-less, or 'serbest' – a kind of written out *gazel*; these normally return to the beginning in an ABA structure (as, for example in "*Aşkın susuz bağında pınar gibi*" – in *nihavent* – with the pattern *aksak-serbest*; or "*Mehtaba bürünmüş gece*" – *nihavent* – *düyek-serbest*; or "*Ne Yaptım Kendimi nasıl andattın*" – *uşşak* – *düyek-serbest*). Some consist of a shift from one to another, and back again, though without structural repetitions, as in "*Batarken ufukta bu akşam güneş*" (*hüzzam* – *sofyan-curcuna-sofyan*), "*O siyah gözleri birde aha*" (*hüzzam* – *aksak-curcuna- aksak*), "*Gönlüm içindedir*" (*hüseyni* – *düyek-aksak-düyek*), and "*Ey İpek Kanatlı Seher Rüzgari*" (*nihavent* – *düyek-devri hindi-düyek*). Many involve three *usûl* shifts; this is the limit – which is only extended to four when the fourth section is a *gazel* or '*serbest*' section, as in "*Menekşelendi Sular*". The *usûl* involved are overwhelmingly *sofyan*, *düyek*, *curcuna*, *aksak* and *semai*. There is only one exception, "*Ey İpek Kanatlı Seher Rüzgari*", which involves a B section in *devri hindi*. In many of these more multi-sectional songs, the first move, or second, is to a *semai*/waltz – none start off in this *usûl*. For an example of this, see "*Damlalar damla damla*" – *kürdilihicazkar* – *sofyan-semai-sofyan-sofyan*; or "*Bir Rüzgardır Gelir Gecer Sanmıştım*" (*segah* – *düyek-semai-serbest*), or "*Kalplerden Dudaklara*" – *düyek-semai-serbest*). And it is, as discussed earlier, the second shift in "Menekşelendi Sular" (*nihavent* – *sofyan-düyek-semai-serbest*).

What questions emerge from this – admittedly superficial – overview? Firstly, I think they raise questions about the relationship between *makam* and *usûl*-

sectionality in this repertory. It is immediately noticeable, as mentioned above, that *nihavent* is prominent. *Nihavent* in this period is a kind of hybrid modal space, bringing together *makam* practice with facets of the western melodic and harmonic minor scale; a space, in performance and composition, where one can be, as it were, 'western' and 'eastern' at the same time. So a question that arises is whether this licenses or, somehow, underwrites other processes of formal exploration, for example, with multi-sectionality and *usûl*. Or is the connection a purely fortuitous one? Was *nihavent* becoming a popular *makam* due, perhaps, to the growing number of western musical instruments circulating in popular music space (for instance the piano)? And were multi-*usûl fantezi* popular for other reasons connected, perhaps, with their function as dubbings/translations of Egyptian film, and did these two developments just happen to coincide?

Secondly, is there any regularity of *usûl* sequencing in these multi-*usûl* songs? The x:*semai*:*serbest* pattern seems relatively common, where x can be any *usûl* other than *semai* (though often *düyek*). How, though, is this to be explained, and interpreted? Are there regular shifts in poetic voice that might explain the shift from *semai* to *serbest*, as in, for example, "*Menekşelendi Sular*"? Where the *semai* section would seem to signify resolution and fortitude, of some kind or another, and the *serbest* section introspection and melancholy? Is one to look at the *usûl* shifts in terms of reflecting the words, or vice-versa – a pattern arrived at as a result of formal experimentation stimulating this kind of play of active and passive poetic voice? Are *düyek*, *curcuna* and *sofyan* associated with any comparable shifts in poetic voice? And how regular might these linkages be?

If questions about form accumulate here that might be answered (or developed) by building up statistical evidence, they also accumulate on the interpretative and explanatory side. What major precedents are there for this in Ottoman Turkish, or other, related Middle Eastern art music practices? If there is not much evidence for precedence in the later 19th-century song repertory (those of the Hacı Arif Bey generation, for example), there are further back, for instance in the classical *kar* and *kar-ı nev*, or in the *Mevlevi ayin-i şerif*. The former linked *usûl* changes to changing *makam*-s in a display of compositional virtuosity and poetic intertextuality. The latter linked *usûl* changes to the complex spiritual and danced significations of *usûl* in the *Mevlevi* tradition. And both involved *usûl* shifts in the context of much larger-scale compositional works, and in a significantly different *usûl* universe, which makes comparisons difficult.

Another candidate for a model for Sadettin Kaynak's *fantezi* style would be the *muwashshahat* and *adwar* of the early recording era in Egypt.[6] This is to say, the song practices of the late nineteenth century *nahda* ('renaissance'), closely associ-

---

6 For the most thorough and systematic historical work on the early Arab recording industry currently available in Arabic and English, please see the podcasts, recordings and transcriptions available on the AMAR Foundation's website (http://www.amar-foundation.org/podcasting/).

ated with Abduh Hamuli and Abd al-Hayy Hilmi, and recorded in the latter years of the nineteenth century and the early twentieth century by such luminaries as Sheikh Muhammad al-Darwish, Sheikh Sayyid al-Safti and Sheikh Yusuf al-Manyalawi, as well as Abduh Hamuli and Abd al-Hayy Hilmi themselves. Recording on wax cylinders and 78 rpm discs, in a lively and competitive market, squeezed the more relaxed performative habits of *waslah* (suite) singing into shorter time units. This generation of vocalists and instrumentalists perfected the art of miniaturizing these performances, so introductory instrumental *dulab*-s could last a matter of seconds, improvised vocal *mawwal*-s and *layali*-s could be highly condensed, and instrumental *taqasim* would be shortened by, for example, beginning with the '*jawab*' section (the upper octave, and descending). The multi-sectional *dawr*, meanwhile, lost a lot of its improvisatory nature, whereby '*ahat*' (the '*ah*' section) and a *henk wa renk* (call and response section) could be generated on the spur of the moment in performance. A more prescriptive sense of form slowly emerged, marked by frequently changing tempi and modulations, and culminating in what one might describe as the 'fully composed' *adwar* of Mohammed Abd al-Wahhab in the 1940s (such as "*Aheb Ashufak Kulli Yom*", for example).

This is more plausible. There seems to have been a lively traffic of recordings from Egypt to Istanbul in the latter Ottoman years, as well as in the border regions of the new republic until the 1950s. As a well-travelled, cosmopolitan, and musically alert individual, Sadettin Kaynak is likely to have been highly familiar with this kind of song practice in its recorded form. The compression of instrumental introductions, the short, written out, vocal improvisations, and the rapid shifts of *usûl* in his *fantezi* may well owe something to his knowledge of, and efforts to reproduce something of this Egyptian aesthetic in Turkish art song practice.

So, questions about *fantezi* necessarily push us away from the space of Turkish art song, conceived in narrowly musicological terms, and into a broader field of exchange, circulation and translation. I will conclude by widening the frame of inquiry even further. What are the cross-cultural implications of this term, and how might it bear on the Turkish practice? *Fantezi* is, after all, a European term (known to musicologists as 'fantasy', 'fancy', 'phantasie', 'fantasia' and other closely related terms). Its Turkish usage, as with the term *arabesk*, is loaded with local meanings and implications, but it also reverberates in a post-colonial space. One cannot fully exclude the non-Turkish meanings of this word. Or, to put it another way, one might legitimately allow oneself to be nudged by them. We might be prompted, firstly, to think of the fantasias and *in nomine*-s of the English viol consort school, Orlando Gibbons, Henry Lawes, Henry Purcell, or of continental European contemporaries – long, multi-sectional pieces, taking one imitative point after another, exploring and playing with them to their limits. Contemporary performers, like Laurence Dreyfus' Oxford-based ensemble Phantasm, introduce a feel of unpredictability and improvisation into their performances, but the fantasy in this context is, of course, a rigorously conceived and highly structured piece, operating within the rules for imitative counterpoint at play in seventeenth-century England, guided "solely", as Luis de Milan had put it a century earlier, by "the fantasy and skill of the author who created it".[7] Fantasias, then, may have been associated with individual subjectivity, but not necessarily with improvisation, or freedom from constraint.

Freedom from constraint was very much at issue a century later, in the German speaking musical world, and remains a matter of debate. Ratner characterizes the eighteenth-century fantasia as an improvisatory *topos* – not improvisation *per se*, but, as it were, a musical representation of the *idea* of improvisation.[8] This, in Ratner's view, would become the driving force in the classical style of the nineteenth century. Scholars with a more focused historical sensibility point out that no matter how central the idea of improvisation might have been to the nineteenth - century understanding of *fantasia*, this was not necessarily how it was seen in the eighteenth century. Matthew Head argues that it is quite problematic to think about the eighteenth century fantasia in terms inspired by topic theory, implying one citable style amongst others.[9] It was, rather, a compositional principle at the heart of composers like CPE Bach's stylistic development. It involved a highly structured exploration of, for example, the idea of modulation, or the implications of figured bass movements. The musical 'sensibility' of this era – the capacity of music to both stir and represent the feelings – was associated more with the idea of formal play, and less with the idea of improvisation, or of freedom from external constraint.

These latter meanings would be aggressively in play in the nineteenth century, but, once again, they are at odds with the musical material. Schubert's "*Wanderer-fantasie*", for instance, uses a single motive to link the four movements of a piano sonata in one his most ambitious formal exercises. Similarly, Schumann's "*Fantasiestücke*" are conceived as the abstract instrumental equivalent of one of his song cycles. Liszt's fantasies are operatic medleys for the piano, such as his "*Reminiscences de Don Juan*", but these too are associated with large-scale formal experimentalism, and constitute some of his more serious music for piano.

These points of reference may seem remote from the world of Sadettin Kaynak, but they constitute *one* context for considering the meanings of *fantezi* in Turkey. The European story connects the word 'fantasia' to new technologies of musical communication (principally the pianoforte), to new political environments in which *sensibility* was paramount, and to a reflexive preoccupation with

---

7 Cited in Field, Christopher et al., 2000, art. "Fantasias", in: *New Grove Dictionary of Music and Musicians*, vol. 8, 2nd ed., Stanley Sadie and John Tyrrell (Eds.), London: Macmillan, 545-558.

8 Ratner, Leonard G. 1980, *Classic Music: Expression, Form and Style*, New York: Schirmer.

9 Head, Matthew 2013, "Fantasia and Sensibility", in: *Oxford Handbooks Online*, Danuta Mirka (Ed.), New York: Oxford University Press.

form and its limits. It is also a story conventional musicology has struggled with, attempting to confine it to specific stylistic or topical parameters or to the idea of improvisation. In his useful review of the term *fantasia*, Matthew Head has recently suggested that this has been problematic for our musicological sense not only of the eighteenth century but of the nineteenth century as well. A narrow stylistic or topical definition either over-extends it through ahistorical ideas about improvisation, or makes it seem merely episodic in western music history, a stage in the development of something more important.

Similar issues are at play, I would suggest, on the Turkish side of the story. Here too is a genre name that comes into play in the 1930s alongside a vital new music technology (the music film), and political environment (the new republic) that invested massively in transforming everyday structures of feeling. And here too is a genre that seems improvisatory, but that, as my brief survey has suggested, is better characterized as a space of compositional formalism with its own rules and conventions, and one actually rather remote from classical Turkish *taksim* and *gazel* practice. The two sides of the story are, of course, intertwined. The West legitimized its musical playfulness and experimentalism with reference to an imagined Orient, as Locke and others show.[10] The 'Orient' reciprocated, and in reciprocating set in play a fractal landscape of east-meets-west difference-making, one that is still very much in motion today.

So the translational contexts of *fantezi* add additional layers of meaning. There are at least two translational dimensions of *fantezi* to consider here: the translation of the Egyptian film 'originals' (themselves, incidentally, often Egyptian versions of western romantic and sentimental classics), and the appropriation of the Western European musical term 'fantasy'. In the context of a new nation state, supposedly busy at work discovering, in the lives of the Anatolian peasants, the elements of a properly 'folkish' national culture, the use of the term *fantezi* by the composers of the period has more than a whiff of postcolonial 'sly civility', to use Homi Bhabha's term.[11] That is to say, it suggests the pleasures and the subtle agencies of translational identities at precisely the moment the new nation-state was purging the Turkish language of its Arabic and Persian elements. The pleasures and subtle agencies on the part of a composer as talented, popular and versatile as Sadettin Kaynak, might involve explorations of songs as a space of internal dialogue, as in the case of "*Menekşelendi Sular*", or reimagining classical *şarkı* form as a mini-suite comprising multiple *usûl*. Wry humour was certainly at play in the choice of an august European musical term to complicate and disguise what was, essentially, a note of cultural appreciation of the regionally dominant Egyptian cultural practice, ranking very low on the scale of values

10 Locke, Ralph 2011, *Musical Exoticism: Images and Reflections*, Cambridge: Cambridge University Press.

11 Bhabha, Homi 2004, *The Location of Culture*, London: Routledge.

espoused by the new nationalist elites. And this would, as Orhan Gencebay discovered, serve as a powerful resource at subsequent moments when wry humor and sly civility would prove to be a very valuable commodity indeed.

Approaches to Folk Music Resulting From Republican Period Music Policies

Songül Karahasanoğlu

The development of Turkish music over the last 100 years has been affected both by influences from within, such as the foundation of the Republic and the coup of 1980, and influences from abroad, particularly ever-changing media technologies. Musical synthesis has been a key feature of Turkish music since the establishment of the Republic in 1923. Westernization and modernization policies that started during the Ottoman period crystallized with the Republic and created a new tradition by ignoring important elements of the tradition as it had hitherto been known.

In the past, the traditional music of Turkey existed as an oral tradition, maintained by people who were accustomed to using music to express their feelings and thoughts. Turkish music, both court and folk, can be classified according to the categories of vocal and instrumental music; the social milieus in which it is used (military music, religious music, classical music, folk music); performance venues (military events, the palace, the mosque, the *tekke* [Sufi lodge], urban or rural environments, entertainment venues) and the style of the performance (composed or improvised). The master-apprentice system of education (*meşk*) is found in every domain of Turkish music. Notation, while being a useful education tool, is not a sufficient medium for transmitting the nuances of Turkish modes (*makam*) and rhythms (*usûl*), which require face-to-face education in the form of *meşk* for a complete understanding. Both *makam* and *usûl* are equally significant in that *makam* regulates melody whereas *usûl* regulates time. In *meşk*, they are interconnected, and the master teaches *makam* immediately after *usûl*.

In republican Turkey, music was used as a means of creating a modern nation state, and therefore education relied on Western-style musical notation. Mistakes and insufficient detail in notation led to a decline in the accuracy of musical performances. The various components of the music, such as mode, beat, form, meter, and rhythm, began to be taught separately with the departure from the *meşk* system, and the wholeness of the music was lost. This situation brought about misguided performance choices and sterility in the music. In my research, I focused on 50 albums and 100 songs recorded between 1995 and 2002. The chart included in the appendix shows the impoverishment and uniformity of meters and rhythms. When I investigated the properties of contemporary pop music rhythms, I found that 4/4 was frequently used and was the most common meter.

At this point, I would like to examine the understanding of *usûl* in the republican period. What is *usûl*? Traditional musicians have made various definitions with reference to *usûl*:

1. Coherence in time. Essentially, *usûl* is a meter consisting of a larger measure which is created by a combination of rhythms.[1]
2. Through the creation of certain rhythms, measures are assigned (*saptanmış*) to a pattern called an *usûl*.[2]
3. All patterns of beats used for measuring musical melodies, whether the beats' musical values are equal to each other or not, are called *usûl*.[3]

A multifunctional concept like this is undoubtedly a fundamental condition for musical forms. *Usûl*, contrary to what is widely accepted, is not only a device that provides shape to the melody. According to Okan Murat Öztürk, who is one of the new generation of theorists, *usûl*, in its broadest sense, is a fundamental and general notion, which provides "time organization" in music in Anatolia and its surrounding countries. At the practical level, *usûl* includes four main concepts, which gives organization to the temporal dimension of music. These are: rhythmic pattern, tempo, meter, and form.[4]

Turkish music is vocal in nature, and large portions of its lyrics are taken from folk and *dîvân* literatures. On the one hand, there is the application of *usûl* which emerges in relation to *dîvân* literature, as well as *dîvân* literature itself; on the other, there is the application of *usûl* in folk and Sufi literature. However, these traditions have been weakened by westernization, the problems of text-setting and the linguistic difficulty of *dîvân* literature. For the same reasons, new pieces are hardly ever composed. Newly composed pieces cannot be attractive for the young generation because of their detachment from tradition and for many other reasons. In contrast, folk music is closely connected with daily life, with its rhythmic variety and the freedom that it offers.

Despite all the mistakes made with regards to the compilation, protection and maintenance of folk music, it still occupies an important place in Turkish life. Moreover, "[f]olk music provided a synthesis between Seljuk and Ottoman civilizations along with the Lydian, Phrygian, Hittite, Hellenistic, Persian, Byzantine and Turkish civilizations that were present in Anatolia, and formed a rich component in the creation of music."[5] The biggest problem in the application of *usûl*

---

1 Özkan, İ. Hakkı 2001, *Türk Musikisi Nazariyatı ve Usûlleri. Kudüm Velveleleri*, Istanbul, p. 561.

2 Ungay, M. Hurşit 1981, *Türk Musikisinde Usûller ve Kudüm*, Istanbul, p. 3.

3 Karadeniz, M. Ekrem 2013, *Türk Musikisinin Nazariye ve Esasları*, Istanbul, p. 30.

4 Öztürk, Okan Murat 2005, "Arif Sağ Üstad'ın 'Davullar Çalınırken' Çalışması Vesilesiyle Anadolu Müziğinde Usuller", http://www.turkuler.com/yazi/anadolumuziginde.asp (accessed 7 May 2014).

5 Karahasanoğlu, Songül 2013, "New Paradigms of Turkish Folk Music", in: *Traditional Music Of The Kazakhs and People of the Central Asia: The Modern Condition, Studying, Perspectives Of Development*, Gulzada Omarova (Ed.), Almaty, 163-170, p. 163.

is the loss caused by a discriminatory approach to Turkish music. Thus, art music and folk music, which in fact developed interdependently, are thought of as the productions of different cultures.

Here I will focus on the notational problems and issues in the performance practice of folk music in Turkey, which has suffered from attempts to shape it according to an artificial theory and the notational system that surrounds it. One of the most important factors for musical change was the transition from the Ottoman Empire to the new Turkish Republic after the First World War. Kemal Atatürk and his compatriots set into motion a process of modernization and secularization that would eventually touch all aspects of Turkish life. Music was no exception to this. While the state-sponsored, modernizing process drew heavily upon European polyphonic art music, there was a strong emphasis on preserving core 'Turkish' features of music. This is not uncommon in instances of musical modernization around the world, and, as Bruno Nettl has pointed out, musical modernization does not necessarily mean only the adaptation of Euro-American technology and culture, but can simultaneously include an insistence on the maintenance of core cultural features.[6] This proactive musical restructuring by the state had a dramatic effect and at times indirectly brought about changes that were not in line with the official vision of Turkish music.

As a result of the new state's cultural policies, folk music collection studies were initiated. But despite the valiant efforts of those involved in music-collecting excursions, all the studies carried out in the historically rich land of Anatolia proved insufficient. Moreover, the materials gathered have still not been adequately evaluated, which is problematic. There are many reasons for this, among them the effect of communications media on folk culture. In 1945, the works that were collected began to be broadcast on what was to become Turkish State Radio (TRT). These broadcasts were of new musical forms based on folk traditions, and this music was deemed appropriate for the newly emerging republic. Myriad attempts were made to create new musical forms for a new Turkish identity. For example, in the 1930s a choir was established to perform older folk songs.

This new ensemble format drew heavily upon European choral traditions, introducing methods of performance such as harmonic counterpoint and Western instruments unheard of in the music of the Ottoman period. Media reproduction of rural folk music was greatly affected by the introduction of this new, large choral format, particularly at the newly formed state radio and television, whose members collected and reformulated folk pieces for performance by large choirs and orchestras. As Gabriel Skoog and I have argued, "this new Europeanized format had a major impact on musical life in the young Republic. One of the effects was a shift from an emphasis on older, rural folk styles of performance to this newer ap-

6 Nettl, Bruno 1983, *The Study of Ethnomusicology: Twenty-nine Issues and Concepts*, Champain, p. 348.

proach, a shift that left the folk poets and musicians behind and gave greater importance to their imitators."[7] Although many people were not enthused by the music being performed on TRT after the 1980s, this choral performance style later became one of the most important contextual factors for music.

While the new communications media proved useful in reaching many individuals, they also became the catalyst for various cultures to be affected by each other, eventually resulting in cultural homogeneity. As songs from every part of Turkey were transcribed in notation and disseminated on a national scale, similar songs started appearing in every region. Eventually, the original songs of particular regions were forgotten. A further problem was that folk songs, which were traditionally sung and interpreted differently for each individual occasion, lost their dynamism due to notation. Moreover, urban musicians performed the songs in a uniform musical style.

The traditional understanding of *usûl* and music has suffered severe losses. *Usûl*, in particular, has been ignored during the notation and performance of folk music, and, because of the application of Western music theory, "rhythm" has become the focus. At the beginning of the republican years, researchers like M. R. Gâzimihal[8], Kemal İlerici[9], and Veysel Arseven[10] made definitions of meter instead of *usûl*. Muzaffer Sarısözen, who made many compilations of folk music, and who disseminated them to radio broadcasting but focused only on meter, was very influential in this field.[11] His work, which was the first of its kind to be published in Turkey, has affected many theorists in this area. Not only first generation theorists but also contemporary researchers such as Cihangir Terzi[12] and Mehmet Ali Özdemir[13] are still focused on the rhythmic and metric system.

---

7 Karahasanoğlu, Songül and Skoog, Gabriel 2009, "Synthesizing Identity: Gestures of Filiation and Affiliation in Turkish Popular Music", *Asian Music 40(2)*, 52–71.

8 Gazimihal, M. Ragıp 1961, *Musiki Sözlüğü*, Istanbul, pp.215- 244. His definitions:
Basic meters: (2, 3, 4)
Mixed meters: (6/8, 9/8, 12/8)
Additive meters: (5 ,7, 9,10).

9 İlerici, Kemal 1981, *Bestecilik Bakımından Türk Müziği ve Armonisi*, Istanbul, p.253: *Küçük* [minor] *usûller* (2, 3, 4, 5, 6/8, 9/8, 12/8, 7, 8, 9, 10)
Büyük major] *usûller* (11 and more).

10 Arseven, Veysel 1957, "Türk Halk Müziğinde Metrik Sistem", *Türk Folklor Araştırmaları Dergisi* 100/101, 1590:
Basic meters : (2, 3, 4)
Mixed meters: (6/8, 9/8, 12/8)
Additive meters: (5, 7, 9,10).

11 Sarısözen, Muzaffer 1962, *Türk Halk Musikisi Usulleri*, Ankara, pp. 1-120.
Ana [basic] *usûller*: (2,3,4 and 6/8, 9/8, 12/8)
Birleşik compound/additive] *usûller*: (5,6,7,8,9)
Karma mixed] *usûller*: (10 and more).

12 Terzi, Cihangir 1992, *Türk Halk Müziği Metrik Yapısının Tespit ve Tasnifinde Karşılaşılan Problemler ve Çözüm Yolları,* Istanbul Technical University, Unpublished Thesis.

13 Özdemir, Mehmet Ali 2005, "Halk müziğini ölçülendirme sorunu", *Folklor-Edebiyat 42*, 39-45.

However, because of its construction and its rhythmic pattern, *usûl* is always primary and fundamental. Local musicians learn the local repertoires through performing, which begins in childhood, and every region has its own rhythmic patterns. On the other hand, the same structures are found in art/*makam* music. It was found necessary to give a different name to each *usûl.* When any *usûl* is named, it is clear which rhythmic pattern is going to be applied; writing only the meter is not sufficient. Moreover, the desire of researchers who study folk music to create new and different music theories has generated exaggerated rhythmic patterns.[14] Here is an example of an incorrectly transcribed rhythm, with the correct transcription provided below:

Fig. 1: "*Ben ağlarım yane yane*"[15]

Fig. 2: "*Ben ağlarım yane yane*" (correct transcription)[16]

There have been very important notational mistakes and omissions with regards to *usûl.* The richness of folk music is due to its dynamic structure. For this reason, we see that several compilers have notated the same piece of music with different *usûl*s and melodic structures. These differences appear in *usûl* as much as in the melodies.

With the transformation of *usûl* to a Western-style time signature, one of the important elements which is lost is the accent.[17] The accent is an important element that defines *usûl* in horizontally enhanced music. Understanding of strong and weak beats has disappeared from notated music. I would like to illustrate this point below with a vocal melody which is notated by TRT as having a 3/8 time signature (the correct transcription is provided underneath):

---

14 That is, there has been an artificial usage of large time-signatures such as 15:8, 17:8, 18:8, 19:8, 20:8, 24:8, 30:8 etc.

15 Transcription according to Muzaffer Sarısözen, TRT (Turkish State Radio and Television) Müzik Dairesi Yay., THM Repertuar No: 667.

16 Koç, Mehmet 2010, *T.R.T. Müzik Dairesi Başkanlığı'nın Halk Müziği Repertuarında Tespit Edilen Sözlü-Sözsüz Ezgilerdeki Usül Sorunları Üzerine Bir Çalışma*, Istanbul Technical University, Unpublished Master's Thesis, p. 7.

17 "A musical piece or a musical sentence is accepted as a well-performed one which reaches the necessary degree of expressiveness by altering some tones and processes this is an accent." (Gâzimihal 1961, p. 268.)

Fig. 3: "*Kız belin incedir ay ince*"[18]

Fig. 4: "*Kız belin incedir ay ince*" (correct transcription)[19]

Due to the dynamic structure of folk music, it is not sufficient to notate a melody from a single recording. Therefore, there have been problems both in the development of musical theory and in writing notation. Here is another example from the folk music repertoire which is incorrectly notated, with a corrected version below:

Fig. 5: "*Belgrad kal'ası*"[20]

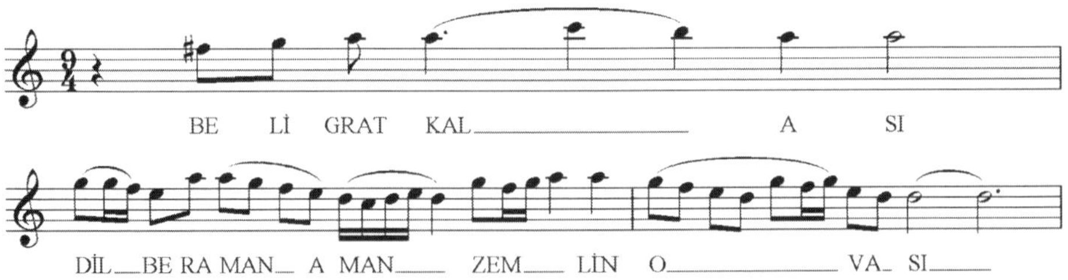

Fig. 6: "*Belgrad kal'ası*" (correct transcription)[21]

---

18 Transcription according to Muzaffer Sarısözen, TRT (Turkish State Radio and Television) Müzik Dairesi Yay., THM Repertuar No: 598.

19 Transcription according to Koç 2010, p. 15.

20 Transcription according to Muzaffer Sarısözen, TRT (Turkish State Radio and Television) Müzik Dairesi Yay., THM Repertuar No: 429.

21 Transcription according to Koç 2010, p.19.

Conclusion and Some Suggestions

Along with *makam*, *usûl* is a very important and basic element in Turkish music. Many mistakes have been made due to the introduction of Western staff notation and a Western-style education system. I would therefore like to suggest the following recommendations for the development of Turkish folk music:

1. We should respect all musical traditions of Anatolia without discriminating between genres.
2. Music should not be simplified by the application of the rules of Western music theory.
3. We must not ignore the traditional education system (*meşk*).
4. Theory should be based not on the meter but on the *usûl*.
5. Pieces should be notated by looking at the melody, lyrics, meter, and rhythm as a whole.
6. We should not disregard the rhythmic instruments (*bağlama*, *kaval*, *zurna* etc.) which accompany the vocals in written notation.
7. Pieces should not be notated on the basis of a single, careless recording when there is a *meşk* system available as a resource.
8. We should not disregard special regional characteristics.
9. We should notate the sounds which are produced by the accompanying rhythm instruments in dance music.
10. Although not absolutely necessary, if the aim is to publish notation, it should be done by people who are experts in their own areas.
11. We should try to reveal local rhythm patterns in Anatolia by leaving aside all known rhythmic structures.
12. If every melody in folk music has its own rules, the *usûl* of every melody also has its own distinctiveness.

Appendix

Singer – Song	**Meter**
Demet Akalın, "*Afedersin*"	4/4
Rafet El Roman, "*Gönül Yarası*"	4/4
Ebru Gündeş, "*Çingenem*"	4/4
Serdar Ortaç, "*Sor*"	4/4
Serdar Ortaç, "*Dansöz*"	4/4
Serdar Ortaç, "*Gel*"	4/4
Tarkan, "Bounce"	4/4
Candan Erçetin, "*Ada sahilleri*"	4/4

Singer – Song	**Meter**
Candan Erçetin, "*Aman doktor*"	4/4
Candan Erçetin, "*Telgrafın tellerine*"	4/4
Duman, "*Aman aman*"	4/4
Duman, "*Halimiz duman*"	4/4
Kenan Doğulu, "*Baş harfi ben*"	4/4
Gökhan Tepe, "*Yürü yüreğim*"	4/4
Gülben Ergen, "*Yalnızlık*"	4/4
Gülşen, "*Bu gece*"	4/4
İsmail YK, "www.bombabomba.com"	4/4
İsmail YK, "*Allah belanı versin*"	4/4
Funda Arar, "*Benim için üzülme*"	4/4
Gülben Ergen, "*Lay la lay la lay*"	4/4
Müslüm Gürses, "*Aşk tesadüfleri sever*"	4/4
Nazan Öncel, "*Aşkım*"	4/4
Hande Yener, "*Kelepçe*"	4/4
Kenan Doğulu, "*Çakkıdı*"	4/4
Hırsız Polis (TV series soundtrack), "*İmkansız aşk*"	4/4
İntizar, "*Ihlamurlar altında*"	4/4
İntizar, "*Uykum firari*"	4/4
Koray Candemir, "*İçini dök*"	4/4
Özcan Deniz, "*Cahildim dünyanın rengine kandım*"	4/4
Sibel Can, "*Lale Devri*"	4/4
Şöhret (TV series soundtrack)	4/4
Baha, "*Ağla halimize*"	4/4
Volkan Konak, "*Cerrahpaşa*"	10/8
Hepsi, "*Tempo*"	4/4
Gülay, "*Ellerini çekip benden*"	4/4
Ebru Gündeş, "*Alev alev*"	4/4
Leman Sam, "*Gönül*"	4/4
Hüseyin Turan, "*Beyaz giyme*"	4/4
Zara, "*Senede bir gün*"	4/4
Onur Akın, "*Seviyorum seni*"	4/4
Gece Yolcuları, "*Unut beni sevgilim*"	4/4
Ahmet Kaya, "*Penceresiz kaldım anne*"	4/4
İntizar, "*Ah senin küsmelerin*"	4/4
Hepsi, "*Kaç yıl geçti*"	4/4

Singer – Song	**Meter**
Hüseyin Turan, "*Ah le yar yar*"	4/4
Nilgül, "*Yazımı kışa çevirdin*"	4/4
Ayna, "*Gesi bağları*"	4/4
Ayna, "*Hekimoğlu*"	4/4
Demet Akalın, "*Herkes hak ettiği gibi yaşıyor*"	4/4
Fatih Erkoç, "*Ellerim bomboş*"	4/4
Fatih Erkoç, "*Elveda tatlım*"	4/4
Fatih Erkoç, "*Hepsi de beni bekler*"	4/4
Mahsun Kırmızıgül, "*Dinle*"	4/4
Mahsun Kırmızıgül, "*Azar azar*"	4/4
Murat Başaran, "*Nankör*"	4/4
Murat Başaran, "*Sana ölürüm*"	4/4
Serdar Ortaç, "*Gitme*"	4/4
Sami Özer, "*Alemler nura gark oldu*"	4/4
Sami Özer, "*Güzel aşık*"	4/4
Zafer Peker, "*Sensiz sabah olmuyor*"	4/4
Sami Özer, "*Hak yarattı alemi*"	4/4
Muazzez Ersoy, "*Kim arar*"	4/4
Sami Yusuf, "*Al muallim*"	4/4
Sami Yusuf, "Who is the loved one"	4/4
Sami Yusuf, "Supplication"	4/4
Murat Kekilli, "*Ahir zaman*"	4/4
Direc-t, "Rambo"	4/4
Vega, "*Hafif müzik*"	4/4
Athena, "*Çatal yürek*"	4/4
Çilekeş, "*Ardıma hiç bakmadım*"	4/4
Déjà vu, "*Oha*"	4/4
Cansu Koç, "*Gamzedeyim deva bulmam*"	4/4
Duman, "*Anlamam*"	4/4
Duman, "*Güller sensiz*"	4/4
Kurban, "*İnsanlar*"	4/4
Kurban, "*Olmalı mı olmamalı mı?*"	4/4
Pinhani, "*Hele bi gel*"	7/8
Replikas, "*Avaz*"	4/4
Şebnem Ferah, "*Cam kırıkları*"	4/4
Serdar Öztop, "*Sükut*"	4/4

Singer – Song	**Meter**
Duman, "*Bebek*"	4/4
Ferhat Göçer, "*Dön diyemedim*"	4/4
Ferhat Göçer, "*Yastayım*"	4/4
Mustafa Özarslan, "*Benim ömrüm*"	7/8
İbrahim Tatlıses, "*Bir taş attım*"	4/4
Oğuz Yılmaz, "*Çekirge*"	4/4
İbrahim Tatlıses, "*Ağrı dağın eteğinde*"	4/4
İbrahim Tatlıses, "*Bileydim*"	4/4
Emre Altuğ, "*Aşk-ı kıyamet*"	4/4
Orhan Ölmez, "*Su misali*"	4/4
Hakan Altun, "*Telefonun başında*"	4/4
Manga, "*Dursun zaman*"	4/4
Mustafa Sandal, "*Pazara kadar*"	4/4
Sezen Aksu, "*Perişanım şimdi*"	4/4
Sezen Aksu, "*İkili delilik*"	4/4
Sertab Erener, "Every way that I can"	4/4
Ferda Anıl Yarkın, "*Ayrılmayalım*"	4/4
Arif Sag, "*Ezo gelin*"	4/4

Bibliography

Abel, Carl 1884, *Über den Gegensinn der Urworte*, Leipzig.

Agayeva, Süreyya and Latif Kerimov 1975, "Avtobiografia v stikhakh Abdulkadira Maragi", *AEA Heberleri, Edebiyyat, Dil ve İncesenet ser.*, vol.4, 119-127.

Agayeva, Süreyya and Recep Uslu 2008, *Ruhperver: Bir XVII.yy Müzik Teorisi Kitabı*, Ankara: Ürün Yayınları.

Akdemir, Kemal Hayrettin 1990, *Die neue türkische Musik: Dargestellt an Volksliedbearbeitungen für mehrstimmigen Chor*, Berlin.

Aksoy, Bülent 2008, *Geçmişin Musikî Mirasına Bakışlar*, Istanbul.

- 2008b, "Fasıl Musikisi Divan Edebiyatının Musikisi midir?", in: *Geçmişin Musiki Mirasına Bakışlar*, Bülent Aksoy (Ed.), Istanbul: Pan Yayıncılık, 17-35.

Apel, Willi (Ed.) 1953, *Harvard Dictionary of Music*, Massachusetts.

Arel, Hüseyin Sadettin 1993,*Türk Musikisi Nazariyatı Dersleri*, (Ed.) Onur Akdoğu, Ankara: Kültür Bakanlığı Yayınları/1347, Sanat-Müzik-Dizisi/33-l.

Arseven, Veysel 1957, "Türk Halk Müziğinde Metrik Sistem", *Türk Folklor Araştırmaları Dergisi 100/101*, 1590.

Arslan, Fazlı 2007, *Safiyyüddîn-i Urmevî ve šerefiyye risâlesi*, Ankara: Atatürk Kültür Merkezi.

Atlığ, Nevzad 1988, *Türk Musikîsi Klasikleri*, Yıl 2, Cilt 2, Sayı 8, Istanbul: Türk Dünyası Araştırmaları Vakfı.

Bar-Yosef, Amatzia 2007, "A Cross Cultural Structural Analogy Between Pitch & Time Constraints", *Music Perception: An Interdisciplinary Journal 24*, 265-280.

Bardakçı, Murat 1986, *Maragalı Abdülkadir*, Istanbul: Pan Yayıncılık.

- (Ed.) 1995, *Refik Bey: Refik Bey ve Hatırları*, Istanbul: Pan Yayıncılık.

Bartlett, Frederic Charles 1995 [1932], *Remembering: A Study in Experimental and Social Psychology*, Cambridge: Cambridge University Press.

Baysal, Ozan 2011, *Phrase Rhythm and Time in Beste-i Kadims, A Cyclical Approach*, PhD thesis, İstanbul Teknik Üniversitesi).

Baysal, Ozan and Beşiroğlu, Şefika Şehvar 2013, "Uzatma Teorilerinin Makam Musikisine Uygulanabilirliği: Döngüsel bir Analiz Modeli", *Porte Akademik 8 (Müzikolojide Güncel Yaklaşımlar Özel Sayısı)*, 155-168.

Behar, Cem 1987, *Klasik Türk Musikisi Üzerine Denemeler*, Istanbul: Bağlam Yayınları.

- 1990, *Ali Ufkî ve Mezmurlar*, Istanbul.

- 1993, *Zaman, Mekân, Müzik: Klâsik Türk Musıkisinde Eğitim (Meşk), İcra ve Aktarım*, Istanbul: AFA Yayınları.

- 1998, *Aşk Olmayınca Meşk Olmaz*, Istanbul: Yapı Kredi Yayınları.

- 2005, *Musıkiden Müziğe – Osmanlı/Türk Müziği: Gelenek ve Modernlik*, Istanbul, 17-56.

- 2008, *Saklı mecmua. Ali Ufkî'nin Bibliothèque Nationale de France'taki [Turc 292] yazması*, Istanbul: Yapı Kredi Yayınları.

Beljaev, Viktor M. (Ed.) 1950-1967, *Shashmaqom* vols. I-V (transcribed in Western notation by Fajzullaev, Sahibov and Shahobov), Moscow.

Bhabha, Homi 2004, *The Location of Culture*, London: Routledge.

al-Biṭār, ʿAbd al-Razzāq 1993, *Ḥilyat al-bashar fī tārīkh al-qarn al-thālith ʿashar*, Muḥammad Bahjat al-Biṭār (Ed.), vol. 1, 2nd ed., Beirut: Dār Ṣādir.

Boldyrev, A.N. and Beljaev, V.M. (Ed.) 1960, *Abduraḥmon Dzomij: Muzika ḥakida traktat / Traktat o muzyke*. Tashkent: Uzbekiston SSR Akademijasi nashriëti.

Borrel, Eugène 1946, "La Musique Turque", in: *La Musique, des origines à nos jours*, Norbert Fourcq et. al. (Ed.), Paris: Librairie Larousse, 433-438.

Bžškean, H. Minas 1997 [1815], *Eražštut'iwn or ē hamaṙōt tełekut'iwn eražštakan skzbanc' elewēǰut'eanc' ełanakac' ew nšanagrac' xazic'*, Aram K'erovbean (Ed.), Erewan: Girk' Hratarakč'ut'iwn.

Cairo Congress 1932, *Recueil des Travaux du Congrès de Musique Arabe qui s'est tenu au Caire en 1932 (Hég. 1350) sous le Haut Patronage de S.M. Fouad 1er, Roi d'Égypte*, Cairo: Royaume d'Égypte. Ministère de l'Instruction Publique.

Çelik, B. 2001, *Hızır bin Abdullah'ın Kitabü'l Edvar'ında Makamlar*, unpublished PhD Thesis, Marmara Üniversitesi Sosyal Bilimler Enstitüsü, Istanbul.

Cemil Bey, Tanburî 1989 [1902], *Rehber-i Mûsikî*, M. Hakan Cevher (Ed.), Izmir: Ege Üniversitesi Basımevi.

Cengiz, Halil E. (Ed.) 1993, *Yaşanmış Olaylarla Atatürk ve Müzik: Riyâset-i Cumhûr İnce Saz Hey'eti Şefi Binbaşı Hâfız Yaşar Okur'un Anıları (1924-1938)*, Ankara: Müzik Ansiklopedisi Yayınları.

Ceyhan, A. 1994, Bedr-i Dilşâdın Muradnâmesi, unpublished PhD Thesis, Marmara Üniversitesi Sosyal Bilimler Enstitüsü, Istanbul.

Cooper, Grosvenor and Leonard B. Meyer 1963, *The Rhythmic Structure of Music*, Chicago: University of Chicago.

Dāniš Pažūh, Muḥammad Taqī 2535/1976, "advār-i sulṭānī", *Hunar va-Mardum 173*, year 15, 18-25.

Dehkhoda, Ali Akbar et al. (Ed.) (?), *Farhang-e motawasset-e Dehkhoda*, 2 vols., Tehran.

Dentler, Hans-Eberhard 2008, *Johann Sebastian Bachs "Musicalisches Opfer". Musik als Abbild der Sphärenharmonie*, Mainz: Schott-Verlag.

Deutsches Wörterbuch von Jacob Grimm und Wilhelm Grimm, accessible online at http://woerterbuchnetz.de/DWB/

Doğrusöz, Nilgün 2012, *Yusuf Kırşehri'nin Müzik Teorisi*, Kırşehir Valiliği, Kırşehir.

Doğrusöz-Dişiaçık, N. and Uruş, D. 2012, "Meşk ile intikalde müzik eseri: III. Selim'in Suzidilara Mevlevi Ayini", *International Journal of Human Sciences* [online], 9(2), 427-445.

Ekinci, Mehmet Uğur 2012, "The *Kevserî Mecmuası* Unveiled: Exploring an Eighteenth-Century Collection of Ottoman Music", *Journal of the Royal Asiatic Society*, Series 3, 22(2), 199-225.

Elçin, Şükrü (Ed.) 1976, *Alî Ufkî, Hayatı, eserleri ve Mecmûa-i Sâz ü Söz (tıpkıbasım)*, Istanbul: Milli Eğitim Basımevi.

d'Erlanger, Baron Rudolph 1930-1959, *La Musique Arabe*, 4 vols., Paris: Paul Geuthner, Paris.

Ezgi, Dr. Subhi Zühtü1933-1953, *Nazarî ve Amelî Türk Musikisi*, 5 vols., Istanbul.

Fallahzadeh, Mehrdad (Ed.) 2009, *Two treatises – two streams: treatises from the post-scholastic era of Persian writings on music theory*, Bethesda, Maryland: Ibex Publishers.

Farmer, Henry George 1976, *Islam – Musikgeschichte in Bildern*, Leipzig: VEB Deutscher Verlag für Musik.

– 1986, *Studies in Oriental Music*, 2 vols., (ed. Eckhard Neubauer), Frankfurt am Main: Institut für Geschichte der Arabisch-Islamischen Wissenschaften.

Feldman, Walter 1996, *Music of the Ottoman court: makam, composition and the early Ottoman instrumental repertoire* (Intercultural Music Studies: 10, ed. Max Peter Baumann), Berlin: VWB.

– 2001, "Structure and Evolution of the Mevlevi Ayin: the Case of the Third Selam" in: *Sufism, Music and Society in Turkey and the Middle East*, Hammarlund, Olson and Özdalga (Ed.), Istanbul: Swedish Research Institute: 49-65.

– 2015, "The Musical 'Renaissance' of Late Seventeenth Century Ottoman Turkey: Reflections on the Musical Materials of Ali Ufki Bey (ca. 1610-1675), Hafiz Post (d. 1694) and the 'Maraghi' Repertoire", in: *Writing the History of "Ottoman Music"*, Martin Greve (Ed.), Istanbuler Texte und Studien: 33, Würzburg: Ergon.

– (forthcoming), "Itri's 'Nühüft Sakil' in the Context of Ottoman Peşrevs of the Seventeenth Century", in: *Tuning the Past: Theory and Practice in the Music of the Islamic World*, Rachel Harris and Martin Stokes (Ed.), SOAS Musicology Series, Farnham: Ashgate.

Field, Christopher et al., 2000, art. "Fantasias", in: *New Grove Dictionary of Music and Musicians*, vol. 8, 2nd ed., Stanley Sadie and John Tyrrell (Eds.), London: Macmillan, 545-558.

Fitrat, Abdura'uf 1993 [1927], *Özbek klassik musiqasi wa uning tarixi*, Tashkent.

Gâzimihal, M.Ragıp 1961, *Musiki Sözlüğü*, Istanbul.

Gökmen, Mustafa 1991, *Eski İstanbul Sinemaları.* Istanbul: İstanbul Kitaplığı Yayınları.

Greve, Martin (Ed.) 2015, *Writing the History of "Ottoman Music"*, Istanbuler Texte und Studien: 33, Würzburg: Ergon.

Haim, S. 2004, *The New Persian-English Dictionary*, Tehran: Moaser Farhang.

Hall, Leslie 1989, *The Turkish Fasıl: Selected Repertoire*, PhD. Dissertation, University of Toronto.

Hakkı Bey, İsmail 1925 [1919], *Solfej yahûd Nota Dersleri*. Istanbul: Haşim Matbaası.

– 1926, *Mûsıkî Tekâmül Dersleri*, 2nd Book, Istanbul: Feniks Matbaası.

Ḥamām, ʿAbd al-Ḥamīd 1409/1989, "Awzān al-ʿarab al-shiʿriyya", in: *Majallat al-Majmaʿ al-lugha al-ʿarabiyya al-urdunnī* , no. 36, ʿAmmān, 233-275.

– 1989, "al-Ahammiyya al-mūsīqiyya li-l-ishbāʿ wa-l-taḥrīk fī l-shiʿr al-ʿarabī", in: *Abḥāth al-Yarmūk (Jāmiʿat al-Yarmūk)*, vol. 5, 287-302.

– 1991, *Muʿāraḍat al-ʿarūḍ*, ʿAmmān.

Hâşim Bey, Hacı Mehmed 1280/1864, *Mecmûa-i Kârhâ ve Nakışhâ ve Şarkıyât [Mûsıkî Mecmûası]*, 2nd edition, Istanbul.

Haug, Judith 2010, *Der Genfer Psalter in den Niederlanden, England, Deutschland und dem Osmanischen Reich (16.-18. Jahrhundert)*, Tutzing.

Head, Matthew 2013, "Fantasia and Sensibility", in: *Oxford Handbooks Online*, Danuta Mirka (Ed.), New York: Oxford University Press.

Hickmann, Regina (Ed.) 1979, *Indische Albumblätter, Miniaturen und Kalligraphien aus der Zeit der Moghul-Kaiser*, Leipzig und Weimar.

al-Ḥijāzī, Muḥammad Shihāb al-Dīn ibn Ismāʿīl 1311/1893, *Safīnat al-mulk wa-nafīsat al-fulk* [1273/1856 or 1857], Kairo: al-Maṭbaʿa al-Jāmiʿa.

Hood, Mantle 1960, "The Challenge of »Bi-Musicality«", *Ethnomusicology 4*, 55-59.

Houle, George 1987, *Meter in Music, 1600-1800. Performance, Perception, and Notation*, Bloomington.

al-Ḥulw, Salīm 1965, *al-Muwashshaḥāt al-andalusiyya – nashʾatuhā wa-taṭawwuruhā,* Beirut: Dār Maktabat al-Ḥayāt.

Hyde, Thomas (Ed.) 1690, *Tractatus Alberti Bobovii Turcarum Imp. Mohammedis IVti olim Interpretis primarii, de Turcarum liturgia* [...], Oxford.

İhsanoğlu, Ekmeleddin (Ed.) 2003, *Osmanlı Musiki Literatürü Tarihi,* Istanbul: IRCICA.

İlerici, Kemal 1981, *Bestecilik Bakımından Türk Müziği ve Armonisi*, Istanbul.

İnal, İbnülemin Mahmut Kemal 1958, *Hoş Sadâ: Son Asır Türk Musikişinasları*, Istanbul: Maarif.

Irsoy, Hafız Ahmed and Dr. Suphi Ezgi 1940/1941/1943, *Zekâi Dede Külliyatı*, 3 vols., Istanbul: İstanbul Konservatuarı.

– 1943, *Türk Mûsikîsi Klasiklerinden*, Istanbul: İstanbul Konservatuarı.

al-Iṣfahānī, Abū l-Faraj 1936, *Kitāb al-Aghānī al-kabīr*, vol. 9, Cairo: Dār al-Kutub al-Miṣriyya.

İstanbul Belediye Konservatuvarı 1954, *Türk Musikisi Klasiklerinden: Sazkâr Faslı*, No: 5, Istanbul.

– 1954b, *Türk Musikisi Klasiklerinden: Mahur Faslı*, No: 6, Istanbul.

Jackson, Maureen 2013, *Mixing Musics: Turkish Jewry and the Urban Landscape of a Sacred Song*, Stanford: Stanford University Press.

Jäger, Ralf Martin 1996, *Türkische Kunstmusik und ihre handschriftlichen Quellen aus dem 19. Jahrhundert* (=*Schriften zur Musikwissenschaft aus Münster* 7, ed. Klaus Hortschansky), Eisenach.

– 1996b, *Katalog der hamparsum-notası-Manuskripte im Archiv des Konservatoriums der Universität İstanbul*, Eisenach: K.D. Wagner.

– 1998, "Die Metamorphosen des Irak Elçi Peşrevi", in: Marianne Bröcker (Ed.), *Berichte aus dem ICTM-Nationalkomitee* VI/VII, Bamberg, 31-57.

– 2004, "The Aesthetic of Time in Traditional Ottoman Art Music", in: Panikos Giorgoudes (Ed.), *Proceedings of the 1st International Conference of the Cyprus Musicological Society*, Nicosia, 75-96.

Jung, Angelika 1984, *Quellen der traditionellen Kunstmusik der Usbeken und Tadshiken Mittelasiens*, Hamburg.

– 1989, *Quellen der traditionellen Kunstmusik der Usbeken und Tadschiken Mittelasiens*, Beiträge zur Ethnomusikologie 23, Hamburg.

– 1995, "Prosaische oder Poetische Melodien? Zu den Begriffen nathr und nazm in der Musik", in: *Iran und Turfan. Werner Sundermann zum 60. Geburtstag gewidmet*, Ch. Reck and P. Zieme (Ed.), Wiesbaden.

– (Ed.) 2010, *Der Shashmaqam aus Buchara. Überliefert von den alten Meistern, notiert von Ari Babakhanov*, Berlin: Schiler-Verlag.

– 2015 (forthcoming), *Der Shashmaqam aus Buchara. Beiträge zum Verständnis der klassischen Musik Mittelasiens*, Berlin: Schiler-Verlag.

Junker, Heinrich and B. Alavi 2002, *Persisch-Deutsch Wörterbuch*, 9th edition, Wiesbaden.

Karabey, Lâika 1966, "Münirin Cesareti", in: *Üstad Münir Nurettin Selçuk'un 50. San'at Yılı Jübilesi* (Anon.), Istanbul: Nebioğlu Yayınevi, 14.

Karadeniz, Ekrem 1965, *Türk Musikîsinin Nazariye ve Esasları*, Ankara, 1981 Ankara: İş Bankası Yayınları, 2013.

Karahasanoğlu, Songül 2013, "New Paradigms of Turkish Folk Music", in: *Traditional Music Of The Kazakhs and People of the Central Asia: The Modern Condition, Studying, Perspectives Of Development*, Gulzada Omarova (Ed.), Almaty, 163-170.

Karahasanoğlu, Songül and Skoog, Gabriel 2009, "Synthesizing Identity: Gestures of Filiation and Affiliation in Turkish Popular Music", *Asian Music 40/2*, 52–71.

Karomatov, Fayzullah and Rajabov, I. (Ed.) 1966-1975, *Shashmaqom* Vol. I-VI (transcribed in Western notation by Junus Rajabi), Tashkent.

Kaygusuz, Nermin 2006, *Muallim İsmail Hakkı Bey ve Mûsıkî Tekâmül Dersleri*, Istanbul: İTÜ Vakfı Yayınları.

Keltzanides, Chatzi Panagiotes 1881, *Μεθοδικη διδασκαλια θεωρητικη τε και πρακτικη προς εκμαθησιν και διαδοσιν του γνησιου εξωτερικου μελους*, Konstantinopel.

Khan, Pir Vilayat Inayat 1982, *Der Ruf des Derwisch*, Essen.

al-Khulaʿī, Muḥammad Kāmil 2000, Kitāb al-mūsīqā al-sharqī [1322/1904], Kairo: Maktabat Madbūlī.

Klebe, Dorit 2006, "Visualization-Forms of the Ottoman-Turkish Rhythmic Mode Usûl from the 17th Century on: Discussed in the Context of the Emic/Etic Concept", in: *Shared Musics and Minority Identities*, Naila Ceribašić and Erica Haskell (Ed.), Zagreb, 141-155.

Kleinmichel, Sigrid 2003, "Nawāʾī-i bī nawā", in: *Mīr ʿAlīshīr Nawāʾī*, Barbara Kellner-Heinkele and Sigrid Kleinmichel (Ed.), Istanbuler Texte und Studien:1, Würzburg, 97-118.

– 2003, "Nawāʾī-i bī nawā", in: *Mīr ʿAlīšīr Nawāʾī. Akten des Symposiums aus Anlaß des 560. Geburtstages und des 500. Jahres des Todes von Mīr ʿAlīšīr Nawāʾī am 23. April 2001*, Barbara Kellner-Heinkele and Sigrid Kleinmichel (Ed.), Würzburg.

Koç, Mehmet 2010, *T.R.T. Müzik Dairesi Başkanlığı'nın Halk Müziği Repertuarında Tespit Edilen Sözlü-Sözsüz Ezgilerdeki Usül Sorunları Üzerine Bir Çalışma*, Istanbul Technical University, Unpublished Master's Thesis.

Konuk, Ahmed Avni 1317/1899, *Hânende*, Istanbul: Mahmud Bey Matbaası.

Kulin, Ayşe 1996, *Bir Tatlı Huzur: Fotoğraflarla Münir Nureddin Selçuk'un Yaşam Öyküsü*, Istanbul: Sel Yayıncılık.

Kurdmāfī, Saʿīd 2013, "Bar rasī-yi barḫī janbahā-yi ʿamalī-yi īqāʿ dar risālāt-i qadīm-i mūsīqī-yi ḥawza-yi islāmī (qurūn-i haftum tā davāzdahum-i hijrī qamarī)", *faṣlnāma-yi mūsīqī-yi māhūr 60*, 167-198.

Lane, Edward William 1968 [1867], *Madd al-Qāmūs. An Arabic-English Lexicon ...*, Book I, part 3, Beirut: Librairie du Liban.

Lerdahl, Fred and Ray Jackendoff 1983, *A Generative Theory of Tonal Music*, Cambridge, MA: MIT Press.

Levin, Theodore 1996, *The hundred thousand fools of God. Musical travels in Central Asia*, Bloomington.

Locke, Ralph 2011, *Musical Exoticism: Images and Reflections*, Cambridge: Cambridge University Press.

London, Justin 2004, *Hearing In Time: Psychological Aspects of Meter*, New York: Oxford University Press.

– 2001, art. "Rhythm", in: *The New Grove Dictionary of Music and Musicians*, 2nd. ed., vol. 21, New York, 277-309.

al-Mahdī, Ṣāliḥ 1990, *Īqāʿāt al-mūsīqā al-ʿarabiyya wa-ashkāluhā* (= Wizārat al-Thaqāfa wa-l-Iʿlām, Silsilat maʿārif li-l-jamīʿ: funūn jamīla), Qarṭāj (Carthago): Bayt al-Ḥikma.

Maraqa, Salah Eddin 2015, *Die traditionelle Kunstmusik in Syrien und Ägypten von 1500 bis 1800. Eine Untersuchung der musiktheoretischen und historisch-biographischen Quellen* (=*Würzburger Beiträge zur Musikforschung* 4, ed. Ulrich Konrad), Tutzing.

Markoff, Irene 2001, art. "Aspects of Folk Music Theory", in: *Garland Encyclopedia of World Music*, vol. 6, New York, 77-88.

Matyakubov, Otanazar 2011, *Bucharskij šašmakom*, Tashkent.

– R. Boltaev and H. Aminov 2009, *Khorazm Tanbur chisighi*, Tashkent.

al-Murādī, Abū al-Faḍl Muḥammad Khalīl ibn ʿAlī ibn Muḥammad 1301/1883, *Silk al-Durar Fī Aʿyān al-Qarn al-Thānī ʿAshar*, ʿārif Bāshā und Aḥmad Beg Asʿad (Ed.), vol. 4, Cairo: al-Maṭbaʿa al-Mīriyya.

Neubauer, Eckhard 1968/69, "Die Theorie vom īqāʿ:I. Übersetzung des Kitāb al-īqāʿāt von Abū Naṣr al-Fārābī", *Oriens 21/22*, 196-232.

– 1994, "Die Theorie vom īqāʿ:II. Übersetzung des "Kitāb Iḥṣā' al-īqāʿāt" von Abū Naṣr al-Fārābī", *Oriens 34*, 103-173.

– 1995, "Al-Ḫalīl ibn Aḥmad und die Frühgeschichte der arabischen Lehre von den 'Tönen' und den musikalischen Metren, mit einer Übersetzung des Kitāb an-naġam von Yaḥyā ibn 'alī al-Munaǧǧim", *Zeitschrift für Geschichte der arabisch-islamischen Wissenschaften* 10, 255-323.

– 1999, *Der Essai sur la musique orientale von Charles Fonton mit Zeichnungen von Adanson*, Frankfurt: Institute for the History of Arabic-Islamic Science.

– 1999/2000, "Glimpses of Arab Music in Ottoman Times from Syrian and Egyptian Sources", *Zeitschrift für Geschichte der arabisch-islamischen Wissenschaften 13*, 317-365.

– 2008-9, "Quṭb al-Dīn Shīrāzī (d. 1311) on musical metres (īqāʿ)", *Zeitschrift für Geschichte der Arabisch-Islamischen Wissenschaften 18*, 357-371.

Neudecker, Hannah 1994. *The Turkish Bible Translation by Yaḥya bin 'Isḥaḳ: also called Ḥaki (1659)*, Leiden.

Nettl, Bruno 1983, *The Study of Ethnomusicology: Twenty-nine Issues and Concepts*, University of Illinois Press.

O'Connell, John M. 2000, "Fine Art, Fine Music: Controlling Turkish Taste at the Fine Arts Academy", *Yearbook for Traditional Music 33*, 117-142.

– 2003, "Song Cycle: The Life and Death of the Turkish Gazel: Review Essay", *Ethnomusicology 47(3)*, 399-414.

– 2013, *Alaturka: Style in Turkish Music (1923-1938)*, SOAS Musicology Series, Farnham: Ashgate.

– (forthcoming), "Concert Platform: A Space for a Style in Turkish Music", in: *Music and Architecture in Islam*, Michael Frishkopf and Federico Spinetti (Eds.), Austin: University of Texas Press.

Oransay, Gültekin 1957, "Das Tonsystem der Türkeitürkischen Kunstmusik", *Die Musikforschung 10(2)*, 250-264.

– 1962, *Die melodische Linie und der Begriff Makam der traditionellen türkischen Kunstmusik vom 15. bis zum 9. Jahrhundert*, Ankara: Küğ.

– 1964, *Die traditionelle türkische Kunstmusik*, Ankara: Küğ.

Ömürlü, Yusuf (?), *Türk Mûsıkîsi Klâsikleri: Muhayyer Makamı*, Cilt 9, No 103, Istanbul: Kubbealtı Mûsıkî Entsitüsü.

Özalp, Nazmi 1986, *Türk Musikisi Tarihi*, 2 vols., Ankara: TRT Müzik Dairesi Başkanlığı.

Özdemir, Mehmet Ali 2005, "Halk müziğini ölçülendirme sorunu", *Folklor-Edebiyat 42*, 39-45.

Özkan, İsmail Hakkı 1987/1990/2011, *Türk Mûsikîsi Nazariyati ve Usûlleri. Kudüm Velveleleri*, Istanbul: Ötüken.

Öztuna, Yılmaz 1987, *Türk Musikisi: Teknik ve Tarihi,* Istanbul: Türk Petrol Vakfı Lale Mecmuası Neşriyatı.

– 1990, *Büyük Türk Mûsikîsi Ansiklopedisi*, 2 vols., Istanbul: Millî Eğitim Basımevi.

– 2006, *Türk Mûsikîsi – Akademik Klasik Türk San'at Mûsikîsi'nin Ansiklopedik Sözlüğü*, 2 vols., Ankara: Orient Yayınları.

Öztürk, Okan Murat, 2005, "Arif Sağ Üstad'ın ‚Davullar Çalınırken', Çalışması Vesilesiyle Anadolu Müziğinde Usuller", http://www.turkuler.com/yazi/anadolu muziginde.asp.

Özyıldırım, Murat 2011, "Türkiye'de Arap Müziği üzerine Düşünceler", *Musiki Dergisi*, http://www.musikidergisi.net/?p=1821.

Paçacı, Gönül (Ed.) 1999, *Cumhuriyet'in Sesleri*, Istanbul: Türkiye İş Bankası.

Popescu-Judetz [Judeţ], Eugenia 1973, *Dimitrie Cantemir: cartea sţinţei muzicii*, Bucharest: Editura Musicala.

– 1981, *Dimitrie Cantemir's Theory of Turkish Art Music*, Studies in Oriental Arts, Pittsburgh, PA: Duquesne University, Tamburitzans Institute of Folk Arts.

– 1998, *Türk Musiki Kültürünün Anlamları* (trans. Bülent Aksoy), Istanbul: Pan Yayıncılık.

– *XVIII. Yüzyıl Musiki Yazmalarından Kevseri Mecmuası Üstüne Karşılaştırmalı Bir İnceleme*, (trans. Bülent Aksoy), Istanbul: Pan Yayıncılık.

– 2002, *Tanburî Küçük Artin: A Musical Treatise of the Eighteenth Century*, Istanbul: Pan Yayıncılık.

Popescu-Judetz, Eugenia and Neubauer, Eckhard (Ed.) 2004, *Seydī's book on music: A 15th century Turkish discourse*, The Science of Music in Islam, vol. 6, Frankfurt am Main: Institute for the History of Arabic-Islamic Science.

Pourjavadiy, Amir Hoseyn [Hosein] 2005, *The musical codex of Amir Khān Gorji (c. 1108-1697)*, PhD dissertation, University of California, Los Angeles.

– (Ed.) 2007, *Nasīm-i Ṭarab (The Breeze of Euphoria). A Sixteenth-Century Persian Musical Treatise by Nasīmī*, Tehran: Iranian Academy of Arts.

Ratner, Leonard G. 1980, *Classic Music: Expression, Form and Style*, New York: Schirmer.

Redhouse, Sir James 1990, *İngilizce – Türkçe Redhouse Sözlüğü*, Istanbul: Redhouse Yayınevi.

Reinhart, Kurt and Ursula 1969, *Les Traditions Musicales: Turquie*, Paris: Buchet/Castel.

Sachs, Curt 1953, *Rhythm and Tempo*, New York.

al-Safarjalānī, Aḥmad Afandī 1308/1890-1, *al-Safīna al-adabiyya fī 'l-mūsīqa al-ʿarabiyya*, Damascus: Maṭbaʿat Wilāyat Sūriyya al-Jalīla.

Safarova, Zemfira1997, *Abdül Qadir Marağayi*, Baku: Tebriz Neşriyatı.

Sahibinin Sesi 1934-1935, *Marconi Radyoları: Sahibinin Sesi'ne Mensuptur* [Istanbul].

Sait, Mekki 1933, "Münir Nurettinin Yuvasında", *Yedigün* 30, 10-12.

Şamlı İskender [Kutmani] [c.1923], *Kürdîli Hicazkâr Faslı*, Istanbul.

Sarısözen, Muzaffer (?), TRT (Turkish State Radio and Television) Müzik Dairesi Yay., THM Repertuar Nos: 667 and 598.

– 1962, *Türk Halk Musikisi Usulleri*, Ankara.

Sawa, George Dimitri 1995, "*Muʿaradat al-ʿArud*, by ʿAbd al-Hamid Hamam",*The World of Music*, vol. 37(2), 106-108.

– 2009, *Rhythmic Theories and Practices in Arabic Writings to 339 AH / 950 CE*. (= Musicological Studies, vol. XCIII), Ottawa: The Institute of Mediaeval Music.

– 2015, *An Arabic Musical and Socio-Cultural Glossary of* Kitāb al-Aghānī, Leiden: Brill.

Saygun, Ahmet Adnan 1960, art. "La Musique Turque", in *Historie de la Musique, Encyclopédie de la Pleiade*, vol. 1, Paris: Editions Gallimard, 573-617.

Schimmel, Annemarie 1992, *Mystische Dimenisonen des Islam*, 2nd edition, München.

– 1995, *Rumi. Ich bin Wind und du bist Feuer. Leben und Werk des großen Mystikers*, 8th edition, München.

Schmid, Manfred Hermann 2012, *Notationskunde. Schrift und Komposition 900-1900*, Kassel-Basel.

Seidel, Heinz-Peter 1972/3, "Studien zum Usul 'Devri kebîr' in den Peşrev der Mevlevi", *Mitteilungen der deutschen Gesellschaft für Musik des Orients 11*, 7-69.

– 1973/74 "Die Notenschrift des Hamparsum Limonciyan. Ein Schlüssel", *Mitteilungen der Deutschen Gesellschaft für Musik des Orients 12*, 72-124.

Selçuk, Münir Nureddin 1947, "Ses Musikimiz", *Türk Musikisi Dergisi*, 1(2), Istanbul.

Semėnov, Anton A. 1946, *Sredneaziatskij traktat po muzyke Darviša Ali* (summarised translation from Persian into Russian, introduction and commentaries), Tashkent.

Shah, Idries 1996, *Die Sufis. Botschaft der Derwische, Weisheit der Magier*, 10th edition, München.

al-Shaṭṭī, Jamīl 1994, *Aʿyān Dimashq fī al-qarn al-thālith ʿashar wa-nisf al-qarn al-rābiʿ ʿashar Min 1201-1350 H.*, Damascus: Dār al-Bashāʾir.

Shaw, Stanford 1977, *History of the Ottoman Empire and Modern Turkey*, 2 vols., Cambridge: Cambridge University Press.

Shiloah, Amnon 1979, *The Theory of Music in Arabic Writings (c. 900-1900) – Descriptive Catalogue of Manuscripts in Libraries of Europe and the U.S.A.*, Répertoire International des Sources Musicales B/X, Munich.

Signell, Karl L. 1977, *Makam: Modal Practice in Turkish Art Music,* Seattle, WA: Asian Music Publications.

Stokes, Martin 2010, *The Republic of Love: Cultural Intimacy in Turkish Popular Music*, Chicago: University of Chicago Press.

Sultanova, Razia 2011, *From Shamanism to Sufism*, London.

Sulzer, Franz Joseph 1781, *Geschichte des transalpinischen Daciens, das ist: der Walachey, Moldau und Bessarabiens, im Zusammenhange mit der Geschichte des übrigen Daciens als ein Versuch einer allgemeinen dacischen Geschichte mit kritischer Freyheit entworfen von Franz Joseph Sulzer, ehemaligem k. k. Hauptmann und Auditor*, vol. 2, Vienna.

Tahsin, Hasan 1906, *Gülzar-ı Musiki*, Istanbul: Şirket-i Mürettibiye Matbaası.

Tanrıkorur, Cinuçen 1990, "Concordance of Prosodic and Musical Meters in Turkish Classical Music", *Turkish Musical Quarterly*, 3(1), 1-7.

Taştan, Yahya Kemal 2006, "Teganni'den Irlamak'a Musikinin Serencamı", *Köprü Dergisi* 99, no. 67.

Terzi, Cihangir 1992, *Türk Halk Müziği Metrik Yapısının Tespit ve Tasnifinde Karşılaşılan Problemler ve Çözüm Yolları,* Istanbul Technical University, Unpublished Thesis.

Töre, Abdülkadir [1913], *Usûl-i Talim-i Keman*, Istanbul.

Trimingham, John Spencer 1998, *The Sufi Orders in Islam*, 2nd ed., Oxford [i.a.]: Oxford Univ. Press.

Tura, Yalçın 1988, *Türk Mûsikîsinin Mes'eleleri*, Istanbul: Pan Yayıncılık.

– 1988b, "Darb-ı Fetih Usûlü ve Bu Usûlle Yapılmış Peşrevler", in: *Türk Mûsıkîsinin Mes'eleleri*, Yalçın Tura (Ed.), Istanbul, 87-103.

– (Ed.) 2001, *Kitābu ʿilmi'l-mūsīḳī ʿalā vechi'l-ḥurūfāt. Mûsikîyi harflerle tesbît ve icrâ ilminin kitabı, I. cilt, Edvâr* (*tıpkıbasım – çevriyazı – çeviri – notlar*), Istanbul: Yapı Kredi Yayınları.

2001b *Kitābu ʿilmi'l-mūsīḳī* […], *II. cilt, Notalar* (*tıpkıbasım –çeviri – notlar*), Istanbul: Yapı Kredi Yayınları.

– (Ed.) 2006, *Nâsır Abdülbâkî Dede: İnceleme ve Gerçeği Araştırma (Tedkîk ü Tahkîk),* Istanbul: Pan Yayıncılık.

Turabı, Ahmet Hakkı (Ed.) 2004, *İbn Sînâ Mûsikî*, Istanbul.

Ungay, M. Hurşit 1981,*Türk Musikisinde Usûller ve Kudüm*, Istanbul.

Üngör, Edhem R. 1980, *Türk Musikisi Güfteler Antolojisi*, Istanbul: Eren Yayınları.

Ünlü, Cemal 2004, *Git Zaman Gel Zaman. Fonograf – Gramofon – Taş Plak*, Istanbul.

Uslu, Recep 2007, *Fatih Sultan Mehmed Döneminde Mûsikî ve Şems-i Rûmî'nin Mecmûa-i Güfte'si*, Istanbul: Istanbul Fetih Cemiyeti Yay. 106.

Uspenskim, V. A. 1924, *Šest' muzykal'nych poėm, zapisannych v Buchare,* Moskau.

Uygun, M. Nuri 1999, *Safiyüddin Abdülmü'min Urmevî ve Kitâbü'l-Edvârı*, Istanbul.

Uz, Kāżım 1964, *al-Iṣṭilāḥāt al-Mūsīqiyya*, (trans. Ibrāhīm al-Dāqūqī), Baghdad: Maṭbaʿat Dār al-Jumhūriyya.

Wadler, Arnold 1997 [1935], *Der Turm von Babel – Urgemeinschaft der Sprachen*, Wiesbaden.

Wehr, Hans 1994, *A Dictionary of Modern Written Arabic*, J. Milton Cowan, ed., Wiesbaden: Otto Harrassowitz.

Wright, Owen 1978, *The Modal System of Arab and Persian Music A.D. 1250-1300*, Oxford: Oxford University Press.

– 1983, "Music and verse", in: *Arabic Literature to the End of the Umayyad Period*, A.F.L. Beeston et al. (Ed.), Cambridge etc.: Cambridge University Press, 433-459.

– 1988, "Aspects of historical change in the Turkish classical repertoire", in: *Musica Asiatica 5*, Richard Widdess (Ed.), Cambridge: Cambridge University Press, 1-108.

– 1992, *Words without Songs. A Musicological Study of an Early Ottoman Anthology and its Precursors*, London: SOAS Musicology Series, vol. 3.

– 1992b, *Demetrius Cantemir: The Collection of Notations. Volume 1:Text*, London: SOAS Musicology Series, vol. 1.

– 1994/95, "Abd al-Qadir al-Maraghi and ʿAli B. Muhammad Binaʾi: Two Fifteenth-Century Examples of Notation", Pts. 1 and 2, *Bulletin of the School of Oriental and African Studies, University of London*, vol, LVII, 1994 and LVIII, 1995.

– 2000, *Demetrius Cantemir, The Collection of Notations, Volume 2: Commentary*. (SOAS Musicology Series), Aldershot: Ashgate.

– 2004-5, "Die melodischen Modi bei Ibn Sīnā und die Entwicklung der Modalpraxis von Ibn al-Munağğim bis zu Ṣafi al-Dīn al-Urmawī", *Zeitschrift für Geschichte der arabisch-islamischen Wissenschaften* Bd. 16, 224-308

– 2007, "Mais qui était «Le compositeur du *péchrev* dans le makam *nihavend*»?", Studii şi cercet. Ist. Art., Teatru, Muzică, Cinematografie, serie nouă, 1(45), 3-45.

– 2013, "Turning a Deaf Ear", in: The Renaissance and the Ottoman World, Anna Contadini and Claire Norton (Eds.), Farnham, 143-165.

– 2014, *Music theory in Mamluk Cairo. The ġāyat al-maṭlūb fī ʿilm al-anġām wa-'l-ḍurūb by Ibn Kurr*, Farnham: Ashgate.

Yekta, Rauf, Ahmed Irsoy and A.R. Çağatay, *Dârülelhan Külliyatı* 1-180, Istanbul.

Yekta, Rauf 19 Şaban 1317/22 December 1899, "Osmanlı Mûsikîsinde Tabîî Sadâlar", *İkdam*, Istanbul.

– 26 Şaban 1317/29 December 1899, "Osmanlı Mûsikîsinde Çâryek, Sülüs ve Nısf Sadâlar", *İkdam*, Istanbul.

– 1922, "La Musique Turque ", in: *Encyclopédie de La Musique V*, Paris.

– 1924, *Türk Mûsikîsi Nazariyâtı*, Istanbul: Mahmud Bey Matbaası.

– 1925 *Şark Mûsikîsi Târihi*, Istanbul: Mahmud Bey Matbaası.

– 1325/1907, "Tanburda Negamâtın Mevâkı-i Fenniyesi", *İkdam*, No. 4667, Istanbul.

– 1986, *Türk Musikisi*, (trans. Orhan Nasuhioğlu), Istanbul: Pan Yayıncılık.

– 1926, *Durülelhân Külliyatı*, Istanbul.

Manuscripts and Editions

Abd al-Muʾmin b. Ṣafī al-Dīn al-Jurjānī, see *bahjat al-rūḥ*

Abdülbâkî Nâsır Dede Efendi, *Tedkîyk ü Tahkîyk*, Süleymaniye Kütüphanesi Nafiz Paşa Kitaplığı No: 1242, Istanbul.

Adwār, see Urmawī

Ali Ufukî [Albert Bobovsky], *[Album de poésies turques [...] de la musique italienne et allemande, et la notation, quelquefois avec transcription, de chansons turques, par 'Ali Beg Bobowski, dit 'Ali Ufkî]*, Paris, Bibliothèque Nationale de France, Ms Turc 292, *http://gallica.bnf.fr/ark:/12148/btv1b84150086*

Behar, Cem 2008, *Saklı mecmua. Ali Ufkî'nin Bibliothèque Nationale de France'taki [Turc 292] yazması*, Istanbul: Yapı Kredi Yayınları.

– 1665, *Mecmûa-i Sâz ü Söz*, British Library, Sloane 3114

Cevher, Hakan (Ed.) 2003, *Ali Ufkî: Hâzâ Mecmûa-i Sâz ü Söz (Çeviriyazım-İnceleme)*, Izmir: Meta Basım Matbaacılık Hiz.

Elçin, Şükrü (Ed.) 1976, *Alî Ufkî, Hayatı, eserleri ve Mecmûa-i Sâz ü Söz (tıpkıbasım)*, Istanbul: Milli Eğitim Basımevi.

– 1665, *Serai Enderun* [...], British Library, MS Harley 3409

Brenner, Nicolaus (trans.) 1667, *Serai Enderun* [...], Vienna.

– 1666, Grammatica Turcicolatna [sic] Alberti Bobovii Leopolitani Linguæ Turcicæ Professoris [...], Oxford, Bodleian Library, MS Hyde 47.

Anonymous, [Untitled collections of Hamparsum notation], İstanbul Üniversitesi Nadir Eserler Kütüphanesi, Y 203-1, Y.212/10b and Y.205/3; İstanbul Arkeoloji Müzeleri Kütüphanesi, İAM 1537.

Awbahī, ʿAlīšāh b. Būka, *muqaddima-yi uṣūl*, MS İstanbul Üniversitesi Kütüphanesi F 1079.

Banāʾī, ʿAlī b. Muḥammad Miʿmār [mašhūr be-Banāʾī] 888/1484, *risāla dar mūsīqī*. [Facsimile] 1368š/1990, Tehran: markaz-i našr-i dānišgāhī.

Bahjat al-rūḥ [ʿAbd al-Muʾmin b. Ṣafī al-Dīn al-Jurjānī (?)], Bodleian MS Ouseley 117.

de Borgomale, H. L. Rabino (Ed.) 1346/1968, *Bahjat al-rūḥ*, Tehran.

Buḫārī, *muḥīṭ al-tawārīḫ*

Fallahzadeh, Mehrdad (Ed.) 2009, *Two treatises – two streams: treatises from the postscholastic era of Persian writings on music theory*, Bethesda, Maryland: Ibex Publishers.

Cantemir, Dimitri [Kantemiroğlu], *Kitâb-ı 'İlmü'l-Mûsıkî 'alâ Vechi'l-Hurûfât*, İstanbul Üniversitesi Türkiyat Araştırmaları Enstitüsü, Arel Kütüphanesi Y 100 (former signature: Nr. 2768); [manuscript copy] İstanbul Üniversitesi Kütüphanesi Nadir Eserler Koleksiyonu (İÜY) 1856.

Tura, Yalçın (Ed.) 2001, *Kitābu 'ilmi'l-mūsīḳī 'alā vechi'l-ḥurūfāt. Mûsikîyi harflerle tesbît ve icrâ ilminin kitabı, I. cilt, Edvâr* (*tıpkıbasım – çevriyazı – çeviri – notlar*),

Istanbul: Yapı Kredi Yayınları; 2001b *Kitābu 'ilmi'l-mūsiḳī* [...], *II. cilt, Notalar (tıpkıbasım -çeviri - notlar)*, Istanbul: Yapı Kredi Yayınları.

Wright, Owen, 1992b, *Demetrius Cantemir: The Collection of Notations. Volume 1: Text*, London: SOAS Musicology Series, vol. 1.; 2000, *Demetrius Cantemir, The Collection of Notations, Volume 2: Commentary*, (SOAS Musicology Series), Aldershot: Ashgate.

dar bayān-i Shashmaqām 1285/1868, Uzbek Academy of Sciences Tashkent, Ms. No. 5734.

Fārābī [Abū Naṣr al-Fārābī (d. 339/950)], see also Sawa 2009.

Neubauer, Eckhard 1968/69, "Die Theorie vom īqāᶜ: I. Übersetzung des Kitāb al-īqāᶜāt von Abū Naṣr al-Fārābī", *Oriens 21/22*, 196-232; 1994, "Die Theorie vom īqāᶜ: II. Übersetzung des "Kitāb Iḥṣā' al-īqāᶜāt" von Abū Naṣr al-Fārābī", *Oriens 34*, 103-173.

Fonton, Charles 1751, *Essai sur la musique orientale compare a la musique Europeene*, Paris.

Neubauer, Eckhard (Ed.) 1999, *Der Essai sur la musique orientale von Charles Fonton mit Zeichnungen von Adanson*, Frankfurt: Institute for the History of Arabic-Islamic Science.

Gorjī, Amīr Khān [ca. 1700].

Pourjavadiy, Amir Hoseyn [Hosein] 2005, *The musical codex of Amir Khān Gorji (c. 1108-1697)*, PhD dissertation, University of California, Los Angeles.

al-Ḥalabī, ᶜAskar al-Ḥanafī al-Qādirī 1083/1672, *Rāḥ al-jām fī shajarat al-anghām*, MS Paris, Bibliothèque Nationale, Arabe 3250.

Hamparsum Limonciyan, İstanbul Üniversitesi, Türkiyat Araştırmaları Enstitüsü, Ms. Arel 110.

- İstanbul Üniversitesi Kütüphanesi Nadir Eserler Koleksiyonu, Y.203/1.
- (?), İstanbul Üniversitesi Kütüphanesi Nadir Eserler Koleksiyonu, Y.211/9.

Hızır Ağa, *Tefhîmü'l-Makamat fî Tevlîdi'n-Negamât* [Edvâr-ı Ḥıżır Aġa], Süleymaniye Kütüphanesi Hafid Efendi Yaz. 291; Topkapı Sarayı Hazine Kütüphanesi 1793

Hızır bin Abdullah, see Khıżır b. ᶜAbdullāh

Ibn al-Sīd [Abū Muḥammad ᶜAbd Allāh b. Muḥammad Ibn al-Sīd al-Baṭalyawsī (d. 521/1127)], *Sharḥ Saqṭ al-zand.*

al-Saqqā, Muṣṭafā et al. (Ed.) 1366/1947, "Sharḥ Saqṭ al-zand", in: *Shurūḥ Saqṭ al-zand*, vol. 3, Cairo: Dār al-Kutub al-Miṣriyya.

Ibn Zayla, *al-Kāfī fī l-mūsīqī*, Zakariyyā Yūsuf (Ed.) 1964, Cairo: Dār al-Qalam.

Jāmī [Nūr al-Dīn ᶜAbd al-Raḥmān Jāmī (d. 898/1492)], *Risāla-i mūsīqī.*

Aᶜlā Khān Afṣaḥzād, Moḥammad Jān 'Omārof and Abū Bakr Ẓohūr al-Dīn 1379/2000, *Bahārestān va-rasā'el-e Jāmī*, Tehran: Mīrāth-e Maktūb, 171-220.

Boldyrev, A. N. and Beljaev, V. M. (Ed.) 1960, *Abduraḥmon Dzomij: Muzika ḥaḳida traktat / Traktat o muzyke.* Tashkent: Uzbekiston SSR Akademijasi nashrīčti.

Kevserî, Muṣṭafâ, [untitled treatise and music collection], Milli Kütüphane (Ankara), Mf1994 A 4941.

Isḥāq al-Mawṣilī, see Mawṣilī

Kawkabī [Najm al-Dīn Kawkabī Bukhārāʾī (early 10th/16th cent.)] 1509, *Risāla-i mūsīqī*.

Rajabov, ʻAskarʻalī (Ed.) 1983 [Persian title page]/1985 [Russian title page], *Risāla-i mūsīqī*, Doshanbe: ʻIrfān.

Khıżır b. ᶜAbdullāh [first half of the 9th/15th cent.], *Edvār [Kitâb-ı Edvâr]*, Ms. İstanbul, Topkapı Sarayı, Revan 1728.

Özçimi, Sadreddin 1999, "Hızır bin Abdullah ve Kitâbü'l-Edvâr", in: *Musiki Mecmuası* no. 466, 61-67; 2000, no. 467, 65-68; 2001, no. 471, 73-77; 2001, no. 472, 77-80.

Çelik, B. 2001, *Hızır bin Abdullah'ın Kitabü'l Edvar'ında Makamlar*, unpublished PhD Thesis, Marmara Üniversitesi Sosyal Bilimler Enstitüsü, Istanbul.

Kırşehrî [Yūsuf b. Niẓāmeddīn b. Yūsuf-i Rūmī-i Ḳırşehrī el-Mevlevī (early 9th/15th cent.)] 1411, *Kitâb-ı Edvâr* [Turkish translation by Harîrî bin Muhammed 1469], Paris Bibliothèque Nationale de France, Suppl. Turc. 1424; Ankara Milli Kütüphane, Nr: 131/1.

Doğrusöz, Nilgün 2012, *Yusuf Kırşehri'nin Müzik Teorisi*, Kırşehir Valiliği, Kırşehir.

al-Kubaysī, Ḥusayn ibn Aḥmad 1200/1786 [1785], [*Safīna*], MS Berlin, Staatsbibliothek, or. oct. 1088; MS Damascus, al-Asad Library (previously at al-Ẓāhiriyya Library), ᶜāmm 4725.

Lādhiqī, [Muḥammad b. ᶜAbd al-Ḥamīd al-Lādhiqī (d. after 890/1485)]: *al-Risāla al-Fatḥiyya* [*Fatḥiyya*].

al-Rajab, Hāshim Muḥammad (Ed.) 1406/1986, *al-Risāla al-Fatḥiyya*, al-Majlis al-Waṭanī li-l-Thaqāfa wa-l-Funūn wa-l-Ādāb. al-Silsila al-turāthiyya, vol. 16, Kuwait.

– *Zayn al-alḥān fī ᶜilm al-taʾlīf wa-l-awzān* [*Zayn*], Ms. Istanbul, Nuruosmaniye 3655.

ʻal-Marāġī, Abd al-Qādir Ġaybī, *jāmiᶜ al-alḥān*, Nuruosmaniye 3644 and 3645.

Bīnesh, Taqī [Taqī Bīniš] (Ed.) 1366/1987, *Jāmiᶜ al-alḥān*, Wezārat-e Farhang va-Āmūzesh-e ᶜĀlī. Moʾassase-ye Moṭṭalāᶜāt va-Taḥqīqāt-e Farhangī, no. 560, Tehran.

Khażrāʾī, Bābak (Ed.) 1388/2009, *Jāmiᶜ al-alḥān*, Tehran: Farhangestān-e Honar-e Jomhūrī-e Eslāmī-e Īrān.

– *Maqāṣid al-alḥān*, Nuruosmaniye 3656.

Bīnesh, Taqī [Taqī Bīniš] (Ed.) 1344/1965, "Maqāṣid al-alḥān", *Majmūᶜe-ye motūn-e fārsī*, no. 26, Tehran: Bongāh-e Tarjoma va-Nashr.

– *Sharḥ-i Adwār*, Nurusmaniye 3651.

Bīnesh, Taqī [Taqī Biniš] (Ed.) 1370/1991, *Sharḥ-i Adwār (including the Zevaidü'l-Fevaid)*, Markaz-e Nashr-e Dāneshgāhī, no. 563: Honar, no. 4, Tehran.

al-Mawṣilī, Isḥāq (d. 235/850), [referred to by Abū Naṣr al-Fārābī (d. 339/950)], see Sawa 2009.

Mortażā Shāmlū [compiled 1659]

Afshār, Īraj and Monzavī, Aḥmad (Eds) 1382/2003, *Jong-e Mortażā Qolī Shāmlū*, Selsele-ye enteshārāt-e ketābkhāne, 15, Tehran: Markaz-e Dā'erato 'l-Maᶜāref-e Bozorg-e Eslāmī.

Nasīmī, *Nasīm-i ṭarab*

Pourjavady, Amir Hosein (Ed.) 2007, *Nasīm-i Ṭarab (The Breeze of Euphoria). A Sixteenth-Century Persian Musical Treatise by Nasīmī*, Tehran: Iranian Academy of Arts.

Qazvīnī, Mīr Ṣadr al-Dīn Muḥammad 2003, *risāla-yi ᶜilm-i mūsīqī*, ed. Rustamī, Āriyū, *faṣlnāma-yi mūsīqī-yi māhūr 18.*

Quṭb al-Dīn [Quṭb al-Dīn (al-) Shīrāzī (d. 710/1311)] *Durrat al-tāj li-ghurrat al-Dubāj*

Mishkāt, Muḥammad (Ed.) 1939-1945, *Durrat al-tāj li-ghurrat al-Dubāj*, 5 vols. Tehran (music chapter in vol. 4, pp. 1-149, section on *īqāᶜ*, pp. 127-140).

Nāṣeḥpūr, Naṣrollāh 1387/2008, *Resāle-ye mūsīqī az Dorrato 't-tāj li-ghorrati 'd-Dabbāj* [sic], 2 vols. Tehran: Enteshārāt-e Farhangestān-e Honar.

Saylakūnī [Alī b. ᶜUbayd Allāh al-Saylakūnī (al-Siyalkūtī? fl. 900/1500)], *Treatise on music*, Ms. Gotha, Forschungsbibliothek, orient. A 39.

Seydī, *Hazâ el-Matla'fi Beyanü'l-Edvar ve'l Makâmat ve fi Ilmü'l Esrâr ve'r-Riyâzat*, ["*Seydî'nin el Matla'ı*"], Topkapi Palace Museum, A 3459.

Popescu-Judetz, Eugenia and Neubauer, Eckhard (Ed.) 2004, *Seydī's book on music: A 15th century Turkish discourse*, The Science of Music in Islam, vol. 6, Frankfurt am Main: Institute for the History of Arabic-Islamic Science.

Sharafiyya, see Urmawī.

Shihāb al-Dīn al-ᶜAjamī [Shihāb al-Dīn al-ᶜAjamī (2nd half of the 9th/15th cent.], *Muqaddima fī ᶜilm al-anghām*, Mss. Paris, Bibliothèque nationale, arabe 2865 (fols. 70a-75b); Istanbul, Süleymaniye, Şehit Ali 1170 (fols. 61a-64a); Tunis, Bibliothèque nationale 18638 (fols. 7a-19b).

al-Shīrāzī, see Quṭb al-Dīn.

al-Širwānī, Fatḥ Allāh al-Muᵓmin, *majalla fī al-mūsīqī*, MS Topkapı Ahmet III 3449.

[facsimile] 1986, in: Publications of the Institute for the History of Arabic-Islamic Science, series C, 29, Frankfurt.

Sulāfat al-ḥān fī 'l-alḥān 1277/1860, MS Damascus, al-Asad Library (previously at al-Ẓāhiriyya Library), ᶜāmm 4013.

Taqsīm al-naġamāt wa-bayān al-daraj wa-'l-šuᶜab wa-'l-maqāmāt [16. cent], Österreichische Staatsbibliothek, A-Wn, MS Flügel 1516 (Mxt. 674).

Urmawī, [Ṣafi al-Dīn al-Urmawī (d. 693/1294)] *Kitāb al-Adwār*, Nurosmaniye 3653 [several editions and translations, i.a.:]

al-Rajab, Hāšim Muḥammad (Ed.) 1980, *Ṣafī al-Dīn al-Urmawī. kitāb al-adwār*, Baghdad.

– *al-Risāla al-Sharafiyya fī l-nisab al-taʾlīfiyya* [several editions and translations, i.a.:]

Quraiʿa [Kriaa], Muḥammad al-Asʿad (Ed.) 2009, *al-Risāla al-Sharafiyya fī l-nisab al-taʾlīfiyya,* Sīdī Bū Saʿīd: Markaz al-Mūsīqā al-ʿArabiyya wa-l-Mutawassiṭiyya, Iṣdārāt an-Najma az-Zahrāʾ.

Yūsuf b. Niẓāmeddīn, see Kırşehrî.

ORIENT-INSTITUT
ISTANBUL

ISTANBULER TEXTE UND STUDIEN

Alle erschienenen Titel sind auch als E-Books erhältlich. Sechs Jahre nach Erscheinen sind sie kostenfrei über www.ergon-verlag.de abrufbar.

1. Barbara Kellner-Heinkele, Sigrid Kleinmichel (Hrsg.), *Mīr ʿAlīšīr Nawāʾī. Akten des Symposiums aus Anlaß des 560. Geburtstages und des 500. Jahres des Todes von Mīr ʿAlīšīr Nawāʾī am 23. April 2001.* Würzburg 2003.
2. Bernard Heyberger, Silvia Naef (Eds.), *La multiplication des images en pays d'Islam. De l'estampe à la télévision (17-21 siècle). Actes du colloque* Images : fonctions et langages. L'incursion de l'image moderne dans l'Orient musulman et sa périphérie. *Istanbul, Université du Bosphore (Boğaziçi Üniversitesi), 25 – 27 mars 1999.* Würzburg 2003.
3. Maurice Cerasi with the collaboration of Emiliano Bugatti and Sabrina D'Agostiono, *The Istanbul Divanyolu. A Case Study in Ottoman Urbanity and Architecture.* Würzburg 2004.
4. Angelika Neuwirth, Michael Hess, Judith Pfeiffer, Börte Sagaster (Eds.), *Ghazal as World Literature II: From a Literary Genre to a Great Tradition. The Ottoman Gazel in Context.* Würzburg 2006.
5. Alihan Töre Şagunî, Kutlukhan-Edikut Şakirov, Oğuz Doğan (Çevirmenler), Kutlukhan-Edikut Şakirov (Editör), *Türkistan Kaygısı.* Würzburg 2006.
6. Olcay Akyıldız, Halim Kara, Börte Sagaster (Eds.), *Autobiographical Themes in Turkish Literature: Theoretical and Comparative Perspectives.* Würzburg 2007.
7. Filiz Kıral, Barbara Pusch, Claus Schönig, Arus Yumul (Eds.), *Cultural Changes in the Turkic World.* Würzburg 2007.
8. Ildikó Bellér-Hann (Ed.), *The Past as Resource in the Turkic Speaking World.* Würzburg 2008.
9. Brigitte Heuer, Barbara Kellner-Heinkele, Claus Schönig (Hrsg.), *„Die Wunder der Schöpfung". Mensch und Natur in der türksprachigen Welt.* Würzburg 2012.
10. Christoph Herzog, Barbara Pusch (Eds.), *Groups, Ideologies and Discourses: Glimpses of the Turkic Speaking World.* Würzburg 2008.
11. D. G. Tor, *Violent Order: Religious Warfare, Chivalry, and the* ʿAyyār *Phenomenon in the Medieval Islamic World.* Würzburg 2007.

12. Christopher Kubaseck, Günter Seufert (Hrsg.), *Deutsche Wissenschaftler im türkischen Exil: Die Wissenschaftsmigration in die Türkei 1933-1945.* Würzburg 2008.

13. Barbara Pusch, Tomas Wilkoszewski (Hrsg.), *Facetten internationaler Migration in die Türkei: Gesellschaftliche Rahmenbedingungen und persönliche Lebenswelten.* Würzburg 2008.

14. Kutlukhan-Edikut Şakirov (Ed.), *Türkistan Kaygısı. Faksimile.* In Vorbereitung.

15. Camilla Adang, Sabine Schmidtke, David Sklare (Eds.), *A Common Rationality: Muʿtazilism in Islam and Judaism.* Würzburg 2007.

16. Edward Badeen, *Sunnitische Theologie in osmanischer Zeit.* Würzburg 2008.

17. Claudia Ulbrich, Richard Wittmann (Eds.): *Fashioning the Self in Transcultural Settings: The Uses and Significance of Dress in Self-Narrative.* Würzburg 2015.

18. Christoph Herzog, Malek Sharif (Eds.), *The First Ottoman Experiment in Democracy.* Würzburg 2010.

19. Dorothée Guillemarre-Acet, *Impérialisme et nationalisme. L'Allemagne, l'Empire ottoman et la Turquie (1908 –1933).* Würzburg 2009.

20. Marcel Geser, *Zwischen Missionierung und „Stärkung des Deutschtums": Der Deutsche Kindergarten in Konstantinopel von seinen Anfängen bis 1918.* Würzburg 2010.

21. Camilla Adang, Sabine Schmidtke (Eds.), *Contacts and Controversies between Muslims, Jews and Christians in the Ottoman Empire and Pre-Modern Iran.* Würzburg 2010.

22. Barbara Pusch, Uğur Tekin (Hrsg.), *Migration und Türkei. Neue Bewegungen am Rande der Europäischen Union.* Würzburg 2011.

23. Tülay Gürler, *Jude sein in der Türkei. Erinnerungen des Ehrenvorsitzenden der Jüdischen Gemeinde der Türkei Bensiyon Pinto.* Herausgegeben von Richard Wittmann. Würzburg 2010.

24. Stefan Leder (Ed.), *Crossroads between Latin Europe and the Near East: Corollaries of the Frankish Presence in the Eastern Mediterranean (12th – 14th centuries).* Würzburg 2011.

25. Börte Sagaster, Karin Schweißgut, Barbara Kellner-Heinkele, Claus Schönig (Hrsg.), *Hoşsohbet: Erika Glassen zu Ehren.* Würzburg 2011.

26. Arnd-Michael Nohl, Barbara Pusch (Hrsg.), *Bildung und gesellschaftlicher Wandel in der Türkei. Historische und aktuelle Aspekte.* Würzburg 2011.

27. Malte Fuhrmann, M. Erdem Kabadayı, Jürgen Mittag (Eds.), *Urban Landscapes of Modernity: Istanbul and the Ruhr.* In Vorbereitung.

28. Kyriakos Kalaitzidis, *Post-Byzantine Music Manuscripts as a Source for Oriental Secular Music (15th to Early 19th Century).* Würzburg 2012.

29. Hüseyin Ağuiçenoğlu, *Zwischen Bindung und Abnabelung. Das „Mutterland" in der Presse der Dobrudscha und der türkischen Zyprioten in postosmanischer Zeit.* Würzburg 2012.

30. Bekim Agai, Olcay Akyıldız, Caspar Hillebrand (Eds.), *Venturing Beyond Borders – Reflections on Genre, Function and Boundaries in Middle Eastern Travel Writing*. Würzburg 2013.
31. Jens Peter Laut (Hrsg.), *Literatur und Gesellschaft. Kleine Schriften von Erika Glassen zur türkischen Literaturgeschichte und zum Kulturwandel in der modernen Türkei*. Würzburg 2014.
32. Tobias Heinzelmann, *Populäre religiöse Literatur und Buchkultur im Osmanischen Reich. Eine Studie zur Nutzung der Werke der Brüder Yazıcıoğlı*. Würzburg 2015.
33. Martin Greve (Ed.), *Writing the History of "Ottoman Music"*. Würzburg 2015.
34. A.C.S. Peacock, Sara Nur Yıldız (Eds.), *Islamic Literature and Intellectual Life in Fourteenth- and Fifteenth-Century Anatolia*. Würzburg 2016.
35. Burcu Yıldız, *Experiencing Armenian Music in Turkey: An Ethnography of Musicultural Memory*. Würzburg 2016.
36. Zeynep Helvacı, Jacob Olley, Ralf Martin Jäger (Eds.), *Rhythmic Cycles and Structures in the Art Music of the Middle East*. Würzburg 2017.
37. Karin Schweißgut, *Das Armutssujet in der türkischen Literatur des 20. Jahrhunderts*. Würzburg 2016.